Empirical Econometric Modelling

Using PcGive for Windows

Empirical Econometric Modelling
Using PcGive for Windows

David F. Hendry
Jurgen A. Doornik

INTERNATIONAL THOMSON BUSINESS PRESS
I(T)P An International Thomson Publishing Company

London • Bonn • Boston • Johannesburg • Madrid • Melbourne • Mexico City • New York • Paris
Singapore • Tokyo • Toronto • Albany, NY • Belmont, CA • Cincinnati, OH • Detroit, MI

Empirical Econometric Modelling: Using PcGive for Windows

First published 1996 by International Thomson Business Press

I(T)P A division of International Thomson Publishing Inc.
The ITP logo is a trademark under licence

PcGive is a computer program designed for Econometric analysis. It is the micro-computer, interactive descendant of GIVE and RALS from the library AUTOREG (Hendry and Srba, 1980). The acronym GIVE is from Generalized Instrumental Variables Estimators (see Sargan, 1959 and Hendry, 1976).

To facilitate replication and validation of empirical findings, **PcGive** should be cited in all reports and publications involving its application.

British Library Cataloguing-in-Publication Data
A catalogue record for this book is available from the British Library

Library of Congress Cataloging-in-Publication Data
A catalog record for this book is available from the Library of Congress

First edition 1996

Printed in the UK by Clays Ltd, St Ives plc

ISBN 1-86152-057-3

International Thomson Business Press
Berkshire House
High Holborn
London WClV 7AA
UK

International Thomson Business Press
20 Park Plaza
14th Floor
Boston MA 02116
USA

http://www.itbp.com

In memory of Denis Sargan

Contents

Figures

Tables

Preface

PcGive for Windows is the latest in a long line of descendants of the original GIVE program. Over its life, many scholars, researchers and students have contributed to its present form. We are grateful to them all for their help and encouragement. Version 9 builds on version 8 by adding many useful new features supported by Windows, but retaining the look and feel of version 8. Version 9 also sees the introduction of Ox as part of PcGive Professional, and a complete separation between front-end (GiveWin) and econometric modules (PcGive now, PcFiml and Stamp later). In addition, the documentation has been improved and expanded again.

The original mainframe ancestor was written in Fortran, PC versions in a mixture of Fortran with some C and Assembly. Version 7 was a complete rewrite in C (with the graphics in Assembly). Version 9 is a mixture of C and C++.

Sections of code in PC-GIVE 6 were contributed by Neil Ericsson, Giuseppe Mazzarino, Adrian Neale, Denis Sargan, Frank Srba and Juri Sylvestrowicz, and their important contributions are gratefully acknowledged. Despite the algorithms having been rewritten in C, their form and structure borrows from the original source. In particular, Adrian Neale's code for graphics from PC-NAIVE was incorporated in PC-GIVE 6.0 and much of that was carried forward to PcGive 7 and 8. The interface of PcGive 7 and 8 was based on D-FLAT, developed by Al Stevens for *Dr. Dobb's Journal*. Version 9 relies on the Microsoft Foundation Class for its interface. We are grateful to Bernard Silverman for permission to include his code for density estimation.

Many people made the development of the program possible by giving their comments and testing out β-versions of version 9 and earlier versions. With the risk of forgetting some, we wish to thank Willem Adema, Peter Boswijk, Gunnar Bårdsen, Mike Clements, Neil Ericsson, Marius Ooms and Neil Shephard for their help. We are also grateful to the Oxford Institute of Economics and Statistics, especially to Gillian Coates, Candy Watts, and Alison Berry for help with earlier versions. We also wish to thank Maureen Baker and Nuffield College.

The documentation for GIVE has evolved dramatically over the years. We are indebted to Mary Morgan and Frank Srba for their help in preparing the first (mainframe) version of a manual for GIVE. Our thanks also to Manuel Arellano, Giorgio Bodo, Peter Boswijk, Julia Campos, Mike Clements, Neil Ericsson, Carlo Favero, Chris Gilbert, Andrew Harvey, Vivien Hendry, Søren Johansen, Siem Jan Koopman, Adrian Neale, Marius Ooms, Robert Parks, Jean-François Richard, Neil Shephard, Timo Teräsvirta and

Giovanni Urga for their many helpful comments on the documentation for PC-GIVE 6 and later versions.

Scientific Word in combination with emTeX and DVIPS eased the development of the documentation for version 9 in LaTeX, further facilitated by the more self-contained nature of PcGive 9 and its in-built help system.

Over the years, many users and generations of students have written with helpful suggestions for improving and extending PcGive, and while version 9 will undoubtedly not yet satisfy all of their wishes, we remain grateful for their comments and hope that they will continue to write with good ideas (and *report any bugs*!).

DFH also owes a considerable debt to Evelyn and Vivien during the long hours he spent on the project: their support and encouragement were essential, even though they could benefit but indirectly from the end product. We hope the benefits derived by others compensate.

We wish you enjoyable and productive use of

PcGive for Windows

Part I

PcGive Prologue

Chapter 1

Introduction to PcGive

1.1 General information

PcGive is an interactive menu-driven program for econometric modelling. Version 9 for Windows, to which this documentation refers, runs on IBM-compatible machines operating under Windows (3.1 after the Win32S extender version 1.30 is installed, but preferably under Windows 95 or NT). There is also a version which works on Dec-Alpha machines running Windows NT. PcGive is part of the AUTOREG Library (see Hendry and Srba, 1980, Hendry, 1986c, 1993, Doornik and Hendry, 1992, and Doornik and Hendry, 1994b, 1994a).

PcGive is designed for modelling economic data when the precise formulation of the relationship is not known *a priori*. The present version is for individual equations with jointly determined, weakly or strongly exogenous, predetermined, and lagged endogenous variables. A wide range of individual equation estimation methods is available. Particular features of the program are its ease of use, edit facilities, flexible data handling, extensive set of preprogrammed diagnostic tests, and its focus on recursive methods, supported by powerful graphics. System estimation methods are incorporated in PcFiml, which is supplied with PcGive Professional (although initially with some delay).

The documentation aims to provide an operational approach to econometric modelling using the most sophisticated yet easy-to-use software available. Thus, this book is especially extensive to fully explain the econometric methods, the modelling approach, and the techniques used, as well as bridge the gap between econometric theory and empirical practice. It transcends the old ideas of 'textbooks' and 'computer manuals' by linking the learning of econometric methods and concepts to the outcomes achieved when they are applied by the user at the computer. Because the program is so easy to learn and use, the main focus is on its econometrics and application to data analysis. Detailed tutorials in Chapters 3–9 teach econometric modelling by walking the user through the program in organised steps. This is supported by clear explanations of econometrics in Chapters 10–15. The material spans the level from introductory to frontier research, with an emphatic orientation to practical modelling. The exact definitions of all statistics calculated by PcGive are described in Chapters 16–18. The manuals in Chapters 19–20 are for reference to details about menus and dialogs. The context-sensitive help system supports this approach by offering help on both the program and the econometrics.

This chapter discusses the special features of PcGive, describes how to use the documentation, provides background information on data storage, interactive operation, help, results storage, and filenames, then outlines the basics of using the program (often just point-and-click with a mouse), and concludes by illustrating some of its capabilities.

1.2 The special features of PcGive

(1) *Ease of use*

- PcGive is **user friendly**, being a **fully interactive and menu-driven** approach to econometric modelling: pull-down menus offer available options, and dialog boxes provide access to the available functions.
- PcGive has a **high level of error protection**, making it suitable for students acquiring experience in econometrics on computers, for live teaching in the classroom, or fraught late-night research.
- PcGive provides an extensive context-sensitive **help system** explaining both the program usage and the econometrics.
- **High quality screen presentations** in edit windows allow documentation of results as analysis proceeds, with easy review of previous results and cutting and pasting within or between windows.
- Both text and graphics can be controlled by a **mouse**, allowing powerful and flexible editing, rapid menu and dialog access, and easy documentation of graphs.
- An **estimation profile** can be set to automatically activate or inhibit model evaluation procedures, set the format for results presentation and control the detail and sophistication of the output.

(2) *Advanced graphics*

- PcGive supports **text and graphics together on screen**, with easy adjustment of graph types, layout and colours.
- As many as **36 graphs** can be shown simultaneously, with easy user control or automatic selection.
- **Graphs can be documented and edited** via direct screen access with reading from the graph.
- **Time series and cross-plots** are supported with flexible adjustment and scaling options, including several bivariate linear regression lines with joint presentation of reverse regressions, or non-parametric fits, as well as spectra, correlograms, histograms and data densities.

- **Descriptive results, recursive statistics, diagnostic tests, likelihood projections and forecasts** can be graphed in many combinations.

(3) *Flexible data handling in GiveWin*

- The **data handling system provides convenient storage** of large data sets with easy loading to PcGive either as a unit, or for subsamples or subsets of variables.
- **Excel and Lotus spreadsheet files** can be loaded directly, or using 'cut and paste' facilities.
- **Large data sets** can be analysed, with with as many variables and observations as memory allows.
- Database variables can be transformed by a **calculator**, or by entering **mathematical formulae** in an editor with easy storage for reuse; the database is easily viewed, incorrect observations are simple to revise, and variables can be documented on-line.
- **Appending** across data sets is simple, and the data used for estimation can be any subset of the data in the database.
- **Several data sets** can be open simultaneously, with easy switching between the database.

(4) *Efficient modelling sequence*

- The underlying **C algorithms** are **fast, efficient, accurate** and carefully **tested**; all **data are stored in double precision**, and numerical operations use 80-bit arithmetic.
- PcGive is designed specifically for **modelling time-series** data, and creates lags, and analyses dynamic responses and long-run relations with ease; it is simple to change sample, or forecast, periods or estimation methods: models are retained for further analysis, and general-to-specific sequential simplifications are monitored for reduction tests.
- The **structured modelling approach** is fully discussed in this book, and guides the ordering of menus and dialogs, but application of the program is completely at the user's control.
- The **estimators** supported include least squares, instrumental variables, error autocorrelation, non-linear least squares, and non-linear maximum likelihood: powerful numerical optimization algorithms are embedded in the program with easy user control and most methods can be calculated recursively over the available sample.

- PcGive offers **powerful preprogrammed testing facilities** for a wide range of hypotheses of interest to econometricians and economists undertaking substantive empirical research, including tests for unit roots, dynamic specification, cointegration, linear restrictions and common factors.
- PcGive is also **applicable to cross-section data** and most of its facilities and tests are available for such analyses.
- **Large models** can be formulated, with no restrictions on size, apart from those imposed by available memory.
- A **Batch language** allows automatic estimation and evaluation of models, and can be used to prepare a PcGive session for teaching.

(5) *Thorough evaluation*

- **Equation mis-specification tests are automatically provided**, including residual autocorrelation, autoregressive conditional heteroscedasticity (ARCH), heteroscedasticity, functional form, parameter constancy, and normality (with residual density functions), as well as a complete set of encompassing tests.
- The **recursive estimators provide easy graphing** of coefficients and residuals with their confidence intervals, or 't'-values: parameter constancy statistics scaled by selected nominal significance levels are also calculated.
- All estimators provide **graphs** of fitted/actual values, residuals, and forecasts against outcomes with 1-step error bars.

(6) *Output*

- **Graphs can be saved** in several file formats including for later recall, further editing, and printing, or for importing into many popular word processors, as well as directly by 'cut and paste'
- **Results window** information can be saved as an ASCII (human readable) document for input to most word processors, or directly input by 'cut and paste'.
- Model residuals and recursive output can be **stored in the database** for additional graphs or evaluation.

We now consider some of these special features in greater detail.

(1) *Advanced graphics*

- Users have full control over **screen and graph colours**. The colour, type (solid, dotted, dashed etc.) and thickness of each line in a graph can be set; graphs can be drawn inside boxes, and with or without grids; axis values can be automatic or user defined; areas highlighted as desired; and so on.
- Up to **36 different graphs** can be shown simultaneously on-screen, which is especially valuable for graphical evaluation of equations and recursive methods. Combinations of graphs displaying different attributes of data can be shown simultaneously — examples are reported below.
- Once on-screen, text can be entered for **graph documentation**, or a mouse used to highlight interesting features during live presentations. Graphs can be both rapidly saved and instantly recalled. Coordinates can be read from each graph, however many are displayed at once.
- Much of PcGive's output is provided in **graphical form** which is why it is written as an interactive (and not a batch) program. Dozens of time series can be graphed together using a wide range of adjustment and prescaling options. Two variables can be cross-plotted as points or joined by lines (to show historical evolution), with least-squares lines for subsamples, selected recursively (so growing in size) or sequentially (a fixed % of the whole sample), showing projections of points from the lines; alternatively, both bivariate regression lines and/or a non-parametric regression can be drawn. Or they can be plotted by the values of a third variable. Spectral densities, correlograms, histograms and interpolated data densities and distributions also can be graphed in groups of up to 36.
- The option to see **multiple graphs** allows for more efficient evaluation of large amounts of information. Blocks of graphs can simultaneously incorporate descriptive results (fitted and actual values, scaled residuals and forecasts etc.) and diagnostic test information; or show many single-parameter likelihood grids.

(2) *Efficient modelling sequence*

- **Dynamic econometrics** involves creating and naming lagged variables, controlling the available sample and forecast period etc., and assigning the appropriate status to all variables, so such operations are either automatic or very easy. The basic PcGive operator is a lag polynomial. Long-run solutions, unit-root tests, cointegration tests, the significance of lagged variables (or groups of lags), the choice between deterministic or stochastic dynamics, roots of lag polynomials, tests for common factors etc. are all calculated. If the recommended general-to-specific approach to model construction is adopted, the sequence of reductions is monitored and F-tests, information criteria etc. are reported.

- This **extensive program book** seeks to bridge the gap between econometric theory and empirical modelling: the tutorials walk the user through every step from inputting data to the final selected econometric model of the variables under analysis. The econometrics chapters explain the theory and methods with reference to the program with detailed explanations of all the estimators and tests. The statistical output chapters carefully define all the estimators and tests used by PcGive.
- The **ordering of the menus and dialogs** is determined by the theory: first establish a data coherent, constant parameter model, investigate cointegration, reduce the model to a stationary, near orthogonal and simplified representation and finally check for parsimonious encompassing of the system: see Hendry and Ericsson (1991) and Hendry (1993, 1995a) for further details. Nevertheless, the application and sequence of the program's facilities remain completely under the user's control.
- **Estimation methods** currently supported include ordinary and recursive least squares, two-stage least squares, instrumental variables and recursive instrumental variables, r^{th}-order autoregressive least squares, non-linear least squares and recursive non-linear least squares and maximum likelihood. models are easily revised, transformed and simplified; up to 15 models are remembered for easy recall and progress evaluation.
- **Powerful testing facilities** for a wide range of specification hypotheses of interest to econometricians and economists undertaking substantive empirical research are preprogrammed for automatic calculation. Available tests include dynamic specification, lag length, cointegration, and tests of reduction or parsimonious encompassing. Wald tests of linear restrictions are easily conducted.

(3) *Thorough evaluation*

- **Evaluation tests** can either be automatically calculated, calculated in a block as a summary test option, or implemented singly or in sets merely by selecting the relevant dialog option. A comprehensive and powerful range of mis-specification tests is offered to sustain the methodological recommendations about model evaluation. Equation mis-specification tests include residual autocorrelation, ARCH, heteroscedasticity, functional form mis-specification and normality. Constancy tests can be computed automatically or via recursive procedures. A range of encompassing tests can be undertaken (just by a single keystroke or click!) once two rival models have been estimated.

- **Graphical diagnostic information** includes plots of residual correlograms, residual density functions and histograms, and QQ plots.
- Much of the power of PcGive resides in its extensive use of **recursive estimators**. These provide voluminous output (coefficients, standard errors, t-values, residual sums of squares, 1-step residuals and their standard errors, constancy tests etc. at every sample size), but recursive statistics can be graphed for easy presentation (up to 36 graphs simultaneously). The size of models is only restricted by the available memory, as long as fewer than 100 variables are involved.
- All estimators provide **graphs** of residuals, fitted and actual values and their cross-plots, as well as 1-step forecasts or forecast errors with 95% confidence intervals shown by error bars.
- Full graphics facilities can be applied to any or all of these graphs (e.g., adding regression lines etc.)

Considerable experience has demonstrated the practicality and value of using PcGive as an operational complement to learning econometrics and conducting empirical studies. It is also easy and helpful to run PcGive live in classroom teaching as an adjunct to theoretical derivations. On the research side, the incisive recursive estimators and the wide range of preprogrammed tests make PcGive the most powerful interactive econometric modelling program available; Chapter 15 discusses its application to a range of important practical econometrics problems. These roles are enhanced by the flexible and informative graphics options provided.

1.3 Documentation conventions

The convention for instructions that you should type is that they are shown in `Typewriter` font. Capitals and lower case are only distinguished as the names of variables in the program and the mathematical formulae you type. Once GiveWin has started, then from the keyboard, the `Alt` key accesses line menus (at the top of the screen); from a mouse, click on the item to be selected using the left button. Common commands have a shortcut on the toolbar, the purpose of which can be ascertained by placing the mouse on the relevant icon. Icons that can currently operate are highlighted. Commands on menus, toolbar buttons, and dialog items (buttons, checkboxes etc.) are shown in Sans Serif font.

Equations are numbered as (chapter.number); for example, (8.1) refers to equation 8.1, which is the first equation in Chapter 8. References to sections have the form §chapter.section, for example, §8.1 is Section 8.1 in Chapter 8. Tables and Figures are shown as Figure chapter.number (e.g.) Figure 5.2 for the second figure in Chapter 5. Multiple graphs are numbered from left to right and top to bottom, so (b) is the top-right graph of four, and (c) the bottom left.

1.4 Using PcGive documentation

The documentation comes in five main parts: Part I comprises this introductory chapter, and instructions on starting the program. Part II then has six extensive tutorials on all aspects of econometric modelling, emphasising the data analytic facilities over simply program usage. Part III has six chapters discussing the econometrics of PcGive from introductory to advanced levels. Part IV offers a detailed description of the statistical and econometric output of PcGive. Part V provides complete information about the menus and dialogs. Finally, Part VI contains appendices. The documentation ends with references and a subject index. As discussed above, the aim is to provide a practical textbook of econometric modelling, linking the econometrics of PcGive to empirical modelling through tutorials which implement applied modelling exercises. In more detail:

(1) A separate book explains and documents the companion program **GiveWin** which records the output and provides data loading and graphing facilities.

(2) The **Prologue** discusses the main feature provided by PcGive, sketches how to use the program and illustrates some of its output.

(3) The **Tutorials** in Chapters 3 to 9 are specifically designed for joint learning of econometric analysis and use of the programs. They describe using the editor, data input, graphics control, dynamic model formulation, estimation and evaluation; dynamic analysis; econometric modelling; and advanced features. By implementing empirical research exercises, they allow rapid mastery of PcGive and an understanding of how the associated econometric theory operates in practice.

(4) The **Econometric overview** in Chapter 10 briefly reviews the background econometrics of PcGive.

(5) Chapters 11–15 explain the **Econometrics** at all levels from elementary, through intermediate to advanced, including Chapter 13 covering statistical theory, as well as a chapter on important practical problems.

(6) The **Statistical Output** in Chapters 16 to 18 explain in detail the econometric and statistical calculations of PcGive.

(7) The **Manuals** in Chapters 19 to 20 document the structure and functioning of PcGive. Chapter 19 gives information about PcGive languages, whereas Chapter 20 documents the menu structure. The **manuals** correspond closely to the information available in the on-line help. They should be needed for reference only, but it may be helpful to read them once.

The appropriate sequence is to first read and follow the instructions in the **installation procedure** to copy and install PcGive 9 on your system. Next, read the remainder of this introduction, then follow the step-by-step guidance given in the **tutorials** to get familiar with the operation of PcGive. Part III explains the required econometrics, starting at an elementary level and building up to advanced tools.

To use the documentation, either check the index for the subject, topic, menu or dialog that seems relevant; or look up the part relevant to your current activity (for example, econometrics, tutorials or description) in the **Contents**, and scan for the most likely keyword. The references point to relevant publications which analyse the methodology and methods embodied in PcGive.

1.5 An overview of PcGive menus

There are five main menus relevant to:

(1) File: which enables exiting the program;
(2) Data: data description and autoregressive distributed-lag models;
(3) Model: model formulation and estimation;
(4) Test: formal and graphical testing;
(5) Help: accesses the help system.

Entry to further dialogs is always via one of these, which pulls down the relevant set of choices.

1.6 Citation

To facilitate replication and validation of empirical findings, PcGive should be cited in all reports and publications involving its application. The appropriate form is to cite PcGive in the list of references.

1.7 World Wide Web

Consult `http://www.nuff.ox.ac.uk/Users/Doornik/` for pointers to additional information relevant to the current and future versions of PcGive.

1.8 Some data sets

The data used in Hendry (1995a) is provided in the files UKM1.IN7/UKM1.BN7. The DHSY data (see Davidson, Hendry, Srba and Yeo, 1978) is supplied in the files DHSY.IN7/DHSY.BN7. An algebra file, DHSY.ALG, contains code to create variables used in the paper. A batch file, DHSY.FL, loads the data, executes algebra code, and estimates the two final equations reported in the paper.

For the data sets used in Hendry and Morgan (1995), consult:
`ftp://hicks.nuff.ox.ac.uk/pub/economic/hendry/histects`.

Chapter 2

Getting Started

We now discuss some of the basic skills required to get started with PcGive. We will give a short introduction to the services provided by GiveWin. Even though PcGive and GiveWin are separate programs they work closely together: GiveWin provides the data which PcGive analyses, and receives all the text output and graphs which you create in PcGive. When you start PcGive, it automatically starts up GiveWin (or will connect to the version which is already active). Then GiveWin will ask PcGive if it can handle batch commands (which it can). Note that GiveWin will *not* automatically start PcGive (when you close GiveWin, you must also close PcGive to restart). The aim of this tutorial is just to load data and create graphs: for instructions on how to transform data using the calculator or algebra, consult the GiveWin book.

The convention for instructions that you should type is that they are shown in `Typewriter` font. Capitals and lower case are only distinguished as the names of variables in the program and the mathematical formulae you type. Once GiveWin and PcGive have started, then from the keyboard, the `Alt` key accesses line menus (at the top of the screen); from a mouse, click on the item to be selected. Commands on menus, toolbar buttons, and dialog items (buttons, checkboxes etc.) are shown in Sans Serif font. Common commands have a shortcut on the toolbar.

We assume that you have the basic skills to operate programs under the Windows operating system (the GiveWin books provides some hints). PcGive works on Windows 3.1, Windows NT or Windows 95, but the screen appearance of the program and dialogs will reflect the operating system you are using. The captures in this book were made under Windows 95.

2.1 Starting PcGive

Start PcGive from the taskbar (or from the GiveWin group). If this is the first time you have used PcGive, you might wish to reduce it to a smaller size. Your initial screen could look like the capture shown on the next page.

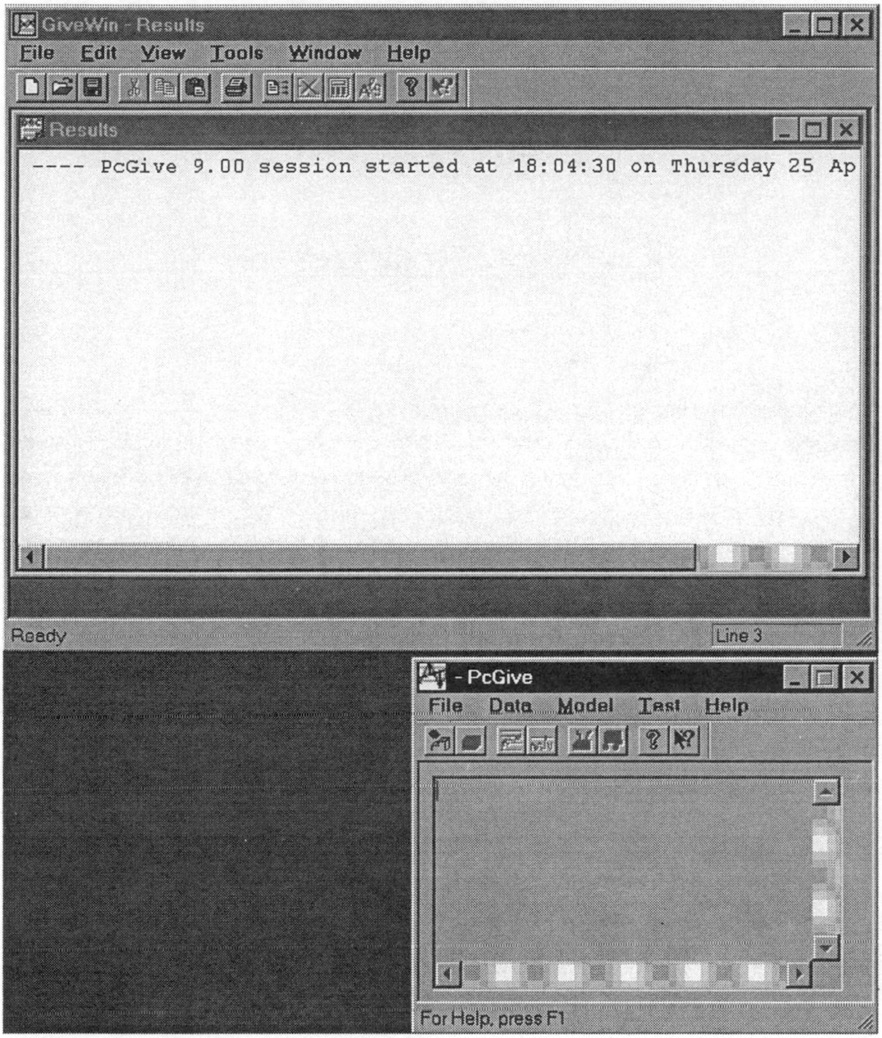

2.2 Loading and viewing the tutorial data set

Without data, PcGive cannot operate, so the first step is to load data into GiveWin which PcGive can then access. All the tutorials use a data set called DATA.IN7. These are artificial data on consumption, income, inflation and output. The IN7 extension indicates a PcGive 7 data file (a format which remained the same for versions 8 and 9). The IN7 file is a human-readable file, describing the data. There is a companion BN7 file, which holds the actual numbers (in binary format, so this file cannot be edited). GiveWin can handle a wide range of data files, among them Excel (.XLS up to version 4) and Lotus files (.WKS and .WK1), and of course plain human-readable (ASCII) files. You can also cut and paste data between Excel and GiveWin. Details are in the GiveWin book.

We shall load the tutorial data set here. Access the File menu in GiveWin:

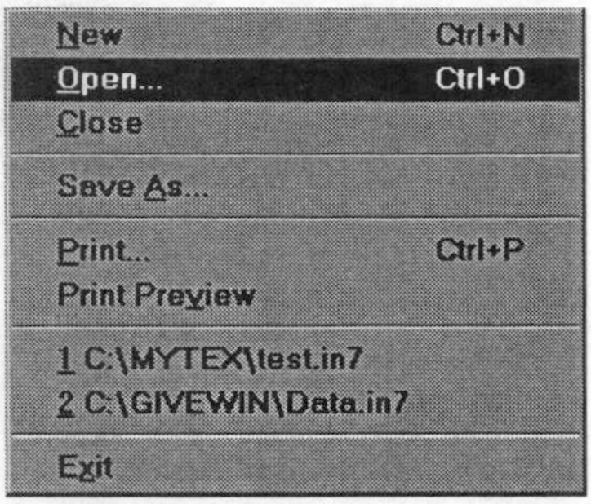

and choose Open. If you installed in the default directory structure the data will be in the `\PcGive` directory, so locate that directory and select Data:

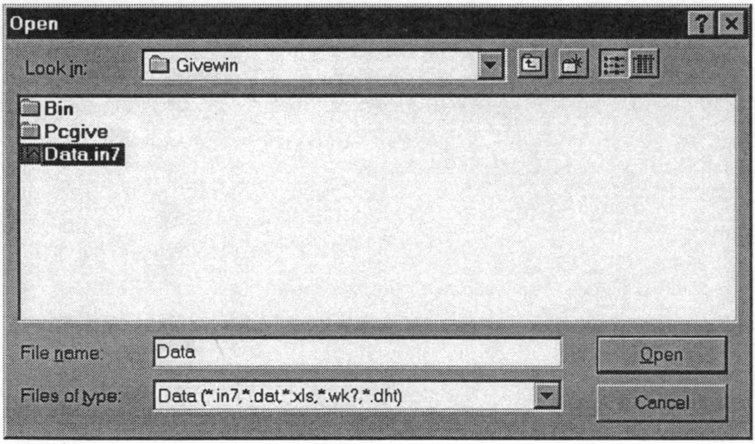

The data file will be loaded, and displayed minimized:

Bring the window into view by clicking on the icon with two overlapping boxes (Windows 95; for Windows 3.1: double click on the database) to show the actual database (note that the left-most panel of the status bar shows the data value with maximum accuracy):

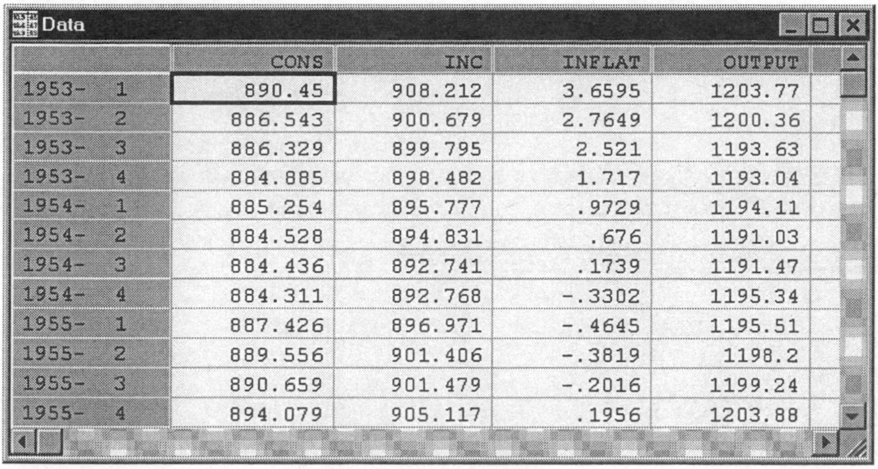

	CONS	INC	INFLAT	OUTPUT
1953- 1	890.45	908.212	3.6595	1203.77
1953- 2	886.543	900.679	2.7649	1200.36
1953- 3	886.329	899.795	2.521	1193.63
1953- 4	884.885	898.482	1.717	1193.04
1954- 1	885.254	895.777	.9729	1194.11
1954- 2	884.528	894.831	.676	1191.03
1954- 3	884.436	892.741	.1739	1191.47
1954- 4	884.311	892.768	-.3302	1195.34
1955- 1	887.426	896.971	-.4645	1195.51
1955- 2	889.556	901.406	-.3819	1198.2
1955- 3	890.659	901.479	-.2016	1199.24
1955- 4	894.079	905.117	.1956	1203.88

Double clicking on the variable name shows the documentation of the variable. For the CONS variable:

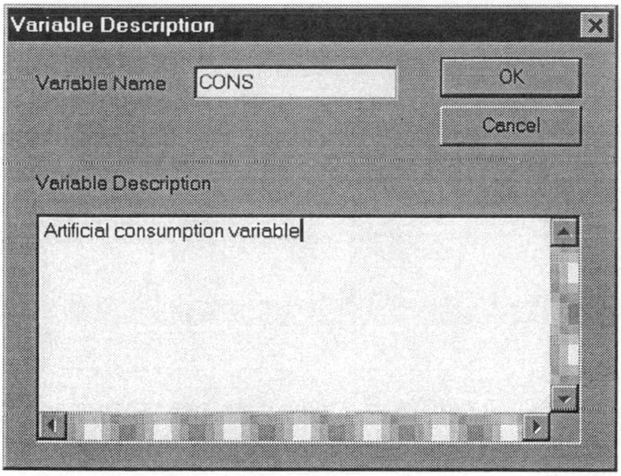

The data can be manipulated, much like in a spreadsheet program. Here we shall not need these facilities, so *minimize* the window again: click on the first button in the right-hand side of the window (Windows 95, Windows 3.1: click on the downward pointing button). Do not click on the cross: this closes the database, thus removing it from GiveWin and so PcGive (which is different from version 8).

2.3 GiveWin graphics

The graphics facilities of GiveWin are powerful yet easy to use. This section will show you how to make time-plots and cross-plots of variables in the database. GiveWin offers automatic selections of scaling etc., but you will be able to edit these graphs, and change the default layout such as line colours and line types. Graphs can also be saved in a variety of formats for later use in a word processor or for reloading to GiveWin.

2.3.1 A first graph

Graphics is the first entry on the Tools menu. Activate the command to see the following dialog box (or click on the cross-plot graphics icon on the toolbar):

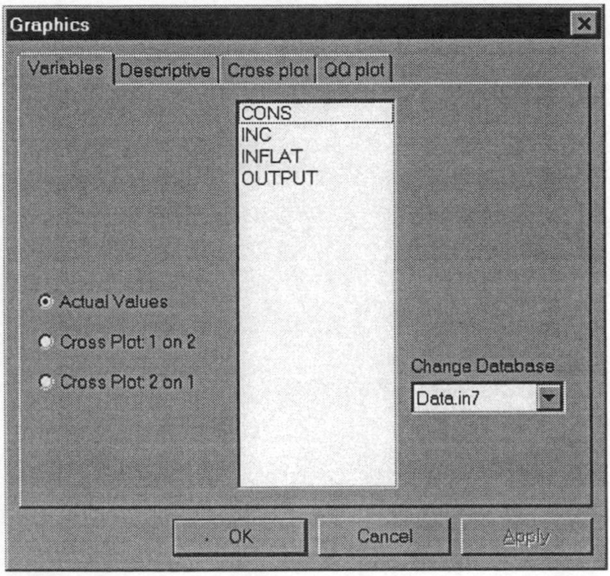

This is the first example of a dialog with a multiple selection list box. In such a list box you can mark as many items as you want. Here we mark all the variables we wish to graph. With the keyboard you can only mark a single variable (by using the arrow up and down keys) or range of variables (hold the shift key down while using the arrow up or down keys).
With the mouse there is more flexibility:

- single click to select one variable;
- hold the left mouse button down to select a range of variables;
- hold the `Ctrl` key down and click to select additional variables;
- hold the `Shift` key down and click to extend the selection range;

In this example we select CONS and INC and then press the OK button. The graph which appears looks very much like Figure 2.1. The only difference is the position of the legend. You can pick that up with the mouse, and move it to another position in the graph.

Most graphs in this book are boxed in, obtainable by choosing Graphics Setup from the View menu, and selecting the Layout page then clicking on Boxed. The View and Edit menu show the available options for graphs.

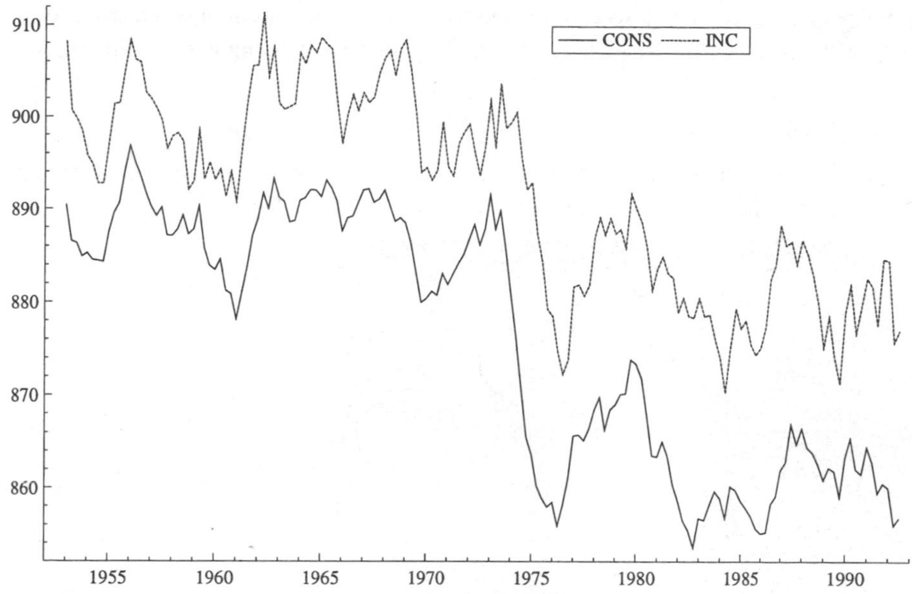

Figure 2.1 Time plot of CONS and INC.

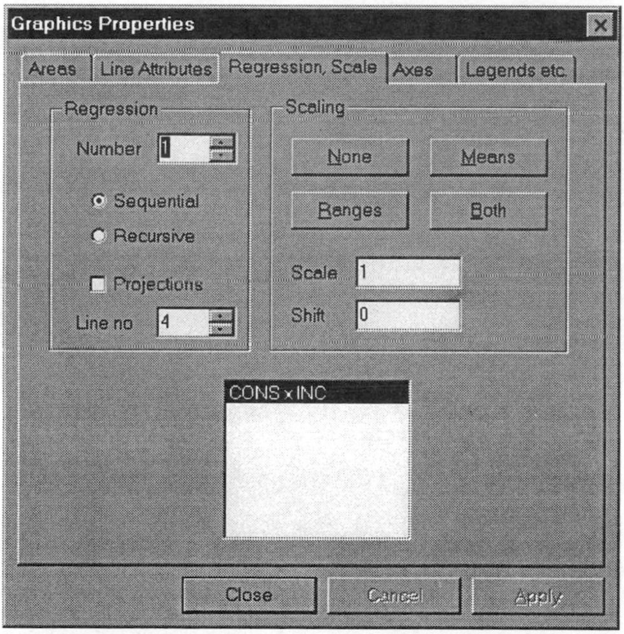

GiveWin can draw multiple graphs simultaneously on-screen: just click on the Graphics toolbar button again, reselect both CONS and INC, and click on Cross plot 1 on 2. Unlike version 8 of PcGive, graphs can be edited while on screen. Double click on the cross plot, select the Regression, Scale page in the Graphics Properties dialog, and add a regression line as shown in Figure 2.2. The GiveWin book describes them in more detail.

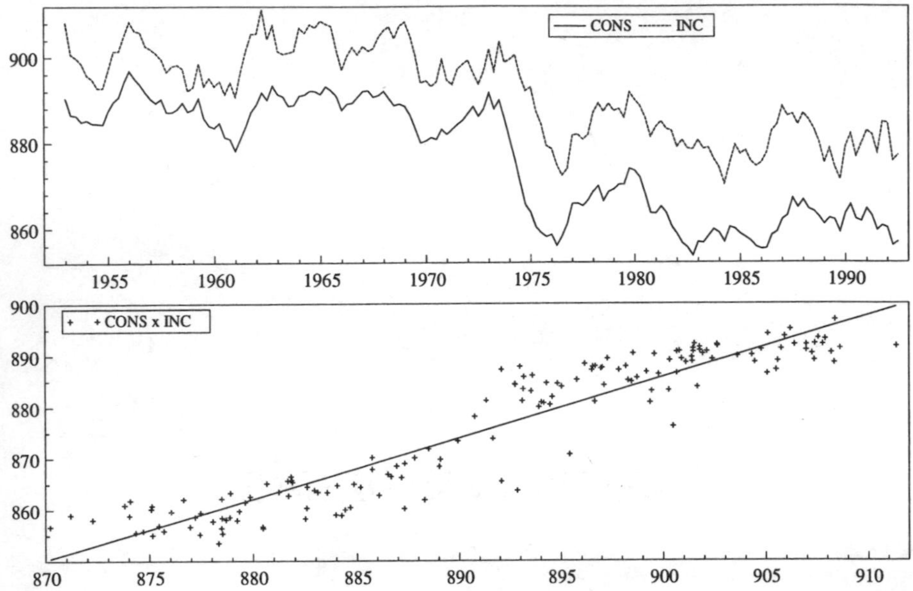

Figure 2.2 Multiple graphs.

2.3.2 Graph saving and printing

To print a graph directly to the printer, click on the printer icon in the toolbar. You can preview the result first using the Print Preview command from the File menu.

Graphs can be saved to disk in various formats:

- Windows metafile (.WMF);
- Enhanced metafile (.EMF, Windows 95 and Windows NT only);
- Encapsulated PostScript (.EPS), this is the format used to produce all the graphs in this book;
- GiveWin Graphics File (.GWG).

The GWG format is particular to GiveWin; no other program can read it and no printer can handle it. However, it is the only format which you can reload into GiveWin for further editing.

This completes the getting started chapter. We hope that you're equipped now for more substantial econometric modelling exercises.

Part II

PcGive Tutorials

Chapter 3

Tutorial on Regression Analysis

3.1 Setting up a regression

The purpose of this tutorial is to explain the use of PcGive for estimating linear regression equations. The background to regression and least squares estimation methods is explained in Chapters 11 and 12. If you are unfamiliar with regression, proceed with this chapter till you feel lost, then read Chapter 11 and return here later.

Start PcGive, and load the DATA.IN7 and DATA.BN7 files in GiveWin as explained earlier, then select the Model menu (`Alt+m`) to bring up the following screen:

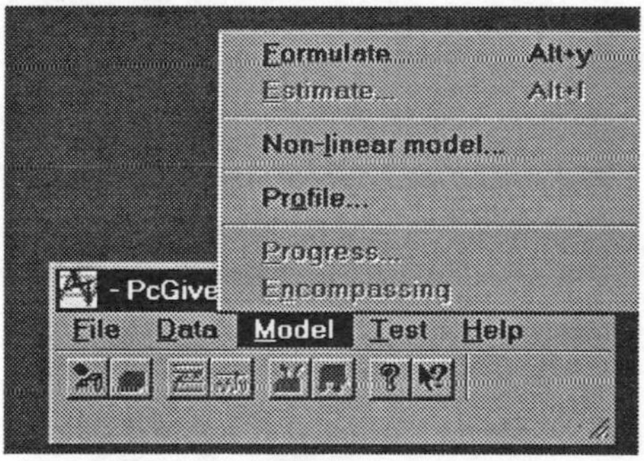

Now select Formulate (`f`) to see the Model Formulation dialog, shown opposite. As a shortcut, you could have clicked on the first toolbar button, which also activates the Model Formulation dialog (the graphical metaphor is that it involves creating the building blocks for a model).

This is a dialog which you will use often, so, at the risk of boring you, we consider it in detail. It consists of four columns: on the right are the three familiar OK, Cancel and Help buttons, the listbox with special variables, and the default lag length setting. Moving to the left, we see the variables in the currently selected database. If more than one database is loaded in GiveWin, you could select any of them. From the currently selected database, we select variables for the model. The next list box, labelled Model has the model specification, empty at the moment. Below it is a Recall button, for recalling previously estimated models. Finally, we have a column of buttons which all act for recalling previously estimated models. Finally, we have a column of buttons which all act on variables in the model.

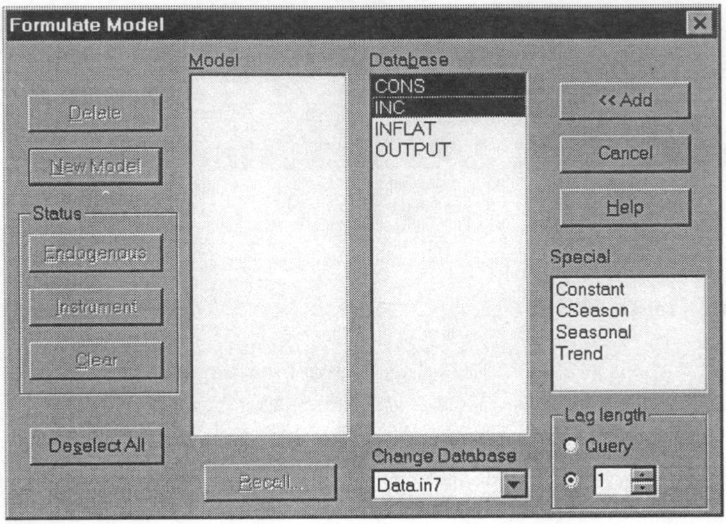

To formulate a model, mark database variables and add them to the model. Mark a variable by clicking on it with the mouse. To select several variables, use the `Ctrl` key with the mouse, to select a range, use `Shift` plus the mouse. Once variables are selected, the OK button changes to Add. Press it to add the variables to the model (or just press the `Enter` key). By default the lag length will be set to one (choosing Query, would result in a little pop-up box, asking the lag length for each variable). The marked variable that is highest in the database becomes the dependent variable, because it is the first to enter the model. A two-step procedure might be required to make a lower variable into the dependent variable: first mark and add the dependent variable, then add the remaining variables. Alternatively, just enter the variables in the order that they occur in the database and change the status of the involved variables later: the requisite buttons are described below.

Select CONS and INC, and add the marked variables to the model.

The default lag length for CONS and INC is one. Also note that a Constant is automatically added, but can be deleted if the scale of the variables lets a regression through the origin have meaning; neither the Constant nor the Trend will be offered for lagging (lagging these would create redundant variables). CONS is marked with an E to show that it is an endogenous (here, the dependent) variable: its status can be cleared by marking it then clicking on the Clear button (and reset by marking and clicking on the Endogenous button).

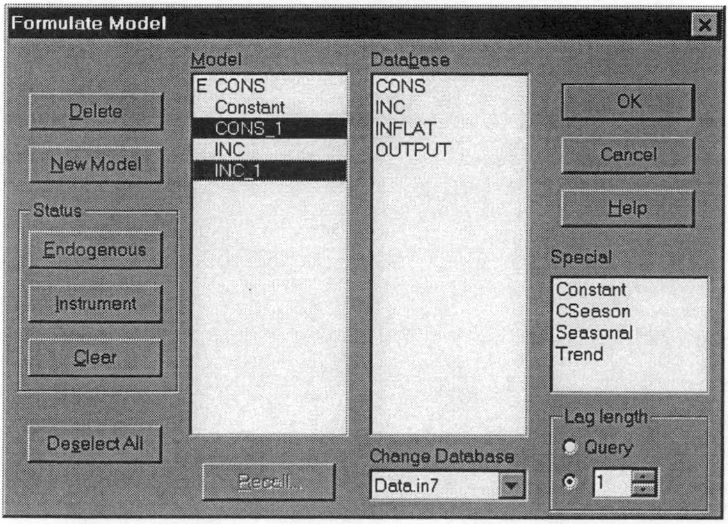

As a first start, we wish to estimate a simple bivariate model, requiring deletion from the model of the lagged variables. Click on 'CONS_1' in the model, then press the `Delete` key, or the Delete button. Do the same for INC_1.

As an additional practice in deleting variables from the model, add Seasonal to the model. As you see, PcGive automatically adds the correct number of seasonals (three here as the data are quarterly: see Chapter 11). It takes the constant term into account; without the constant, four seasonals would have been added. You can rely on the fact that Seasonal is always unity in the first period (quarter here). So Seasonal_1 is one in the second quarter. Delete the seasonals from the model.

The next button of note is New Model which will delete all the model variables to start a new model. If you pressed it by accident, an earlier model can be recalled by clicking the Recall button at the foot of the dialog. The remaining three buttons on the left assign and change the status of model variables. These could be used to change the dependent variable. Otherwise they are mainly relevant for instrumental variables estimation, and will be considered in Chapter 6.

Once the model formulation is complete, click on OK or press `Enter` to bring up the Estimation dialog.

3.2 Regression estimation

Estimation methods are discussed in Part III. Here we restrict ourselves to regression which is implemented by ordinary least squares (OLS) (examples of the other estimation methods are shown in Chapter 6). Pressing the OK button in the Model Formulation dialog immediately jumps to the Estimation dialog. Other ways of activating the Estimation dialog are the short-cut key `Alt+l`, in which the `l` stands for least squares;

however, the toolbar button (the second: putting the blocks together) will be the most convenient way of activating the dialog.

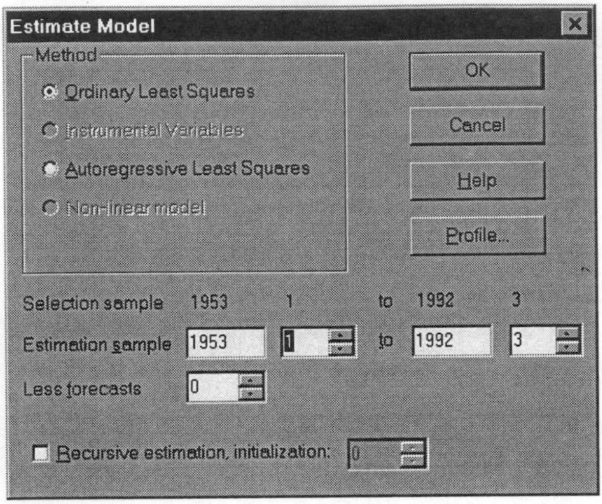

Any one estimation method can be selected: `Alt+o` marks ordinary least squares (the default). The dialog allows you to retain some data for forecasting. The sample period can be adjusted, but the one shown is always admissible and will either be the maximum available or the one used in the previous model. *Please verify that the sample size on your screen corresponds to the one shown here*: 1953 (1) – 1992 (3) with no forecasts. Here we use no forecasts, and the full sample. Press the OK button (or `Enter`) to estimate the model. Providing the profile has not been reset, this brings up the Graphical analysis dialog. Exit this dialog by pressing the `Escape` key; we shall return to it shortly.

The equation we fitted is:

$$\text{CONS}_t = a + b\text{INC}_t + u_t$$

where a and b are selected to minimize the sum of squares of the $\{u_t\}$. The resulting estimated values for a and b are written $\hat{a}$ and $\hat{b}$. During estimation, the actions of PcGive are recorded in its main dialog:

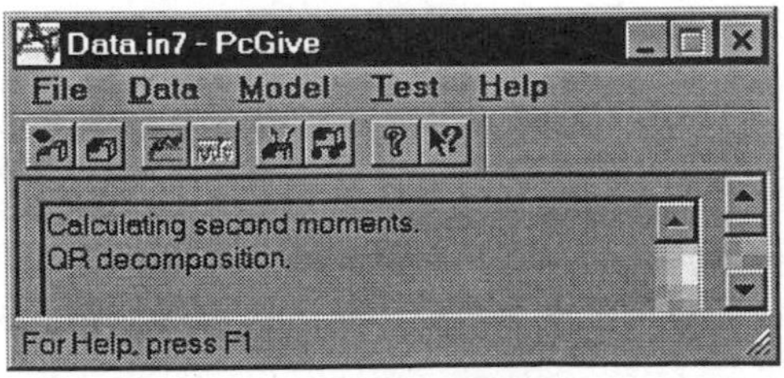

3.3 Bivariate regression output

3.3.1 Regression estimates

The regression results are written to the Results window. As you know from Chapter 2, this window does not reside in PcGive, but in GiveWin. Set focus to GiveWin, and to the Results window. The output is:

```
EQ( 1) Modelling CONS by OLS  (using Data.in7)
The present sample is:  1953 (1) to 1992 (3)

Variable       Coefficient     Std.Error  t-value  t-prob PartR^2
Constant           -181.27        30.028   -6.037  0.0000  0.1884
INC                 1.1856      0.033673   35.210  0.0000  0.8876

R^2=0.887596  F(1,157)=1239.8 [0.0000]  \sigma=4.5537 DW=0.365
RSS = 3255.584443 for 2 variables and 159 observations
```

These results cannot be regarded as substantive but their meaning can be described. To do so, we remain in GiveWin, and turn to a cross-plot of CONS and INC. Access the Graphics dialog and graph a cross plot of CONS against INC. Then double click on the graph to add a regression line with projections: the outcome is shown in Figure 3.1.

The slope of the line is the tangent of the angle at b: a tangent is calculated by the ratio of the length opposite over the length adjacent. Using the point facility (`Alt+p`) to read off the values at the two extremes of the line as drawn, we find the approximate slope:

$$\hat{b} = \frac{(896.864 - 853.136)}{(909.367 - 872.379)} = \frac{43.728}{36.988} = 1.182.$$

This value closely matches the coefficient just reported.

The intercept is the value of CONS when INC equals zero, or more usefully, using an overbar $^-$ to denote the mean value, a is given by:

$$\hat{a} = \overline{\text{CONS}} - \hat{b} \times \overline{\text{INC}}.$$

To calculate the mean values, select the Data menu in PcGive and choose the Descriptive Statistics command. Mark CONS and INC and Correlations as shown here:

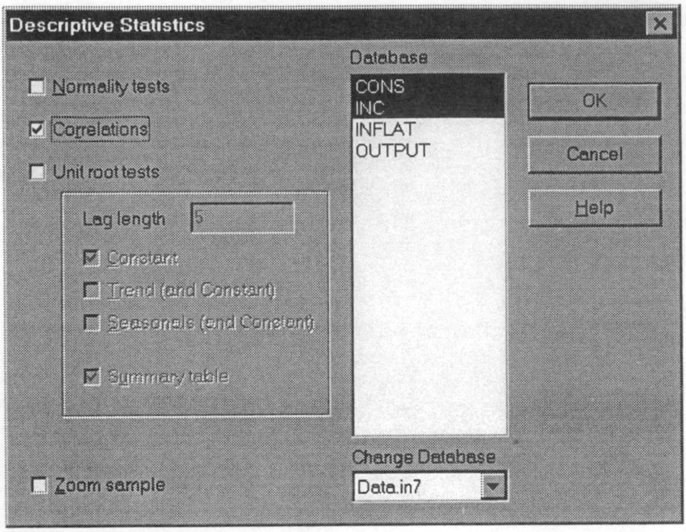

The results from the descriptive statistics are:

```
The present sample is:  1953 (1) to 1992 (3)
Descriptive statistics
Means
        CONS          INC
      875.94       891.69

Standard Deviations
        CONS          INC
      13.539       10.759

Correlation matrix
                   CONS          INC
CONS             1.0000
INC             0.94212       1.0000
```

Substituting the means of the variables into our formula, we obtain:

$$\hat{a} = 875.94 - 1.182 \times 891.69 = -178.$$

Thus, the regression coefficients simply show the values of the slope and intercept needed to draw the line in Figure 3.1. Their interpretation is that a unit increase in INC is associated with a 1.18 unit increase in CONS. If the data purport to be consumption expenditure and income, we should be suspicious of such a finding taken at face value. However, there is nothing mysterious about multiple regression: it is simply a procedure for fitting straight lines to data.

Next, the standard errors (SEs) of the coefficients reflect the best estimate of the variability likely to occur in repeated random sampling from the same population: the coefficient ± 2SE provides a 95% confidence interval. When that interval does not include

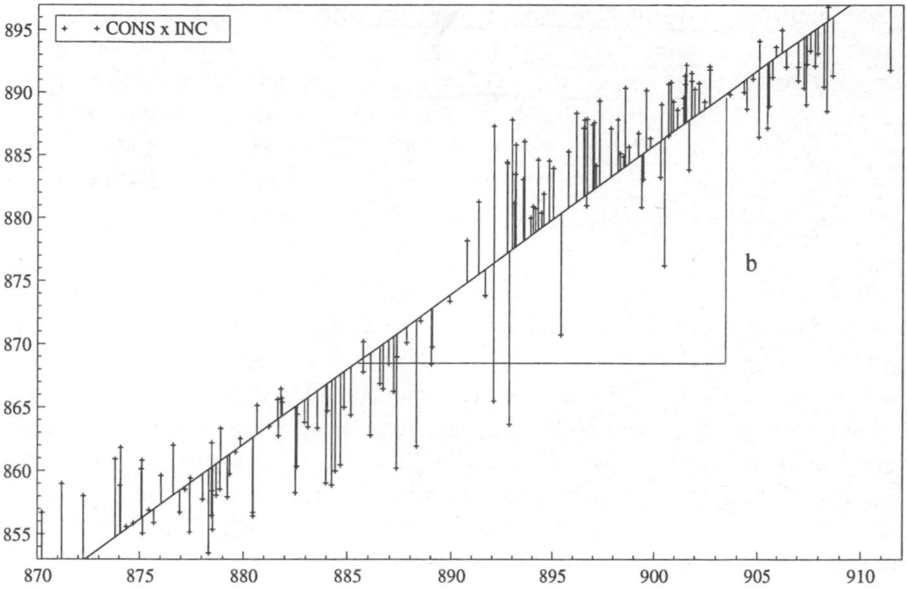

Figure 3.1 Cross-plot of CONS against INC.

zero, the coefficient is often called 'significant' (at the 5% level). The t-value is the ratio of the estimated coefficient to its standard error, so values with $|t| > 2$ are significant. Here, the non-random residuals manifest in Figure 3.1 make the interpretation of the SEs suspect (in fact, they are downwards biased here, and hence the reported 't'-values are artificially inflated – despite that, they are so large that even the 'correct' SEs would yield t-values greater than 2 in absolute value).

The last statistic in the regression array is the partial r^2. This is the squared correlation between the relevant explanatory variable and the dependent variable (often called regressor and regressand respectively), holding all other variables fixed. For the regression of CONS on INC, there are no other variables (after all, the Constant is not called that for nothing!), so the partial r^2 equals the simple correlation squared (shown above in the descriptive statistics output). As can be seen, that is also the value of the coefficient of multiple correlation squared, R^2, which measures the correlation between the actual values $CONS_t$ and the fitted values $\widehat{CONS}_t$, and is reported immediately below the regression output. When there are several regressors, r^2 and R^2 differ. Here:

$$\widehat{CONS}_t = \hat{a} + \hat{b}\, INC_t.$$

Moving along the R^2 row of output, the F-test is a test of $R^2 = 0$. For a bivariate regression, that corresponds precisely to a test of $b = 0$ and can be checked using the fact that $t^2(k) = F(1, k)$. Here, $(35.21)^2 = 1239.74$ which is close for a hand calculation. The next item [0.0000] is the probability that $F = 0$, and the ** denotes that the outcome is significant at the 1% level or less.

The value of $\hat{\sigma}$ is the standard deviation, usually called the equation standard error. Since the errors are assumed to be drawn independently from the same distribution with mean zero and constant variance σ, an approximate 95% confidence interval for any one error is $0 \pm 2\hat{\sigma}$. That represents the likely interval from the fitted regression line of the observations. When $\hat{\sigma} = 4.55$, the 95% interval is a huge 18.2% of CONS – the government would not thank you for a model that poor, as it knows that consumers' expenditure rarely changes by more than 5% from one year to the next even without your model. We learn that not all regressions are useful.

The last statistic in that row of output is the DW (Durbin–Watson) test statistic. That checks whether the residuals are indeed successively related (called serial correlation): tables of significance values are presented in many textbooks, but the assumptions needed to justify the application of the test in economics are rarely satisfied. It is reported more as a historical relic than as a fundamental test. Here, it is invalid but nevertheless suggests non-random residuals (values outside $[1, 3]$ are usually significant: its mean is 2 and its extreme lower and upper values are zero and 4 respectively). Finally, RSS is the acronym from residual sum of squares, namely $\sum_{t=1}^{T} \hat{u}_t^2$, which can be useful for hand calculations of tests between different equations for the same variable.

3.3.2 Regression graphics

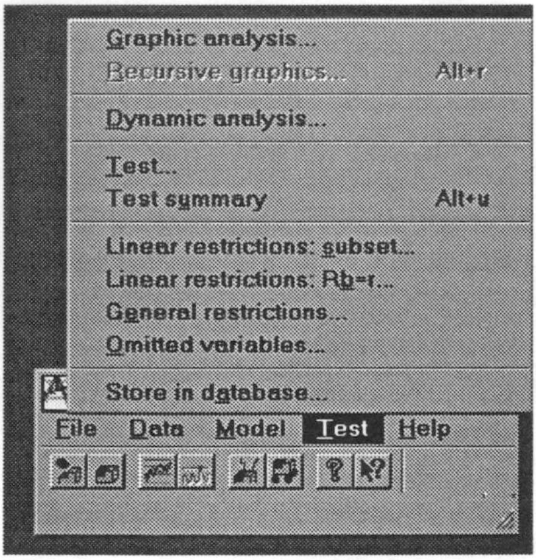

Of course, there are other ways to represent the findings, and one of the more useful is a time-series graph of the fitted values, namely $\widehat{\text{CONS}}_t$, with the outcomes, a cross-plot of the same two variables, and the scaled residuals:

$$\hat{u}_t = \frac{\left(\text{CONS}_t - \widehat{\text{CONS}}_t\right)}{\hat{\sigma}}.$$

Select the Test menu (Alt+t) to produce the menu shown at the beginning of this section. Choose Graphic analysis (this dialog has a shortcut on the toolbar, the third button):

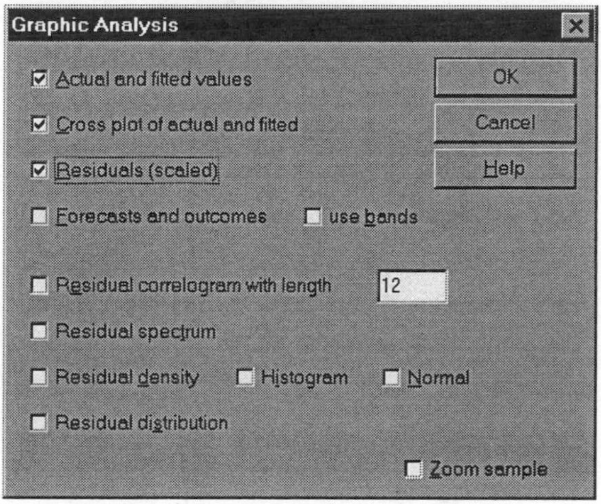

The Graphic analysis dialog lets you plot and/or cross-plot the actual and fitted values for the whole sample, the residuals scaled by $\hat{\sigma}$, the forecasts if any were assigned, and a variety of graphical diagnostics to which we return below.

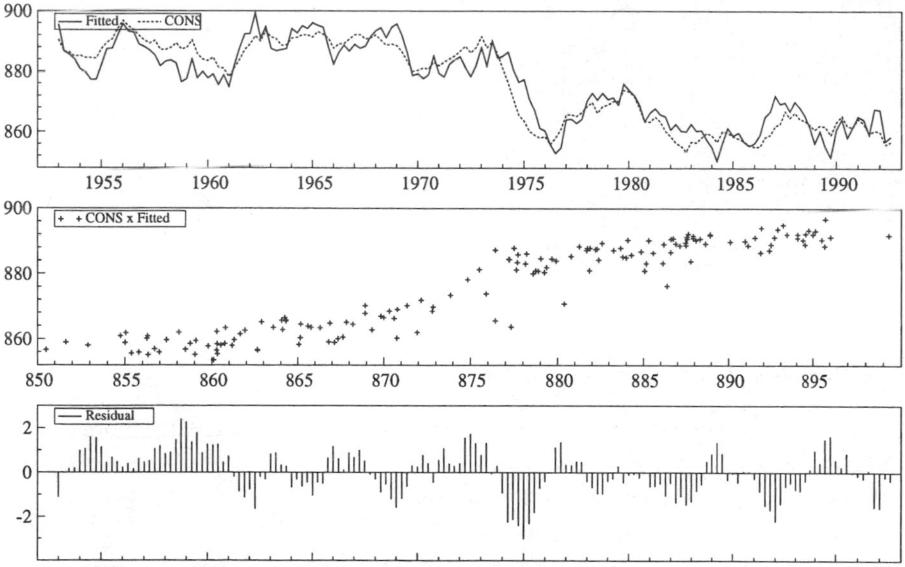

Figure 3.2 Goodness-of-fit graphs for bivariate model of CONS.

Mark Actual, Cross-plot and Scaled residuals as shown: the necessary keystrokes are `Alt+a`, `Alt+p`, `Alt+c` (or click as desired with the mouse). Accepting (`Enter`) produces Figure 3.2 in GiveWin. As before, any graphs can be saved, edited or printed.

The first plot shows the 'track' of the outcome by the fitted model as time series. The overall tracking is fair, but is not very precise. This is perhaps easier to see here from the cross-plot, where two groups of scatters can be seen on either side of 875: the outcome would be a straight line for a perfect fit. Finally, the scaled residuals do not look very random: when the value is high in one period, you can see that it is more likely to be high again in the next period, and similarly low (that is, large negative) values are followed by other low values.

3.4 Test output

We will only compute two tests in this part of the tutorial: the first is for a subset of the regressors being zero. With only one actual variable, there is not much scope, but we can check that the test yields the same outcome as the (squared) t-test already reported. Select the Test menu, and Linear restrictions: subset, and mark INC:

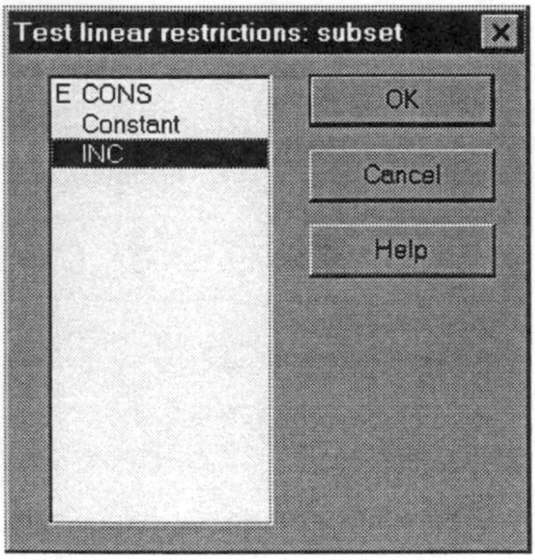

Now accept to produce:

```
Wald test for linear restrictions (Subset)
LinRes F(1,157) =     1239.8 [0.0000] **

Zero restrictions on:  INC
```

This is identical to the F-test value above.

As a second test, we consider adding a variable to the existing model. Select Test/Omitted variables and mark INFLAT so that:

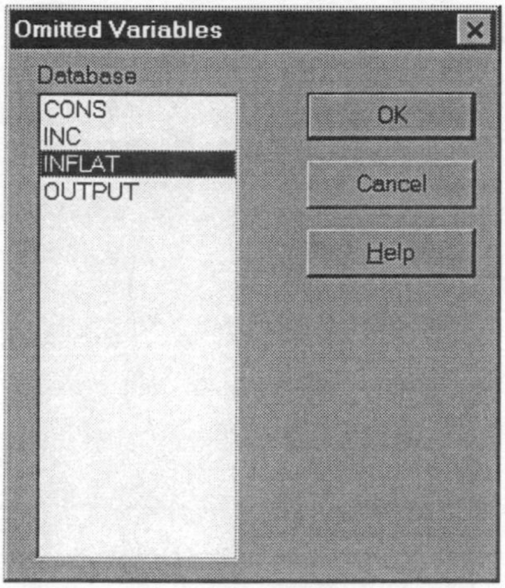

Accept (if lagged observations are available, this dialog offers a choice of lag length) to obtain:

```
LM test for omitted variables
Add      F( 1,156) =      149.07 [0.0000] **

Added variables: INFLAT
```

This result strongly suggests that INFLAT has an important impact on the relation between CONS and INC, as the hypothesis that the effect is zero would essentially never produce such a large test outcome by chance.

3.5 Multiple regression

That last result suggests using a multiple explanatory variable model, with both INC and INFLAT as regressors. From a methodological viewpoint, expanding a model in response to test rejections is not a good way to do research: we could have found 10 different flaws with the first regression, and where we finally ended up would depend critically on the order in which we 'fixed' them. However, in a tutorial on the use of the program, we can claim some poetic licence and proceed to the more interesting stage of a multiple regression by adding INFLAT to the set of regressors. Select Model, Formulate using the toolbar button, or the 'hot-key' `Alt+y` (remember y_t is usually the symbol for the dependent variable in econometrics since Koopmans, 1950).

Either click on INFLAT with the mouse or type `Alt+b` and use the arrows (↓) to move down and highlight INFLAT. Then press the `Enter` key to accept (simply double clicking on INFLAT would have done the job too). We still do not want any lags at this stage: so delete the unwanted variable from the model. Either click on INFLAT_1 or type `Alt+m`, and use the arrow keys to highlight it, and press the Delete button (click with the mouse or `Alt+d`). Now we can accept the model and estimate it (`Enter` – or click on OK – then `Enter` again at the Estimation dialog) to obtain:

```
EQ( 2) Modelling CONS by OLS  (using Data.in7)
The present sample is:  1953 (1) to 1992 (3)

Variable      Coefficient    Std.Error  t-value  t-prob PartR^2
Constant          -147.39       21.719   -6.786  0.0000  0.2279
INC                1.1526     0.024307   47.420  0.0000  0.9351
INFLAT            -2.4747      0.20268  -12.210  0.0000  0.4886

R^2=0.942522  F(2,156)=1279 [0.0000]  \sigma=3.26673  DW=0.605
RSS = 1664.758208 for 3 variables and 159 observations
```

The added variable is apparently highly significant (but DW remains too low to allow any trust in the standard errors reported).

The square of the t-test on INFLAT is precisely the Omitted variable F-test. Otherwise, the INC coefficient is not greatly altered, and still exceeds unity, but $\hat{\sigma}$ is somewhat smaller, allowing a 95% confidence around the line of about 13% of CONS, which remains too large for the model to be useful.

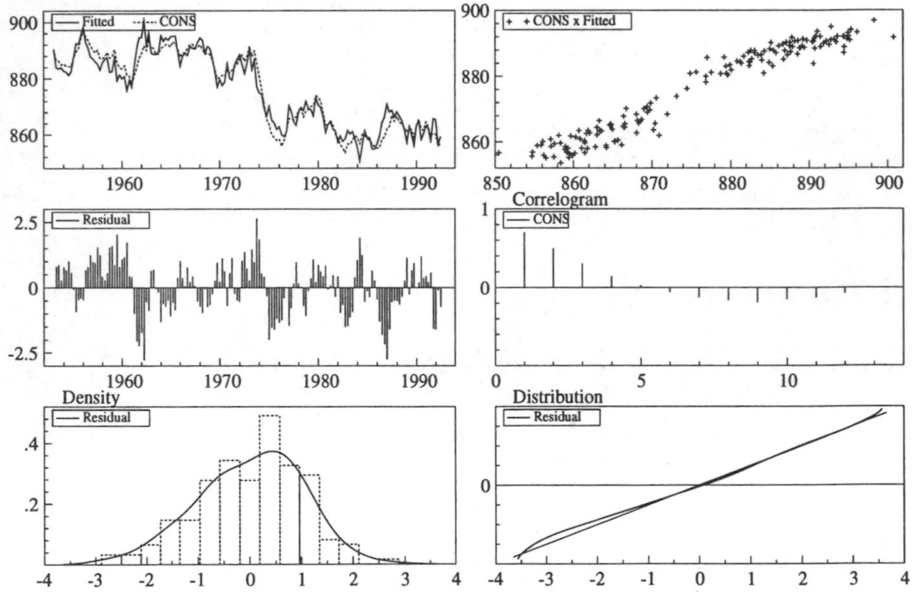

Figure 3.3 Goodness-of-fit graphs for extended model of CONS.

The partial r^2 for INC has risen relative to the simpler regression despite adding INFLAT: in fact INC only has a correlation of -0.11 with INFLAT. Nevertheless, some of the explanation of CONS is being spread across the two regressor variables although more is being explained in total. Replot the graphical output, this time marking the options for Actual and fitted values, Cross-plot of actual and fitted, Residuals (scaled), residual correlogram, Residual density and Histogram, and finally, Residual QQ plot. The graphs now appear as in Figure 3.3.

The improvement in the fit over Figure 3.1 should be clear. There are three new graphs. The first is the correlogram, which extends the idea behind the DW test to plot the correlations between successive lagged residuals (that is, the correlation of $\hat{u}_t$ with $\hat{u}_{t-1}$, then with $\hat{u}_{t-2}$, $\hat{u}_{t-3}$ and so on up to $\hat{u}_{t-12}$). A random (independent) residual would have most such correlations close to zero: visually, the dependence between successive residuals is clear. The next new plot is the histogram with an interpolation of the underlying density. This lets us see the extent to which the residuals are symmetric around zero, or have outliers etc.; more generally, it suggests the form of the density. The final plot is a QQ-plot of the cumulative distribution with the standardized normal represented by the 45° line (see Chapter 13 for more details). The departure from normality is not very marked here.

3.6 Formal tests

Econometricians have constructed formal tests of such hypotheses as serial correlation or normality, and these are easily implemented in PcGive. For example, to test normality of the errors, select the Test command from the Test menu and the Test dialog appears. Mark Normality (click on it or type `Alt+n`) as shown below, and accept.

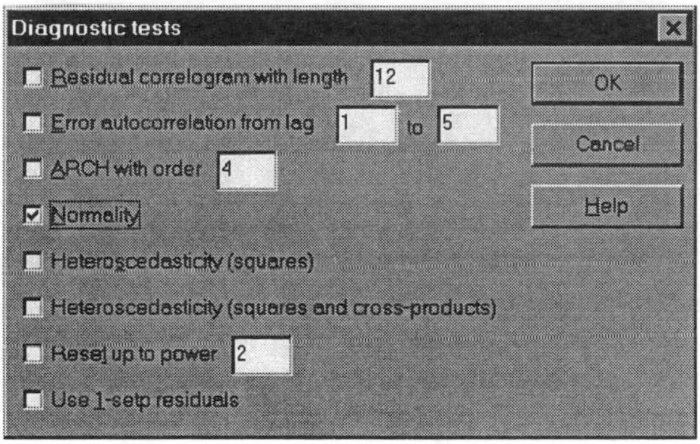


```
Normality test for Residual
The present sample is:  1953 (1) to 1992 (3)
Sample Size      159

Mean                    -0.000000
Std.Devn.                3.235765
Skewness                -0.324150
Excess Kurtosis         -0.083166
Minimum                 -9.049097
Maximum                  8.602543
Normality Chi^2(2)=      3.2519 [0.1967]
```

```
(asymptotic form of normality test: 2.8303)
```

The output comprises the first four moments of the residuals and a χ^2 test for these being from a normal distribution. Note that the mean of the residuals is zero by construction when an intercept is included, and the standard deviation is the equation standard error (but uses the wrong degrees of freedom, as it only allows for a mean). The skewness statistic measures the deviation from symmetry, and the excess kurtosis measures how 'fat' the tails of the distribution are: fat tails mean that outliers or extreme values are more common than in a normal distribution. Finally, the largest and smallest values are reported. Here, the normality χ^2 test does not reject: the probability of such a value or larger is 0.1967.

This concludes the first tutorial on regression estimation. We now move on to formulating and estimating dynamic models. The mechanics of the program remain the same, although the level of technique needed is higher. Chapter 12 describes the analysis of linear dynamic models, with the objective of learning the econometrics. Chapter 5 shows how to do it in PcGive.

Chapter 4

Tutorial on Data Description

The previous tutorial was mainly concerned with the mechanics of operating PcGive. We have mastered the skills to start the program, access menus and operate dialogs, load, save and transform data, use graphics, including saving and printing and estimate simple regression models. And remember, there is always help available if you get stuck: just press `F1`. Now we're ready to move to more substantial activities. Usually, a data analysis starts by exploring the data and transforming it to more interpretable forms. These activities are the subject of this chapter. The GiveWin book describes the 'Calculator' and 'Algebra'.

If you're not inside PcGive at the moment, restart and load the tutorial data set DATA.IN7/DATA.BN7 into GiveWin.

4.1 Descriptive data analysis

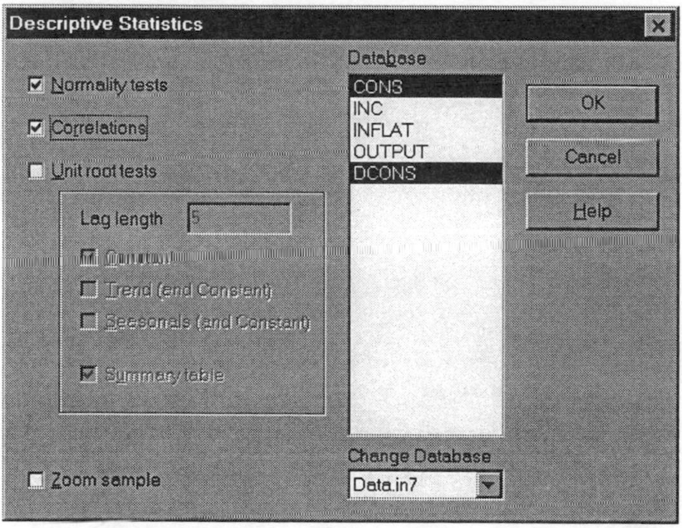

Select Data/Describe/Descriptive data analysis. Select CONS and DCONS and correlations and normality as shown above (the unit-root tests are described in §4.3). Press OK. The normality test output consists of the first four moments, extrema and a test statistic.

```
Normality test for CONS
The present sample is:   1953 (2) to 1992 (3)
Sample Size      158
Mean                     875.848087
Std.Devn.                 13.489677
Skewness                  -0.171954
Excess Kurtosis           -1.625105
Minimum                  853.503723
Maximum                  896.830872
Normality Chi^2(2)=      52.808 [0.0000] **
(asymptotic form of normality test: 18.165)

Normality test for DCONS
The present sample is:   1953 (2) to 1992 (3)
Sample Size      158
Mean                      -0.213409
Std.Devn.                  2.203097
Skewness                  -0.112075
Excess Kurtosis           -0.553022
Minimum                   -5.489685
Maximum                    4.739258
Normality Chi^2(2)=      2.2958 [0.3173]
(asymptotic form of normality test: 2.3442)
```

For a standard normal distribution (denoted by $\mathsf{N}(0,1)$) the numbers would be:

mean	0
standard deviation	1
skewness	0
excess kurtosis	0

The normality test statistic is a function of the skewness and excess kurtosis. The value of the test for CONS is 52.81. The probability of getting a number at least as large if CONS would really have a normal distribution is given between the square brackets. It is zero (not exactly, but so close to zero that we need not bother how close). The two stars indicate that the test is significant at the 1% level, in other words it tells us that 0% (the p-value) $< 1\%$. It is extremely unlikely that CONS was generated by a normal distribution. DCONS is another picture, as we saw before: its shape is not significantly different from an $\mathsf{N}(-0.21, (2.2)^2)$ distribution.

```
The present sample is:   1953 (2) to 1992 (3)
Descriptive statistics
Means
        CONS         DCONS
      875.85      -0.21341
```

```
Standard Deviations
          CONS          DCONS
        13.533         2.2101

Correlation matrix
                       CONS          DCONS
CONS                 1.0000
DCONS              0.098638         1.0000
```

Finally, we have the mean and standard deviation again, with one less significant digit, and the correlations. Note the difference between the standard deviation of CONS under the normality test and here. This can be explained by:

$$\hat{\sigma} = \sqrt{\frac{1}{T}\sum_{t=1}^{T}(x_t - \bar{x})^2} \text{ versus } s = \sqrt{\frac{1}{T-1}\sum_{t=1}^{T}(x_t - \bar{x})^2}.$$

The normality test reports the former:

$$13.489677 \times \sqrt{\frac{158}{157}} = 13.533.$$

CONS is hardly correlated with its difference, matching its high correlation with its own one-lagged value.

4.2 Autoregressive distributed lag

The graphs showed that CONS is highly correlated with its own lags, but that not much autocorrelation is present in DCONS, the distribution of which resembled an independent normal distribution. From this, we could entertain the hypothesis that CONS is appropriately described by a first-order autoregressive process, denoted by AR(1). In mathematical form:

$$y_t = \alpha + \beta y_{t-1} + \epsilon_t, \quad t = 1, \ldots, T. \tag{4.1}$$

The coefficient α is the intercept. If β were zero, y_t would be perturbed by a random disturbance around a constant. When $\beta = 1$, then Δy_t is random. Assumptions about the error term are that it has mean 0 and variance which is constant over time:

$$\mathsf{E}\left[\epsilon_t\right] = 0,\ \mathsf{V}\left[\epsilon_t\right] = \mathsf{E}\left[\epsilon_t - \mathsf{E}\left[\epsilon_t\right]\right]^2 = \mathsf{E}\left[\epsilon_t^2\right] = \sigma^2.$$

Autoregressions are a subset of autoregressive-distributed lag (ADL) models, and are easily estimated in PcGive. Select the Data menu, and then Autoregressive-distributed lag. Double click on CONS and set the ending lag of CONS to 1. The dialog should look like:

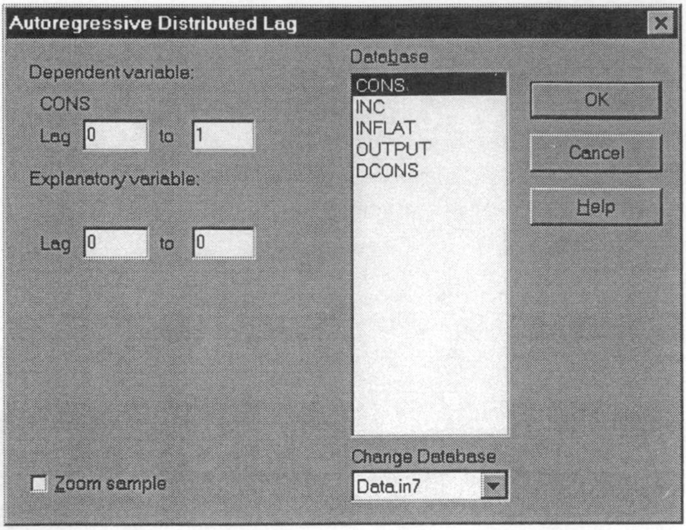

Press OK to accept and estimate the AR(1) model. The results are:

```
Autoregression  for CONS: lags from 1 to 1
The present sample is:  1953 (2) to 1992 (3)
          Constant     Lag  1
Coeff.       9.092     0.9894
Std.Err      11.46    0.01308

RSS = 763.6482142  \sigma = 2.21251  R^2 = 0.97344
F(1, 156) = 5717.42 [0.0000] **
```

The first line of numbers gives $\hat{\alpha}$ and $\hat{\beta}$. Below that are their estimated standard errors, from which we could derive a rough 95% confidence interval, for $\hat{\beta}$: $(0.9894 \pm 2 \times 0.01308)$. The number 2 derives from the assumption that $\hat{\beta}$ has a student-t distribution with $T - k = 158 - 2 = 156$ degrees of freedom. This, in turn, we know to be quite close to a standard normal distribution, and: $\mathsf{P}(|Z| > 2) \approx 95\%$ where $Z \sim \mathsf{N}(0, 1)$. Soon we shall see that this assumption might not be valid; if so, the confidence interval will change. Not reported but easy to compute is the so-called t-value of $\hat{\beta}$:

$$\mathsf{t}_\beta = \frac{\hat{\beta}}{\mathsf{SE}\left(\hat{\beta}\right)} = \frac{0.9894}{0.01308} = 75.6.$$

This can be used to test the hypothesis that β is zero (expressed as $\mathsf{H}_0 : \beta = 0$). Under the current assumptions we reject the hypothesis if $\mathsf{t}_\beta > 2$ or $\mathsf{t}_\beta < -2$ (again, using a 95% confidence interval, in other words, a 5% significance level). The observed value of 75.6 is very much larger than 2, making it highly unlikely that β is zero.

RSS stands for residual sums of squares. The residuals are $\hat{\epsilon}_t = y_t - \hat{\alpha} - \hat{\beta} y_{t-1}$, and

$$RSS = \sum_{t=1}^{T} \hat{\epsilon}_t, \quad \hat{\sigma} = \sqrt{\frac{RSS}{T-k}},$$

$\hat{\sigma}$ is the residual standard deviation (also called equation standard error or SEE: standard error of the equation), R^2 is the (squared) coefficient of multiple correlation. The F-statistic tests the hypothesis that all coefficients, apart from the constant term, are zero. Here it coincides with $H_0 : \beta = 0$, and the square of the t-value equals the F-test value. The number in square brackets is the 'p-value' of the test. It tells us how likely we are to get at least such a test outcome if H_0 were true. This is extremely unlikely, and leads us to reject the null hypothesis. The two stars indicate that the p-value is less than 1%.

4.3 Unit-root tests

It is more interesting to test whether β equals one, $H_0 : \beta - 1 = 0$. The t-value is computed as

$$\frac{0.9894 - 1}{0.01308} = -0.8.$$

It is convenient to rewrite (4.1) by subtracting y_{t-1} from both sides:

$$y_t - y_{t-1} = \alpha + \beta y_{t-1} - y_{t-1} + \epsilon_t,$$

or:

$$\Delta y_t = \alpha + (\beta - 1)\, y_{t-1} + \epsilon_t. \tag{4.2}$$

With DCONS in the database, we can check whether (4.2) is identical to (4.1). Select Data/Autoregressive-distributed lag. Put the cursor on DCONS, press ↩, put the cursor on CONS, ↩. Set both the start lag and the end lag for CONS to 1. Accept to see:

```
Distributed Lag of DCONS on CONS: lags from 1 to 1
The present sample is:  1953 (3) to 1992 (3)
          Constant      Lag  1
Coeff.        7.533  -0.008816
Std.Err       11.45    0.01306

RSS = 750.9419745  \sigma = 2.20109  R^2 = 0.00292911
F(1, 155) = 0.455346 [0.5008]
```

Tip When you try to replicate previous results, and the outcomes are close but not close enough, check the sample size of the estimation.

Redo (4.1) for the same sample: select CONS with lags 0 to 1, mark the Zoom check box, take 1953(2) as the starting point (this is adjusted to 1953(3) to allow for the lag, and thus working differently from specifying a sample in the model estimation dialog):

```
Autoregression  for CONS: lags from 1 to 1
The present sample is:  1953 (3) to 1992 (3)
           Constant     Lag  1
Coeff.        7.533     0.9912
Std.Err       11.45    0.01306

RSS = 750.9419745  \sigma = 2.20109  R^2 = 0.973777
F(1, 155) = 5755.76 [0.0000] **
```

Comparing RSS shows that the outcomes are identical. What has changed are R^2 and the F-statistic, corresponding to switching between y_t and Δy_t as dependent variables.

The hypothesis $H_0 : \beta = 1$ is called the unit-root hypothesis (which implies that y_t is non-stationary). It is of special interest, because under the null hypothesis, it is incorrect to use the student-t distribution. Moreover, many economic variables appear to have a unit root, consistent with the typical spectral shape noted above. If CONS has one unit root, we say that CONS is integrated of order 1, denoted I(1); this corresponds to saying that DCONS is I(0). The correct distribution to use for the t-value is the 'Dickey-Fuller' distribution. Unfortunately, the precise distributional form depends on the presence or absence of a Constant or Trend term. (If the distribution of a test depends on other ('nuisance') parameters, it is called 'not similar'.)

To obtain correct critical values, use Data/Descriptive Statistics/Unit root tests to re-estimate (4.2). Select CONS, check Unit-root tests, set the lag length to 0 to select no additional lags, and switch off the summary table, keep the default of just using a constant term:

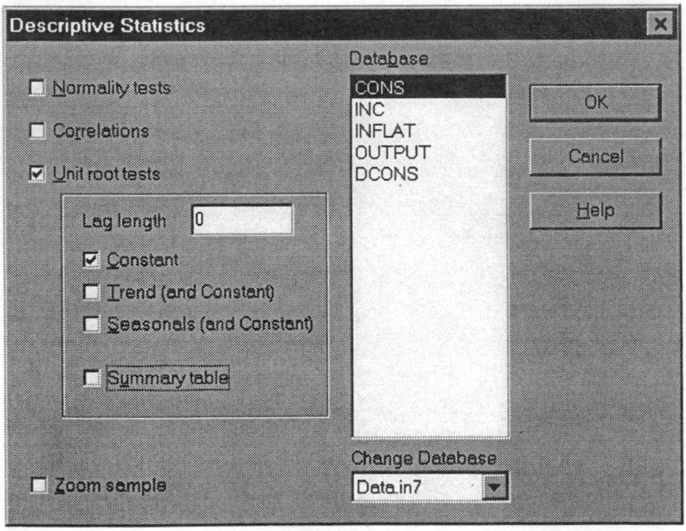

OK to accept. This uses the full sample as you can see:

```
Unit-root tests for CONS
The present sample is:  1953 (2) to 1992 (3)

Dickey-Fuller test for CONS; DCONS on
Variable     Coefficient    Std.Error  t-value
Constant          9.0922       11.464    0.793
CONS_1         -0.010622     0.013085   -0.812

\sigma=2.21251  DW=1.60  DW(CONS)=0.02639  DF(CONS)=-0.8118
Critical values used in DF test: 5%=-2.88 1%=-3.473
RSS = 763.6482142  for 2 variables and 158 observations
```

DW is the Durbin-Watson statistic of the OLS regression residuals, whereas DW(CONS) is the Durbin-Watson of CONS (see Chapter 16). DF(CONS) is the t-statistic we computed earlier. The 5% critical value for the Dickey-Fuller test is reported as -2.88. The negative number is given, because the interesting alternative hypothesis is that $\hat{\beta} < 1$; $\hat{\beta} > 1$ corresponds to an exploding process, which we tend not to see in economic variables. The critical values are based on response surfaces in MacKinnon (1991); 5% significance is marked by *, 1% by **. Here we can *not* reject the hypothesis that $\beta - 1 = 0$: CONS appears to have a unit root (is I(1)). As with all statistical tests, some caution is required. It can be seen in the time-series graph of CONS that it has a break around 1975, and it has been found that a break can cause I(0) variables to appear I(1) in DF tests.

The augmented Dickey-Fuller (ADF) test derives from the DF test by adding lagged differences, for example, for the ADF(1) test:

$$\Delta y_t = \alpha + (\beta - 1)\, y_{t-1} + \gamma \Delta y_{t-1} + \epsilon_t,$$

or more general for the ADF(s):

$$\Delta y_t = \alpha + (\beta - 1)\, y_{t-1} + \sum_{i=1}^{s} \gamma_i \Delta y_{t-i} + \epsilon_t.$$

ADF(0) corresponds to the DF test. The purpose of these additional lags is to 'whiten' the residuals.

Tip The null hypothesis is that of a unit root. A significant test statistic would reject that hypothesis and suggest stationarity.

To facilitate the computation of ADF tests, and the decision about the lag length, PcGive can be instructed to print a summary table of ADF tests. Select Data/Descriptive Statistics/Unit-root tests, mark INFLAT and CONS. The default is the summary table starting from lag 5. The output consists of the sequence of ADF(5)..ADF(0) tests:

```
Unit-root tests 1954 (3) to 1992 (3)
Critical values: 5%=-2.88 1%=-3.474; Constant included

            t-adf  beta Y_1    \sigma lag t-DY_lag  t-prob  F-prob
CONS      -1.1173   0.98530   2.1164   5  -2.7761  0.0062
CONS      -1.4594   0.98053   2.1642   4   1.2563  0.2110  0.0062
CONS      -1.2927   0.98289   2.1684   3   1.4446  0.1507  0.0107
CONS      -1.1199   0.98524   2.1763   2   1.6951  0.0921  0.0109
CONS     -0.92848   0.98776   2.1899   1   2.4864  0.0140  0.0073
CONS     -0.63520   0.99154   2.2271   0                  0.0013
INFLAT -4.6116**   0.85365  0.35557   5 -0.20467  0.8381
INFLAT -5.0960**   0.85116  0.35441   4  0.58714  0.5580  0.8381
INFLAT -5.3165**   0.85802  0.35362   3   1.0548  0.2932  0.8254
INFLAT -5.3392**   0.86931  0.35375   2   1.1100  0.2688  0.6863
INFLAT -5.3365**   0.88017  0.35403   1   11.324  0.0000  0.6096
INFLAT -2.4297     0.92722  0.48057   0                  0.0000
```

The first column is the t-value, which is the ADF test statistic, the second column is the equation standard error, followed by the lag length (the value of s). The last two columns give the t-value of the highest lag (of γ_s, $s = 5, 4, 3, 2, 1$), followed by the p-value of that lag. The suggested strategy is to select the highest s with a significant last γ_s (the distribution of $\hat{\gamma}_s$ is the conventional student-t distribution). So for INFLAT we use an ADF(1) test, for CONS an ADF(5) test. The only place where it makes a difference is in using ADF(1) or ADF(0) for INFLAT. Using the lag criterion we conclude that INFLAT is stationary, so if we did not check for the importance of lagged values of INFLAT, we might mistakenly think that it is non-stationary. Note that all tests used the same sample period.

We have avoided the issue of including a constant, or a constant and trend. The implications are as follows:

$$
\begin{array}{l|l|l}
 & \beta = 1 & \beta < 1 \\
\Delta y_t = (\beta - 1)\, y_{t-1} + \epsilon_t & \text{zero growth} & \text{mean zero} \\
\Delta y_t = \alpha + (\beta - 1)\, y_{t-1} + \epsilon_t & \text{trend in } y_t & \text{non-zero mean} \\
\Delta y_t = \alpha + (\beta - 1)\, y_{t-1} + \mu t + \epsilon_t & \text{quadratic trend in } y_t & \text{trend in } y_t
\end{array}
\qquad (4.3)
$$

Few variables have quadratic trends, but it is often advisable to include t in case the variable is stationary around a linear trend. Equally, include an intercept unless it is clear that the variable has a zero mean. Technically, including a polynomial in time of order n (for example, having α and μt corresponds to $n = 1$) makes the test similar despite the presence of the nuisance parameters of a polynomial of order $n - 1$.

Some variables could be thought to be I(2). Then you could start with checking whether the second differences are stationary. If so, move on to test stationarity of the first differences.

That concludes the data description. The PcGive unit-root test and issues of cointegration are also discussed in §12.5.

Chapter 5

Tutorial on Dynamic Modelling

Dynamic modelling normally consists of a cycle of three steps: formulation or reformulation, estimation and evaluation. The modelling process takes place within the Model and the Test menus described in the previous tutorial, but we reproduce several dialogs here for convenience. This tutorial will guide you through a simple model sequence based on the artificial data set. Hopefully you will agree at the end that PcGive combines sophistication with great simplicity.

5.1 Model formulation

Start PcGive, and load DATA.IN7 in GiveWin, if you are starting this tutorial afresh. Click on the first icon on the toolbar (or select the Formulate command on the Model menu; if you prefer to use the keyboard, you can use `Alt+y` as the short-cut key: 'model the y variable'). This initiates the Formulate a Model dialog, discussed extensively in Chapter 3. The first model to formulate is CONS on a Constant, CONS lagged, INC, INC lagged and inflation, as shown overleaf.

The Constant is automatically included. There are various ways of formulating such a model, including:

- Double click on CONS, INC, INFLAT respectively. Then select INFLAT_1 in the Model list box, and delete (using the `Delete` key or pressing the Delete button).
- Set lag length to Query, and repeat the previous actions. Now you are prompted to specify a lag length.
- Still using the mouse, select the CONS, INC, INFLAT variables. Note that a single click only selects one variable. To select a range, drag the mouse from CONS to INC. Alternatively, hold the `Ctrl` key down, and click on the three variables. Finally, you could click on CONS, then hold the `Shift` key down and click on INFLAT. With the three variables selected, the OK button changes to '<<Add'; press this button, or press the Enter key.
  Lastly, just using the keyboard: type `Alt+b` to set focus to the database list box, then select a variable (using the arrow keys), and press `Enter` each time.

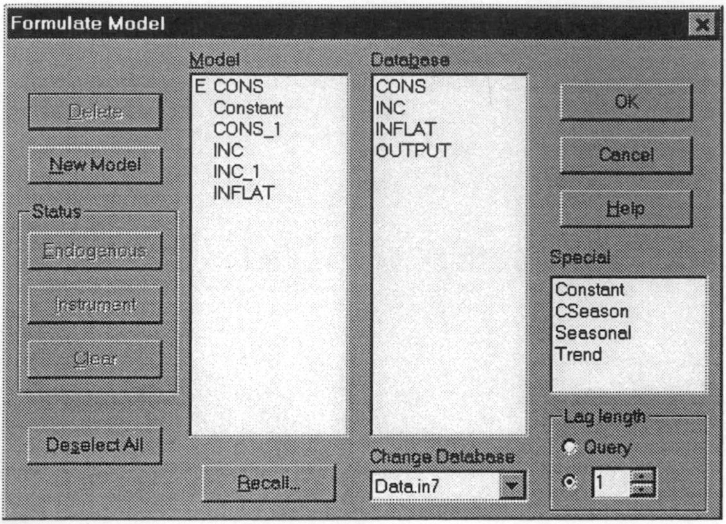

A brief digression on lags is called for. PcGive names lagged variables by appending an underscore and then the lag length. So CONS_1 is CONS one period lagged. PcGive uses this naming scheme to keep track of the lag length. Suppose the database holds both a CONS and a CONS_1 variable. Then, when formulating a model involving the first lag of CONS, PcGive will use CONS, to create that lag. So the database CONS_1 variable is never used. When CONS_1 is the only CONS variable in the database, PcGive will start using it.

5.2 Model estimation

Estimation methods are discussed in Chapter 12; Chapter 17 reviews the statistical output reported following estimation. Here we only need OLS; examples of the other estimation methods are given in the next chapter. The short-cut key for model estimation is `Alt+l`, in which the `l` stands for least squares. However, pressing OK in the Model Formulation dialog takes us directly to the Estimation dialog.

Retain eight observations for parameter constancy using the Less forecasts text entry field (the default is none, and the maximum is determined by the sample size).

Tip It is easy to refit models to subsamples and hence conduct tests of constancy based on the residual sums of squares. The RLS/RIV options allow testing over the entire set of subsamples.

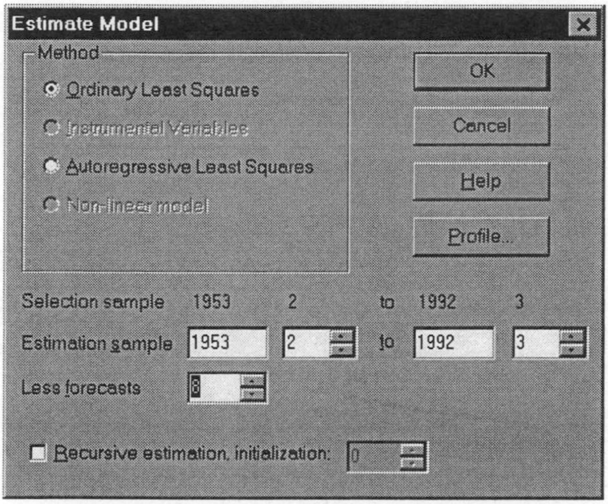

The model, the sample or the estimation method can be altered later, either separately or together. During estimation, the progress report flashes briefly in the main dialog window as noted in Chapter 3:

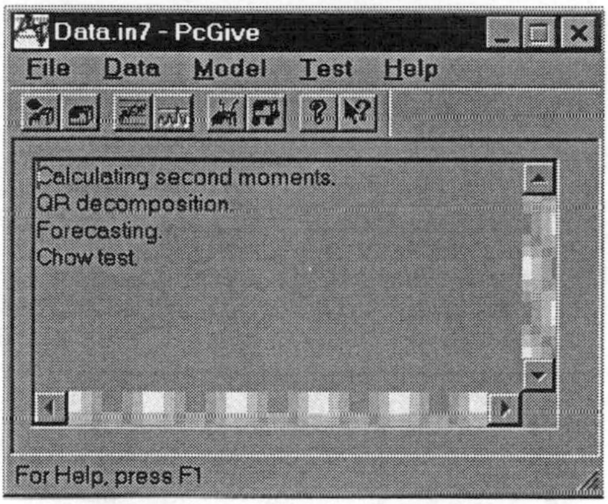

By default the Graphic Analysis dialog appears after estimation, hiding the progress report. We shall turn to this dialog shortly, after looking at the estimation results.

5.3 Model output

5.3.1 Equation estimates

The equation estimation results are written to the GiveWin Results window where further editing is easy. We assume that you have the default profile setting, which generates the minimum number of statistics. Section 5.6 discusses the profile. The reported results include coefficient estimates; standard errors; t-values; the squared partial correlation of every regressor with the dependent variable; the squared multiple correlation coefficient (denoted R^2); an F-test on R^2 equalling zero; the equation standard error (σ); the residual Durbin–Watson statistic (DW); the Residual Sum of Squares (RSS); the sample size.

```
EQ( 1) Modelling CONS by OLS  (using Data.in7)
The present sample is:  1953 (2) to 1992 (3) less 8 forecasts
The forecast period is: 1990 (4) to 1992 (3)

Variable      Coefficient     Std.Error  t-value   t-prob PartR^2
Constant          -18.518        8.7265   -2.122   0.0355  0.0301
CONS_1            0.80909      0.025478   31.756   0.0000  0.8743
INC               0.50669      0.028822   17.580   0.0000  0.6807
INC_1            -0.29649      0.035595   -8.330   0.0000  0.3236
INFLAT           -0.99257      0.086183  -11.517   0.0000  0.4777

R^2=0.993693  F(4,145)=5711.6 [0.0000]  \sigma=1.07598 DW=1.96
RSS = 167.8723959 for 5 variables and 150 observations
```

The sample period was automatically adjusted for the lags created on CONS and INC. The figure in $[\cdot]$ after the F $(\cdot)$ value is the probability of obtaining that value from a central F-distribution with the degrees of freedom shown. Should it be desired, an equation form can be set in the Profile, as shown in §5.6.

5.3.2 Analysis of 1-step forecast statistics

The forecast tests are a Chow test and a forecast Chi^2 (8) which is an index of numerical parameter constancy. For H forecasts, values $> 2H$ imply poor *ex ante* accuracy. The χ^2 value always exceeds that of H times the Chow test. Later, we will graph the outcomes, forecasts and the error bars for ± 2 standard errors of the 1-step forecasts. The reported forecast results are:

```
      Analysis of 1-step forecasts
   Date      Actual   Forecast   Y - Yhat Forecast SE    t-value
1990  4    861.484    862.235  -0.751532     1.09660  -0.685329
1991  1    864.444    862.136    2.30801     1.09018    2.11709
1991  2    862.750    863.237  -0.487490     1.08517  -0.449230
1991  3    859.413    860.146  -0.732399     1.09117  -0.671208
1991  4    860.480    862.243   -1.76260     1.10609   -1.59355
1992  1    860.002    860.796  -0.793439     1.09158  -0.726870
1992  2    855.908    856.477  -0.568310     1.11262  -0.510787
1992  3    856.731    856.995  -0.264312     1.08946  -0.242607

Tests of parameter constancy over:  1990 (4) to 1992 (3)

Forecast Chi^2( 8)=     9.3241 [0.3157]
Chow     F( 8,145) =      1.15 [0.3337]
```

5.4 Testing and evaluation

The next major step is to evaluate the estimated model. If you do not still have the Graphic Analysis dialog on screen, choose it from the Test menu (or press the third toolbar button).

5.4.1 Graphical evaluation

The dialog lets you plot or cross-plot the actual and fitted values for the whole sample, the residuals scaled by σ, so that values outside the range $[-2, +2]$ suggest outlier problems, the forecasts, and some graphical diagnostic information about the residuals (their spectrum, correlogram, histogram, density and cumulative distribution). The forecast period start is marked by a vertical line (see Figure 5.1). Notice the good fit: the earlier high R^2, and good Chow test are consistent with this. As before, any graphs can be saved for later recall, editing and printing. Six graphs have been selected here (if you wish to use a non-default sample size, check the Zoom sample box):

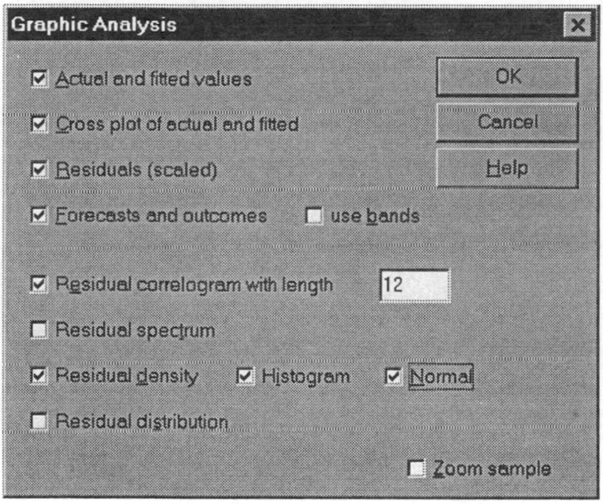

accept this, and the graphs appear in the PcGive Graphics window in GiveWin, as in Figure 5.1.

5.4.2 Dynamic analysis

Next, the toolbar button with the box on wheels leads to the dynamic analysis (also on the Test menu). Select Static long-run solution, Lag structure analysis, and both Normalized weights and Cumulative normalized weights, as shown:

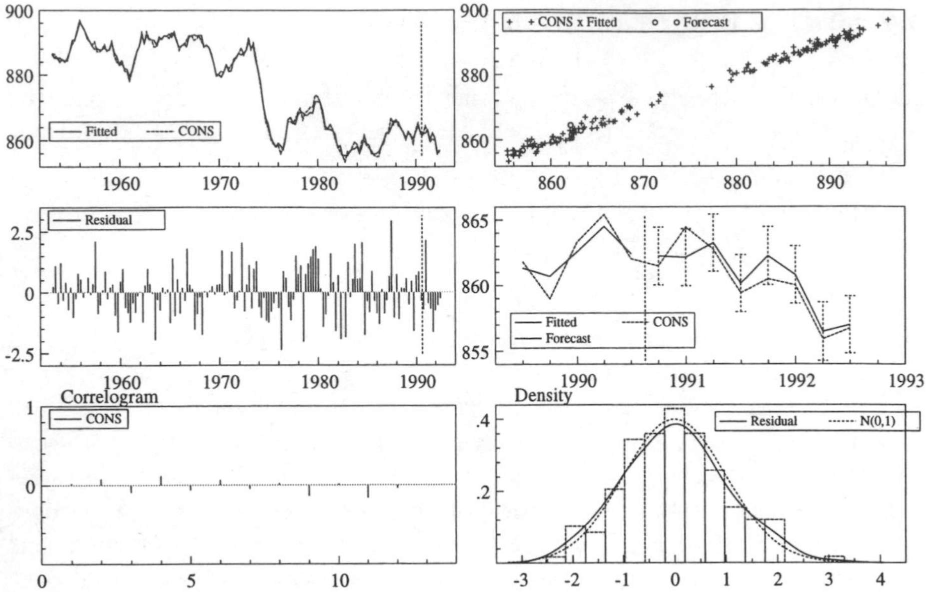

Figure 5.1 Graphical evaluation of CONS model.

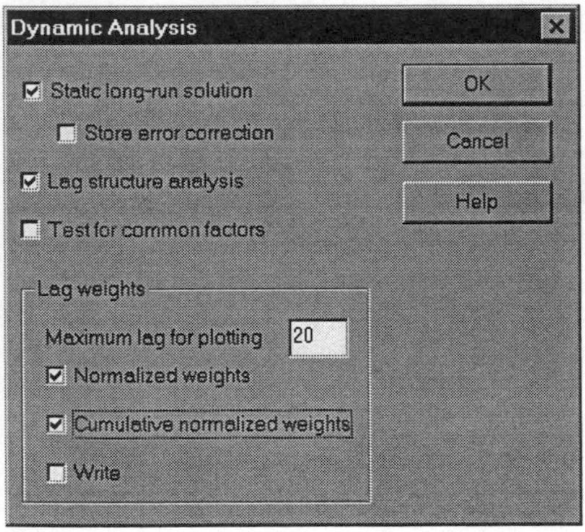

The dynamic analysis commences with the long-run solution. Chapter 12 provides an explanation. The solved long-run model (or static solution) is calculated, together with the relevant standard errors as follows. Write the dynamic equation as

$$a\,(L)\,y_t = b\,(L)\,x_t + \epsilon_t,$$

where L is the lag operator so that $Lx_t = x_{t-1}$ and $b(L) = \sum_{i=0}^{n} b_i L^i$ is a scalar polynomial in L of order n, the longest lag length. With $a(1) = \sum_{i=0}^{n} a_i$ (that is, $a(L)$

evaluated at $L = 1$), then if $a(1) \neq 0$ the long run is:

$$y = \frac{b(1)}{a(1)} x = Kx.$$

Under stationarity (or cointegration inducing a stationary linear relation), standard errors for derived coefficients like K can be calculated from those of $a(\cdot)$ and $b(\cdot)$. Here the long-run coefficients are well determined, and the null that they are all zero (excluding the constant term) is rejected.

```
Solved Static Long Run equation
CONS =          -97             +1.101 INC          -5.199 INFLAT
(SE)      (   40.68)        (  0.04534)         (   0.5558)

ECM = CONS + 96.9979 - 1.10102*INC + 5.19917*INFLAT;

WALD test Chi^2(2) = 824.78 [0.0000] **
```

Next, the lag polynomials are analysed to yield $a(1)$, $b(1)$, etc. and their standard errors, as well as F-tests of the joint significance of each variable's lag polynomial. The hypothesis that $a(1) = 0$ can be rejected, suggesting cointegration between the variables in the model in levels (see Banerjee, Dolado, Galbraith and Hendry, 1993, or Johansen, 1995).

Finally, tests on the significance of each lag length are provided (here we deleted three columns with zeros):

```
Analysis of lag structure
        Lag           0        1      2        Sum
CONS                 -1    0.809      0     -0.191
     StdErr           0   0.0255      0     0.0255
Constant          -18.5        0      0      -18.5
     StdErr        8.73        0      0       8.73
INC               0.507   -0.296      0       0.21
     StdErr      0.0288   0.0356      0     0.0313
INFLAT           -0.993        0      0     -0.993
     StdErr      0.0862        0      0     0.0862

Tests on the significance of each variable
Variable    F(num,denom) Value   Probability  Unit root t-test
  CONS      F( 1,145) =  1008.5 [0.0000] **       -7.4931**
  Constant  F( 1,145) =   4.503 [0.0355] *
  INC       F( 2,145) =  155.67 [0.0000] **        6.7226
  INFLAT    F( 1,145) =  132.64 [0.0000] **       -11.517

Tests on the significance of each lag
Lag              F(num,denom)     Value  Probability
  1              F( 2,145) =      617.11 [0.0000] **
```

The unit-root t-test (also called the PcGive unit-root test) does not in fact have a t-distribution, but the marked significance (* for 5%, ** for 1%, dependent variable only) is based on the correct critical values, see Banerjee, Dolado and Mestre (1992).

Since we also chose Lag weights, there are four new graphs in the PcGive Graphics window, as in Figure 5.2.

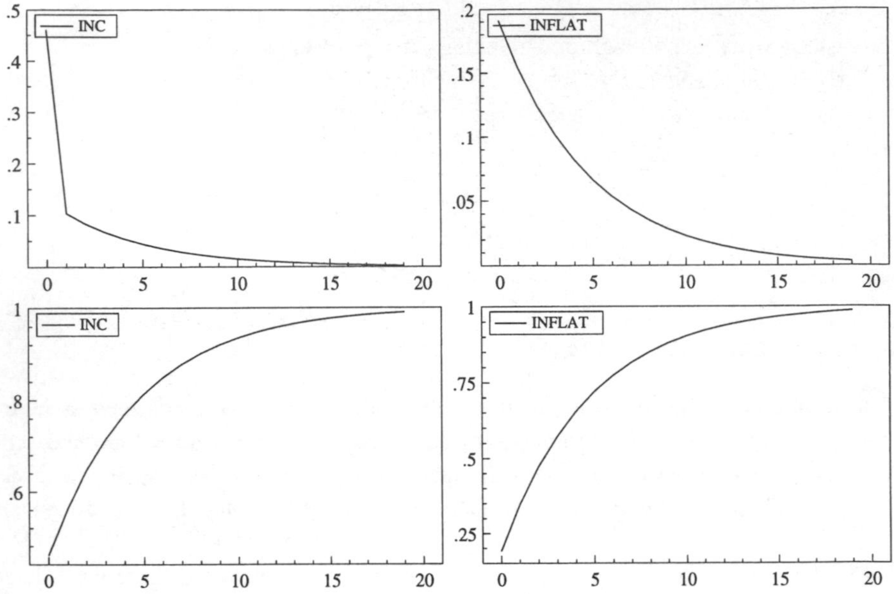

Figure 5.2 Lag weights from CONS model.

5.4.3 Mis-specification tests

`Alt+t,u` or just `Alt+u` (or the toolbar button of the box with sparks coming out of it) conducts a summary testing sequence on the residuals for a range of null hypotheses of interest, including: autocorrelation, autoregressive conditional heteroscedasticity (ARCH), the normality of the distribution of the residuals, heteroscedasticity, and functional form mis-specification. The output is:

```
AR 1- 5 F( 5,140) =      0.90705 [0.4784]
ARCH 4  F( 4,137) =      0.55687 [0.6943]
Normality Chi^2(2)=      0.67529 [0.7134]
Xi^2    F( 8,136) =       1.0169 [0.4263]
Xi*Xj   F(14,130) =      0.93848 [0.5199]
RESET   F( 1,144) =       1.8231 [0.1791]
```

Note how easy these tests are to calculate; and to see how informative they are about the match of model and evidence, try computing them when any regressor is dropped (why does dropping INC not lead to rejection?).

Tests can also be undertaken individually, or in different groups from that embodied in the test summary. From the Test menu, select Test, which brings up the Diagnostic tests dialog:

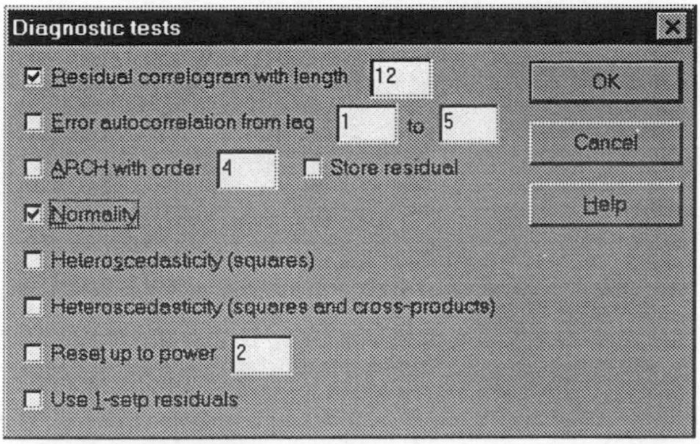

Any or all available tests can be selected (`Alt+r` for the residual correlogram, or click with the mouse, etc.).

Tip The values for lag lengths and Reset order are set to the default value for the first model, thereafter only reset when choosing a new data set. So any new number you type will remain in force (and will also be used in the test summary).

The output is rather more extensive than with batch tests. For example, the residual correlogram test produces:

```
Residual correlogram
Portmanteau statistic for 12 lags and 150 observations: 13.55
Autocorrelation coefficients
 0.020549  0.077548 -0.093157   0.11184 -0.063847  0.063623
-0.047705  0.024609  -0.13859  0.014902  -0.16190 -0.039129
```

followed by:

```
Autoregression  for Residual: lags from 1 to 12
The present sample is:  1956 (2) to 1990 (3)
        Constant   Lag  1    Lag  2    Lag  3    Lag  4    Lag  5
Coeff.  -0.01434  0.05073  0.02813  -0.0814   0.1017  -0.0343
Std.Err  0.09342  0.08958  0.08883  0.08883  0.08914  0.08972

          Lag  6    Lag  7    Lag  8    Lag  9   Lag 10    Lag 11
Coeff.   0.03178 -0.00889 0.003383  -0.1199  0.01529   -0.1371
Std.Err   0.0897  0.08973  0.08976  0.08883  0.08937  0.08924

          Lag 12
Coeff.  -0.05365
Std.Err  0.09018

RSS = 150.366698  \sigma = 1.09678  R^2 = 0.0673234
F(12, 125) = 0.751906 [0.6982]
```

Similarly, the normality test leads to the low-order moments being reported.

```
Normality test for Residual
The present sample is:  1953 (2) to 1990 (3)
Sample Size      150
Mean                     0.000000
Std.Devn.                1.057899
Skewness                 0.157618
Excess Kurtosis         -0.118517
Minimum                 -2.541566
Maximum                  3.169125
Normality Chi^2(2)=      0.67529 [0.7134]
(asymptotic form of normality test: 0.70887)
```

The density of the scaled residuals was shown in Figure 5.1 and revealed slight skewness and somewhat fatter tails than the standard normal distribution.

These mis-specification test outcomes are satisfactory, consistent with the equation being a congruent model, so we now consider some specification tests.

5.4.4 Specification tests

First, we test whether a subset of the coefficients is zero. Choose Linear restrictions: subset from the Test menu to conduct a subset linear restrictions test At the dialog mark INC and INC_1 and accept:

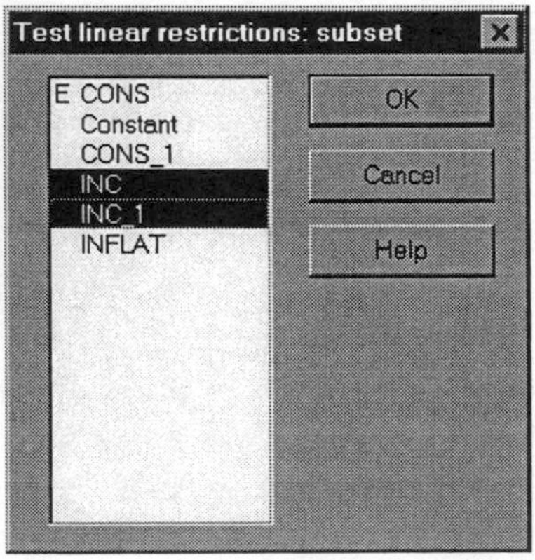

Before looking at the subset test result, we shall also do a linear restrictions test on homogeneity of CONS with respect to INC. This time, select Linear restrictions: Rb=r. Highlight CONS_1, and press the Set to zero button. This formulates the restriction that the coefficient on CONS_1 is zero. To complete, edit the restrictions as follows:

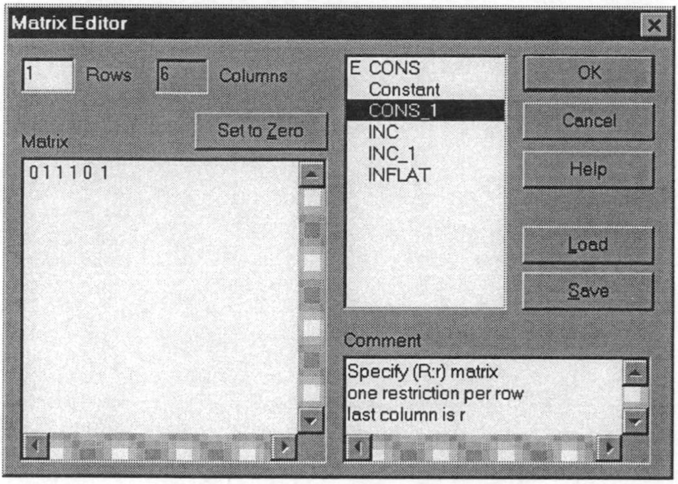

This formulates one restriction. The last element is the r vector, specifying what the restriction should add up to.

One further way of implementing this test is in the form of general restrictions. These are expressed as $\mathbf{f}(\boldsymbol{\theta}) = \mathbf{0}$. Complete the dialog as follows, and accept:

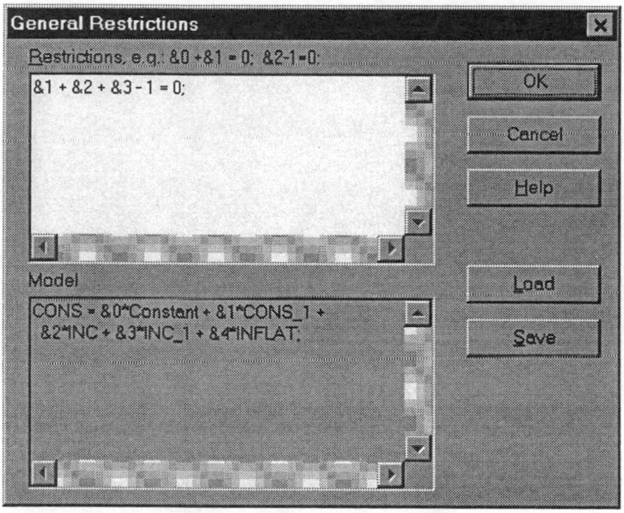

The results of the three tests are:

```
Wald test for linear restrictions: Subset
LinRes  F( 2,145) =     155.67 [0.0000] **

Zero restrictions on:  INC INC_1

Wald test for linear restrictions: Rb=r
LinRes  F( 1,145) =     4.0348 [0.0464] *
```

```
R matrix
    Constant        CONS_1         INC        INC_1      INFLAT
     0.00000        1.0000      1.0000       1.0000     0.00000
r vector
      1.0000


Wald test for general restrictions
GenRes Chi^2( 1) =     4.0348 [0.0446] *

Restrictions:  &1 + &2 + &3 - 1 = 0;
```

The output of the homogeneity test shows slight evidence of rejection of long-run homogeneity if conventional critical values are used. The previous subset test reveals strong rejection of the null.

Finally, we conduct an omitted variables test for INFLAT_1. At the dialog, mark INFLAT, accept, input 1 lag at the mini-dialog for lag length, accept and see:

```
LM test for omitted variables
Add     F(1,144) =     1.4489 [0.2307]

Added variables:        INFLAT_1
```

The additional lag is indeed irrelevant.

5.5 COMFAC and encompassing tests

To select COMFAC tests (see Chapter 12), the minimum lag length must be unity for all non-redundant variables (variables that are redundant when lagged can occur without lags: PcGive notices the Constant and Trend if such terms occur). First, we must revise the model to have one lag on INFLAT: select the Model Formulation dialog, mark INFLAT in the database, press `Enter` to add it to the model, using a lag length of 1. PcGive notices that current INFLAT is already in the model and doesn't add it a second time. Accept, and accept again in the Estimation dialog, to implement over the previously selected sample. Now select Dynamic analysis, and mark Test for common factors. Since the lag polynomials are first-order, only the Wald test of one common-factor restriction is presented following the roots of the lag polynomials. When the dynamic equation is:

$$a(L)\,y_t = b(L)\,x_t + c(L)\,z_t + \epsilon_t$$

COMFAC involves testing whether $a(L) = a(1 - \rho L)$ when $b(L) = b(1 - \rho L)$ and $c(L) = c(1 - \rho L)$ so that $(1 - \rho L)$ is the factor of the lag polynomials in common. COMFAC is discussed by Hendry and Mizon (1978); here the restriction is rejected so the dynamics do not have an autoregressive error representation, matching the very different roots of the lag polynomials. The output is:

```
Roots of the lag polynomials
CONS          lags 0 - 1
                  0.7964
INC           lags 0 - 1
                  0.5526
INFLAT        lags 0 - 1
                 -0.3084

COMFAC WALD test statistic table
Order Chi^2df Value  p-value    Incr.df Value  p-value
  1      2    102.8 [0.0000]**     2    102.8 [0.0000]**
```

The final set of tests we will consider are for encompassing. This necessitates two non-nested models.

For the first, delete INFLAT but keep INFLAT_1 and re-estimate.

For the second model, delete INFLAT_1, and re-introduce current INFLAT. That is the model with which we started this chapter, so we can recall the specification. In the Formulate a model dialog, press the Recall button, and then Previous until you see:

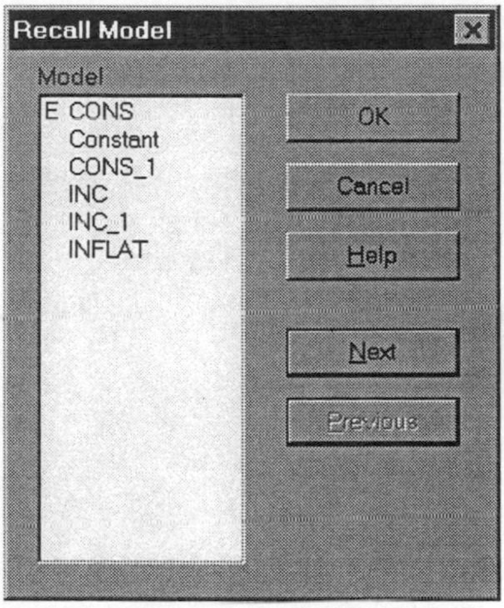

Accept that, and the model is recalled for re-estimation. Re-estimate and then select Encompassing from the Model menu. The output comprises:

```
Encompassing test statistics
       The present sample is:  1953 (2) to 1990 (3)

M1 is:          CONS on
  Constant  CONS_1  INC  INC_1  INFLAT_1

M2 is:          CONS on
  Constant  CONS_1  INC  INC_1  INFLAT

Instruments used:
  Constant  CONS_1  INC  INC_1  INFLAT_1   INFLAT
```

```
\sigma[M1]=1.13726  \sigma[M2]=1.07598  \sigma[Joint]=1.07432

 Model 1 v                                           Model 2 v
   Model 2    Form       Test            Form          Model 1
  -5.16986    N(0,1)     Cox             N(0,1)       -1.3002
   4.48786    N(0,1)     Ericsson IV     N(0,1)        1.23475
   16.4986    Chi^2(1)   Sargan          Chi^2(1)      1.4443
   18.4887    F(1,144)   Joint Model     F(1,144)      1.44901
  [ 0.0000]                                          [ 0.2307]
```

All the tests listed are automatically computed; none rejects model 2 and all reject model 1 (see Chapter 12 for details). How many hours would that have taken with another program? And we have many tools yet untried to dig deeper into the performance of econometric equations. Naturally you can extend, contract, transform or abandon your model, switch sample period or estimation methods, save the model's predictions, etc.

5.6 Profile

The Profile allows you to select automatic model evaluation options, and control the generation of estimation results. Chapter 20 explains how the profile settings for automatic model evaluation affect the operation of PcGive.

The equation format may prove more convenient for direct inclusion in final reports. To make PcGive write the output in equation format, activate the Profile, (on the Model menu) and mark as:

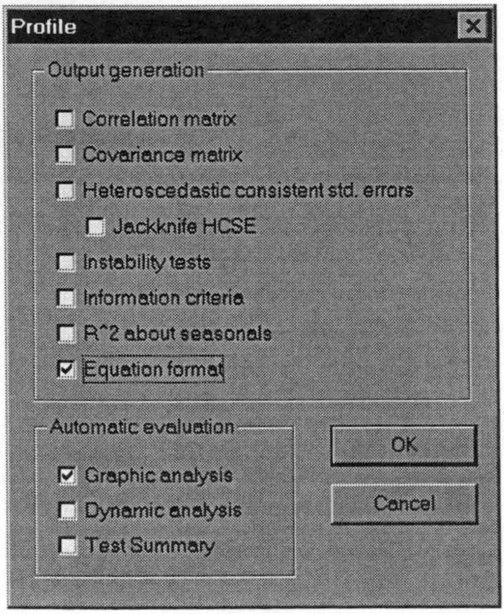

Reporting only the changed equation format, this produces:

```
EQ( 5) Modelling CONS by OLS
The present sample is:  1953 (2) to 1992 (3) less 8 forecasts


      CONS =    -18.52             +0.8091 CONS_1       +0.5067 INC
(SE)         (   8.726)          (  0.02548)          (  0.02882)
              -0.2965 INC_1        -0.9926 INFLAT
             (  0.0356)          (  0.08618)
```

Switch equation format off, and activate computation of HCSE, instability tests and information criteria to see after re-estimation:

```
EQ( 6) Modelling CONS by OLS  (using Data.in7)
The present sample is:  1953 (2) to 1992 (3) less 8 forecasts
The forecast period is: 1990 (4) to 1992 (3)

Variable Coefficient Std.Error t-value     HCSE PartR^2 Instab
Constant     -18.518    8.7265  -2.122   8.4559  0.0301   0.08
CONS_1       0.80909  0.025478  31.756 0.024930  0.8743   0.08
INC          0.50669  0.028822  17.580 0.026076  0.6807   0.08
INC_1       -0.29649  0.035595  -8.330 0.034473  0.3236   0.08
INFLAT      -0.99257  0.086183 -11.517 0.085654  0.4777   0.07

R^2=0.993693  F(4, 145)=5711.6 [0.0000]  \sigma=1.07598 DW=1.96
RSS = 167.8723959 for 5 variables and 150 observations

Variance instability test:0.761958*; Joint instab.test:1.39207
Information Criteria:   SC=0.27959;  HQ=0.220006;  FPE=1.19633
```

The t-prob entry has disappeared, to make space for columns with HCSEs (heteroscedastic-consistent standard errors) and instability statistics. Also new are various Information Criteria (SC = Schwarz, HQ = Hannan–Quinn, FPE = Final Prediction Error). See Chapters 12 and 17.

Profile settings are saved between runs, so reset them to the original settings (only Graphic analysis marked) for the remaining tutorials.

The next stage is to try some of the other estimators, which either produce different output or need different input instructions.

Chapter 6

Tutorial on Estimation Methods

Four main groups of estimation methods will be explained. The first is recursive estimation where we describe recursive least squares in detail. This approach was noted briefly in Chapter 5; you can investigate other possibilities at your leisure later. Next, we examine instrumental variables then turn to estimating models with autoregressive errors. That provides a convenient introduction to non-linear optimization and the tutorial concludes by considering non-linear least squares methods. Maximum likelihood estimation is considered separately in Chapter 9.

6.1 Recursive estimation

Formulate a model consisting of CONS on Constant, CONS_1, INC and INC_1, as explained in the previous chapter. Move to the model estimation dialog, set the maximum possible estimation sample, and keep 8 observations for forecasting. Now choose Recursive Least Squares (`Alt+r`). Chapter 13 explains the algebra of recursive estimation; the logic is simply to fit the model to an initial sample of $M-1$ points and then fit the equation to samples of $M,\ M+1, ...$ up to T observations. The main output will be graphs of coefficients, $\hat{\sigma}$ etc. over the sample. This is a powerful way to study parameter constancy (especially in its absence!).

The number of observations for intitialization (the $M-1$ above) is set to 15. Press the OK button to estimate. In a trice, all $T-M$ estimates and associated statistics are computed. The final (full sample) estimates are shown in the Results window.

The one new statistic reported to the Results window is for the mean of the innovations being zero. Here we have:

```
t(7) for a zero Forecast innovation mean =  -1.49
```

so that this test does not detect any non-constancy. Interestingly, neither do the instability statistics (based on Hansen, 1992): see the final section of Chapter 5 for the reported outcomes (switch these on at the Profile if you want to see the numbers).

The main new option on the Test menu is the Recursive graphics dialog. Cancelling the Graphic analysis dialog takes us straight there:

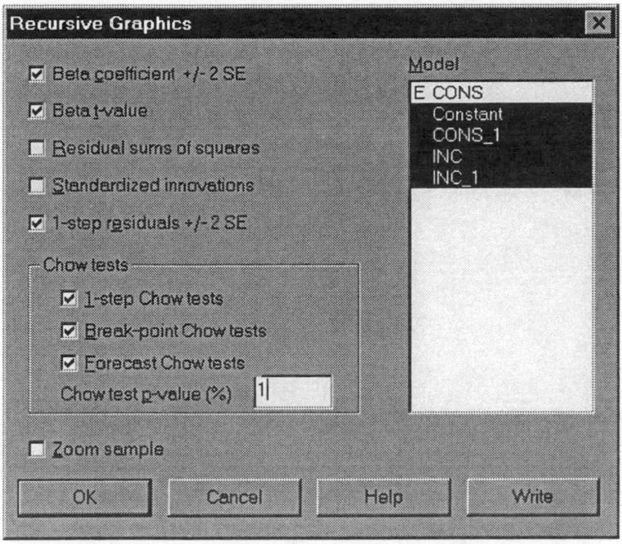

Mark all the variables to be plotted, then select the options by which they are to be plotted (Beta coefficients are already selected as shown above). Alter the significance level to 1%. First, the graph of the coefficient of CONS_1 over the sample in Figure 6.1 shows that after 1978, $\hat{\beta}_t$ lies outside of the previous confidence interval which an investigator pre-1974 would have calculated as the basis for forecasting. Other coefficients are also non-constant. Further, the 1-step residuals show major outliers around 1974.

The 1-step residuals are $\tilde{u}_t = y_t - \mathbf{x}_t'\hat{\beta}_t$ and they are plotted with $\pm 2\hat{\sigma}_t$ shown on either side of zero. Thus $\tilde{u}_t$ which are outside of the error bars are either outliers or are associated with changes in $\hat{\sigma}$. Note the increase in $\hat{\sigma}_t$ around 1974 (the oil crisis ...). The 1-step Chow tests amply reflects this. A further summary graph is the break-point Chow test graph. Each point is the value of the Chow F-test for that date against the final period, here 1990(3), scaled by its 1% critical value (which becomes the line at unity), so the forecast horizon N is decreasing from left to right (hence the name Ndn tests). Figure 6.1 illustrates. Note that the critical value can be set for any desired probability level.

Peruse other options as you wish: see how the standardized innovations often highlight the outliers, or how the residual sums of squares confirm that a break occurred in 1974. Any of these graphs can be edited and printed, or saved for later recall and printing.

Next, select the Graphic analysis dialog and look at the full sample residuals:

$$\hat{u}_t = y_t - \mathbf{x}_t'\hat{\beta}_T$$

where $\hat{\beta}_T$ is the usual full-sample OLS estimate. The full-sample estimates somewhat smooth the outliers evident in the recursive figures, so now the largest is not much more than 3.5 standard errors (partly because $\hat{\sigma}$ increased by about 50% over the sample).

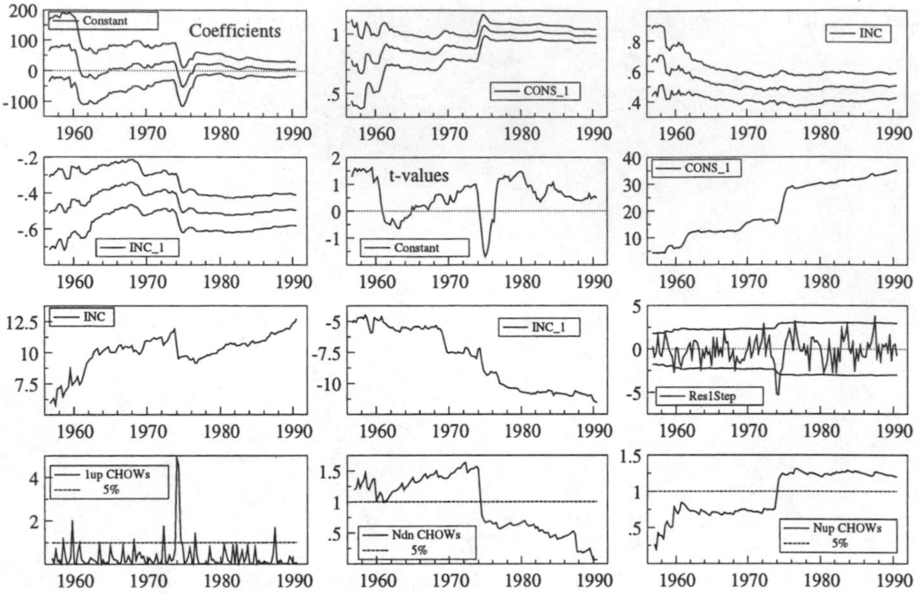

Figure 6.1 Recursive least squares graphical constancy statistics.

For the diagnostic tests, first select normality to see the distribution of $\{\hat{u}_t\}$ and note the value of the χ^2 test (12.58). Now select 1-step residuals to switch over to the $\{\tilde{u}_t\}$ and repeat the normality test for the 136 available observations (12.75). The various statistics can be computed for either or both choices.

That completes RLS. Note that RLS can be used to check the constancy of pre-tests such as (Augmented) Dickey-Fuller tests for the order of integration of a time series, and the recursive graphs may help to discriminate between genuine unit roots and autoregressive coefficients driven towards unity by a failure to model a regime shift.

6.2 Instrumental variables

In many situations it may not be legitimate to treat all regressors as valid conditioning variables, hence instrumental variables (IV) (which for extraneous reasons are known to be valid) must be used. Reselect Model/Formulate as a first step towards the IV option. To compute instrumental variables, PcGive needs to know the status (dependent – or normalized – variable, endogenous, and exogenous or lagged) that you wish to assign to each variable. Given the present model, with a predefined dependent variable (CONS), known lags (CONS_1, INC_1) and a known status for the Constant (exogenous, as it is deterministic), only INC needs a status. Thus, make INC endogenous (mark, then press the Endogenous button) Next, the instruments must be selected. The lag polynomial choices for instruments must be sufficient to identify the equation: add OUTPUT with one lag to the model. Highlight both in the model, and press the Instrument button. The screen should be:

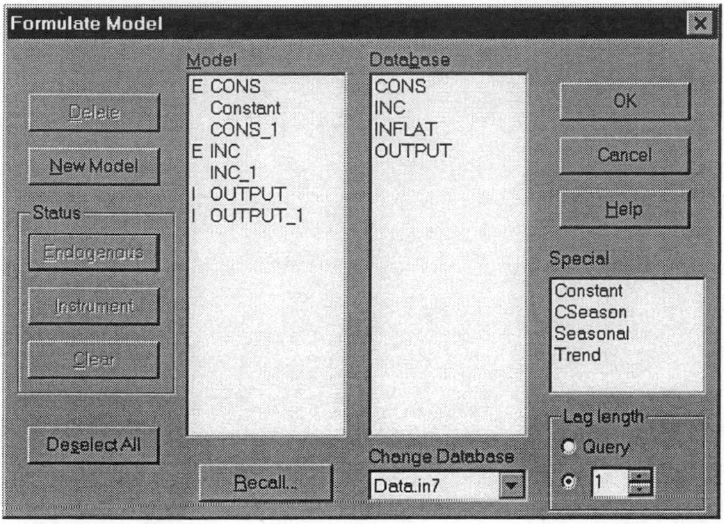

OK to accept and bring up the Estimation dialog, switch to instrumental variables, and press OK again.

6.2.1 Reduced forms

The first statistics reported are the Reduced Form Estimates. These are the regressions of each endogenous variable on the instruments alone, so there are two equations (for CONS and INC). The Results window is positioned at the structural estimates, so press ↑ until you see the reduced form estimates.

```
Modelling Reduced Form for CONS
Variable      Coefficient     Std.Error  t-value
CONS_1             1.0171      0.046472   21.886
Constant           6.2285        25.118    0.248
INC_1           -0.079785      0.050468   -1.581
OUTPUT            0.20994      0.053144    3.950
OUTPUT_1         -0.16812      0.054809   -3.067

R^2=0.977095 F(4,145)=1546.4 [0.0000] RF\sigma=2.05053 DW=1.70
RSS = 609.6757058 for 5 variables and 150 observations

Modelling Reduced Form for INC
Variable      Coefficient     Std.Error  t-value
CONS_1           0.023619      0.064342    0.367
Constant          -58.808        34.777   -1.691
INC_1             0.72756      0.069875   10.412
OUTPUT            0.26855      0.073581    3.650
OUTPUT_1        -0.032723      0.075885   -0.431
```

```
R^2=0.930736 F(4,145)=487.11 [0.0000] RF\sigma=2.83904 DW=2.06
RSS = 1168.724048 for 5 variables and 150 observations
```

If these reduced form equations fit badly (in terms of their $\hat{\sigma}s$), the IV estimates will be poorly determined later. Note that these equations are unrestricted; once the structural model (here CONS on CONS_1, INC, INC_1 and a Constant) is estimated, the reduced form equation for INC can be used to eliminate it from the structural equation to produce a restricted reduced form for CONS. Thus, a comparison of the unrestricted and restricted reduced forms allows a test for the validity of the instruments (see Sargan, 1964). This will be shown below: do you expect a good or bad outcome on such a test from what you have seen so far?

6.2.2 Structural estimates

The structural estimates appear following the reduced forms just shown:

```
EQ( 3) Modelling CONS by IVE  (using Data.in7)
The present sample is:  1953 (2) to 1992 (3) less 8 forecasts
The forecast period is: 1990 (4) to 1992 (3)

Variable       Coefficient     Std.Error  t-value  t-prob
INC                0.37335       0.10250    3.643  0.0004
CONS_1              1.0156      0.036328   27.957  0.0000
Constant            16.656        14.383    1.158  0.2487
INC_1             -0.40746      0.077712   -5.243  0.0000

Additional Instruments used:
   OUTPUT  OUTPUT_1

\sigma = 1.53761   DW = 1.32
RSS = 345.1792451 for 4 variabless and 150 observations
2 endogenous and 3 exogenous variables with 5 instruments

Reduced Form \sigma = 2.05053
Specification  Chi^2(1)   =      14.883 [0.0001] **
Testing \beta=0:Chi^2(3) =        10986 [0.0000] **

Forecast Chi^2( 8)=     6.5087 [0.5904]
```

The specification χ^2-test is for the validity of the instruments – and strongly rejects. Did you anticipate that? If so, which variables are the culprits? The χ^2 (3) testing $\beta = 0$ is the analogue of the OLS F-test of R^2 equal to zero (so testing whether all the coefficients except the constant term are zero). Note how the coefficient of CONS_1 is larger than unity. All of these counter indicators suggest serious mis-specification.

Next we test the model for other problems, similar to the approach and methods used for least squares. The test summary produces:

```
AR 1- 5 F( 5,141) =      7.244 [0.0000] **
ARCH 4   F( 4,138) =    7.3218 [0.0000] **
Normality Chi^2(2)=       5.09 [0.0785]
Xi^2     F( 6,139) =    1.1346 [0.3455]
Xi*Xj    F( 9,136) =    1.1152 [0.3562]
```

Note the significant residual autocorrelation, invalidating most of the inferences you may have been tempted to make *en route*. The use of IVs may correct a simultaneity or measurement error problem, but the basic model specification must be sound before their use.

6.3 Autoregressive least squares

In this section we require the first difference of CONS. If you do not have this in the database yet, switch to GiveWin, and use the Calculator to create DCONS (or use Algebra: `DCONS = diff(CONS,1);`).

The following assumes that ΔCONS is the dependent variable and that the regressors are only Constant, CONS_1, INC and INC_1: if you do not wish to create DCONS, simply add unity to the coefficient of CONS_1 below; if any INFLAT variables remain, delete these.

To access RALS (r^{th} order autoregressive least squares), check the Autoregressive least squares option in the estimation dialog. If recursive estimation is still checked, uncheck it to allow RALS estimation (RALS is not available recursively). As usual, PcGive offers the sample period for your approval. Change it to 1953 (3) to 1992 (3) using 8 forecasts. RALS requires lagged information, prior to the estimation sample. Here there is one observation, 1953 (2), so we can only do first order RALS.

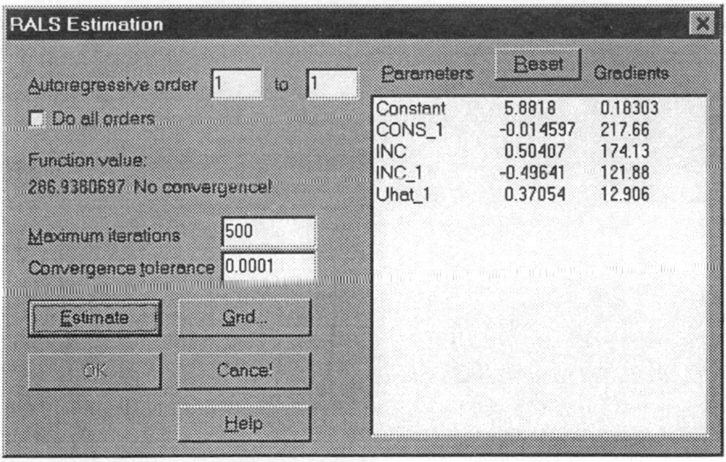

The initial values for RALS are provided by OLS. The parameters are the coefficients from OLS estimation, followed by an nth-order autoregressive error process (initialized by an LM-test, the order being set at the frequency+1, or the maximum lag length, whichever is smaller) and the function is the residual sum of squares (the grid plots show RSS/T).

6.3.1 Optimization

The available options are:

(1) Choose the orders (s, r) of the error process:

$$u_t = \sum_{j=s}^{r} \alpha_j u_{t-j} + \epsilon_t$$

(2) Reset the initial values to those at dialog entry.
(3) Regression coefficients can also be set to any particular desired value.
(4) Optimize
(5) Fix the maximum number of iterations (that is, steps in which the function value reduces); if this number is reached, the optimization process will abort, despite not finding the minimum yet.
(6) Set the convergence criterion; and
(7) Conduct a grid search over α_p for $1 \leq p \leq n \leq 13$, graphing the function over α_p.

All current defaults are shown on-screen. If you wish to skip, then `Esc` jumps back to the main window.

Begin with a grid, to view the graph of the function against the first-order autoregressive parameter. The dialog allows you to select the region for the grid search, as well as the resolution of the search. Press OK once, to accept the default for the first plot. The Grid dialogs returns. Do the second grid around 0.9, in steps of 0.01:

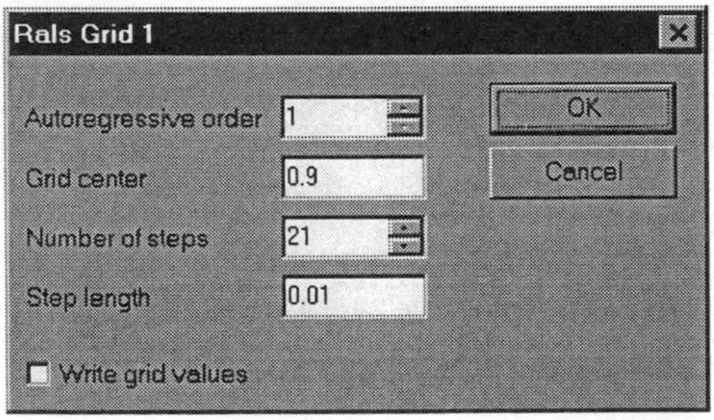

The results are in Figure 6.2. There is a local minimum around 0.4, but the line goes down again after 0.8. The second graph inspects the rightmost section of the grid: centred at 0.9. Use the point facility when the graph is on the screen (View/Point): a minimum of about 1.86 seems to be around 0.97. We can also do a more accurate grid around 0.4 and read the minimum off the screen. Centre the grid around 0.4 and select a

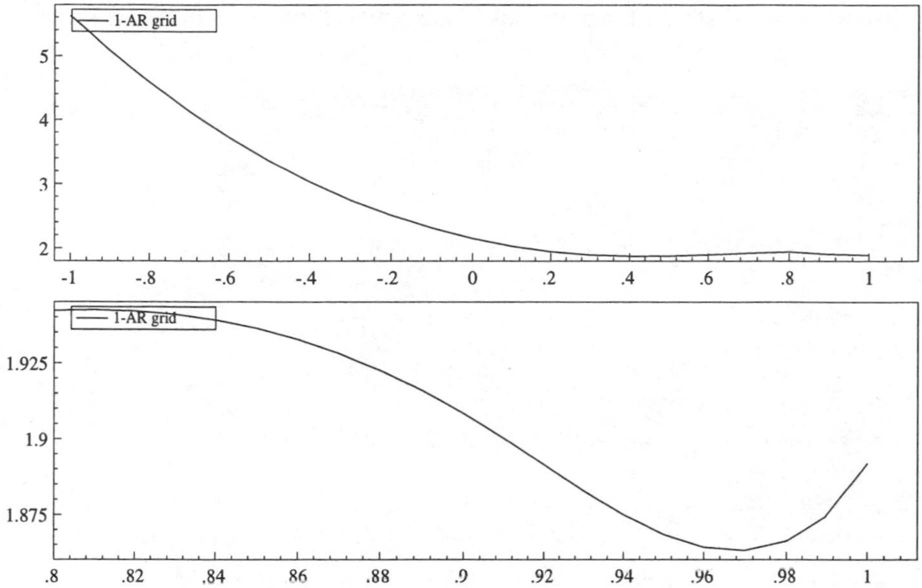

Figure 6.2 Autoregressive least squares grids.

step length of 0.01. Here we find a minimum of 1.87 around 0.43 to 0.44. The optimum appears to be at 0.97, but the two minima have similar function values.

On completion of the grid, the RALS estimation dialog reappears. Now select `Alt+e` for estimation. Note that iterations can be interrupted by pressing a key (for example, if too slow or diverging). After convergence, the OK button lights up. Press OK to write the RALS output to the Results window (we have omitted the detailed forecast output here).

```
EQ( 4) Modelling DCONS by RALS  (using Data.in7)
The present sample is:  1953 (3) to 1992 (3) less 8 forecasts
The forecast period is: 1990 (4) to 1992 (3)

Variable      Coefficient    Std.Error  t-value  t-prob
Constant          -11.283       18.520   -0.609  0.5433
CONS_1           -0.10150     0.053300   -1.904  0.0589
INC               0.50535     0.037158   13.600  0.0000
INC_1            -0.39306     0.055402   -7.095  0.0000
Uhat_1            0.43634     0.098596    4.426  0.0000

\Sum y(t)^2 = 712.915  \sigma = 1.39231
\Phi=279.147933 for 4 variables and 149 obs.(5 parameters)

Roots of the Error Polynomial   0.4363
Tests of parameter constancy over:  1990 (4) to 1992 (3)
Forecast Chi^2( 8)=    0.97324 [0.9984]
Chow    F( 8,143) =    0.95328 [0.4751]
```

Return to the RALS estimation dialog. Double click on Uhat_1 in the parameters list box and type in the desired new value (0.97 here, which we read off Figure 6.2):

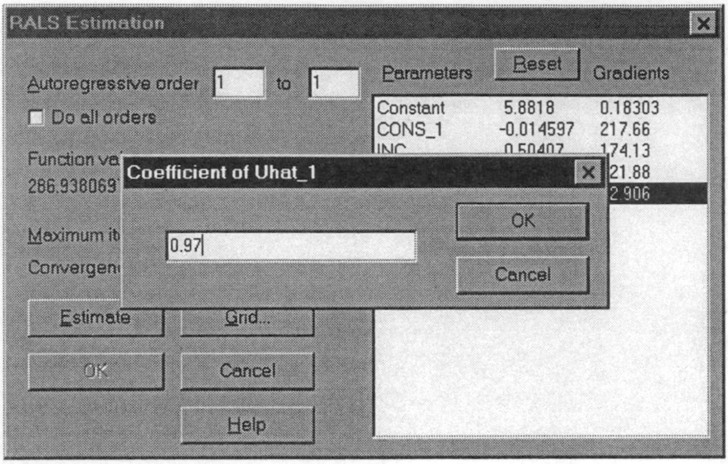

In this way the iteration can be recommenced from any point to check for multiple maxima – note what happens here:

```
EQ( 5) Modelling DCONS by RALS  (using Data.in7)
The present sample is:  1953 (3) to 1992 (3) less 8 forecasts

Variable       Coefficient     Std.Error  t-value  t-prob
Constant            209.68        60.390    3.472  0.0007
CONS_1            -0.64541      0.084785   -7.612  0.0000
INC                0.50513      0.036354   13.895  0.0000
INC_1             -0.10724      0.054246   -1.977  0.0500
Uhat_1             0.96256      0.026054   36.946  0.0000

\Sum y(t)^2 = 712.915  \sigma = 1.38908
\Phi = 277.8554465 for 4 variables and 149 obs.(5 parameters)
```

Thus, the existence of the two optima is real and the latter delivers the smaller RSS (reported as `\Phi`). The function value in the grid is RSS/T, which with $277.855/149 = 1.865$ corresponds to what we read off the graph. Note that the RALS grid is different from the grids in non-linear estimation. In the first-order RALS case, all the OLS parameters are concentrated out, so that we can read the maximum off the screen. In the non-linear model case, all the other parameters are kept constant, and we cannot read the overall maximum off the screen (the graphs are just thin slices of the cake).

Now exit RALS estimation, re-enter the Model estimation dialog, and add an additional observation at the start, beginning estimation at 1953 (4). This allows a second order RALS model. Again, convergence is rapid and both $\{\hat{\alpha}_i\}$ are significant. In fact, if one of the roots of the error polynomial $\left(1 - \hat{\alpha}_1 L - \hat{\alpha}_2 L^2\right)$ is close to unity, this would suggest a specification problem. As before, forecasts and fitted graphics can be perused as in Figure 6.3.

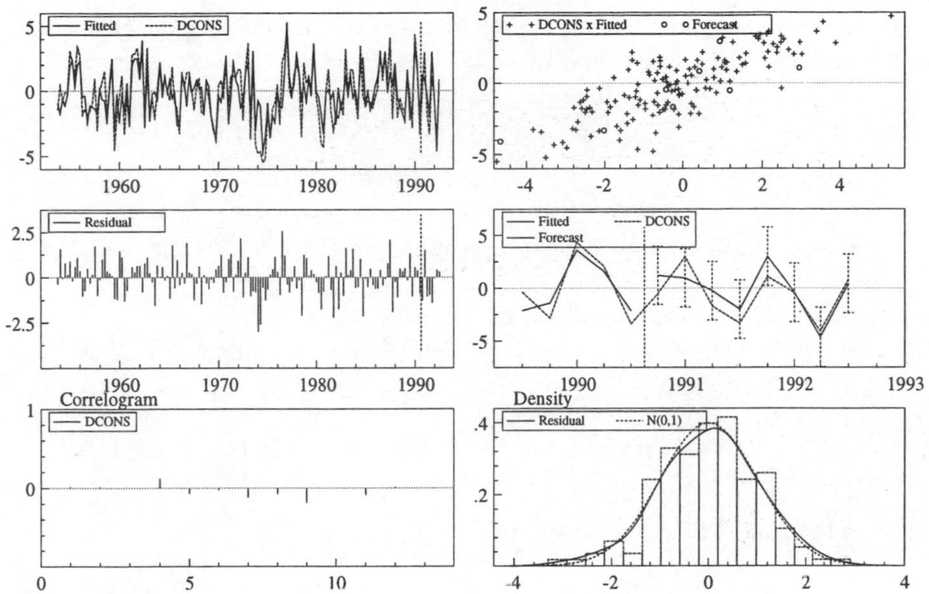

Figure 6.3 Autoregressive least squares graphical statistics.

6.3.2 RALS model evaluation

`Alt+t,t` brings up the usual Test dialog; select some or all options and observe the output (only valid selections will be calculated, others are simply ignored). The residual correlogram and autoregression show that the residuals are close to white noise once the second-order error process is removed, although they are not in fact an innovation process (see Chapter 14). The results for the second-order model are:

```
Residual correlogram
Portmanteau statistic for 12 lags and 148 observations: 12.49

Autocorrelation coefficients
0.015021  0.010052 0.00030269   0.11717 -0.067001 -0.022336
-0.11705 -0.072981   -0.18489 0.0028649 -0.087286  0.011099


Autoregression  for Residual: 12 lags from 1 to 12
The present sample is:  1956 (4) to 1990 (3)
        Constant     Lag  1    Lag  2    Lag  3  Lag  4    Lag  5
Coeff.  -0.04112 -0.003787 -0.04182 0.006077 0.09836   -0.0499
Std.Err   0.1172   0.09054  0.09012  0.09015 0.08871   0.08908

           Lag  6    Lag  7    Lag  8    Lag  9  Lag 10    Lag 11
Coeff.  -0.02273   -0.1151 -0.07865  -0.1667 0.01827 -0.07379
Std.Err  0.08888   0.08878  0.08943  0.08889 0.09062  0.08972
```

```
          Lag 12
Coeff.   0.02199
Std.Err  0.09127

RSS = 228.4256626  \sigma = 1.36276  R^2 = 0.0704094
F(12, 123) = 0.77636 [0.6737]
```

The summary results are (activating the Equation format on the Profile):

```
EQ( 6) Modelling DCONS by RALS  (using Data.in7)
The present sample is:  1953 (4) to 1992 (3) less 8 forecasts

   DCONS = -4.533          -0.1544 CONS_1    +0.5154 INC
(SE)    (   24.86)      ( 0.08168)        (  0.03651)
          -0.3586 INC_1   +0.3743 Uhat_1    +0.2786 Uhat_2
       ( 0.06869)      (    0.1161)       (  0.09126)

\Sum y(t)^2 = 712.912  \sigma = 1.35112
\Phi = 259.2248143 for 4 variables and 148 obs.(6 parameters)

0.7472 and   -0.3729

Tests of parameter constancy over:  1990 (4) to 1992 (3)
Forecast Chi^2( 8)=     1.0265 [0.9981]
Chow     F( 8,140) =    1.0109 [0.4307]

ARCH 4   F( 4,136) =    1.6821 [0.1577]
Normality Chi^2(2)=     1.4527 [0.4837]
Xi^2     F( 6,137) =   0.28748 [0.9421]
Xi*Xj    F( 9,134) =   0.86621 [0.5572]
```

6.4 Non-linear least squares

We now turn to non-linear least squares (NLS) estimation. This method is shown directly on the Model menu since it requires a different method of equation formulation.

To facilitate the model formulation, first do OLS of CONS on a Constant, CONS_1, INC and INC_1 over 1953 (2) to 1992 (3) less 8 forecasts.

Then bring up the Non-linear model formulation dialog by selecting the command from the Model menu. The non-linear model formulation is based on algebra code. Press Paste linear. This formulates the model we just estimated in algebraic code, complete with starting values:

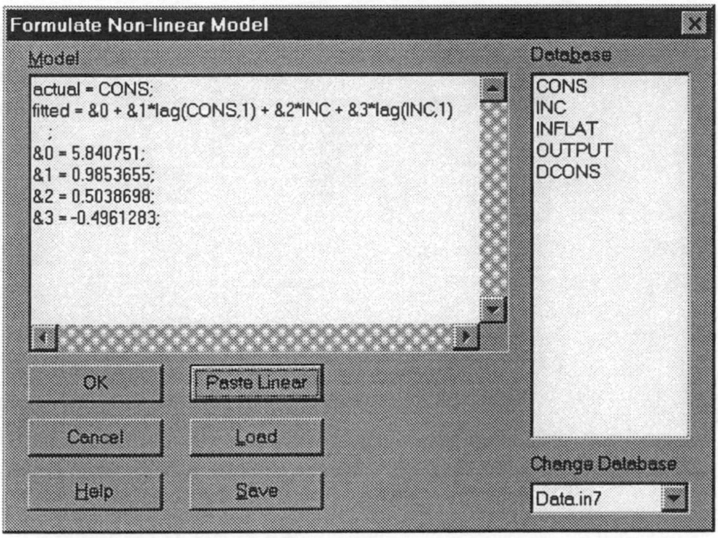

PcGive expects us to define a variable called 'actual' and a variable called 'fitted'. The program can then go ahead to minimize the sum of squares (more precisely, PcGive maximizes $-\sigma$, see Chapter 17):

$$\min \sum_{t=1}^{T} \hat{u}_t^2,$$

with $\hat{u}_t^2$ defined as:

$$\hat{u}_t = actual - \widehat{fitted},$$

and $\widehat{fitted}$ is fitted evaluated at the current parameter values. Parameters are written as `&0`, `&1`, ..., although the numbering does not have to be consecutive. Starting values must always be provided with the code.

We have already considered one method requiring non-linear optimization, namely RALS. The principles behind NLS are similar except that the flexibility needed in formulation to cover a wide class of possible models makes the initial specification more complex. We are cheating here initially and have simply set up a linear-least squares equation.

Accepting the model as shown in the capture above leads to the Non-linear model estimation dialog. This is the standard estimation dialog, with no option to change estimation method. Sample periods and recursive estimation can still be set here. We will just use NLS first. OK brings up an optimization dialog similar to that seen above for RALS:

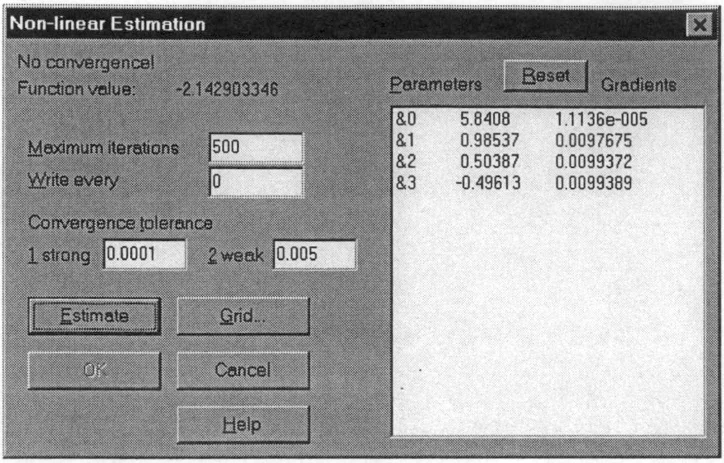

The starting values are shown, together with the gradients at those values. Here starting values are not so important, since OLS has a quadratic sum of squares function (we have good ones anyway from the earlier OLS estimation). Press estimate to commence the optimization. Press the OK button after convergence. The output produced is:

```
EQ( 9) Modelling actual by NLS  (using Data.in7)
The present sample is:  1953 (2) to 1992 (3) less 8 forecasts
The forecast period is: 1990 (4) to 1992 (3)

Variable      Coefficient    Std.Error  t-value  t-prob PartR^2
&0                 5.8408       10.166    0.575  0.5665  0.0023
&1                0.98537     0.027243   36.170  0.0000  0.8996
&2                0.50387     0.039470   12.766  0.0000  0.5275
&3               -0.49613     0.042318  -11.724  0.0000  0.4849

R^2=0.987924  F(3,146)=3981.4 [0.0000]  \sigma=1.48378 DW=1.34
RSS = 321.4355018 for 4 variables and 150 observations
```

Now we return to undertake a more interesting non-linear estimation, namely mimicking RALS. Reselect non-linear estimation, which will show the model we had before. This time, restrict the coefficients of the dynamic relation to satisfy the autoregressive error (that is, COMFAC) restriction for a static regression of CONS on INC, namely &3 = –&1 * &2:

```
actual = CONS;
fitted = &0 + &1*lag(CONS,1) + &2*INC - &1*&2*lag(INC,1);
```

Delete the starting value for &3, and accept this formulation; then in the estimation dialog, check recursive estimation and set the initialization number to 50. OK to move to the Non-linear estimation dialog. Estimate to estimate, and OK to start recursive estimation.

This is a rather time-consuming computation. If it takes too long, press any key to interrupt, showing for example:

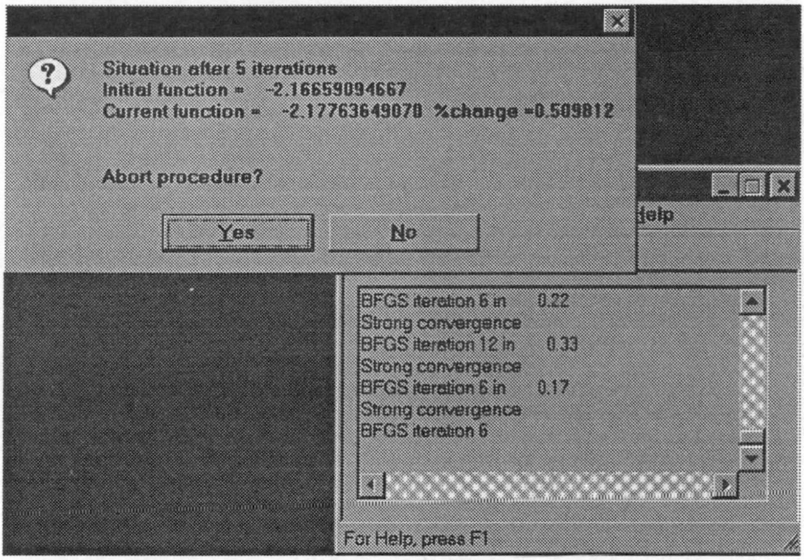

If you abort, the recursive results up to that point will still be available.

```
EQ( 9) Modelling actual by RNLS  (using Data.in7)
The present sample is:  1953 (2) to 1992 (3) less 8 forecasts
The forecast period is: 1990 (4) to 1992 (3)

Variable     Coefficient     Std.Error  t-value  t-prob PartR^2
&0                6.0031        6.0679    0.989  0.3241  0.0066
&1               0.98576      0.014255   69.152  0.0000  0.9702
&2               0.50365      0.037327   13.493  0.0000  0.5533

R^2=0.987924  F(2,147)=6013 [0.0000]  \sigma=1.47873  DW=1.34
RSS = 321.4360874 for 3 variables and 150 observations

Forecast Chi^2( 8)=       7.562 [0.4774]
```

Occasionally, recursive estimation may suffer from a problem in that the RSS value drops from one period to the next. This is signalled by the warning:

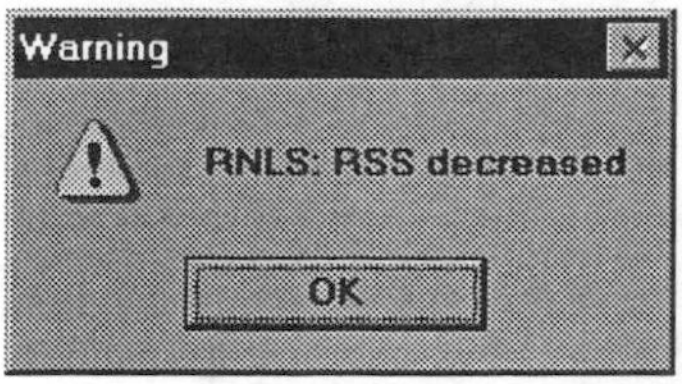

This could then be caused by multiple optima at the full sample size, which either disappear, or we moved from one local optimum to another.

The Recursive graphics dialog has fewer options from that for RLS/RIV:

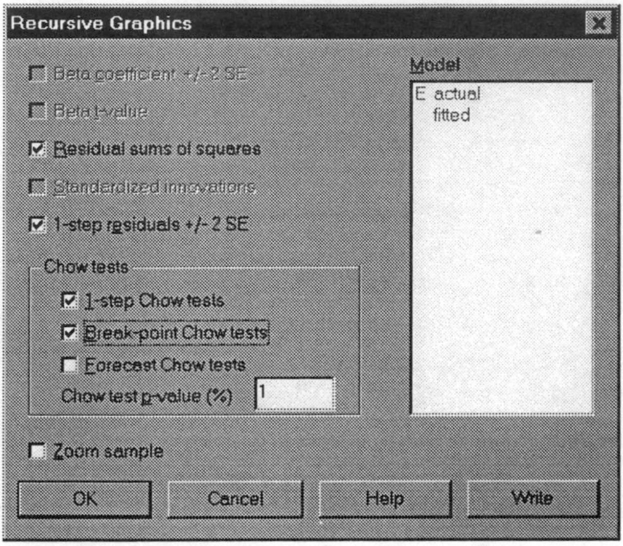

Several steps required a large number of iterations, which already indicated large parameter changes. In addition, parameter non-constancy is obvious from the two Chow-test sequences in Figure 6.4.

We could also have taken our initial values for the parameters from RALS on the static model, giving:

```
EQ(13) Modelling CONS by RALS  (using Data.in7)
The present sample is:  1953 (3) to 1992 (3) less 8 forecasts

     CONS =  +421.3   +0.5039 INC   +0.9857 Uhat_1
(SE)         (34.6)  (0.03811)     (0.01435)

\Sum y(t)^2 = 26520.1  \sigma = 1.48378
\Phi = 321.4333529 for 2 variables and 149 obs.(3 parameters)
```

but note the difference in the intercept: in RALS this is &0*(1–&1) so is much larger than the value for &0 in the NLS formulation we have adopted. Which form is used can substantially affect convergence when &1 is close to unity. Indeed, if you want to create a very badly behaved problem, alter the definition of the intercept to &0/(1–&1) and plot the grid over a wide range! Great care is needed in formulating the function to be minimized. Note also the huge time advantage of specifically programmed methods (e.g. RALS) over doing the equivalent in a generic NLS algorithm. Also note that the alternative specification of the constant term (&0*(1–&1) will lead to different recursive behaviour. The constant in the former vanishes when &1 becomes one. If this happens

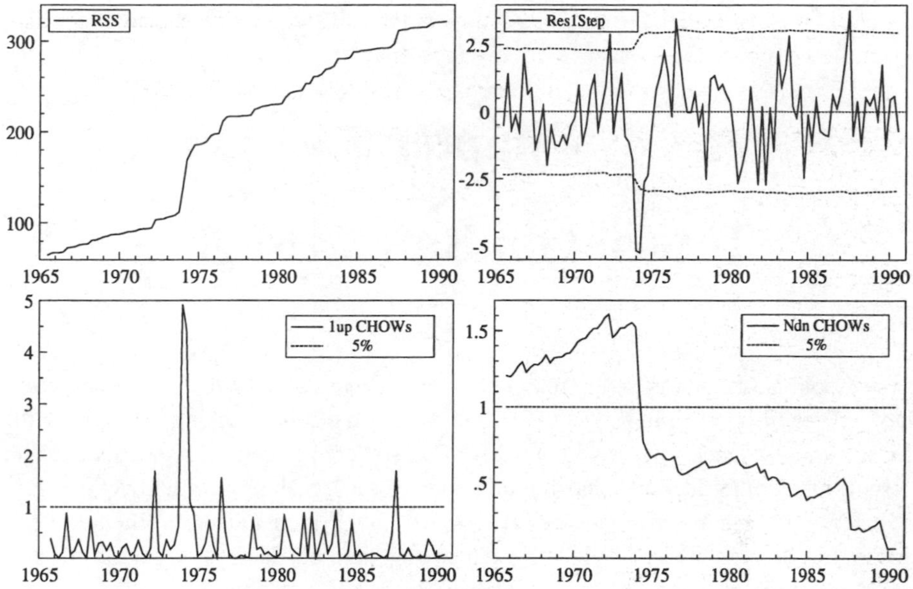

Figure 6.4 Recursive non-linear least squares constancy statistics.

in the RNLS estimation, parameter &1 will not be able to get away from 1.

This concludes our tutorial on estimation methods. There are many others to be explored, and the disk provides several .ALG files for formulating some of the more common non-linear models. Further examples are given in Chapter 9.

Chapter 7

Tutorial on Batch Usage

In this book, the emphasis is very much on interactive use of PcGive. Sometimes, command driven operation can be useful, e.g. as a method of documenting research, or for preparation of a teaching session. For this purpose PcGive supports a batch language. As with many other facilities, batch mode operates in cooperation with GiveWin. It is in GiveWin that the batch commands are issued. GiveWin then decides whether it can handle the command (e.g. data loading and saving, algebra, database selection). If not, the command is passed on to the active module (use the module command to switch between e.g. PcGive and PcFiml when both are open).

To see an example, estimate the familiar model of CONS on a Constant, CONS_1, INC, INC_1, and INFLAT, using the maximum sample with 8 forecasts. Then switch to GiveWin, and activate the batch editor: Tools/Batch Editor or use the toolbar button. The edit dialog appears, with the current model already formulated in the PcGive batch language:

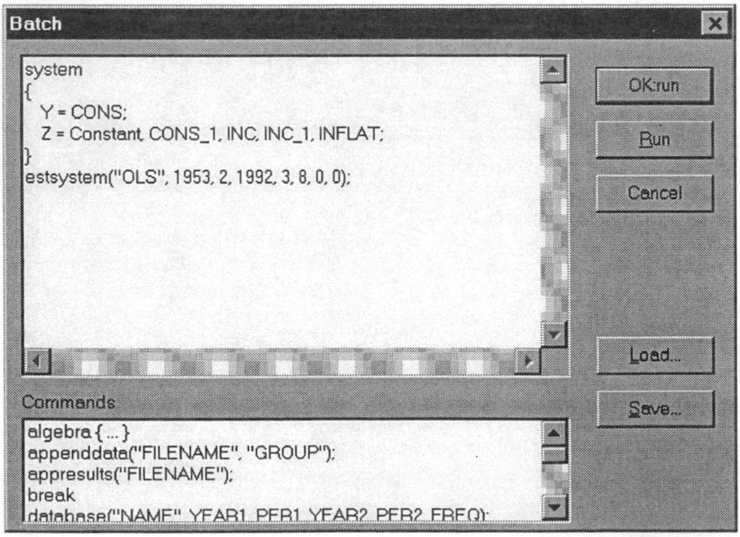

Add some algebra code to create DCONS and DINC, replace CONS and INC in the model by the first differences, and add the testsummary command, as shown in the capture below.

```
algebra
{
  DCONS = diff(CONS,1);
  DINC = diff(INC,1);
}
system
{
  Y = DCONS;
  Z = Constant, CONS_1, DINC, INC_1, INFLAT;
}
estsystem("OLS", 1953, 2, 1992, 3, 8, 0, 0);
testsummary;
```

Press OK:run to execute the batch file. Once saved to disk, a batch file can also be run directly using File/Open, or even by double clicking on the batch file in the Explorer or File Manager. Batch files have the .FL extension, which originally stood for Fiml Language.

As a last example, activate Model/Non-linear model to re-estimate the model using NLS. Then activate the Batch editor in GiveWin. Again, an outline batch file has already been written by GiveWin:

```
nonlinear
{
actual = DCONS;
fitted = &0 + &1*lag(CONS,1) + &2*DINC +
  &3*lag(INC,1) + &4*INFLAT;
&0 = -18.51778;
&1 = -0.190909;
&2 = 0.5066865;
&3 = 0.2101939;
&4 = -0.9925675;
}
estsystem("NLS", 1953, 2, 1992, 3, 8, 0, 0);
```

Chapter 19 documents the PcGive batch commands.

Chapter 8

Tutorial on Model Reduction

8.1 The problems of simple-to-general modelling

While the models used above were mainly selected as illustrations of the use of PcGive, they actually highlighted four important issues:

(1) Powerful tests can reveal model inadequacies: it is not sensible to skip testing in the hope that the model is valid.
(2) A reject outcome on any test invalidates all earlier inferences, rendering useless the time spent up to then – empirical research becomes highly inefficient if done that way.
(3) Once a problem is revealed by a test, how do you proceed? It is a dangerous *non sequitur* to adopt the alternative hypothesis of the test which rejected: did you nearly do this with residual autocorrelation, by assuming it was error autoregression and looking for Cochrane–Orcutt [that is, RALS here]?
(4) What can be done if two or more statistics reject? Which has caused what? Do both or only one need to be corrected? Or should third factors be sought?

As discussed in Chapters 12 and 14, the whole paradigm of postulating a simple model and seeking to generalize it in the light of test rejections or anomalies is suspect, and in fact makes sub-optimal use of PcGive's structure and functioning. Let us now switch to its mode of general-to-specific modelling.

8.2 Formulating general models

We wish to start this chapter with a clean modelling sheet. So exit PcGive and re-enter if you want your model numbering to coincide with the output presented in this chapter. All the output will be presented in equation format, with HCSEs, instability statistics and information criteria. Access the profile to obtain these settings.

Turn to the formulation dialog to create a completely new, general specification. In substantive research, the starting point should be based on previous empirical research evidence (to test in due course that earlier findings are parsimoniously encompassed), economic (or other relevant subject matter) theory, the data frequency – and common sense. Here, we base the initial model on Davidson, Hendry, Srba and Yeo (1978) (denoted DHSY below) and begin by formulating an equation with CONS, INC, INFLAT and Constant as its basic variables (you can add in OUTPUT too if you like, but logic suggests it should be irrelevant given income).

Choose CONS, INC, and INFLAT with two lags each: please note that we are still only illustrating – in practice, five lags would be a better initial lag length for quarterly data, but in a tutorial, the mass of detail could swamp the principles if we reported all the numbers for a long lag length. Do not retain any forecasts for this run and select full sample OLS:

```
EQ( 1) Modelling CONS by OLS  (using Data.in7)
The present sample is:  1953 (3) to 1992 (3)

 CONS =    -20.74          +0.8233 CONS_1     -0.03155 CONS_2
[HCSE]    [9.046]        [0.07751]          [0.07025]
         +0.5001 INC       -0.2959 INC_1      +0.02556 INC_2
       [0.02793]         [0.05294]          [0.04565]
         -0.8441 INFLAT  -0.08015 INFLAT_1   -0.1377 INFLAT_2
        [0.2542]           [0.463]           [0.2798]

R^2=0.993857  F(8,148)=2992.8 [0.0000]  \sigma=1.09027  DW=2.02
RSS = 175.9266198 for 9 variables and 157 observations

Variance instability test: 0.551228*; Joint instab.test: 1.9477
Information Criteria:  SC=0.40367;  HQ=0.299625;  FPE=1.25684
```

Scan the output, noting the coefficient estimates *en route* (e.g. four t-values are small). Select the dynamic analysis to compute the static long-run solution:

```
Solved Static Long Run equation
    CONS =    -99.63       +1.104 INC     -5.101 INFLAT
(SE)         (38.05)    (0.04237)       (0.5484)

ECM = CONS + 99.6282 - 1.10372*INC + 5.10074*INFLAT;

WALD test Chi^2(2) = 981.09 [0.0000] **
```

Note the coefficient values (for example, INC is close to unity, INFLAT to −5) and their small standard errors (so INC is apparently significantly different from unity).

8.3 Analysing general models

The analysis of the lag structure is now more interesting: the unit-root t-tests show that the three basic variables matter as long-run levels (less so if very long lags were selected initially), which rejects a lack of cointegration. The F-tests on the (whole) lag polynomials show that each also matters dynamically. However, lag length 2 is irrelevant, whereas the first lag cannot be removed without a significant deterioration in fit.

```
Analysis of lag structure
          Lag         0         1         2  3  4  5        Sum
CONS                 -1     0.823   -0.0315  0  0  0     -0.208
     StdErr           0    0.0822    0.0715  0  0  0     0.0322
Constant          -20.7         0         0  0  0  0      -20.7
     StdErr        9.07         0         0  0  0  0       9.07
INC                 0.5    -0.296    0.0256  0  0  0       0.23
     StdErr      0.0292    0.0557    0.0447  0  0  0      0.038
INFLAT           -0.844   -0.0802    -0.138  0  0  0      -1.06
     StdErr       0.252     0.435     0.263  0  0  0      0.132

Tests on the significance of each variable
Variable     F(num,denom) Value  Probability Unit root t-test
  CONS       F( 2,148) =  306.93 [0.0000] **         -6.4716**
  Constant   F( 1,148) =  5.2302 [0.0236] *
  INC        F( 3,148) =  102.74 [0.0000] **          6.0458
  INFLAT     F( 3,148) =  32.254 [0.0000] **         -8.039

Tests on the significance of each lag
Lag            F(num,denom)      Value  Probability
   1           F( 3,148) =      38.745 [0.0000] **
   2           F( 3,148) =     0.17158 [0.9155]

Tests on the significance of all lags up to 2
Lag            F(num,denom)      Value  Probability
   1- 2        F( 6,148) =      207.76 [0.0000] **
   2- 2        F( 3,148) =     0.17158 [0.9155]
```

These four perspectives on the model highlight which reductions are consistent with the data, although they do not tell you in what order to simplify. That issue can be resolved in part by more experienced researchers (for one example see the discussion in Hendry, 1987). For the moment, we will follow a sequential simplification route, although generally it is better to transform to near orthogonality prior to simplification.

Can we trust the tests just viewed? The natural attack on that issue is to test all of the congruency requirements listed in the Help: so test using the test summary. Many of these tests will already have been conducted during earlier tutorials. The residual plot looks normal, and no test rejects, although either of the autocorrelation or RESET tests suggests a possible problem may be lurking in the background (the former option gives significant negative autocorrelation possibly owing to overfitting – keep an eye on how that evolves as simplification proceeds). COMFAC accepts that one common factor can be extracted (matching the insignificant 2nd order lag, which would imply that the common factor had a coefficient of zero) but strongly rejects extracting two. The omitted variables test reveals that OUTPUT is indeed irrelevant. And the linear restrictions test confirms that long-run homogeneity of CONS with respect to INC is rejected at the 5% level. Tentatively, therefore, we accept the general or statistical model as data-congruent, with no need for the second lag.

```
AR 1- 5 F( 5,143) =      2.1861 [0.0589]
ARCH 4  F( 4,140) =     0.95118 [0.4365]
Normality Chi^2(2)=      1.6495 [0.4384]
Xi^2    F(16,131) =     0.69832 [0.7916]
Xi*Xj   F(44,103) =     0.74453 [0.8634]
RESET   F( 1,147) =      3.5244 [0.0625]

Roots of the lag polynomials
CONS            lags 0 - 2
  0.7831 and     0.0403
INC             lags 0 - 2
  0.4866 and     0.1050
INFLAT          lags 0 - 2
  -0.0475 \pm 0.4012i = \alpha(0.4040^t)COS{1.6886t+\pi}

COMFAC WALD test statistic table
Order Chi^2df    Value  p-value   Incr.df   Value  p-value
  2       2    0.39429 [0.8211]      2    0.39429 [0.8211]
  1       4     84.071 [0.0000]**    2     83.676 [0.0000]**

LM test for omitted variables
Add     F( 2,146) =     0.25212 [0.7775]

Added variables:  OUTPUT OUTPUT_1

Wald test for linear restrictions: Rb=r
LinRes  F( 1,148) =      4.7143 [0.0315] *
       R matrix
 Constant     CONS_1     CONS_2        INC      INC_1      INC_2
  0.00000     1.0000     1.0000     1.0000     1.0000     1.0000
   INFLAT   INFLAT_1   INFLAT_2
  0.00000    0.00000    0.00000

       r vector
      1.0000
```

8.4 Sequential simplification

For comparability with later models, to transform the dependent variable to DCONS = ΔCONS. Use the GiveWin calculator to create DCONS, return to model formulation, delete CONS from the model, then add DCONS and mark it as endogenous. Now delete all the lags at 2 periods and repeat estimation, keeping the sample starting point to 1953(3) to match the initial model (this is the default behaviour of PcGive: sample periods are sticky). Note the coefficient estimates as you proceed:

```
EQ( 2) Modelling DCONS by OLS  (using Data.in7)
The present sample is:  1953 (3) to 1992 (3)

  DCONS = -0.2021 CONS_1   +0.5002 INC       -0.2773 INC_1
[HCSE]  [0.02608]         [0.02707]          [0.0375]
          -0.784 INFLAT     -0.263 INFLAT_1    -19.94
         [0.1606]          [0.1837]           [8.298]

R^2=0.765599  F(5,151)=98.639 [0.0000]  \sigma=1.08126 DW=1.95
RSS = 176.538482 for 6 variables and 157 observations

Variance instability test:0.549378*; Joint instab.test:1.67364
Information Criteria:  SC=0.310525;  HQ=0.241162;  FPE=1.21381
```

The lag analysis and test options can be reused although the model has been modified by a valid deletion – later, the Progress dialog will be used to take care of testing the validity of reductions. Using test summaries, few keystrokes or mouse clicks are needed to completely re-estimate, regraph and retest the simplified model. Now the apparent residual autocorrelation has gone, suggesting that the earlier interpretation of overfitting was valid. RESET, too, is a little better. After testing whatever hypotheses are desired, select Model/Progress. A dialog appears, listing all the estimated models (excluding non-linear models). The models marked with the = symbols form part of a nesting sequence, based on: with decreasing RSS, increasing number of parameters, the same sample period and regressors forming a subset of the previous models. PcGive does not always get the best nesting sequence, and you can enter or remove a model from the sequence by double clicking. You can also start nesting at an older model, by selecting a model, and then clicking on nest from.

In this case, PcGive infers that both models effectively have the same dependent variable:

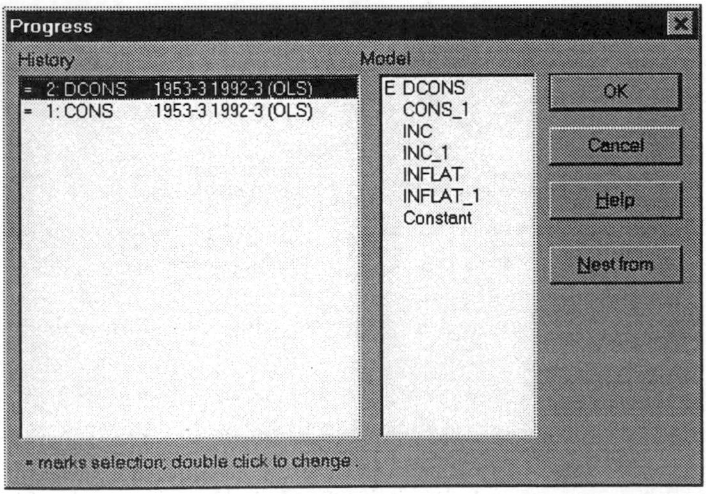

Press OK to see the progress output:

```
Model statistics
    dep.var              T   k    df        RSS      \sigma     Schwarz
 2: DCONS        OLS   157   6   151    176.538     1.08126    0.310525
 1: CONS         OLS   157   9   148    175.927     1.09027     0.40367

Progress to date for modelling DCONS:
Model    1 -->  2: F( 3, 148) =    0.17158 [0.9155]
```

RSS is the residual sum of squares, σ the equation standard error and Schwarz is SC from earlier. The F-test is identical to that in §8.3 for deleting all 2-lagged variables.

Next, we will transform the model to a more interpretable specification, similar to DHSY. Bring up the calculator to transform the variables to sustain a new model of the form:

$$\begin{aligned}\Delta\text{CONS}_t = \beta_0 + \beta_1\Delta\text{INC}_t + \beta_2(\text{INC} - \text{CONS})_{t-1} + \beta_3\text{INFLAT}_t\\ +\beta_4\text{INC}_{t-1} + \beta_5\text{INFLAT}_{t-1};\end{aligned}$$

Create (INC-CONS) by subtracting CONS from INC; call it SAVING, These new variables need to be added to the model: add DINC and SAVING with one lag. Then INC, current SAVING and CONS_1 (or INC_1) must be deleted. Note that it is exactly the same model as model 2 but with a different parameterization and hence a different extent of collinearity (see Chapter 15). We will not estimate this model, but delete INFLAT_1 to retain only DCONS, Constant, DINC, SAVING_1, INFLAT and INC_1 (that is, 5 regressors). Re-estimate over the same sample period as previous models, to get model 3. In Equation format:

```
EQ( 3) Modelling DCONS by OLS  (using Data.in7)
The present sample is:   1953 (3) to 1992 (3)

   DCONS = +0.02054 INC_1       -0.9949 INFLAT    -19.62
[HCSE]    [0.009037]           [0.08372]          [8.214]
            +0.1887 SAVING_1    +0.5074 DINC
          [0.02421]            [0.02604]

R^2=0.763061  F(4,152)=122.38 [0.0000]  \sigma=1.08352 DW=1.95
RSS = 178.4498726 for 5 variables and 157 observations

Variance instability test:0.686029*; Joint instab.test:1.23702
Information Criteria:  SC=0.289089;  HQ=0.231286;  FPE=1.2114
```

The theory behind HCSE is explained in Chapter 12. Test as before and return to check the reduction sequence (again acceptable). Note the greater interpretability of the regression parameters in this differences and levels form; also note that the effect of INC_1 is small, but matching the earlier static long run, is significantly different from zero when conventional critical values are used (but see, for example, Banerjee, Dolado, Galbraith and Hendry, 1993 for an analysis). In fact, the DGP for CONS does have a long-run coefficient of unity for INC, so we will next delete that variable (albeit anticipating a 'significant' reduction this time: in fact, INC is endogenous here, and given the number of tests we planned to use, a 1% level for each would be sensible so the deletion is not deleterious). Thus, delete INC_1, and go back through estimation and testing (note the greatly improved precision of the coefficients estimates in exchange for the cost of an increase in the residual standard error). Again select the nesting sequence in the Progress dialog:

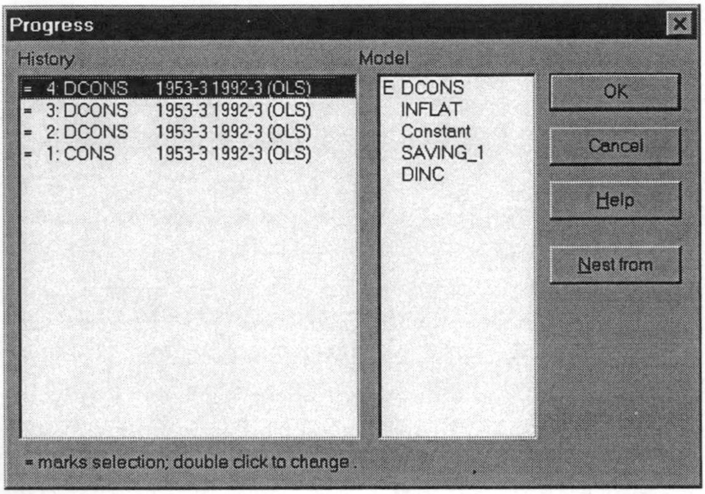

All the diagnostic tests are acceptable from the test summary, and the Progress report is:

```
Model statistics
    dep.var              T   k   df        RSS      \sigma    Schwarz
 4: DCONS        OLS   157   4  153    183.989      1.0966   0.287451
 3: DCONS        OLS   157   5  152     178.45     1.08352   0.289089
 2: DCONS        OLS   157   6  151    176.538     1.08126   0.310525
 1: CONS         OLS   157   9  148    175.927     1.09027    0.40367

Progress to date for modelling DCONS:
Model    1 -->  2: F( 3, 148) =    0.17158 [0.9155]

Model    1 -->  3: F( 4, 148) =    0.53068 [0.7134]
Model    2 -->  3: F( 1, 151) =     1.6349 [0.2030]

Model    1 -->  4: F( 5, 148) =     1.3565 [0.2441]
Model    2 -->  4: F( 2, 151) =     3.1863 [0.0441] *
Model    3 -->  4: F( 1, 152) =      4.718 [0.0314] *
```

At the 5% level, Model 4 is 'significantly' worse than both models 2 and 3 but not than model 1; however, its SC is smaller ($\log T \approx 5.0$ here, so SC falls for all values of F less than about 5) and hence model selection depends in this sample on the choice of criterion and the level of significance. All further reductions by elimination will be significant, although other transformations plus reductions might prove successful: try using the saved ECM which imposes the long-run inflation coefficient as well.

Finally, the resulting model can be re-estimated by RLS to test recursively for parameter constancy (actually, the above model is not fully congruent, and the anomalous results are reflections of that, although the estimates are quite close to those used in the DGP). Figure 8.1 shows the graphical analysis of this final model, re-estimated with 12 forecasts.

Tip Until a data set is saved, all changes within a run are transient; thus, changes will not be kept if you exit prior to saving your data. This is important if new transformations have been created and so automatically added to the database. GiveWin will enquire as you exit if you wish to save the data. If you forget to save the transformed data, you will still have a record of the transformations in the results file. You could then paste the code of the transformations to the Algebra editor, save it and then load the algebra file to transform on each run. This economizes on disk space for data storage, and if you alter the base data, transformed variables are easily recreated.

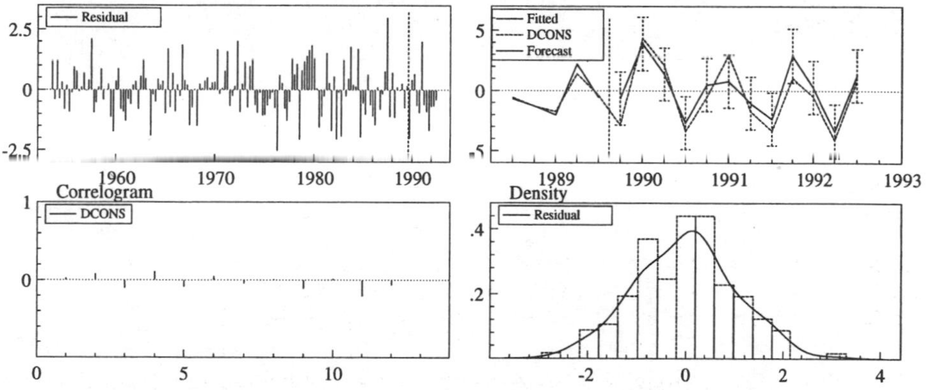

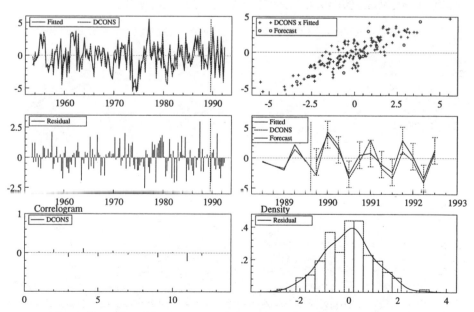

Figure 8.1 Graphical statistics for the final model with 12 forecasts.

8.5 Model revision

If you have made it this far, you can manage on your own for a bit. We hope you enjoyed doing empirical econometrics using PcGive and found it easy, powerful and friendly to use. It is well worth reading through the manuals in Part V before commencing on your own; also read the econometrics Chapters 11–15, although we hope that PcGive provides enough help and menus to be self-explanatory. Or read the final tutorial chapter to delve further into non-linear models. As a final powerful illustration of PcGive, select recursive instrumental variables and reanalyse your model. You will learn a great deal about the inadequacy of conventional methods when you see what you can investigate about claimed models.

Chapter 9

Cross-section Analysis and Non-linear Models

9.1 Cross-section analysis

The emphasis of this book is mainly on time-series econometrics. However, the basic method of ordinary least squares can also be applied to cross-section data. Formulating and estimating a regression model is so easy in PcGive that you will also want to use it for your cross-section regressions. Classify your data as annual in that case, and never select lags of variables. Unlike time-series data, it is common in cross-section data to have missing values spread through the data set. PcGive only works on samples without missing values, but offers sorting facilities to push missing values to the end, or select specific cases. An example will be given in §9.4.

Statistics that test time-series properties of residuals are of less value, but for example, the test for autocorrelation can be used to test for spatial correlation (maybe in combination with the sorting capability). Also, much of the model-building strategy remains valid: just because the data are a cross-section sample doesn't imply that we can suddenly pretend to know the data generation process.

In the remainder of this chapter we shall focus on advanced estimation, using the non-linear model option. Both time-series and cross-section examples will be considered. We assume you are familiar with preceding tutorials, especially with the material in Chapters 4 and 6.

9.2 Non-linear model estimation

Several examples of non-linear least squares estimation were given in Chapter 6. In particular, we saw that a linear model can be set up as a non-linear model, but that direct estimation by OLS is much more efficient. Estimating RALS and NLS models confronted us with some of the potential problems of estimating non-linear models:

(1) choosing bad starting values;
(2) multiple optima;

(3) for recursive NLS: RSS which is not monotonically increasing with sample size;
(4) optima which are hard to locate, maybe resulting in failure to converge;
(5) choosing a 'difficult' parameterization (for example, maximizing a concentrated likelihood might be easier than the original likelihood).

We can add to that:

(1) programming errors, as we have to program the function ourselves (just try reversing the sign of the 'loglik' function);
(2) reaching a region of the parameter space where the function is not defined (such as taking the logarithm of a negative number);
(3) failure to compute numerical first derivatives (these are essential for finding an upward direction);
(4) upon convergence: failure to compute numerical second derivatives (these provide standard errors);

The following four precautions could make the difference between a diverging and converging estimation:

(1) **scale the parameters**, so that they fall between 0.1 and 1 (as a rule of thumb: scale the explanatory variables to be in the range 0.1–1);
(2) **find good starting values**, maybe solving a closely related problem which can be estimated by OLS;
(3) use a careful implementation, e.g. take the absolute value (or square) of parameters that must be positive (such as variances);
(4) in case of divergence, estimate first with fewer parameters.

All these problems have to be taken into account, making non-linear estimation an option for the advanced user. But it is a powerful feature, and a lot of fun to experiment with. Many examples are given below.

Sometimes we can show that the log-likelihood is concave, in which case there is only one maximum. This makes it easier to locate the maximum, and if we find one, we know that it's the only one. Some things can still go wrong, in the case where the starting values are too far away from the maximum, or when reaching an area where the function is numerically flat. Numerical issues must be considered throughout: e^{10000} does exist, but our computer cannot handle such a large number.

9.3 Maximizing a function

The third non-linear estimation method (following NLS and RNLS) is called ML, which stands for maximum likelihood. This option maximizes a function of the parameters. This does not need to be a likelihood function. Consider, for example, minimizing the so-called Rosenbrock function (see Fletcher, 1987):

$$f(\alpha, \beta) = 100 * \left(\beta - \alpha^2\right)^2 + (1 - \alpha)^2 .$$

No data are involved. It is easily seen that the minimum is at $(1,1)$ with function value 0. The contours are rather banana-shaped. To estimate, create a database of just one single observation in GiveWin, then in PcGive select Model/Non-linear model and load the tutorial file TUTROSEN.ALG:

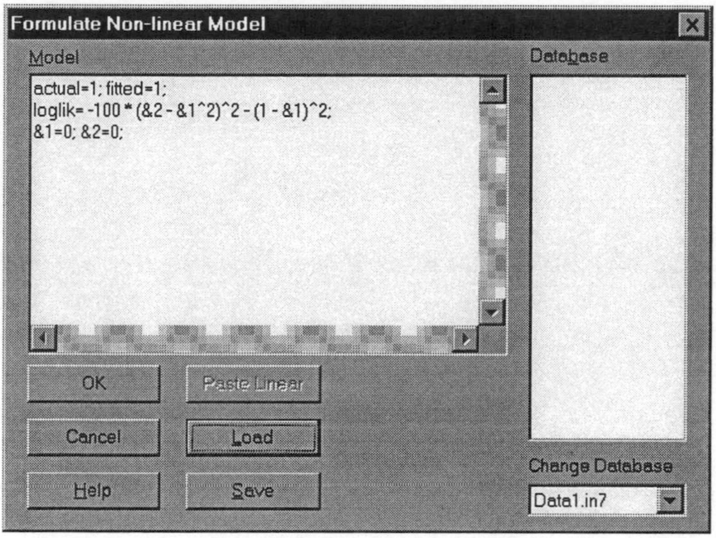

The variables labelled 'actual' and 'fitted' are required by PcGive, but serve no other purpose here (they are used in the graphic analysis). The 'loglik' variable is summed over the sample size, and this sum is minimized. Non-linear modelling requires us to provide starting values, here we choose zero. Accept, and accept the default sample size of one observation. This leads to the Non-linear Estimation dialog; the top line says 'No convergence!', because the maximization has not started yet. Push the Estimate button, leading to convergence quickly (the message changes to 'Strong convergence'):

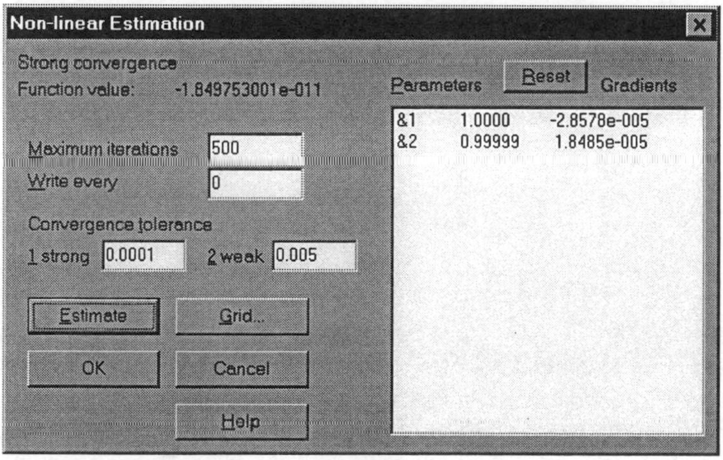

The grid option allows a grid search over one parameter, holding all other parameters at their current value (such a grid is different from RALS, which graphs the concentrated likelihood). Note the very distinct appearances of the function depending on the scale over which the grid is plotted, as in the second line of graphs.

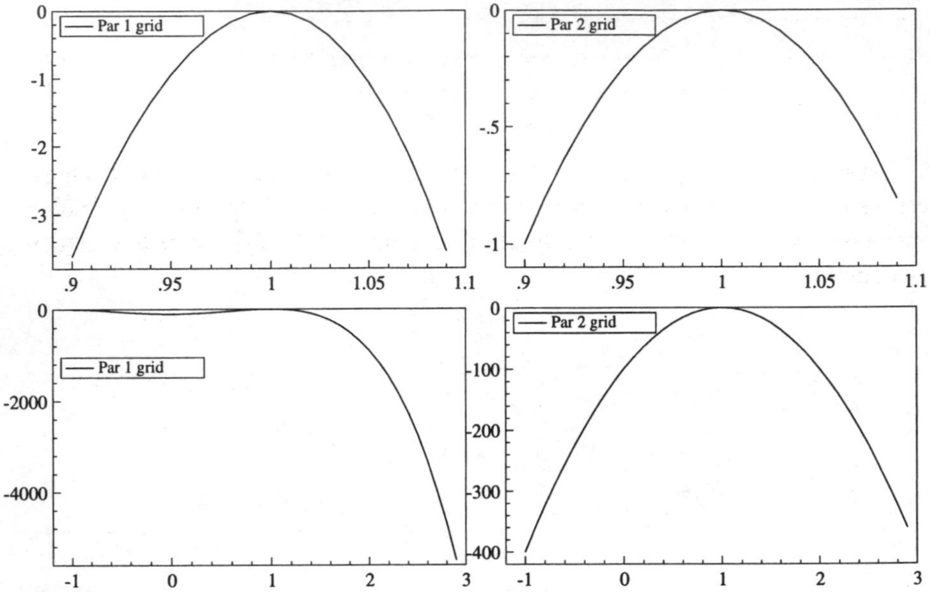

Figure 9.1 Rosenbrock function parameter grid.

Choosing OK gives the output:

```
EQ( 1) Modelling actual by ML  (using Data1.in7)
The present sample is:  1 to 1

Variable       Coefficient    Std.Error  t-value
&1                  1.0000      0.70710    1.414
&2                 0.99999       1.4160    0.706

loglik = -1.849705101e-011 for 1 observations and 2 parameters

Code used for estimation:
actual=1; fitted=1;
loglik= -100 * (&2 - &1^2)^2 - (1 - &1)^2;
&1=0; &2=0;
```

9.4 Logit and probit estimation

A discrete choice model is one where the dependent variable is discrete, and denotes a category. In this section we use this type of model to do maximum likelihood estimation in PcGive. General references are Cramer (1991), McFadden (1984) and Amemiya (1981) among others. Examples of categorical dependent variables are:

$$y_i = 0 \quad \text{if household } i \text{ owns no car,}$$
$$y_i = 1 \quad \text{otherwise,}$$

or

$$y_i = 0 \quad \text{if individual } i \text{ travels to work by car,}$$
$$y_i = 1 \quad \text{if } i \text{ travels to work by bike,}$$
$$y_i = 2 \quad \text{otherwise.}$$

The first example is a binary choice problem (two categories), the second is multinomial. Here we restrict ourselves to the former: the dependent variable is a dummy. With a discrete dependent variable, interest lies in modelling the probabilities of observing a certain outcome. Write

$$p_i = \mathsf{P}\{y_i = 1\}.$$

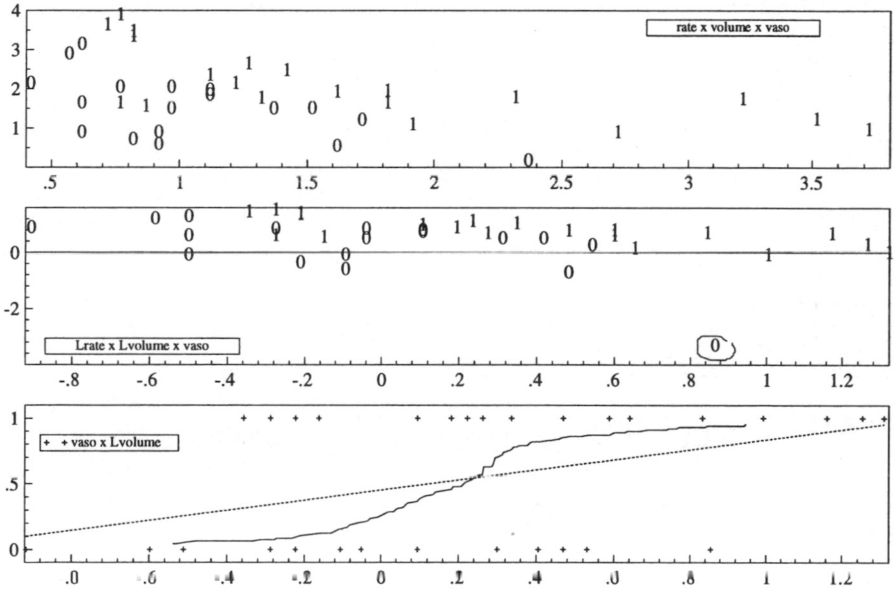

Figure 9.2 Finney's data.

To illustrate this method we use the data from Finney (1947), provided in the files FINNEY.IN7 and FINNEY.BN7. This data set holds 39 observations on the occurrence of vaso-constriction (the dummy variable, called 'vaso') in the skin of the fingers after taking a single deep breath. The dose is measured by the volume of air inspired ('volume') and the average rate of inspiration ('rate'). Load the data set into PcGive. A graphical inspection is provided by Figure 9.2. Figure 9.2(a) shows a cross-plot of volume and rate by vaso; a 1 indicates the occurrence of vaso-constriction. This graph suggests that response is determined by the product of rate and volume. The next graph uses log(rate) and log(volume). The point inside the circle appears to be an outlier. The data are taken from the table in Finney (1947), which has a typing error for observation 32. The correct value is (presumably) 0.3 instead of 0.03 (0.3 corresponds to the graph in the paper). The straight line in Fig. 9.2(c) shows what regressing vaso on log(volume) would lead to; the hand-drawn line shows a better approach, corresponding to a cumulative distribution function. Applying the straight line (that is, OLS) has several disadvantages here. First, it doesn't yield proper probabilities, as it is not restricted to lie between 0 and 1 (OLS is called the linear probability model: $p_i = \mathbf{x}_i'\boldsymbol{\beta}$). Secondly, the disturbances cannot be normally distributed, as they only take on two values: $\epsilon_i = 1 - p_i$ or $\epsilon_i = 0 - p_i$. Finally, they are also heteroscedastic: $\mathsf{E}[\epsilon_i] = (1-p_i)p_i + (0-p_i)(1-p_i) = 0$, $\mathsf{E}[\epsilon_i^2] = (1-p_i)^2 p_i + (0-p_i)^2(1-p_i) = (1-p_i)p_i$.

A simple solution is to introduce an underlying continuous variable y_i^*, which is not observed. Observed is:

$$y_i = \begin{cases} 0 & \text{if } y_i^* < 0, \\ 1 & \text{if } y_i^* \geq 0. \end{cases} \tag{9.1}$$

Now we can introduce explanatory variables:

$$y_i^* = \mathbf{x}_i'\boldsymbol{\beta} - \epsilon_i.$$

and write

$$p_i = \mathsf{P}\{y_i = 1\} = \mathsf{P}\{\mathbf{x}_i'\boldsymbol{\beta} - \epsilon_i \geq 0\} = F_\epsilon(\mathbf{x}_i'\boldsymbol{\beta}).$$

Observations with $y_i = 1$ contribute p_i to the likelihood, observations with $y_i = 0$ contribute $1 - p_i$:

$$L(\boldsymbol{\beta} \mid \mathbf{X}) = \prod_{\{y_i=0\}} (1-p_i) \prod_{\{y_i=1\}} p_i,$$

and the log-likelihood becomes:

$$\ell(\boldsymbol{\beta} \mid \mathbf{X}) = \sum_{i=1}^{N} \left[(1-y_i)\log(1-p_i) + y_i \log p_i\right].$$

The choice of F_ϵ determines the method. Using the logistic distribution:

$$F_\epsilon(z) = \frac{e^z}{1+e^z}$$

leads to *logit*. Logit has a linear *log-odds ratio*:

$$\log\left(\frac{p_i}{1-p_i}\right) = \mathbf{x}_i'\boldsymbol{\beta}.$$

The standard normal gives *probit*. As we can multiply y_i^* by any non-zero constant without changing the outcome, the scale of these distributions is fixed: the logistic has variance $\pi^2/3$, the standard normal has variance equal to 1. The corresponding Algebra code for our application is :

```
actual = vaso;
xbeta = &0 + &1 * Lrate + &2 * Lvolume;
fitted = 1 / (1 + exp(-xbeta));
loglik = actual * log(fitted) + (1 - actual) * log(1 - fitted);
// starting values:
&0 = -0.744;  &1 = 1.346;  &2 = 2.303;
```

and for probit:

```
actual = vaso;
xbeta = &0 + &1 * Lrate + &2 * Lvolume;
fitted = probn(xbeta);
loglik = actual * log(fitted) + (1-actual) * log(tailn(xbeta));
// starting values:
&0 = -0.465;  &1 = 0.842;  &2 = 1.439;
```

The starting values for both problems were obtained from an OLS regression of vaso on a constant, Lrate and Lvolume, and then transforming the parameters following Amemiya (1981) as:

	constant	rest
logit	$4\,(\alpha_{OLS} - 0.5)$	$4\beta_{OLS}$
probit	$2.5\,(\alpha_{OLS} - 0.5)$	$2.5\beta_{OLS}$

First estimate the binary logit model: load the FINNEY data set in GiveWin, in PcGive type `Alt+m,1` to activate Model/Non-linear model. Change database to finney.in7, then load TUTLOGIT.ALG, accept (if you get the message 'vaso not found in database' you forgot to change to the finney database) and accept again. In the Non-linear estimation dialog press `Estimate` to start estimating, and OK to accept the result after convergence. The results are:

```
EQ( 1) Modelling actual by ML
The present sample is:   1 to 39

Variable       Coefficient      Std.Error  t-value  t-prob
&0                 -2.8754         1.3208   -2.177  0.0361
&1                  4.5617         1.8380    2.482  0.0179
&2                  5.1793         1.8648    2.777  0.0086

loglik = -14.61368764 for 39 observations and 3 parameters
```

A graphic analysis which will use the variables 'actual' and 'fitted' as we defined them is not so interesting here. Better is Figure 9.3. Select Test/Store in database, and tick Fitted values and Log-likelihood. Press OK, and rename Fitted to plogit (the probabilities estimated by the logit model), and loglik to liklogit. Next, switch to GiveWin and graph vaso, plogit and liklogit. This graph looks different from 9.3, which is sorted by 'liklogit'. This is achieved by sorting the whole database by the 'liklogit' variable using Algebra; enter:

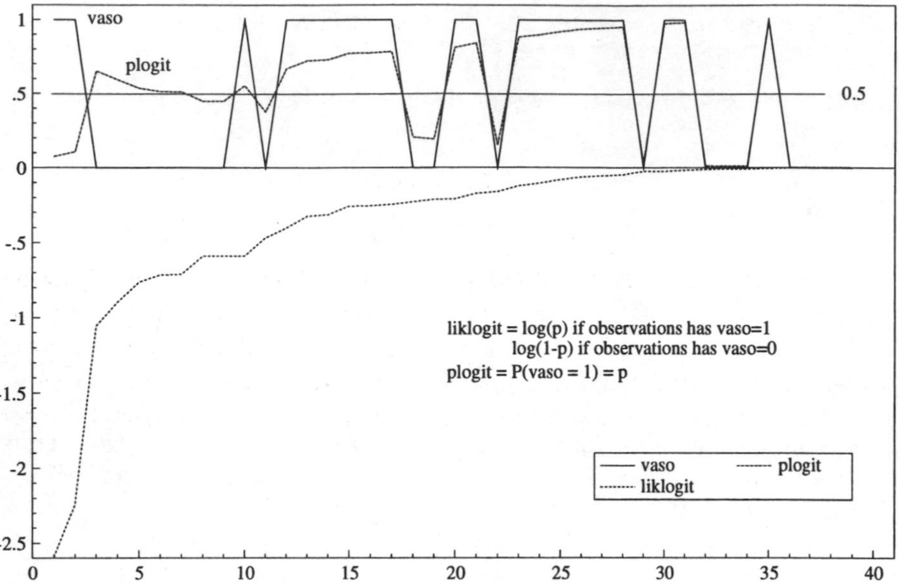

Figure 9.3 Log-likelihoods, probabilities and outcomes for the logit model.

```
index = trend();
_sortallby(loglik);
```

in the Algebra editor and execute. The index variable allows us to undo the sorting operation. The 'plogit' variable is p_i, whereas 'liklogit' is the log-likelihood contribution of observation i: the log of the probability of being in the observed state. Ideally, we predict a probability of one, corresponding to a likelihood of 0. So as we move from left to right, the 'fit' improves. From the top part of the graph we see that if for $p_i > 0.5$ we would classify the outcome as a 1, then the misclassifications are on the left.

To see whether the typo in observation 32 matters much, move it to the end of the database through:

```
deselect = (index == 32);
_sortallby(deselect);
```

deselect will be 1 for observation 32 and 0 otherwise, and sorting all variables by deselect moves number 32 to the bottom. Do a logit model over the sample 1–38: there is hardly any difference at all.

The index variable corresponds to the original observation index, so to restore the original order in the database, execute:

```
_sortallby(index);
```

and turn to the probit estimation using TUPROBIT.ALG:

```
EQ( 1) Modelling actual by ML  (using FINNEY.IN7)
The present sample is:   1 to 39

Variable      Coefficient    Std.Error  t-value  t-prob
&0                -1.5044      0.63751   -2.360  0.0238
&1                 2.5123      0.93651    2.683  0.0110
&2                 2.8620      0.90812    3.152  0.0033

loglik = -14.64353075 for 39 observations and 3 parameters
```

Although the coefficients of logit and probit are quite different, this is mainly owing to the choice of scaling parameter. It is more useful to compare probabilities (or derivatives of probabilities with respect to explanatory variables). Sorting the database again, and combining logit and probit results, gives Figure 9.4. Here we see that the differences between the results are very small indeed: there is no reason to prefer one over the other (also see Chambers and Cox, 1967).

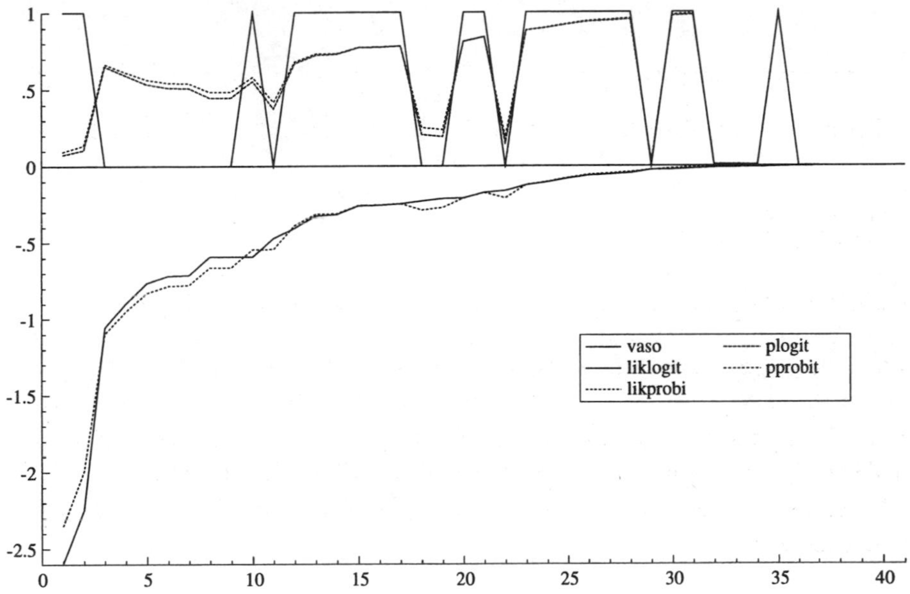

Figure 9.4 Comparison of the probit and logit models.

As an illustration of the possibilities and drawbacks of PcGive's ML option we did a multinomial logit with 4 states (numbered 0,1,2,3), 1700 observations and 24 parameters. The probabilities of observation i to be in state j are defined as:

$$\mathsf{p}_{ij} = \frac{e^{\mathbf{x}_i'\boldsymbol{\beta}_j}}{\sum_{j=0}^{3} e^{\mathbf{x}_i'\boldsymbol{\beta}_j}}, \quad j = 0, \ldots, 3, \quad \text{with } \boldsymbol{\beta}_0 = 0.$$

The code rearranges this somewhat, to provide a numerically more stable calculation, see MNLOGIT.ALG. On a 90 Mhz Pentium this takes 10 minutes to converge (with strong convergence tolerance of 0.001), plus nearly 5 minutes to evaluate the variance numerically. We also implemented the method in a separate program, with analytical first and second derivatives using Newton's method: convergence takes 4 seconds. Most of the penalty comes out of having to evaluate the algebra code over and over again, rather than being able to use the hard-coded function.

9.5 Tobit estimation

In the standard tobit model (see, for example, Amemiya, 1985, Chapter 10, or Cramer, 1991, Chapter 11), the observations on the dependent variable are censored: the positive values are observed, but instead of negative values, we see only zeros. The analogue to (9.1) is:

$$y_i = \begin{cases} 0 & \text{if } y_i^* \leq 0, \\ y_i^* & \text{if } y_i^* > 0, \end{cases}$$

using

$$y_i^* = \mathbf{x}_i'\boldsymbol{\beta} + \epsilon_i, \quad \text{with } \epsilon_i \sim \mathsf{IN}\left(0, \sigma^2\right).$$

Now $\mathsf{P}\{y_i^* \leq 0\} = \mathsf{P}(\mathbf{x}_i'\boldsymbol{\beta} + \epsilon_i \leq 0) = 1 - F_\epsilon(\mathbf{x}_i'\boldsymbol{\beta})$ (F_ϵ is symmetric). The log-likelihood can be seen to consist of a probit part and an OLS part:

$$\ell\left(\boldsymbol{\beta} \mid \mathbf{X}\right) = \sum_{\{y_i=0\}} \log\left(1 - F_\epsilon\left(\mathbf{x}_i'\boldsymbol{\beta}\right)\right) + \sum_{\{y_i>0\}} \log\left(f_\epsilon\left(y_i - \mathbf{x}_i'\boldsymbol{\beta}\right)\right).$$

Using (13.102):

$$\ell\left(\boldsymbol{\beta} \mid \mathbf{X}\right) = \sum_{\{y_i=0\}} \log\left(1 - F_\epsilon\left(\mathbf{x}_i'\boldsymbol{\beta}\right)\right) + c + \sum_{\{y_i>0\}} \left[\log\left(\sigma^{-1}\right) - \frac{1}{2}\frac{\left(y_i - \mathbf{x}_i'\boldsymbol{\beta}\right)^2}{\sigma^2}\right]$$

Write Φ for the standard normal cdf:

$$1 - F_\epsilon(\mathbf{x}_i'\boldsymbol{\beta}) = 1 - \Phi\left(\mathbf{x}_i'\boldsymbol{\beta}/\sigma\right).$$

Using the indicator function $\mathcal{I}(\cdot)$ to indicate whether the outcome was observed, $\ell_i(\boldsymbol{\beta}|\mathbf{x}_i)$, the likelihood for individual i may be written as:

$$\mathcal{I}\left(y_i = 0\right) \log\left[1 - \Phi\left(\mathbf{x}_i'\boldsymbol{\beta}/\sigma\right)\right] + \mathcal{I}\left(y_i > 0\right)\left[\tfrac{1}{2}\log\left(\sigma^{-1}\right) - \tfrac{1}{2}\left(y_i/\sigma - \mathbf{x}_i'\boldsymbol{\beta}/\sigma\right)^2\right].$$

It is convenient to scale by σ, writing $\boldsymbol{\alpha} = \boldsymbol{\beta}/\sigma$, so that $\ell_i(\boldsymbol{\alpha}|\mathbf{x}_i)$ is:

$$\mathcal{I}\left(y_i = 0\right) \log\left[1 - \Phi\left(\mathbf{x}_i'\boldsymbol{\alpha}\right)\right] + \mathcal{I}\left(y_i > 0\right)\left[\tfrac{1}{2}\log\left(\sigma^{-1}\right) - \tfrac{1}{2}\left(y_i/\sigma - \mathbf{x}_i'\boldsymbol{\alpha}\right)^2\right].$$

The data set is TUTTOBIT.IN7, which holds data on expenditure on clothing for 150 individuals, with income and age. In algebra code, the likelihood is expressed as (the code is given in the file TUTTOBIT.ALG):

```
actual = expen;                                  // y
fitted = &0 + &1 * inc/1000 + &2 * age/10;      // x'alpha
loglik = (actual <= 0)
  ? log( max(1.e-20, tailn(fitted)) )            // probit part
  : log(fabs(&3)) - 0.5 * (actual * fabs(&3) - fitted)^2;

&0=-3.3; &1=1.3; &2=2.3; &3=0.022;              // starting values
fitted = fitted/&3;// undo scaling, fitted is no longer needed
```

First of all, scaling of the parameters is important, preferably so that they fall between 0.1 and 1. Without that, the numerical derivatives are much more likely to fail. Also use good starting values (here based on OLS). Secondly, &3 is σ^{-1}, and the remaining parameters estimate $\alpha = \beta/\sigma$. More importantly, we take the absolute value of &3, reducing the singularity to a small region around 0. Consequently, it is possible to find a negative value for &3; in that case restart at the optimum, but with the absolute value of &3, which converges immediately. Finally, we don't allow $1 - F_\epsilon$ to get smaller than 10^{-20}. This helps with bad starting values, but should not make any difference close to the optimum.

The starting values were found from a full-sample OLS estimation:

```
Variable      Coefficient     Std.Error  t-value   t-prob PartR^2
Constant          -151.48        48.557   -3.120   0.0022  0.0621
inc              0.060824      0.017102    3.557   0.0005  0.0792
age                10.439        3.1130    3.353   0.0010  0.0711

R^2=0.23024  F(2, 147)=21.984 [0.0000]  \sigma=46.3493
```

So: &0 $= -151.48/46.3439$, &1 $= (1000 \times 0.060824)/46.3439$, &2 $= (100 \times 10.439)/46.3439$, &3 $= 1/46.3439$.

The final results are:

```
EQ( 2) Modelling actual by ML  (using TUTTOBIT.IN7)
The present sample is:   1 to 150

Variable      Coefficient     Std.Error  t-value   t-prob
&0                -4.7819        1.2066   -3.963   0.0001
&1                 1.2779       0.40526    3.153   0.0020
&2                 2.6729       0.76527    3.493   0.0006
&3              -0.012230     0.0011673  -10.477   0.0000

loglik = -374.9303539 for 150 observations and 4 parameters
```

Figure 9.5 gives a plot of the fitted values from the Tobit model and from OLS in the upper half, and expenditure in the lower half (both after sorting the database by expenditure).

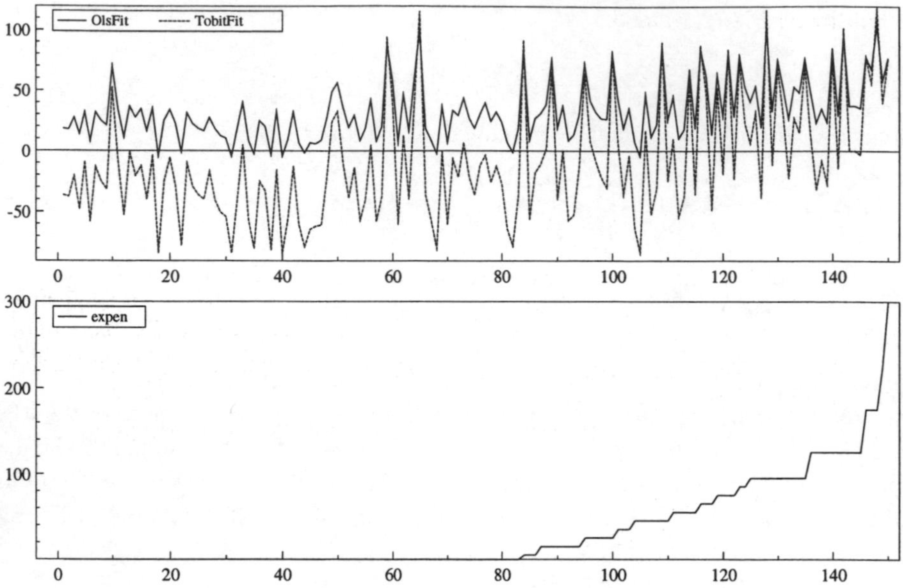

Figure 9.5 Comparison of fitted values from OLS and Tobit.

9.6 ARMA estimation

Here we fit a model to generated ARMA(2, 2) and in the next section to ARCH data. First run the batch file TUTARMA.FL in GiveWin:

```
database("tutarma", 1, 1, 120, 1, 1);
algebra
{
    ranseed(-1);

    eps = rann();
    arma22 = year() >= 3
       ? -1.4 * lag(arma22,1) - .5 * lag(arma22,2) + eps
        - .2 * lag(eps,1) - .1 * lag(eps,2)
       : 0;
    arch = year() >= 3
       ? sqrt(1 + 0.6 * lag(arch,1)^2) * eps
       : 0;

    arma22 = insample(1, 1, 17, 1) ? MISSING;
    arch = insample(1, 1, 17, 1) ? MISSING;
}
```

This creates a database of 120 observations on an ARMA(2, 2) and an ARCH process (the first 17 observations are thrown away).

For the ARMA(2, 2) model

$$y_t = \theta_0 y_{t-1} + \theta_1 y_{t-2} + \epsilon_t + \theta_2 \epsilon_{t-1} + \theta_3 \epsilon_{t-2},$$

we can use NLS to mimimize the conditional sum of squares (CSS):

$$\sum_{t=3}^{T} \left(y_t - \theta_0 y_{t-1} - \theta_1 y_{t-2} - \theta_2 \epsilon_{t-1} - \theta_3 \epsilon_{t-2}\right)^2$$

with $\epsilon_1 = \epsilon_2 = 0$. This treatment of the initial disturbances simplifies the estimation procedure. Exact maximum likelihood estimation requires specifying the distribution for the initial observations and disturbances. See Box and Jenkins (1976) or Harvey (1993) among others.
The code for estimating the ARMA(2, 2) model is given in TUTARMA.ALG:

```
actual = arma22;
fitted = (lag(actual,2) != MISSING)
       ?  &1*lag(actual,1) + &2*lag(actual,2)
        +  &3*(lag(actual,1) - lag(fitted,1))
        +  &4*(lag(actual,2) - lag(fitted,2))
       : actual;
// starting values:
&1 = -1.4; &2 = -0.5; &3 = -0.2; &4 = -0.1;
```

Algebra is a vector language: each line can be interpreted as having an observation loop around it. This enables us to define 'fitted' recursively: when computing 'fitted' at time t, the value at $t-1$ already exists. But we have to be careful, as this doesn't work for $t = 1$ and $t = 2$ where the second lag of 'fitted' cannot exist. The work-around is the conditional statement: in those two cases we assign the observed value, corresponding to a residual of zero. The final line gives the starting values. These lines can occur anywhere in the code, but are executed when the code is analysed for errors, so before the proper algebra statements are executed. The syntax is restricted to '*parameter=value*;', as used in the code. In pseudo language the code can be interpreted as:

initialize	$\hat\theta_0 = -1.4, \hat\theta_1 = -0.5, \hat\theta_2 = -0.2, \hat\theta_3 = -0.1;$
	set actual, fitted to missing for the whole database period;
statement 1	for $t = T_1, \ldots, T_2$: actual $\leftarrow y_t$;
	for $t = T_1, \ldots, T_1 + 2$: fitted $(\hat y_t) \leftarrow y_t$;
statement 2	for $t = T_1 + 3, \ldots, T_2$: fitted $(\hat y_t) \leftarrow \hat\theta_0 y_{t-1} - \hat\theta_1 y_{t-2} -$
	$\hat\theta_2 \left(y_{t-1} - \hat y_{t-1}\right) - \hat\theta_3 \left(y_{t-2} - \hat y_{t-2}\right).$

$T_1, \ldots, T_2$ is the sample used for estimation, and the result is that the first three ϵs in that sample are zero.

Estimation from observation 18 gives (remember that information criteria, etc. are switched off by default):

```
EQ( 2) Modelling actual by NLS  (using tutarma)
       The present sample is:  18 to 120

Variable       Coefficient    Std.Error  t-value  t-prob PartR^2
&1                 -1.6556      0.20794   -7.962  0.0000  0.3904
&2                -0.70008      0.18852   -3.714  0.0003  0.1223
&3                0.079800      0.23571    0.339  0.7357  0.0012
&4                -0.30143      0.18705   -1.611  0.1103  0.0256

R^2=0.942942  F(3, 99)=545.35 [0.0000]  \sigma=0.963591 DW=2.0
RSS = 91.92219251 for 4 variables and 103 observations
```

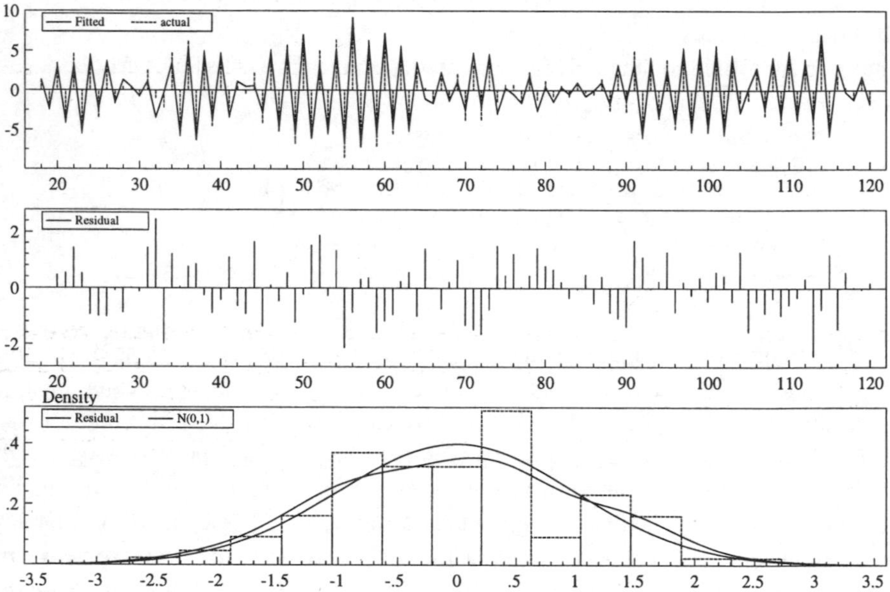

Figure 9.6 Graphical analysis of ARMA(2,2) model.

Graphic analysis is based on the 'actual' and 'fitted' values, with the residuals defined as the difference, see Figure 9.6. Tests are also available:

```
ARCH 1  F( 1, 97) =      5.5024 [0.0210] *
Normality Chi^2(2)=     0.48109 [0.7862]
AR 1- 2 F( 2, 97) =     0.16366 [0.8493]
Xi^2    F( 6, 92) =      1.1827 [0.3225]
Xi*Xj   F( 9, 89) =      1.1557 [0.3332]
```

Tests that require an auxiliary regression use the derivatives of 'fitted' with respect to the parameters evaluated at the optimum, see §18.4.9.

9.7 ARCH estimation

Specify an ARCH(q) model as:

$$y_t = \mathbf{x}_t'\boldsymbol{\beta} + u_t, \quad \text{with } u_t = \sigma_t \epsilon_t, \quad \text{and } \sigma_t^2 = \alpha_0 + \sum_{j=1}^{q} \alpha_j u_{t-j}^2.$$

See, for example, Engle (1982) or Bollerslev, Chou and Kroner (1992). Assuming $\epsilon_t \sim \mathsf{IN}(0,1)$ gives $u_t | u_{t-1} \cdots u_{t-q} \sim \mathsf{N}(0, \sigma_t^2)$. So conditional on the past, the model is normal but heteroscedastic. The log-likelihood for observation t follows from (13.103)

$$\ell_t\left(\boldsymbol{\theta}|\mathcal{I}_{t-1}\right) = c - \tfrac{1}{2}\log\left(\sigma_t^2\right) - \tfrac{1}{2}\frac{\left(y_t - \mathbf{x}_t'\boldsymbol{\beta}\right)^2}{\sigma_t^2}.$$

Fitting an ARCH(1) model to the generated data, with only a constant in the mean (that is, the only x is the intercept), is achieved by formulating:

```
actual = arch;
fitted = &0;
res    = actual - fitted;
condv  = fabs(&1 + &2 * lag(res,1)^2);
loglik = -0.5 * (log(condv) + res^2/condv);
&0 = -0.05; &1 = 1.47; &2 = 0.56;      // starting values
```

with $\beta_0 = \&0$, $\alpha_0 = \&1$, $\alpha_1 = \&2$. The fabs() function takes the absolute value of its argument. This forces the variance to be positive, and improves the numerical behaviour of the optimization process considerably. The starting values are the coefficients from the ARCH test on the residuals from regressing the arch variable on a constant. The estimated model is, using 8 forecasts:

```
EQ( 2) Modelling actual by ML  (using tutarma)
The present sample is:  19 to 120 less 8 forecasts
The forecast period is: 113 to 120

Variable      Coefficient    Std.Error  t-value  t-prob
&0              -0.015010     0.095341   -0.157  0.8753
&1                0.70828      0.18300    3.870  0.0002
&2                0.76772      0.22907    3.351  0.0012

loglik = -69.92337936 for 94 observations and 3 parameters
```

Graphic analysis and some tests are available, but this is not very helpful here because of the definition of 'actual' and 'fitted': the latter is only a constant. The result is that ARCH effects are not removed from 'actual'–'fitted', as seen from the test:

```
ARCH 1  F( 1, 89) =        36.93 [0.0000] **
Normality Chi^2(2)=       8.2419 [0.0162] *
```

More useful information is obtained from actual values $y_t/\hat{\sigma}_t$ and fitted values $\mathbf{x}_t'\hat{\boldsymbol{\beta}}/\hat{\sigma}_t$. Re-estimate adding the following to lines at the bottom of the algebra code:

```
actual = arch / sqrt(condv);
fitted = &0 / sqrt(condv);
```

The ARCH test has become insignificant:

```
ARCH 1  F( 1, 89) =       1.9815 [0.1627]
Normality Chi^2(2)=       3.4009 [0.1826]
```

Some graphical results are in Figure 9.7.

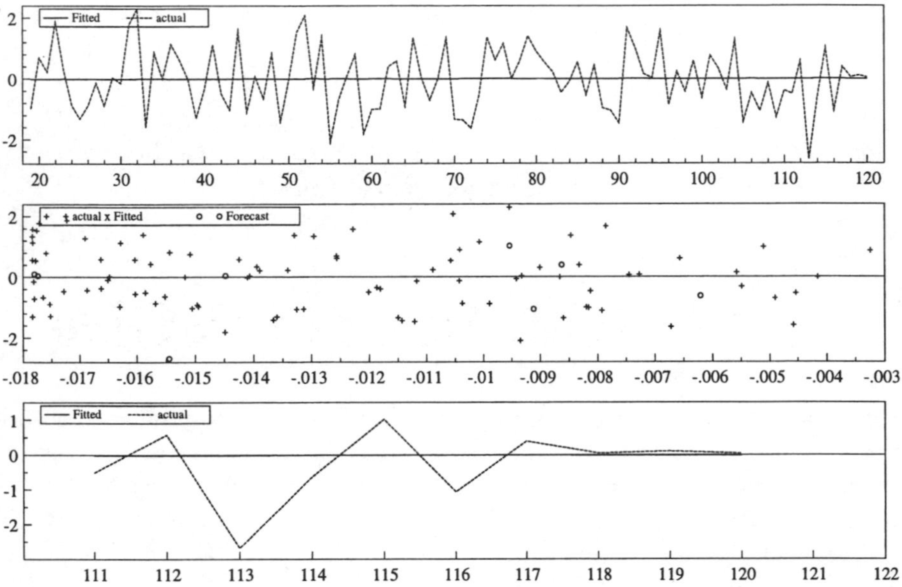

Figure 9.7 Graphical analysis for ARCH model using scaled actual and fitted.

As in the ARMA case, it makes a difference how the initial values are treated. In the ARCH algebra code, the first observations in the estimation use a value determined as actual–fitted when the algebra is run to determine the potential sample period, but left untouched during estimation (the value used in this case is 1.4714). It could be fixed by:

```
                                   // loglik must already exist
condv  = lag(loglik,1) != MISSING && lag(res,1) != MISSING
  ? fabs(&1 + &2 * lag(res,1)^2) : 1;
```

This finishes our discussion of non-linear estimation using PcGive. We are confident that you can now experiment successfully with your own models.

Part III

The Econometrics of PcGive

Chapter 10

An Overview

The purpose of Part III is to explain the concepts, models, methods and methodology embodied in PcGive, and how to interpret its statistical and econometrics output. For completeness, we occasionally refer to PcFiml, the module for system modelling which is fully described in a separate book, see Doornik and Hendry (1994a).

There are seven chapters on the econometrics of PcGive. First, PcGive offers excellent facilities for learning econometrics at all levels from elementary courses, through intermediate stages to advanced graduate standard. Its ease of use, menu interface and virtual uncrashability make it a straightforward tool even for beginning economists and econometricians. The present chapter provides a brief overview and is followed by an elementary explanation of econometrics, which also serves as the background to many of the features examined in the tutorials. The discussion is intuitive and discursive, and although mathematics is used, this is not at an advanced level. Chapter 13 then describes the statistical theory of the normal distribution, of maximum likelihood estimation and of least squares, linking that to regression analysis (a distinction discussed shortly). The third 'learning' chapter is 12 which is at an intermediate level and considers the bulk of the features offered by PcGive.

These chapters establish the main econometric tools, leading in Chapter 14 to an overview of the approach embodied in PcGive to sustain efficient econometric modelling. Chapter 15 considers nine important practical problems. The detailed discussion of the actual statistics reported in PcGive is in Chapters 16–17, relating respectively to data description and single equation evaluation. As such, they are a reference to be used as needed, rather than read throughout at a single sitting. Conversely, it is advisable to read Chapters 12–14 prior to using PcGive for substantive research. The detailed table of contents is intended as a quick reference guide for locating explanations about any results obtained. References to sections are denoted by chapter.section, for example, §1.1, §2.4 etc. Equations are denoted by (chapter.number), for example, (12.17). Finally, figures are shown as chapter.number, for example, Figure 13.2.

The philosophy underlying PcGive is that economic time-series data are generated by a process of immense generality and complexity owing to the interacting behaviours and conflicting objectives of millions of individuals. The outcomes produced by the economic mechanism are measured with varying degrees of accuracy, but rarely perfectly and sometimes not very well. The combination of the mechanism (the processes of production, transaction and consumption) and the measurement system is called the data generation process (DGP). The econometrician seeks to model the main features of the DGP in a simplified representation based on the observables and related to prior economic theory. Since many important data features are inevitably assumed absent in any economic theory, empirical models have to be developed interactively to characterize the data while being consistent with the theory. For example, a theory model might assume white-noise errors, whereas aggregation and the lack of a mapping of decision periods to data observation intervals may mean that the estimated model manifests substantial residual serial correlation (perhaps of a seasonal form). Equally, the parameters of the theory may correspond to model coefficients which are not empirically constant over time. PcGive is designed to facilitate the process of model design, reveal problems with potential models, and test models destructively to highlight their strengths and weaknesses.

Current research suggests that an important component of any modelling exercise is to estimate the most general model that it is reasonable to entertain *a priori*. Thus, PcGive facilitates formulating general linear dynamic models, while still offering protection against the possibility that the initial generality is in fact too specific to adequately characterize the available data. This approach corresponds loosely to a constructive aspect of empirical modelling. Both aspects of model construction and destruction are analysed in Chapter 14.

Many econometrics packages focus on the estimation of economic models of varying degrees of complexity assuming that their qualitative characteristics are known beforehand, but the numerical values of their parameters need calibration from empirical evidence. While estimation represents a necessary ingredient in econometrics research, it is far from sufficient for practical empirical modelling. PcGive has been developed to aid the process of discovering 'good' models by offering a wide range of evaluation tools, some of which are sophisticated estimation methods reoriented to highlight potential model weaknesses. There is no royal road to developing good models, but some considerations which have proved helpful in related studies are discussed below, including an analysis of the criteria by which empirical models might be judged. A more extensive discussion is provided in Hendry (1993) and Hendry (1995a).

Just as there is no 'best' way to drive a car, but many obviously bad ways (for example, with your eyes closed), so there are many necessary, but no sufficient, conditions for model validity. Delineating these necessary conditions, and analysing the links between them, the available information and statistics for evaluating model adequacy is the focus for the discussion in Chapter 14. Here, we begin with data description as the first step towards mastering modern econometrics.

Chapter 11

Learning Elementary Econometrics Using PcGive

11.1 Introduction

This chapter explains how to use GiveWin and PcGive as a complement to conventional elementary econometrics textbooks. Chapters 14–17 of this manual will be referenced frequently as they have been structured to complement the ideas in the present chapter.

The chapter assumes that you have sufficient knowledge to operate PCs running under Windows, and are familiar with GiveWin/PcGive in terms of its menus, mouse and keyboard. The Tutorials in Part II explain the mechanics of using the program. On-line, context-sensitive help about the program usage and the econometrics is always available. To load the data used in this chapter, access PCGTUT1.IN7 and PCGTUT1.BN7.

The chapter is also designed to help instructors in teaching econometrics. It is assumed that the instructor has prepared an appropriate data set in an .IN7 + .BN7 format: the PCGTUT data set used below is derived from DATA.IN7, DATA.BN7. Also, it is obvious that the teacher must have explained enough of the usage of PcGive and the rudiments of Windows so that students can use the program. An overhead computer projection panel can be linked to a PC for classroom displays. The authors have found this to be an admirable and easy vehicle for illustrating econometrics concepts, models, and methods at all levels. As PcGive is esentially uncrashable and models can be formulated in batch files in advance of exercises as required, there is little risk of a serious problem developing — and should the worst happen, it can be turned into a salutory lesson on some of the real difficulties the students will face in undertaking empirical research!

As an initial small data set, we have selected 30 observations on the two variables *cons* and *inc*, which are artificial (computer-generated) data interpreted as aggregate consumers' expenditure and income in constant prices. First we view the data in the database, to see the numbers and determine their meaning, measurement, units and sample period. The data are quarterly (four times per year) over 1986(1)–1993(2), and the variables are in 100 log units. This means that the change between any two points in time, say t to $t+1$, is approximately a percentage change: from 1993(1) to 1993(2), *cons* increased by 3 units from 407.23 to 410.23, which is therefore a 3% increase. Working back to the original units, divide by 100 and take antilogs (exponentials) to see that they are around 60, which is £billions (per quarter). Since consumers' expenditure must be positive, it is safe to take logs; the scaling by 100 converts changes to percentages. The reason for taking logs is to make economic time series more homogenous: back in 1900, consumers' expenditure was under £1billion, so a £1billion change then would have been 100% as against 1.5% now.

11.2 Variation over time

Graphical inspection can highlight the salient features of the variables and reveal any peculiarities in the data, such as typing, or recording, errors. Those in Figure 11.1[1] also show the use of grid lines.

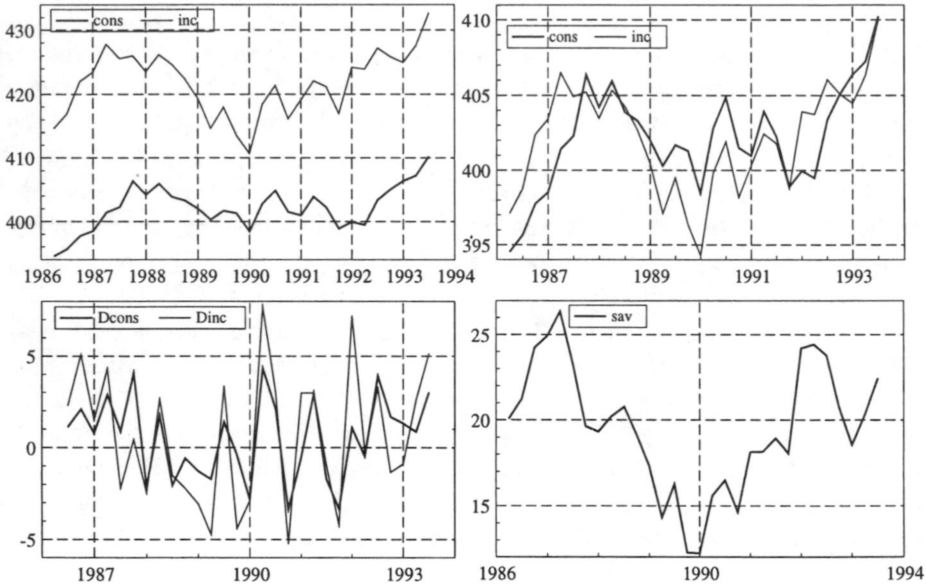

Figure 11.1 Time-series graphs of *cons* and *inc*.

The graph of *cons* and *inc* in Figure 11.1(a) reveals that they have gone through a boom-recession-boom cycle, and have ended higher than the initial observations (about 16% and 18% higher in fact). Further, they show no obvious signs of seasonality (regular variation across the quarters of the year).

Now copy *cons* to a new variable, then revise the observation in 1987(1) from 401.41 to 301.41; it is hard to notice the error in the database – and would be very hard amongst

[1]Multiple graphs are numbered from left to right and top to bottom, so (b) is the top-right graph of four, and (c) the bottom left.

400 data points – but a glance at the graph makes it clear. Remember to change the mistake back if you did not use a copy of *cons*.

Time-series graphs of the differences of each variable highlight the periods of positive and negative growth and show any synchrony between the series. For example, Figure 11.1(a) plots *cons* and *inc* in their original units, Figure 11.1(b) matches them by means and ranges to maximize their closeness, Figure 11.1(c) shows the changes in them, unmatched, and clearly very close, and Figure 11.1(d) plots the difference *inc–cons* which is called *sav* (actually, this is 100 times the savings ratio).

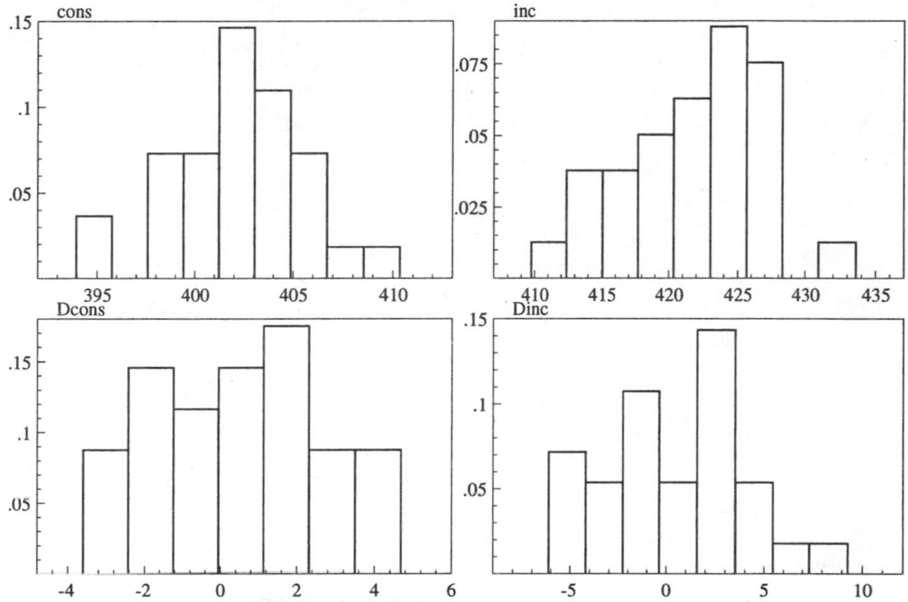

Figure 11.2 Histograms of *cons* and *inc*.

11.3 Variation across a variable

It is also useful to summarize data in terms of their distributional shape and low-order moments, and we illustrate this using the graph/descriptive dialog. Click the option to draw Histograms for *cons*, *inc* and their changes, which leads to the outcome in Figure 11.2(a)–(d). Here, there are too few data points to make the shape of the distributions very clear other than near symmetry. Next, use data/descriptive analysis in PcGive, and mark Correlation for the same four variables to produce the calculation of their means and standard deviations (we return to the correlations below). Since the data are in 100 logs, the standard deviations s of (3.2, 4.9, 2.2, 3.6) are in percentages of the original levels of the variables. Thus, the sample standard deviation (denoted by $\hat{\sigma}$ where the $\hat{}$ denotes that it is estimated from the data) is about 50% as large for the level as the change in *cons*, and 30% larger still for the level of *inc*. Roughly 95% of a symmetric distribution lies between $\bar{x} - 2s$ and $\bar{x} + 2s$ where $\bar{x}$ is the sample mean, so we might expect most changes in *cons* to fall in the range -4 to $+5$ (all of them actually do).

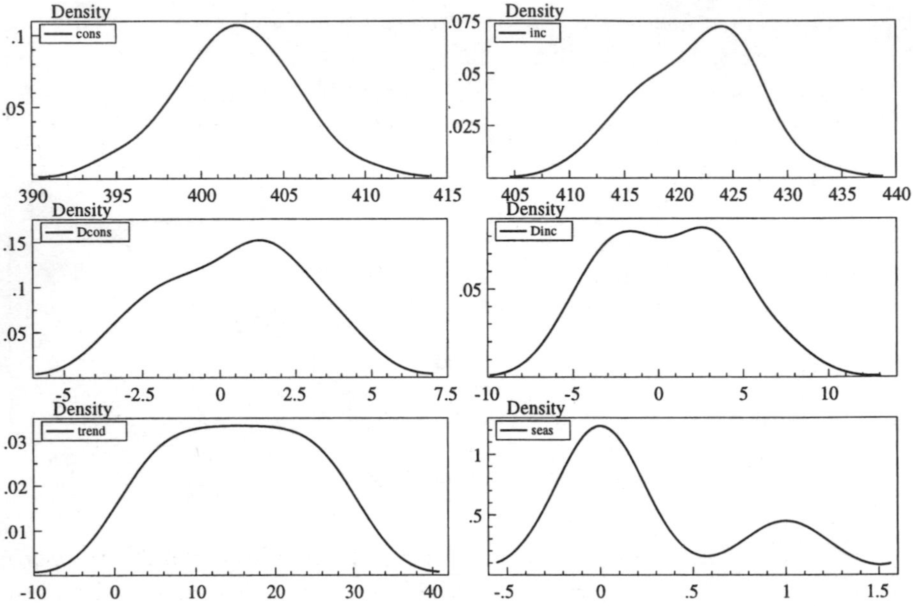

Figure 11.3 Densities for *cons* and *inc*.

The formulae for the mean and standard deviation of a sample $(x_1 \ldots x_T)$ of T observations are:

$$\bar{x} = \frac{1}{T}\sum_{t=1}^{T} x_t \text{ and } s = \sqrt{\frac{1}{T-1}\sum_{t=1}^{T}(x_t - \bar{x})^2}.$$

11.4 Populations, samples and shapes of distributions

Next, we relate the sample of data we observed to the population of possible outcomes that might have occurred. We can use interpolated data densities to show the underlying shapes of the distributions (see Chapter 17 for details). As Figure 11.3 reveals, *cons* is unimodal and close to a normal distribution whereas Δ*cons* (the first difference) is nearer to a uniform distribution; *inc* and Δ*inc* are more erratic and the latter is nearly bimodal, whereas the seasonal (called seas) is clearly bimodal, with one bump much larger than the other, and the trend is nearly uniform (can you explain these last two outcomes?).[2]

[2]To create these in the database use the algebra code: one = 1; trend = trend(); seas = season();. Note that they are automatically provided when estimating a model.

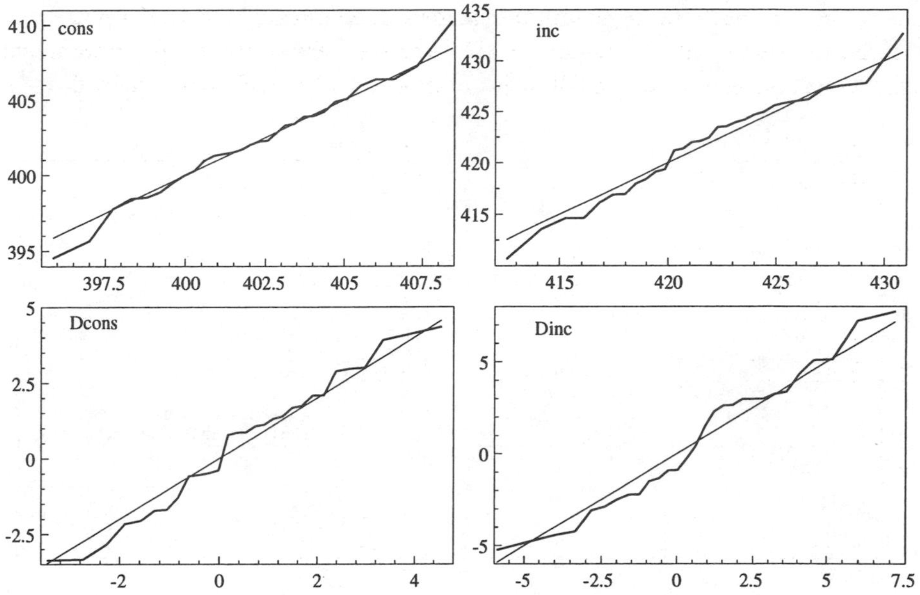

Figure 11.4 QQ plots for *cons* and *inc*.

The (cumulative) distribution function is one of the most basic probability ideas, as it contains all the information about the probability behaviour of a random variable. Plot these for the same six variables (note that the normal is plotted automatically as well) and compare; the GiveWin book discusses creating densities and distributions for the standard statistical distributional forms. So-called QQ plots offer a picture of the closeness to normality of a variable: those in Figure 11.4 show the transformed cumulative distribution of the sample data with that for the normal (which is a straight line). There are departures in the tails but otherwise little evidence against normality.

11.5 Correlation and scalar regression

Figure 11.1(b) highlighted the common movements in the two series in Figure 11.1(a) by plotting them with a standard mean and range. There are many possible measures of co-movement, and correlation is a standardized measure of the closeness of a linear relationship, constructed to lie between -1 and $+1$. We have already computed a set of correlations above and these yielded the table shown below. All of them are positive (increases in any one series are associated with increases – rather than falls – in all of the others), and matching Figure 11.1, the correlation is higher between Δ*cons* and Δ*inc* than between *cons* and *inc*. To understand the units (that is, when is a correlation high?), cross plot the pairs of variables (*cons*,*inc*) and (Δ*cons*,Δ*inc*), first with points, then with a line showing the correlation (four graphs in all) as in Figure 11.5.

Correlation matrix

	cons	inc	Dcons	Dinc
cons	1.000			
inc	0.6455	1.000		
Dcons	0.3677	0.5476	1.000	
Dinc	0.1258	0.4409	0.7647	1.000

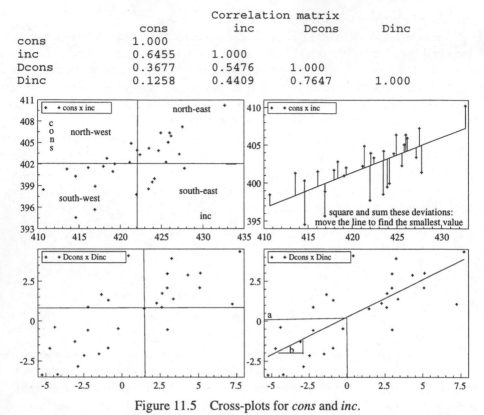

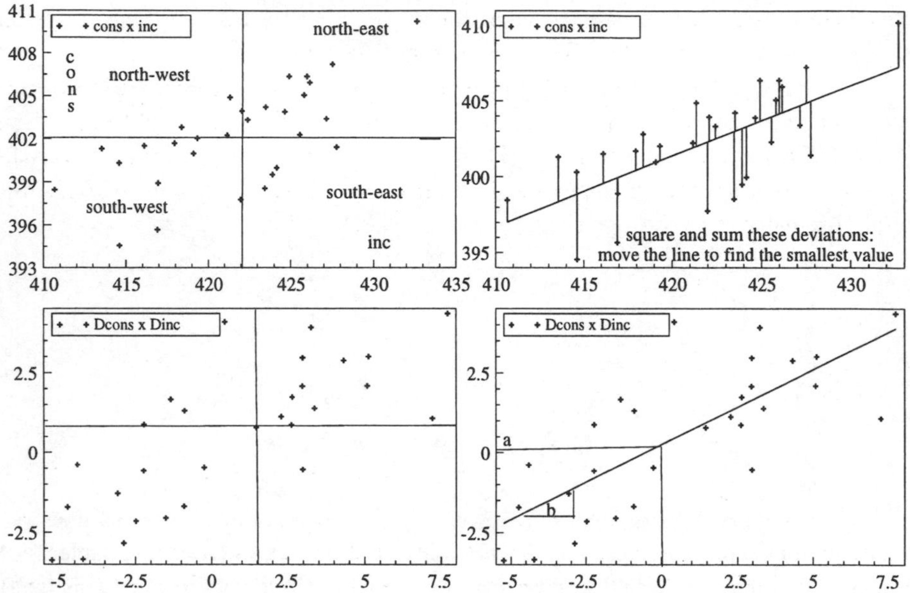

Figure 11.5 Cross-plots for *cons* and *inc*.

We have used the on-screen edit facilities to map out the region in Figure 11.5(a) into four quadrants using line drawing, placing the lines at the means of the variables (402, 422). The positive co-movement is clear from the excess of points in the north-east and south-west corners; a lack of correlation would be reflected by nearly equal numbers of points in each quadrant. Here we find the numbers of points to be:

Numbers of points for *cons*, *inc*

North-west	North-east
5	11
South-west	South-east
10	4

The preponderance of positively related points is clear. For ($\Delta cons$,Δinc) we have:

Numbers of points for $\Delta cons$, Δinc

North-west	North-east
4	12
South-west	South-east
12	1

matching the higher correlation.

The straight line shown in Figure 11.5(b) is defined by $y_t = a + bx_t$ where y_t denotes the variable on the vertical axis (*cons* here) and x_t is the variable on the horizontal axis (i.e. *inc*). The point a (called the intercept) is where the line cuts the y-axis when $x_t = 0$, and b is the slope (measured relative to the positive direction of the x-axis). A unit change in x_t is associated with a change of b in y_t: Figure 11.5(d) illustrates. Now, the closer all the points are to the line, the higher the correlation.

A natural question concerns why the line is drawn as shown, rather than some other line. The answer is that we have picked 'the line of best fit' to the given data set. This is defined by minimizing the squared deviations of the points from the line: the vertical distances from the line are squared and summed and the values of a and b selected to minimize that sum as shown on Figure 11.5(b). We must find:

$$\min_{a,b} \sum_{t=1}^{T} (y_t - a - bx_t)^2 .$$

The values that do so are given by the famous formula:

$$\hat{a} = \bar{y} - \hat{b}\bar{x} \text{ and } \hat{b} = \frac{\sum_{t=1}^{T} (y_t - \bar{y})(x_t - \bar{x})}{\sum_{t=1}^{T} (x_t - \bar{x})^2}, \tag{11.1}$$

where the ^ denotes that these are the best values and $\bar{y}$ and $\bar{x}$ are the sample means. A value of $\hat{b} = 0$ implies no slope, so the line is flat (that is, parallel to the horizontal axis); $\hat{a} = 0$ forces the line through the origin.

Of course, we could have had the variables in the other order (*inc* first then *cons*) and that would have led to a different line: use the cross-plot facility to redraw the figure with both lines of best fit (the second, steeper line, defined by $x_t = c + dy_t$). The distance for the second line on the new figure is the horizontal distance as shown, so it is no surprise that the line is somewhat different as we are minimizing a different sum of squared deviations. Indeed:

$$\hat{c} = \bar{x} - \hat{d}\bar{y} \text{ and } \hat{d} = \frac{\sum_{t=1}^{T} (x_t - \bar{x})(y_t - \bar{y})}{\sum_{t=1}^{T} (y_t - \bar{y})^2}. \tag{11.2}$$

These two possible lines are closely related to the correlation coefficient, which we denote by r:

$$\mathsf{r} = \frac{\sum_{t=1}^{T} (x_t - \bar{x})(y_t - \bar{y})}{\sqrt{\sum_{t=1}^{T} (x_t - \bar{x})^2 \sum_{t=1}^{T} (y_t - \bar{y})^2}}. \tag{11.3}$$

From (11.1) and (11.2), it can be seen that $\hat{b}\hat{d} = \mathsf{r}^2$. When $\mathsf{r} = 1$ (or -1) the two lines coincide; when $\mathsf{r} = 0$, they are both parallel to their respective axes, so are at right angles to each other.

Using PcGive, it is easy to calculate the outcomes from fitting the line shown in the graph. The procedure is often called regression (somewhat loosely as we will see later). Access the Data/Autoregressive-Distributed Lag option and select *cons* as dependent (y_t) and *inc* as explanatory (x_t), leading to:

```
Distributed Lag of cons on inc: lags from 0 to 0
       The present sample is:  1986 (1) to 1993 (2)
          Constant      Lag  0
Coeff.         206      0.4651
Std.Err      40.36     0.09571

RSS = 187.707974    s = 2.58918     Rsq = 0.457558
F(1, 28) = 23.6184 [0.0000] **
```

Later we will explain the meaning of the title 'Distributed Lag of *cons* on *inc:* lags from 0 to 0'; the important information for the present is that the intercept (called Constant) is $\hat{a} = 206$ and the slope $\hat{b} = 0.465$. The numbers denoted Std.Err are the standard errors or the standard deviations of the estimated coefficients of the intercept and slope, so $\pm 2 \times 0.09571$ is an approximate 95% confidence interval around the central value $\hat{b} = 0.4651$. The symbol Rsq (R^2 on screen) is just the square of r = 0.676 and s (\sigma on-screen) denotes the standard deviation of the residuals from the line, where the residuals are:

$$\hat{u}_t = y_t - \hat{a} - \hat{b}x_t \text{ so } s = \sqrt{\frac{1}{T-2}\sum_{t=1}^{T} \hat{u}_t^2}. \tag{11.4}$$

Thus, the line is picked to yield the smallest value of s. RSS denotes the residual sum of squares, namely:

$$RSS = \sum_{t=1}^{T} \hat{u}_t^2.$$

The symbol F is a test of whether the correlation is zero, and ** denotes that it is definitely not (the probability is essentially zero of getting the value 23.6184 for F when r = 0 – shown as [0.0000]).

The final issue is why $\hat{a}$ and $\hat{b}$ have standard errors or standard deviations. This happens because we view the data set as a sample from a much larger population that might have occurred. Had another sample been drawn, different values for $(\hat{a}, \hat{b})$ would result, and the standard errors measure how much variability might be expected on repeated sampling from the same population. Since the data here are computer generated, it is easy to imagine drawing many other sets and plotting the distribution of the outcomes as a density as in Figure 11.3: the standard deviation of that density is the coefficient standard error (Std.Err). Chapter 13 describes the theoretical analysis that delivers the formula for calculating the standard error: note the magic – we actually only have one sample, yet from that one sample, we can estimate how uncertain we are about the values $(\hat{a}, \hat{b})$ that themselves estimate the intercept and slope of the line in the population.

11.6 Interdependence

The concept of economic interdependence has already been illustrated by computing the matrix of correlations between all of the variables. In many economic data sets, all the correlations will be positive and many will exceed 0.9. This salient data feature is discussed below: it raises obvious dangers of confusing 'genuine' correlations between connected variables with those that arise from the gradual evolution of the whole economy. The correlations are smaller for the changes in the variables, and this aspect will recur below as well. The formula in (11.3) explains part of the story, writing r as:

$$\mathsf{r} = \frac{\mathsf{C}\left(x_t, y_t\right)}{\hat{\sigma}\left(x_t\right)\hat{\sigma}\left(y_t\right)} \quad \text{where} \quad \mathsf{C}\left(x_t, y_t\right) = \frac{1}{T-1}\sum_{t=1}^{T}\left(x_t - \bar{x}\right)\left(y_t - \bar{y}\right). \tag{11.5}$$

$\mathsf{C}(x_t, y_t)$ is called the covariance of x_t with y_t. Thus, the correlation coefficient is the ratio of the covariance to the product of the two variables' standard deviations. We know from above that the standard deviations are smaller after differencing; the covariances are as well, but fall by proportionately more owing to removing the 'common' trends and cycles from the data. However, correlations could also increase on differencing if (say) a trend masked opposite sign short-run correlations (see, for example, Hooker, 1901; this is a long-standing issue!).

11.7 Time dependence

Correlations (or dependencies) between successive values of the same variable often occur in economic time series. These are called serial (or auto) correlations. From Figure 11.1, when *cons* was high, the next value was also high, and when low, so was the next value. In general, we denote the current value of a variable by y_t and its previous (or lagged) value by y_{t-1}. The difference is then $\Delta y_t = y_t - y_{t-1}$.

Figure 11.1 also revealed that Δ*cons* jumped around considerably: high values were not followed by other high values very often. By simple algebra, when Δy_t is independent over time, then $y_t \simeq y_{t-1}$ and hence y_t is serially correlated.

A useful way to see time dependence is to cross plot y_t against y_{t-1}, and Δy_t against Δy_{t-1} both without and with a least-squares line (as in Figure 11.6). You may need to create the lagged values using the calculator. It is clear that *cons* and *inc* are both highly correlated with their own lagged values (Figure 11.6(a) and 11.6(b)), whereas Δ*cons* and Δ*inc* are nearly unrelated (horizontal regression lines).

This idea can be generalized to two-period relations, namely the correlation of y_t with y_{t-2}. To summarize all such correlations at once, we plot a correlogram with the correlations $\mathsf{r}_j = \mathsf{corr}(y_t, y_{t-j})$ on the vertical axis and j on the horizontal, illustrated for four terms ($j = 1, \ldots, 4$) in Figure 11.7. This idea relates back to the salient feature of serial dependence of the time-series graphs of the variables in Figure 11.1, and

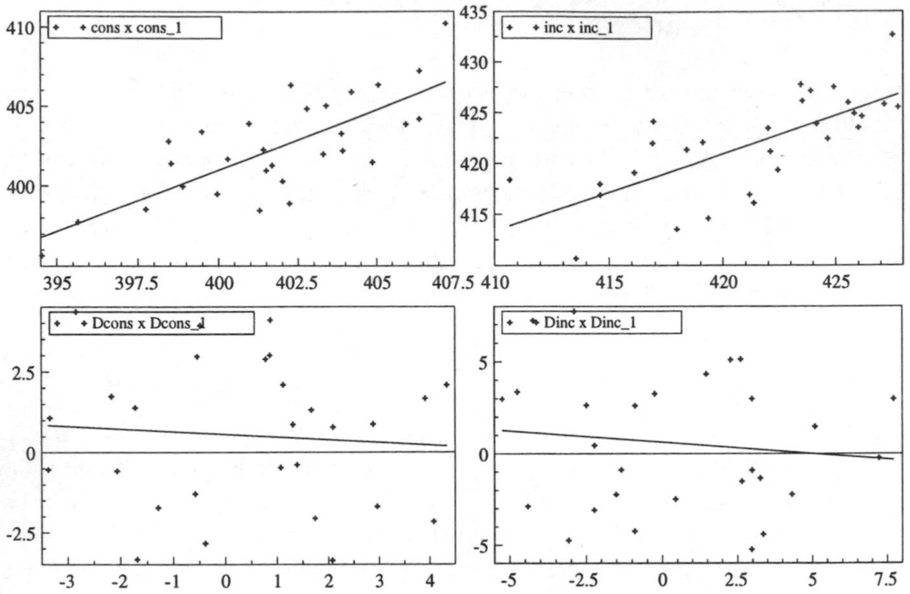

Figure 11.6 Lagged cross-plots for *cons* and *inc*.

provides a quantitative measurement of that aspect. Here, the correlograms for *cons* and *inc* have several large positive terms, whereas those for $\Delta cons$ and Δinc are nearly zero at all lags. The values of r_1 reflect the slopes of the plots in Figure 11.6.

We are in fact implicitly using regression, and can compute the slope coefficient for y_t on y_{t-1}, called a first order autoregression (regression on itself), using that method. Select the autoregressive-distributed lag option for *cons*, choose one lag, and accept to obtain:

```
Autoregression for cons: lags from 1 to 1
       The present sample is:  1986 (2) to 1993 (2)
          Constant       Lag  1
Coeff.         95.28      0.7643
Std.Err        51.51      0.1282
RSS = 123.5016142    s = 2.13872      Rsq = 0.568417
F(1, 27) = 35.5603 [0.0000] **
```

By now the statistics should be becoming more familiar: the intercept is 95.28 and the slope (i.e. the autoregressive coefficient) is 0.7643 which is approximately equal to the autocorrelation of $r_1 = 0.754$ (i.e. the square root of R^2). The value of r_1 is, therefore, just that of the correlation coefficient calculated as in (11.3) for *cons* and $cons_1$, and shows the slope of the regression line in the graph of that variable against its lagged value. Try to prove these connections for a first-order autoregression.

Returning to the correlogram $\{r_j\}$, a new idea occurs: we know $\mathsf{corr}(y_t, y_{t-1})$ and $\mathsf{corr}(y_t, y_{t-2})$ but part of each of these may be owing to the other – can we sort out

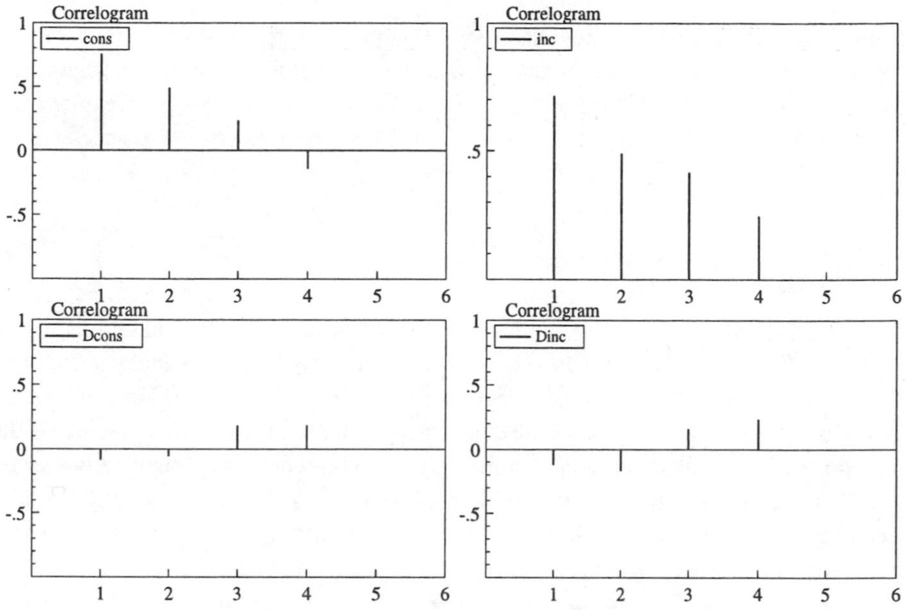

Figure 11.7 Correlograms for *cons* and *inc*.

the 'net' contributions of the one and two period lags? One notion might be to use the residuals from the first-order autoregression and correlate these with y_{t-2}; this approach gets close, but on reflection you can probably see that it takes out too much of y_{t-1} at the first step (that is, it also takes out the bit of y_{t-2} in y_{t-1}). We believe the easiest way to understand the notion is to fit the regression of y_t on both y_{t-1} and y_{t-2} which is simple to perform in PcGive. Select the autoregressive distributed lag option for *cons* again but this time choose two lags and accept to obtain:

```
Autoregression for cons: lags from 1 to 2
       The present sample is:  1986 (3) to 1993 (2)
          Constant      Lag  1      Lag  2
Coeff.         113.9     0.7476    -0.02959
Std.Err         62.5     0.2129     0.2015

RSS = 121.6081159    s = 2.20625     Rsq = 0.490759
F(2, 25) = 12.0464 [0.0002] **
```

The first slope coefficient is almost the same as that obtained when y_{t-1} alone was used, and consistent with that, the second is close to zero. We learn that most of corr (y_t, y_{t-2}) is due to the effect of y_{t-1}, and no 'net' 2-period lag operates. This is important in understanding the pattern we observed in the correlogram. The generalization we have developed is called the partial autocorrelation. The first slope coefficient shows the change in y_t from a change in y_{t-1} when y_{t-2} does not change: the second slope coefficient shows the change in y_t from a change in y_{t-2} when y_{t-1} does not change. Each shows the net effect of its variable – together they show the total effect. A great advantage of regression methods is this ease of generalization to any number of variables where each coefficient measures the effects on the dependent variable of changing that explanatory variable when all other variables are held fixed. Chapter 13 describes the necessary algebra.

11.8 Dummy variables

Dummy variables are artificial creations with their non-zero values determined by us rather than by nature. They are often called indicator variables as they indicate the presence of some state. We have already met two, namely the Constant and Trend (where the former does not vary, so indicates the constant state!). Another common dummy is the indicator variable called Seasonal (for non-annual data) which is automatically created by PcGive to be unity in the first period of the year and zero elsewhere. PcGive only needs one seasonal from which the remaining seasonals for other periods are created by lagging: Seasonal_2 is Seasonal two periods lagged, and so has a unity in the third period of each year. Using the calculator or algebra, other dummies are easily created in a variety of forms for impulse effects (a 'blip' which is zero except for perhaps a couple of quarters where it is unity, often called a (0,1) dummy); and step changes where the dummy is zero until a certain date and unity thereafter. Note that the scale of measurement of a dummy is ordinal ('on' differs from 'off') in that the 'on' effect can bear any relation to the 'off'. It is dangerous to create a dummy which takes three or more values (for example, some 0s, some 1s and some 2s) unless you are certain that the effect of the third is twice that of the second. However, we will do just that – for a specific purpose. Use the algebra to create the variable `qrtr=period();` and using cross plot, graph *cons*, *inc* and qrtr (after highlighting qrtr, click Z, then click by value). The figure will show the points as 1,2,3,4 depending on the quarter of the year, so the relation of *cons* to *inc* in each quarter can be viewed. For the present data the picture is not too informative, but see Davidson, Hendry, Srba and Yeo (1978) for a clearer example.

Next, graph *cons*, apply; then plot *cons* and the trend over time, match for mean and range; next also cross plot them with the points joined; finally cross-plot them again and insert a regression line to see Figure 11.8. The first cross plot (Figure 11.8c) shows precisely the same as the time-series plot of *cons*; and the second cross plot shows the best-fitting trend line, which clearly differs from that obtained by just matching means and ranges (which is almost inevitably too steep).

Finally, a complete set of indicator variables is never needed (for example, a dummy for 'on' and a second dummy for 'off') and is said to be perfectly collinear. Try using the autoregressive-distributed lag option to compute a regression of *cons* on the quarterly seasonal with three lags: contrast the outcome with what happens when you use only two lags, noting that a constant is always included.

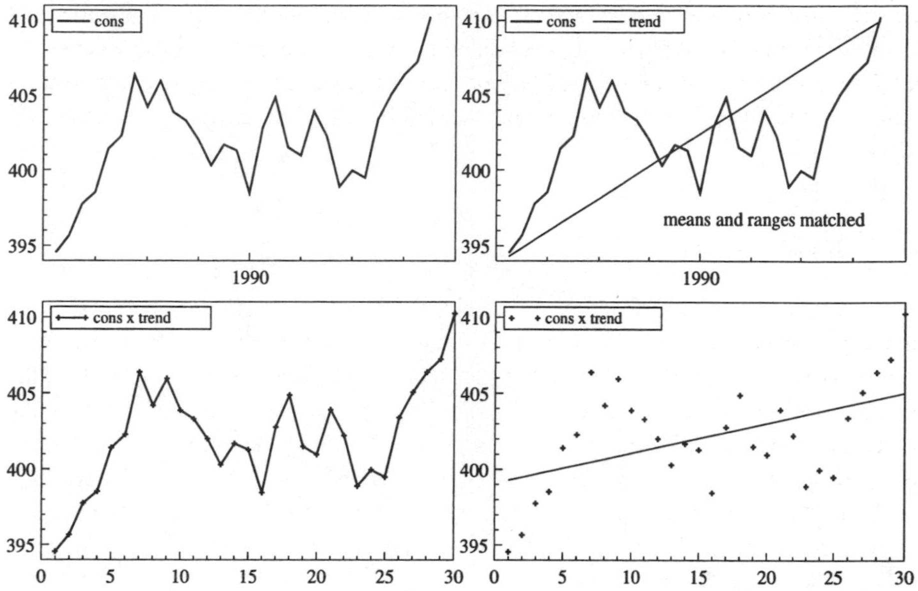

Figure 11.8 Relating time series and cross-plots using dummy variables.

11.9 Sample variability

Histograms and densities showed the data variability; this section focuses on the variability in the sample statistics. Use the zoom sample check box to cross plot *cons* against *inc* with a single regression line for the first half of the data only (to 1989(3)), then for the second half only. Now redo the cross plot for the whole sample period twice, but first fit two sequential lines then two recursive lines. The outcome is shown in Figure 11.9. The regression lines for the two subsamples clearly differ in slope and intercept (compute these numerically using the autoregressive-distributed lag option to check), as Figure 11.9c makes clear. Nevertheless, as Figure 11.9d reveals, the first sample line is close to that obtained for the whole period.

Try fitting a number of sequential lines (four, for example) and consider the outcome, perhaps using several trend lines, to show growth-rate changes. This should clarify the need to report coefficient standard errors.

11.10 Collinearity

Perfect linear dependence was shown in §11.8 above; this item relates to 'near linear dependence' between regressors – a more rigorous analysis is provided in §15.1. We introduced multiple regression above using the example of partial autocorrelation, and now use a finite distributed lag to show the effects of adding x_{t-1} to the regression of

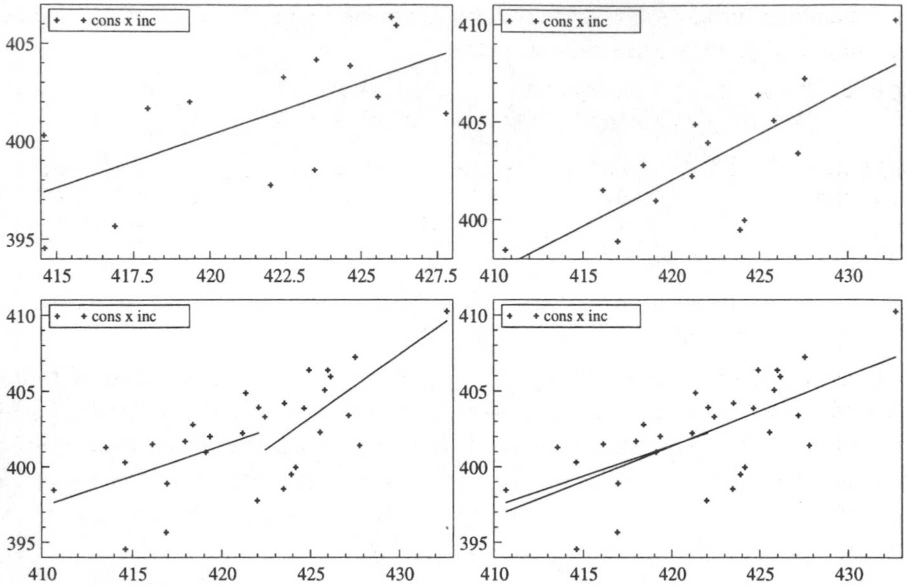

Figure 11.9 Changing regression lines.

y_t on x_t. This is called a distributed lag model because the lag coefficients on x show the distribution of the response of y over time (and when they are all positive, the coefficients can be normalized to add to unity, and hence are like a probability distribution). When x_t is highly autoregressive, a large increase in coefficient uncertainty usually results as the 'explanation' of y_t gets spread between x_t and x_{t-1} rather than concentrated on the former. Choose *cons* for y_t and *inc* for x_t and use the autoregressive-distributed lag option with one lag on *inc* to produce:

```
Distributed Lag of cons on inc: lags from 0 to 1
       The present sample is:  1986 (2) to 1993 (2)
          Constant      Lag  0     Lag  1
Coeff.       202.1      0.3012     0.1739
Std.Err      44.39      0.1352     0.1432

RSS = 157.948781    s = 2.46474    Rsq = 0.448039
F(2, 26) = 10.5524 [0.0004] **
```

Now we can explain why the earlier title in §11.5 was 'Distributed Lag of cons on inc': the option allows any number of lagged xs and we just used the simplest example of x_t only (see §12.2 for more detail). The standard error of the coefficient of x_t has increased by almost 50% from the simple regression: this effect is often called collinearity, and is viewed as deriving from the high correlation between x_t and x_{t-1} when both are used to explain y_t.

At a somewhat more advanced level, use the model option to add Δx_t to the regression of y_t on x_t and consider the new output:

```
EQ( 1) Modelling cons by OLS
       The present sample is:  1986 (2) to 1993 (2)

Variable     Coefficient    Std.Error  t-value  t-prob  PartRsq
Constant          202.06       44.390    4.552  0.0001  0.4435
inc              0.47510      0.10529    4.512  0.0001  0.4392
Dinc            -0.17390      0.14315   -1.215  0.2354  0.0537

Rsq = 0.448039 F(2,26)=10.552 [0.0004] s = 2.46474  DW = 0.463
RSS = 157.948781 for 3 variables and 29 observations
```

A glance establishes that all the regression statistics R^2, s, F etc. are identical to the earlier distributed lag estimates, and apart from the sign, so is the coefficient and standard error of Δ*inc*. Only the coefficient and standard error of *inc* have altered, the former to the sum of the coefficients in the distributed lag, the latter to a value close to that found in the simple regression of *cons* on *inc*. In fact, the two models are equivalent, as is easily seen algebraically:

$$d_1 x_t + d_2 x_{t-1} \equiv (d_1 + d_2) x_t - d_2 (x_t - x_{t-1}).$$

The differences between the two equivalent parameterizations are owing to the relatively low correlation between x_t and Δx_t which must happen when x_t and x_{t-1} are highly correlated. This highlights the advantages of orthogonal parameterizations (ones where explanatory variables are not correlated) where these are feasible.

The new statistics in the above results are the t-values and their probabilities, which test if the coefficients are zero by seeing if the estimated coefficient's 95% confidence interval includes zero, and the PartRsq which are the partial correlations of each variable with the dependent variable, holding the remaining variables fixed, as explained above. When there is a lot of 'spreading' of the explanatory power between variables, the PartRsq will be low even when the R^2 value is high: this reveals that the explanatory variables are substitutes rather than complements. Ignore the statistic called DW for the moment. Finally OLS is an acronym from ordinary least squares, which is a synonym for regression in the present context!

An alternative way to create collinearity is to add y_{t-1} to the regression of y_t on x_t; again use *cons* and *inc* to obtain:

```
EQ( 2) Modelling cons by OLS
       The present sample is:  1986 (2) to 1993 (2)

Variable     Coefficient    Std.Error  t-value  t-prob  PartRsq
Constant          16.557       40.585    0.408  0.6866  0.0064
inc              0.31006     0.061840    5.014  0.0000  0.4916
cons_1           0.63461     0.096648    6.566  0.0000  0.6238

Rsq = 0.780575 F(2,26) = 46.246 [0.0000] s = 1.55403  DW = 1.71
```

```
RSS = 62.79041562 for 3 variables and 29 observations
```

This time, despite the correlation between the explanatory variables, there is almost no increase in the standard error of the coefficient of *inc* (in fact *cons* lagged and *inc* are only correlated 0.27). Notice the counterbalancing effects of the improvement in fit from the added variable against its high interrelation with the previously included variable. Contrast this outcome to that found from (say) regressing Δy_t on Δx_t (or that with Δy_{t-1} added).

11.11 Nonsense regressions

Even at an elementary level, a critical appreciation of econometric evidence is essential, especially for time-series econometrics. First the issue of invalidly 'inferring causes from correlations' must be discussed: high (low) correlations do not by themselves confirm (refute) causal links. Rather, theory-models with well-defined causality links can be tested from data by checking on the presence and/or absence of certain correlations predicted by those models. This is a deductive exercise. Rigorously tested yet acceptable models are then used in later analytical work, but causes are never inferred from correlations.

The most extreme cases of misleading correlations arise in what is known as the nonsense regressions problem. From an early date, economists discovered high correlations between what ought to be unrelated series and puzzled over these (for example, a high positive correlation between the murder rate and membership of the Church of England!: an early analysis is Yule, 1926, so again this is a long-standing issue). We have regularly challenged our econometrics classes to select any two variables from a large data set (being careful to exclude dummies other than constant and trend) and guarantee to produce a correlation of over 0.95 between the two chosen variables after at most one transformation on each variable selected. If the variables are trend free, we use the option to integrate the two series chosen (or cumulate; the Stock function performs this operation); otherwise we take the trending series as selected. Now a cross plot, or even a time series graph with the ranges matched, shows the obviously high correlation, which can be confirmed using the `Data description` calculations. A similar effect is achievable by adding trends to both series. In economics, one is unlikely to lose this challenge.

The underlying statistical problem was analysed by Yule (1926) and arises from either:

(1) integrated but mutually independent time series (*nonsense regressions*); or
(2) data depending on common third factors (*spurious regressions*).

In the former, the high level of serial correlation in each series individually is sufficient to ensure that it is highly correlated with other similarly integrated series; Section 12.2 presents the relevant concepts. Hendry and Morgan (1995) trace the history of the analysis.[3] The latter is more obvious, especially when variables both depend on a linear trend. Econometrics is a powerful body of knowledge precisely because one can (for example) predictably create nonsense regressions outcomes, as in Hendry (1980). Already we have moved towards an intermediate level where we apply PcGive to a further range of topics. An exciting route lies ahead if you pursue the subject to a more advanced level where you will learn how to detect and hence counter such problems (see, for example, Hendry, 1995a). This requires an investment in some econometric theory to understand both the problems and their solutions, and Chapter 13 addresses that need.

[3] All the historical data sets used in their study, and that in Hendry (1995a) can be downloaded in PcGive format from Nuffield ftp: `ftp://hicks.nuff.ox.ac.uk/economic/hendry`

Chapter 12

Intermediate Econometrics

12.1 Introduction

The level envisaged in this chapter corresponds to a course involving *inter alia*, the properties of dynamic models and model types (see §12.2 and §12.3), interpreting linear equations (§12.4), multiple regression (§12.5, which builds on the algebra in Chapter 13), time-series concepts (§12.5.4), instrumental-variables estimation (§12.7), and inference and diagnostic testing (§12.8), leading on to model selection issues (§12.9).[1] Throughout, the econometric theory is illustrated by empirical applications which seek to highlight and explain how to resolve some of the central problems of econometrics. As might be anticipated in a book on a computer program, the emphasis is on practical procedures and solutions. Chapter 15 is devoted to an analysis of the last of these; this section concentrates on the other aspects. In fact, at an intermediate level where formal proofs are usually possible only for restrictive special cases (such as fixed regressors), Monte Carlo is almost certainly a better adjunct to theory derivations than empirical examples.[2] Nevertheless, an easy-to-use regression package also has an important role for illustrating concepts, methods and problems. To reiterate an earlier point, the discussion herein is intended to complement, and not substitute for, formal derivations of estimators, tests and their distributions. Chapter 13 provides an introduction to the necessary background material.

---

[1]The estimation and identification of simultaneous equations systems, vector autoregressions for cointegrated processes, and forecasting are considered in the PcFiml book. PcFiml provides the software for empirically analysing linear dynamic systems.

[2]PcNaive was released in 1991 as a Monte Carlo program specifically oriented to teaching econometrics: see Hendry and Neale (1987), and Hendry, Neale and Ericsson (1991). A Windows module accessible within GiveWin is in preparation; the Ox language included with PcGive allows Monte Carlo programs to be written by users.

12.2 Linear dynamic equations

This section describes the forms of linear dynamic single equation models that occur frequently in time-series econometrics. A typology of possible equation forms is then analysed in §12.3. Chapter 14 briefly generalizes the analysis to dynamic sytems.

The class of models basic to PcGive is that of individual linear dynamic equations. Dynamic linear equation analysis follows from the use of lag operators (denoted by L) such that $L^r x_t = x_{t-r}$ for a variable x_t. Scalar polynomials in L are denoted by:

$$a(L) = a_m L^m + a_{m+1} L^{m+1} + \cdots + a_r L^r = \sum_{r=m}^{n} a_r L^r.$$

It follows that:

$$a(1) = \left(\sum_{r=m}^{n} a_r L^r \right)_{\rfloor L=1} = \sum_{r=m}^{n} a_r,$$

so $a(1)$ denotes the sum of the coefficients, where $a_0 = 1$ is usually imposed to normalize the polynomial. The impact of $a(L)$ on x_t is then:

$$a(L) x_t = \sum_{r=m}^{n} a_r L^r x_t = \sum_{r=m}^{n} a_r x_{t-r}.$$

Lag polynomials like $a(L)$ define autoregressions when the equation is of the form (with $m = 0$ and $a_0 = 1$):

$$a(L) y_t = \sum_{r=0}^{n} a_r y_{t-r} = \epsilon_t \qquad (12.1)$$

and ϵ_t is a serially uncorrelated error (that is, white noise) often taken to be normal and independently distributed, with mean zero and constant variance:

$$\epsilon_t \sim \mathsf{IN}\left(0, \sigma_\epsilon^2\right).$$

Alternatively, $a(L)$ defines a finite distributed lag when the model has the form:

$$y_t = b(L) x_t + \epsilon_t = \sum_{r=0}^{p} b_r x_{t-r} + \epsilon_t. \qquad (12.2)$$

The autoregressive-distributed lag (ADL) class is given by:

$$a(L) y_t = b(L) x_t + \epsilon_t \text{ or } \sum_{j=0}^{n} a_j y_{t-j} = \sum_{r=0}^{p} b_r x_{t-r} + \epsilon_t. \qquad (12.3)$$

Many different xs may be used conjointly if required in models like (12.3), in which case the equation is written in a more convenient notation as:

$$b_0(L)\, y_t = \sum_{i=1}^{k} b_i(L)\, x_{it} + \epsilon_t \tag{12.4}$$

when there are k explanatory variables $(x_{1t} \ldots x_{kt})$.

Many important properties of the dynamic model (12.3) are determined by the polynomials $a(L)$ and $b(L)$. First, any polynomial of degree n has n (real or complex) roots and can be expressed as the product of its roots:

$$a(L) = \sum_{r=0}^{n} a_r L^r = \prod_{i=1}^{n} (1 - \lambda_i L).$$

For example, the models in (12.1) and (12.3) are stable if all the roots λ_i of the polynomial $a(L)$ satisfy $|\lambda_i| < 1$ and PcGive will calculate these.[3] Further, (12.3) has common factors (denoted COMFAC) if some of the roots of $a(L)$ coincide with roots of $b(L)$. For example, when:

$$a(L) = (1 - \rho L)\, a^*(L) = \rho(L)\, a^*(L),$$

and at the same time:

$$b(L) = \rho(L)\, b^*(L),$$

then (12.4) can be written as:

$$\rho(L)\, a^*(L)\, y_t = \rho(L)\, b^*(L)\, x_t + \epsilon_t,$$

or dividing both sides by $\rho(L)$:

$$a^*(L)\, y_t = b^*(L)\, x_t + u_t \;\text{ where }\; u_t = \rho u_{t-1} + \epsilon_t. \tag{12.5}$$

The error $\{u_t\}$ is therefore an autoregressive process, and is generated from the common factor in the structural lag polynomials (see Sargan, 1980b, and §12.3.7).

The other important property of $a(L)$ in (12.3) is the value of $a(1)$; when $a(1) \neq 0$, it is possible to solve for the long-run outcome of the process. In particular, when (y_t, x_t) are jointly weakly stationarity (so their first two moments are finite and constant over time), then:

$$\mathsf{E}\left[y_t - \frac{b(1)}{a(1)} x_t\right] = \mathsf{E}\left[y_t - K x_t\right] = 0 \tag{12.6}$$

[3]The actual roots of $a(L) = 0$ are the inverse of the $\{\lambda_i\}$, and the term root here is a shorthand for eigenroot, where $a(L)$ is viewed as a scalar matrix polynomial, for consistency with eigenroots of dynamic systems below.

is the long-run average solution to (12.3). Clearly, (12.6) requires that no $\lambda_i = 1$ in order to be well defined, and $b(1) \neq 0$ to be non-trivial. In this case, we can also write (12.6) as:

$$\mathsf{E}[y_t] = K\mathsf{E}[x_t]. \quad (12.7)$$

However, if in (12.1) r roots of $a(L)$ are equal to unity in absolute value, then y_t is non-stationary and is said to be integrated of order r, denoted $\mathsf{I}(r)$, as it then needs to be differenced r times to remove the unit roots and become weakly stationary. If $a(1) \neq 0$ and $b(1) \neq 0$ in (12.3) when y_t and x_t are both I(1), yet $\{y_t - Kx_t\}$ is I(0), then y_t and x_t are said to be cointegrated (the literature is vast: see *inter alia,* Engle and Granger, 1987, Granger, 1986, Hendry, 1986b, Banerjee and Hendry, 1992a, Banerjee, Dolado, Galbraith and Hendry, 1993, Hendry, 1995a, and Johansen, 1995). Thus, cointegration is the property that linear combinations of variables also remove the unit roots. The solution in (12.6) remains valid in the cointegrated case. Section 12.3 assumes that x_t is I(1) and that y_t and x_t are cointegrated. Empirical evidence suggests that many economic time series are better regarded as integrated process than as stationary.

Most dynamic equations have an intercept, and may have additional deterministic variables. In the general case of (12.4), simply interpret one of the regressors as the required variable. However, with integrated data, estimation and inference depend on which deterministic terms enter the model and the economic system, so care is required, but we leave a formal analysis to the PcFiml book.

PcGive is specifically designed to formulate, estimate, test, and analyse linear dynamic equations, and computes all of the statistics described above, and many more discussed in later sections. The empirical cloth on the present theory skeleton is presented in later sections once a few more concepts have been introduced.

12.3 A typology of simple dynamic models

Hendry, Pagan and Sargan (1984) provide a detailed analysis of single equation models like (12.4), and show that most of the widely-used empirical models are special cases of (12.4). There are nine distinct model types embedded in (12.4), a point most easily seen by considering the special case of $k = n = 1$ and $m = 0$, so that all of the polynomials are first order, and only one x variable is involved:

$$y_t = \alpha_1 y_{t-1} + \beta_0 x_t + \beta_1 x_{t-1} + \epsilon_t \text{ where } \epsilon_t \sim \mathsf{IN}\left(0, \sigma_\epsilon^2\right) \quad (12.8)$$

and $\mathsf{IN}\left(\mu, \sigma^2\right)$ denotes an independent normal random variable with mean μ and constant variance σ^2.

All nine of the following models are obtainable by further restrictions on this extremely simple case:

(1) static relationships;
(2) autoregressive processes;
(3) leading indicators;
(4) growth-rate models;
(5) distributed lags;
(6) partial adjustments;
(7) autoregressive-error models (COMFAC);
(8) equilibrium-correction mechanisms (ECM);
(9) dead-start models.

Equation (12.8) is a specialization of the special case of a linear, single-equation dynamic model, with the apparently restrictive assumption that $\{\epsilon_t\}$ is a white-noise process. Yet most widely-used model types are schematically represented in (12.8), and the typology highlights their distinct characteristics, strengths and weaknesses.

To clarify the approach, we consider the nine cases in turn, deriving each via restrictions on the parameter vector

$$\boldsymbol{\theta}' = (\alpha_1, \beta_0, \beta_1)$$

of (12.8), noting that an intercept and an error variance can be included without loss of generality in all models, and are omitted for simplicity of exposition. Four of the cases impose two restrictions on $\boldsymbol{\theta}$ and five impose one, and these will be referred to respectively as one and two parameter models since σ^2 is common to all stochastic models. Table 12.1 lists the outcomes.

Table 12.1 Model Typology.

Type of Model	$\boldsymbol{\theta}'$	Entailed Restrictions on (12.8)	
static regression	$(0, \beta_0, 0)$	$\alpha_1 = \beta_1 = 0$	no dynamics
autoregressive process	$(\alpha_1, 0, 0)$	$\beta_0 = \beta_1 = 0$	no covariates
leading indicator	$(0, 0, \beta_1)$	$\alpha_1 = \beta_0 = 0$	no contemporaneity
growth rate	$(1, \beta_0, -\beta_0)$	$\alpha_1 = 1,$ $\beta_1 = -\beta_0$	no levels
distributed lag	$(0, \beta_0, \beta_1)$	$\alpha_1 = 0$	finite lags
partial adjustment	$(\alpha_1, \beta_0, 0)$	$\beta_1 = 0$	no lagged x
autoregressive error	$(\alpha_1, \beta_0, -\alpha_1\beta_0)$	$\beta_1 = -\alpha_1\beta_0$	one common factor
error correction	(α_1, β_0, K)	$K = \dfrac{\beta_0 + \beta_1}{1 - \alpha_1}$	long-run response
dead-start	$(\alpha_1, 0, \beta_1)$	$\beta_0 = 0$	lagged variables

Three important issues must be clarified before proceeding: the status of $\{x_t\}$; the dependence of the model's properties on the data properties; and whether each model type is being treated as correctly specified or as an approximation to a more general

DGP such as (12.4). These three problems arise in part because the analysis has not commenced from the most general system needed to characterize the observed data adequately, and in part because the DGP is unknown in practice, so we do not know which data properties to take as salient features in an analytical treatment (not to mention in empirical studies). The system formulation is offered in Chapter 14.

For the present, we treat $\{x_t\}$ as if it were (weakly) exogenous for the parameters of interest in $\boldsymbol{\theta}$ (see Engle, Hendry and Richard, 1983, and §14.5.2). Heuristically, weak exogeneity ensures that we can take the conditioning variables as valid, and so analyse the conditional equation (12.8) without loss of any relevant information about $\boldsymbol{\theta}$ despite not also modelling the process determining x_t: this would be false if the model of x_t depended on $\boldsymbol{\theta}$. When x_t in (12.8) is weakly exogenous for its parameters, then if any member of the typology is valid, so must be every *less restricted*, but identifiable, member. That statement has profound implications not only for the general methodology of modelling, but also for such major issues of current contention as the practice of 'allowing for residual autocorrelation', the validity of analysing over-identified simultaneous systems (the Sims critique: see Sims, 1980, and Hendry and Mizon, 1993), and the imposition of restrictions based on prior theory, including the Lucas critique (see Lucas, 1976, and Favero and Hendry, 1992).

As noted earlier, x_t is assumed $\mathsf{I}(1)$, and for convenience we take $\{\Delta x_t\}$ to be a stationary process. This determines the answer to the second issue; but since some economic time series seem to be $\mathsf{I}(0)$ (e.g. unemployment), the case $x_t \sim \mathsf{I}(0)$ remains relevant. If x_t and y_t are cointegrated, then $u_t = (y_t - Kx_t) \sim \mathsf{I}(0)$, but such a belief may be false, and the case $u_t \sim \mathsf{I}(1)\ \forall K$ must be noted. The typology treats each case in turn, as if it were the correct specification, but notes both the historical success of such an assumption and the likely consequences when it is incorrect.

12.3.1 Static regression

Equations of the form

$$y_t = b_0 x_t + u_t$$

(with b_0 and x_t vectors in general) have played a large role in many macro-econometric systems as erstwhile 'structural' equations (i.e., embodying the fundamental parameters of the behaviour of economic agents). In practice, $\{u_t\}$ has usually been quite highly autocorrelated (reminiscent of nonsense correlations – see Yule, 1926), so that inference about b_0 is invalid (see, for example, Granger and Newbold, 1974, and Phillips, 1986). Recently, however, static equations have reappeared as part of a two-stage strategy for investigating cointegration, with the focus on testing whether or not $\{u_t\}$ is $\mathsf{I}(1)$ against the alternative that it is $\mathsf{I}(0)$ (see Engle and Granger, 1987). Then, b_0 would be a direct estimator of K in (12.6). Even so, the success of such an estimator in finite samples has been questioned (see Banerjee, Dolado, Hendry and Smith, 1986), and is dependent on the mean lag between y and x, noting that a static equation imposes that mean lag at zero. Alternatively, the strategy of removing the autocorrelation in $\{u_t\}$ by fitting an autoregressive process is considered in §12.3.7. Finally, viewed as a structural equation, all of the restrictions on dynamics and covariates are testable against (12.4), as are the implicit restrictions highlighted in §14.5.

12.3.2 Univariate autoregressive processes

The equation

$$y_t = a_1 y_{t-1} + e_t$$

serves as our representative of univariate time-series models (see Box and Jenkins, 1976). If y_t is I(1), $a_1 = 1$, inducing a random walk when e_t is white noise. Autoregressive equations are widely used for *ex ante* forecasting and have proved a powerful challenger to econometrics systems in that domain (see, for example, Nelson, 1972, and the vector analogues in Doan, Litterman and Sims, 1984.) In economics, the interdependence of economic decisions (for example, one person's income is another's expenditure) entails that univariate autoregressions must be derived, and hence are not autonomous processes – where an equation for y_t is autonomous if changes in the process generating x_t do not alter it. Here, the autoregression is obtained by eliminating, or marginalizing with respect to, x_t. For example, let $x_t = x_{t-1} + \nu_t$ where $\nu_t \sim \mathsf{IN}\left(0,\ \sigma_t^2\right)$ when in fact $\alpha_1 = 1$ and $\beta_1 = -\beta_0$, then $y_t = y_{t-1} + \epsilon_t + \beta_0 \nu_t$ has a non-constant variance $\sigma_\epsilon^2 + \beta_0^2 \sigma_t^2$. Consequently, econometric models should both fit better than autoregressions (or else they are at least dynamically mis-specified), and should forecast better (or else the constancy of the econometric model must be suspect).

That both these requirements are sometimes not satisfied is owing in part to the inappropriateness of some current empirical methodological practices. A major objective of PcGive is to offer an alternative approach which circumvents such difficulties by commencing from a general dynamic specification that automatically embeds the relevant special cases.

12.3.3 Leading indicators

Models of the form

$$y_t = c_1 x_{t-1} + v_t$$

can be used in forecasting if x leads y with sufficient reliability (for example, orders arrive ahead of output). In the absence of a sound behavioural theory, however, c_1 need not be constant. If it is not, that will lead to poor forecasting, especially in periods of change when good forecasts are most needed. Moreover, there seems no good reason for excluding lagged *y*s, and if a general dynamic model is postulated, then the econometric considerations in §14.4, §14.5, §14.6 and §14.7 apply: see Emerson and Hendry (1994).

12.3.4 Growth-rate models

The evolutionary and trend-like behaviour of many economic time series led earlier investigators to recommend differencing data prior to statistical analysis. One example is Granger and Newbold (1977) although, as argued in Hendry and Anderson (1977), there are other transformations (such as ratios) which potentially could also remove trends. That leads on to the concept of cointegration discussed in §12.3.8.

Growth-rate models have the form

$$\Delta y_t = d_0 \Delta x_t + \eta_t.$$

Such models successfully avoid nonsense regressions problems in I(1) data, and from the transformed dependent variable, a useful measure of goodness of fit can be calculated. Nevertheless, if the variance of Δx_t is large relative to that of Δy_t, d_0 must be small even if y_t and x_t are cointegrated with $K = 1$ (this is the permanent income issue in one guise: see Davidson, Hendry, Srba and Yeo, 1978). Further, although $y_t = Kx_t$ implies $\Delta y_t = K\Delta x_t$, the converse is false in a stochastic world owing to integrating the error.

Alternatively, there are no *a priori* grounds for excluding levels from economic relationships since initial disequilibria cannot be assumed to be irrelevant: that is, the time path of Δy_t for a given sequence Δx_t will also depend in general on the relationship between y_0 and x_0. Two further insights into the drawbacks of growth-rate models are discussed below in §12.3.7 and §12.3.8.

On the methodological level, a mistake sometimes committed in applied economics is to begin with a linear approximation to a steady-state theory of the form: $y_t = f(x_t)$, fit a static model thereto, discover severe residual autocorrelation and 'correct' that either by differencing or by using 'Cochrane–Orcutt' (but see their 1949 article, Cochrane and Orcutt, 1949) and finding an autoregressive parameter near unity. While the goodness of fit may not be greatly worsened by imposing differencing, dynamic responses can be substantially distorted and ignoring long-run feedbacks may distort policy strategies.

12.3.5 Distributed lags

Although using only one lag makes the resulting model highly schematic, the equation

$$y_t = f_0 x_t + f_1 x_{t-1} + \xi_t$$

is representative of the class of finite distributed lags. Such models remain open to the objections noted in §12.3.1 above, are highly dependent on whether x_t is weakly, or strongly, exogenous unless ξ_t is white noise (which in practice it rarely is in this class), and tend to suffer from collinearity owing to the inappropriate parameterization of including many levels of the regressor (see Chapter 15). Imposing so-called *a priori* restrictions on the lag coefficients to reduce the profligate parameterization has little to recommend it, although such restrictions are at least potentially testable. It is hard to see any theoretical grounds for excluding lagged *ys*, given that they are another way of representing a distributed lag relationship; and as shown in §12.3.7, considerable dangers exist in arbitrarily removing any residual autocorrelation from ξ_t.

12.3.6 Partial adjustment

The equation

$$y_t = g_0 x_t + g_1 y_{t-1} + \zeta_t$$

occurs regularly in empirical macro-economics, and can be derived from assuming a long-run desired target of the form $y_t = K x_t$ subject to quadratic adjustment costs (see, for example, Eisner and Strotz, 1963, and Nickell, 1985). While such a model type seems reasonable in principle, it does not entail that the y and x variables which agents use in their decision rules are precisely the levels under study by the economist. For example, agents may use the (log of the) consumption-income ratio as their y_t, and the growth rate of income as their x_t, rather than the levels of both.[4] The resulting econometric specification, however, is wholly different despite the common element of partial adjustment.

Even when y_t and x_t are cointegrated in levels, the partial adjustment model has little to recommend it unless it happens to coincide with the DGP. The mean lag is $g_1 / (1 - g_1)$ whereas the median lag (the number of periods to reach the half-way stage towards equilibrium) is zero for $g_0 \leq \frac{1}{2}$ and is $-\log(2g_1) / \log(g_1)$ for $g_0 > \frac{1}{2}$, so that a skewed distribution is imposed without consulting the data (see, for example, Hendry, 1995a, for the derivation of these formulae). When g_1 is near unity, both measures entail extremely slow adjustment, exacerbated by any untreated positive residual autocorrelation. Further, x_t and y_{t-1} are usually highly correlated, so again an unfortunate parameterization is being selected. Since there are no good arguments for *a priori* excluding all the lagged *xs*, and plenty of empirical evidence to show that they do matter in many cases, this model type again seems suspect.[5]

12.3.7 Autoregressive errors or COMFAC models

As noted in §12.2, some of the roots of $a(L)$ and $b(L)$ in (12.3) may be equal, allowing cancellation. In the case of (12.8) with $\beta_0 \neq 0$, we can write the equation as:

$$(1 - \alpha_1 L) y_t = \beta_0 \left(1 + \frac{\beta_1}{\beta_0} L\right) x_t + \epsilon_t.$$

[4] The latter anyway seems suspect since few consumers appear to suffer great adjustment costs in response to increases in their expenditure when income has risen.

[5] Lags would arise naturally in the postulated model if the agents' y and x were not the levels the economist selects.

Thus, if and only if $\alpha_1 = -\beta_1/\beta_0$ or $\beta_1 + \alpha_1\beta_0 = 0$ then on dividing both sides by $(1 - \alpha_1 L)$, the equation can be rewritten as:

$$y_t = \beta_0 x_t + \frac{\epsilon_t}{(1 - \alpha_1 L)},$$

or letting $\rho = \alpha_1$:

$$y_t = \beta_0 x_t + u_t \text{ where } u_t = \rho u_{t-1} + \epsilon_t, \tag{12.9}$$

yielding a static model with an autoregressive error. The term $(1 - \alpha_1 L)$ is a factor (in this simple case, the only factor) of $a(L)$ and similarly $(1 + (\beta_1/\beta_0) L)$ is a factor of $b(L)$, so that when these are equal there is a factor in common in $a(L)$ and $b(L)$ (leading to the name COMFAC). The converse that (12.9) induces a common factor is obvious, so there is an isomorphism between autoregressive errors and common factors in the lag polynomials: if you believe one, you must believe the other. Since (12.9) imposes restrictions on (12.8), these are testable, and rejection entails discarding the supposed reduction to (12.9) (see Hendry and Mizon, 1978). Thus, the ADL class includes all models with autoregressive errors.

Perhaps the greatest *non sequitur* in the history of econometrics is the assumption that autocorrelated residuals entail autoregressive errors, as is entailed in 'correcting serial correlation using Cochrane–Orcutt'. Dozens of mis-specifications in time-series data will induce residual autocorrelation without corresponding to common factors in the lag polynomials of the underlying general model (12.3). Indeed, the order of testing is incorrect: to estimate any models like (12.9) first necessitates establishing the validity of (12.3), then showing that $a(L)$ and $b(L)$ have common factors, and finally testing H_0: $\rho = 0$. Showing that $\rho \neq 0$ in equations like (12.9) does not prove that there are valid common-factor restrictions. PcGive offers algorithms for testing common-factor restrictions in equations like (12.4) using the Wald-test approach in Sargan (1980b). If such restrictions are accepted, generalizations of (12.9) are estimable using the RALS estimator described in Chapter 17.

Two points of importance from (12.9) are that: (a) it imposes a zero mean lag irrespective of the actual lag latencies, since the short-run and long-run responses are forced to be equal by the choice of model type; and (b) the growth-rate model of §12.3.4 can be reinterpreted as imposing a common factor then setting ρ to unity. We concur with the advice in the title of the paper by Mizon (1993).

12.3.8 Equilibrium-correction mechanisms

The issue of appropriate reparameterizations of $\boldsymbol{\theta}$ has arisen on several occasions above, and many alternatives are conceivable. One natural choice follows from rearranging (12.8) as:

$$\begin{aligned} \Delta y_t &= (\alpha_1 - 1)\, y_{t-1} + \beta_0 \Delta x_t + (\beta_1 + \beta_0)\, x_{t-1} + \epsilon_t \\ &= \beta_0 \Delta x_t + (\alpha_1 - 1)\,(y_{t-1} - K x_{t-1}) + \epsilon_t, \end{aligned} \tag{12.10}$$

where $K = (\beta_0 + \beta_1) / (1 - \alpha_1)$ is the long-run response in (12.6) above. The new parameters in $f(\boldsymbol{\theta}) = \boldsymbol{\psi} = (\beta_0, (1 - \alpha_1), K)'$ correspond to the impact effect, the feedback effect and the long-run response: no restrictions are imposed in this transformation. The term $(y - Kx)_{t-1}$ was called an error-correction mechanism (ECM) in Davidson *et al.* (1978) since it reflected the deviation from the long-run equilibrium outcome, with agents correcting $(1 - \alpha_1)$ of the resulting disequilibrium each period. However, such a mechanism does not error correct between equilibria, so equilibrium-correction mechanism is more apposite – and has the same acronym. Sargan (1964) provides a real-wage example, and Hendry and Anderson (1977) considered some non-unit ECMs. The special case $K = 1$ is of interest in econometrics as it corresponds to long-run proportionality (or homogeneity in log-linear models), but ECMs are well defined for $K \neq 1$, although usually K will then need to be estimated. As Hendry *et al.* (1984) note, logistic formulations or more general functions may be necessary to model agents' behaviour if they adjust more or less rapidly depending on the extent of disequilibrium (see Escribano, 1985).

Engle and Granger (1987) establish an isomorphism between ECMs and cointegrated processes: if y_t and x_t are each I(1) and are cointegrated, then there exists an ECM of the form $(y - Kx)$ and conversely. The former does not entail that the ECM necessarily enters the y_t equation, rather than the x_t equation, and may enter both (which would violate weak exogeneity: see Hendry and Mizon (1993) for an example).

In our simple typology, the only ECM case to impose any restrictions on (12.10) is $K = 1$ or $\alpha_1 + \beta_0 + \beta_1 = 1$, revealing that all long-run proportionality theories can be reproduced in static equilibrium by an appropriate ECM. Here, this restriction yields:

$$\Delta y_t = \gamma_0 \Delta x_t - \gamma_1 (y - x)_{t-1} + \omega_t. \tag{12.11}$$

Thus another interpretation of the growth-rate model §12.3.4 is revealed, namely, it corresponds to imposing long-run homogeneity $(\alpha_1 + \beta_0 + \beta_1 = 1)$ and the absence of feedback from the level $(1 - \alpha_1 = 0)$, which together entail a unit root. Consequently, small values of γ_0 are compatible with long-run proportionality. Since partial adjustment corresponds to the special case where $x = y^*$ (the desired target), it imposes $\gamma_0 = -\gamma_1$ to exclude the lagged x.

The parameterization in (12.11) has several advantages beyond being more interpretable: the regressors Δx_t and $(y - x)_{t-1}$ will not usually be highly correlated, being a current change and a lagged disequilibrium; and proportionality is easily tested by adding x_{t-1} as a (relatively non-collinear) regressor (however, such a test must allow for the possibility that $\{x_t\}$ may be I(1)). Further, a less strong lag shape is being imposed, since the mean lag is $(1 - \gamma_0) / \gamma_1$, which depends on both parameters, and can be small even if $(1 - \gamma_1)$ is around 0.9, whereas the median lag is zero for $\gamma_0 \geq \frac{1}{2}$ and is $-\log 2 (1 - \gamma_0) / \log (1 - \gamma_1)$ for $\gamma_0 < \frac{1}{2}$.

When the ECM is the correct specification, the partial adjustment model may suffer from severe biases, and possibly residual autocorrelation, since it omits x_{t-1} which is highly correlated with x_t: because the coefficients of x_t and x_{t-1} are of similar magnitudes but opposite signs, this will drive the coefficient of x_t in the partial adjustment model close to zero (a common empirical problem), so that $g_0 \simeq 1-g_1$ results. Note that $\beta_1 < 0$ in (12.8) need not entail any negative weights $\{w_i\}$ in the solved representation:

$$y_t = \sum_{i=0}^{\infty} w_i x_{t-i} + u_t.$$

Thus, do not delete lagged *x*s because their coefficients appear to have 'wrong signs', since on a reparameterization they may have the correct sign.

Finally, ECMs can be confused with COMFAC models despite their different implications for lag responses. This arises because COMFAC is an ECM with the restriction that long-run and short-run responses are equal, as can be seen by rewriting (12.9) in the form:

$$y_t = \beta_0 x_t + \rho\,(y_{t-1} - \beta_0 x_{t-1}) + \epsilon_t,$$

or:

$$\Delta y_t = \beta_0 \Delta x_t + (\rho - 1)\,(y - \beta_0 x)_{t-1} + \epsilon_t. \tag{12.12}$$

Thus, the degree of mis-specification of (12.12) for (12.10) depends on the extent to which $(\alpha_1 - 1)\,(K - \beta_0) \neq 0$, which could be small even if $K = 1$ and, for example, $\beta_0 = 0.4$. Nevertheless, despite (12.10) and (12.12) having similar goodness of fit, the mean lag in (12.10) when $K = 1$ could be large at the same time as (12.12) imposes it at zero.

12.3.9 Dead-start models

The main consideration arising for this type of model is its exclusion of contemporaneous information. This could be because:

$$y_t = \alpha_1 y_{t-1} + \beta_1 x_{t-1} + \epsilon_t \tag{12.13}$$

is structural, and hence is a partial adjustment type. Alternatively, (12.13) could be a derived form, from which x_t has been eliminated, in which case (12.13) is unlikely to be autonomous, and its parameters would be susceptible to alter with changes in the behaviour of the x_t process. In this second case, the coefficients are not interpretable since they are (unknown) functions of the correlations between x_t and $(y_{t-1},\ x_{t-1})$.

Care is obviously required in selecting an appropriate type of model to characterize both a given theory and the associated data; some of the methodological considerations discussed below help clarify that choice.

12.4 Interpreting linear models

The notation for the linear model is the same as that in Chapter 13:

$$y_t = \sum_{i=1}^{k} \beta_i x_{i,t} + \epsilon_t = \boldsymbol{\beta}'\mathbf{x}_t + \epsilon_t \text{ with } \epsilon_t \sim \mathsf{IN}\left(0, \sigma_\epsilon^2\right), \tag{12.14}$$

where $\boldsymbol{\beta}$ is $k \times 1$ and $\mathsf{E}\left[\mathbf{x}_t \epsilon_t\right] = \mathbf{0}$. Grouping all the T observations:

$$\mathbf{y} = \mathbf{X}\boldsymbol{\beta} + \boldsymbol{\epsilon} \text{ with } \boldsymbol{\epsilon} \sim \mathsf{N}\left(\mathbf{0}, \sigma_\epsilon^2 \mathbf{I}_T\right) \tag{12.15}$$

where $\mathbf{y}, \mathbf{X}, \boldsymbol{\epsilon}$ are respectively $T \times 1, T \times k$ and $T \times 1$.

First, we discuss the four distinct interpretations of (12.14), see Richard (1980) or Hendry *et al.* (1984):

12.4.1 (11.14) is a regression equation

The regression is the conditional expectation of y_t given $\mathbf{x}_t$ (denoted by $\mathsf{E}\left[y_t|\mathbf{x}_t\right]$). Taking the conditional expectation in (12.14):

$$\mathsf{E}\left[y_t \mid \mathbf{x}_t\right] = \boldsymbol{\beta}'\mathbf{x}_t \tag{12.16}$$

where $\boldsymbol{\beta}$ is a parameter of interest. Sufficient conditions to sustain that interpretation of (12.14) are a jointly stationary, multivariate normal distribution for $(y_t, \mathbf{x}_t)$ with $\mathbf{x}_t$ weakly exogenous for $\boldsymbol{\beta}$. (A formal derivation of a conditional equation in a bivariate normal distribution is provided in Chapter 13.) The properties of regression estimators are also discussed in that chapter (for example, that $\mathsf{V}\left[y_t - \boldsymbol{\beta}'\mathbf{x}_t\right]$ is minimized by the choice of $\widehat{\boldsymbol{\beta}}$). The minimal conditions needed to justify (12.16) are not sufficient to sustain $\mathsf{E}\left[\mathbf{y}|\mathbf{X}\right] = \mathbf{X}\boldsymbol{\beta}$, which is used in Chapter 13, as that involves conditioning past ys on future xs.

12.4.2 (11.14) is a (linear) least-squares approximation

Here the approximation is to a postulated general function:

$$y_t = \mathbf{f}\left(\mathbf{x}_t\right) + e_t,$$

chosen on the criteria that: (a) (12.14) is linear in $\mathbf{x}_t$; and (b) $\sum_{t=1}^{T} \epsilon_t^2$ is to be minimized. Graphically, $\boldsymbol{\beta}$ in (12.14) is not $\partial\mathbf{f}/\partial\mathbf{x}'$ (the tangent), owing to the second criterion, but must be a chord. If ϵ_t is non-normal, the regression would not be linear, whereas a linear approximation must be, so §12.4.1 and §12.4.2 are distinct. If, in practice, $\mathbf{f}$ is non-linear then (12.14) may be a poor approximation, $\{\epsilon_t\}$ could be autocorrelated and forecasts could be poor (since $\partial\mathbf{f}/\partial\mathbf{x}_t'$ need not be constant). Of course, a quadratic or even a higher-order approximation to $\mathbf{f}\left(\mathbf{x}\right)$ could be used. White (1980) provides a formal analysis of this case.

12.4.3 (11.14) is an autonomous contingent plan

In this interpretation:

$$y_t^p = \mathbf{x}_t'\boldsymbol{\beta}$$

is the planned value and:

$$y_t = y_t^p + u_t$$

is the outcome, which deviates randomly from the plan (see Marschak, 1953, Bentzel and Hansen, 1955, and Hendry and Richard, 1983). Thus, (12.14) characterizes how agents form plans and $\boldsymbol{\beta}$ is an invariant parameter (see Frisch, 1938). Since $\{u_t\}$ need not have a joint normal distribution, §12.4.3 and §12.4.1 are different; and $\mathbf{f}(\mathbf{x})$ might be approximated by a non-linear function of $\mathbf{x}_t$, so §12.4.2 and §12.4.3 also differ. For example, ARCH errors would be one instance where $\{u_t\}$ is not jointly normal, so that $\mathsf{E}[\mathbf{y}|\mathbf{X}] \neq \mathbf{X}\boldsymbol{\beta}$ need not hold although (12.14) could still be correct.

12.4.4 (11.14) is derived from a behavioural relationship

The final interpretation is:

$$\mathsf{E}[y_t \mid \mathcal{I}_{t-1}] = \boldsymbol{\beta}'\mathsf{E}[\mathbf{x}_t \mid \mathcal{I}_{t-1}],$$

or:

$$y_t^p = \boldsymbol{\beta}'\mathbf{x}_t^e,$$

where $\mathcal{I}_{t-1}$ denotes the universe of information available to agents at the time their plans are formulated, and the distinction is drawn between a plan (which is made about a variable that the relevant agent controls), and an expectation (which is formed about an uncontrolled variable). Let $\boldsymbol{\nu}_t = \mathbf{x}_t - \mathbf{x}_t^e$ and $\eta_t = y_t - y_t^p$ be the vector of expectational errors and the departure of the outcome from the plan respectively, with $\mathsf{E}[\boldsymbol{\nu}_t|\mathcal{I}_{t-1}] = \mathbf{0}$ and $\mathsf{E}[\eta_t|\mathcal{I}_{t-1}] = 0$, then:

$$y_t = \boldsymbol{\beta}'\mathbf{x}_t + \epsilon_t \ \text{ with } \ \epsilon_t = \eta_t - \boldsymbol{\beta}'\boldsymbol{\nu}_t,$$

so that $\mathsf{E}[\epsilon_t|\mathcal{I}_{t-1}] = 0$ but $\mathsf{E}[\epsilon_t|\mathbf{x}_t] \neq 0$ owing to their sharing the common component $\boldsymbol{\nu}_t$. In this setting, regression is inconsistent (and biased) for the parameter of interest $\boldsymbol{\beta}$, and may deliver non-constant estimates even when $\boldsymbol{\beta}$ is invariant but the process determining $\mathbf{x}_t$ alters. Clearly, §12.4.4 is distinct from §12.4.1–§12.4.3.

Merely asserting $y_t = \boldsymbol{\beta}'\mathbf{x}_t + \epsilon_t$ is not an adequate basis for econometric analysis, given the four distinct interpretations of equation (12.14) just described. Although the four interpretations happen to coincide in stationary, linear models with normal errors, the distinctions in §12.4.1–§12.4.4 are not formal: in practice, which one is valid entails quite different prognoses for the success (or failure) of any empirical study. When the $\mathbf{x}_t$ process varies enough, some discrimination is possible owing to the non-constancy of $\boldsymbol{\beta}$, and this is both the usual situation and that in which discrimination actually matters.

12.5 Multiple regression

The algebra of least-squares estimation is established in matrix notation in Chapter 13, and we merely record some of the most relevant formulae here. First:

$$\hat{\beta} = (\mathbf{X}'\mathbf{X})^{-1}\mathbf{X}'\mathbf{y} \text{ with } \widehat{\mathsf{V}\left[\hat{\beta}\right]} = \hat{\sigma}^2_\epsilon (\mathbf{X}'\mathbf{X})^{-1}$$

and:

$$\hat{\sigma}^2_\epsilon = \frac{RSS}{(T-k)} \text{ when } RSS = \left(\mathbf{y}-\mathbf{X}\hat{\beta}\right)'\left(\mathbf{y}-\mathbf{X}\hat{\beta}\right).$$

Further, $\mathbf{M} = \mathbf{I}_T - \mathbf{X}(\mathbf{X}'\mathbf{X})^{-1}\mathbf{X}'$ is a symmetric idempotent matrix which annihilates $\mathbf{X}$, so $\mathbf{MX} = \mathbf{0}$ implying $\mathbf{My} = \mathbf{M}\epsilon = \hat{\mathbf{u}}$ (the vector of residuals $\mathbf{y} - \mathbf{X}\hat{\beta}$). Tests of H_0: $\boldsymbol{\beta} = \mathbf{0}$, or components thereof, are developed in Chapter 13. A simple empirical example with a constant and two other regressors is presented in §11.10.

It is a brave (foolhardy?) investigator who deems their model to coincide with the DGP, and most econometricians consider the possibility of various mis-specifications when appraising empirical research. A number of possibilities can be shown algebraically, such as omitting a relevant regressor. Denoting the OLS estimator of the mis-specified model by $\sim$, partition $\mathbf{X} = (\mathbf{X}_a : \mathbf{X}_b)$, and conformably let $\beta = (\beta_a' : \beta_b')'$ which are $k_a \times 1$ and $k_b \times 1$ so that $k_a + k_b = k$. Then:

$$\tilde{\beta} = (\mathbf{X}_a'\mathbf{X}_a)^{-1}\mathbf{X}_a'\mathbf{y} \text{ and } \widetilde{\mathsf{V}\left[\tilde{\beta}_a\right]} = \tilde{\sigma}^2_\epsilon (\mathbf{X}_a'\mathbf{X}_a)^{-1} \text{ when } \tilde{\sigma}^2_\epsilon = \frac{\mathbf{y}'\mathbf{M}_a\mathbf{y}}{(T-k_a)}$$

and $\mathbf{M}_a$ has the same form as $\mathbf{M}$ but using only $\mathbf{X}_a$. Partitioned inversion of $(\mathbf{X}'\mathbf{X})$ leads to the important numerical identity that:

$$\tilde{\beta}_a \equiv \hat{\beta}_a + \mathbf{B}\hat{\beta}_b \text{ where } \mathbf{B} = (\mathbf{X}_a'\mathbf{X}_a)^{-1}\mathbf{X}_a'\mathbf{X}_b.$$

If $\{\mathbf{x}_t\}$ is a stationary stochastic process, then:

$$\mathsf{E}\left[\tilde{\sigma}^2_\epsilon\right] \geq \mathsf{E}\left[\hat{\sigma}^2_\epsilon\right]$$

since there is a component of $\mathbf{x}_{bt}$ in the residual. Both the bias in $\tilde{\beta}_a$ and in the error variance were illustrated by the comparative regression results in §11.10. Tests for the significance of omitted variables can be undertaken from the Test menu; what would you conclude after getting two significant test results?

Despite a high correlation between $\mathbf{x}_{at}$ and $\mathbf{x}$, it is possible that:

$$\widehat{\mathsf{V}\left[\hat{\beta}\right]} < \widetilde{\mathsf{V}\left[\tilde{\beta}_a\right]},$$

owing to the reduction in $\hat{\sigma}^2_\epsilon$ from $\tilde{\sigma}^2_\epsilon$ when $\mathbf{x}_{bt}$ is added to the regression of y_t on $\mathbf{x}_{at}$. A more extensive treatment of collinearity is provided in Chapter 15. Finally, the Durbin–Watson test (DW: see Durbin and Watson, 1951) is often used to test for mis-specifications which result in residual autocorrelation: see §12.3.7.

12.5.1 Estimating partial adjustment

All these issues can be illustrated empirically, and we do so using the artificial data set called DATA.IN7 and DATA.BN7, with the four variables CONS, INC, INFLAT and OUTPUT. The first regression is of CONS on INC and CONS lagged (that is, a partial adjustment form) which yields:[6]

```
EQ(1) Modelling CONS by OLS
The present sample is:   1953 (2) to 1992 (3)

Variable Coefficient Std.Error t-value  t-prob    HCSE    PartRsq
Constant     -45.604    14.647   -3.114  0.0022   13.642   0.0589
CONS_1       0.82387  0.033004   24.962  0.0000  0.032659  0.8008
INC          0.22398  0.041582    5.386  0.0000  0.040992  0.1577

Rsq = 0.977627 F(2,155) = 3386.6 [0.0000] s = 2.03715  DW = 1.13
RSS = 643.2438296 for 3 variables and 158 observations
```

At first sight, the coefficients seem well determined, and the long-run effect of INC on CONS is close to unity. However, the DW statistic is low (especially as the model has a lagged dependent variable which biases DW towards 2). We will test the specification in the next section.

The new column above labelled HCSE denotes heteroscedastic-consistent standard errors (see Eicker, 1967, and White, 1980). Relative to the usual standard errors reported for regression estimation, HCSEs reflect any heteroscedasticity in the residuals which is related to the regressors. Consider OLS estimation in (12.14) when $\epsilon_t \sim \mathsf{IN}\left(0, \sigma_t^2\right)$ with $\mathsf{E}\left[\mathbf{x}_t \epsilon_s\right] = \mathbf{0}\ \forall t, s$ but we mistakenly believe that:

$$\epsilon_t \underset{h}{\sim} \mathsf{IN}\left(0, \sigma_\epsilon^2\right),$$

where $\underset{h}{\sim}$ denotes 'is hypothesised to be distributed as'. To estimate $\boldsymbol{\beta}$, we set to zero:

$$\sum_{t=1}^{T} \mathbf{x}_t \epsilon_t = \mathbf{0}. \tag{12.17}$$

Then, to derive the variance, we should analytically calculate:

$$\mathsf{E}\left[\sum_{t=1}^{T} \mathbf{x}_t \epsilon_t \left(\sum_{t=1}^{T} \mathbf{x}_t \epsilon_t\right)'\right] = \mathsf{E}\left[\sum_{t=1}^{T}\sum_{s=1}^{T} \mathbf{x}_t \epsilon_t \epsilon_s \mathbf{x}_s'\right] = \sum_{t=1}^{T} \sigma_t^2 \mathbf{x}_t \mathbf{x}_t',$$

from which the variance of $\widehat{\boldsymbol{\beta}}$ is given by:

$$\mathbf{V} = \mathsf{V}\left[\widehat{\boldsymbol{\beta}}\right] = \left(\mathbf{X}'\mathbf{X}\right)^{-1} \left(\sum_{t=1}^{T} \sigma_t^2 \mathbf{x}_t \mathbf{x}_t'\right) \left(\mathbf{X}'\mathbf{X}\right)^{-1} \tag{12.18}$$

[6]The exact form of the output depends on the profile settings.

This involves a weighted average of the xs with weights σ_t^2 proportional to the heteroscedastic error variances. The conventional variance estimator is:

$$\mathsf{V}\widehat{\left[\hat{\beta}\right]} = \hat{\sigma}_\epsilon \left(\sum_{t=1}^{T} \mathbf{x}_t\mathbf{x}_t'\right)^{-1}.$$

When the weights in (12.18) are not constant, the conventional variance estimator does not correctly reflect the estimation uncertainty.

Surprisingly, the correct variance formula in (12.18) can be estimated from the sample by replacing the unknown σ_t^2 by $\hat{\epsilon}_t^2$ (see White, 1980):

$$\hat{\mathbf{V}} = \left(\mathbf{X}'\mathbf{X}\right)^{-1} \left(\sum_{t=1}^{T} \hat{\epsilon}_t^2\mathbf{x}_t\mathbf{x}_t'\right) \left(\mathbf{X}'\mathbf{X}\right)^{-1}. \qquad (12.19)$$

$\hat{\mathbf{V}}$ is consistent for $\mathbf{V}$ (see White, 1980) and the conventional estimator of $\mathbf{V}$ arises when all $\left\{\sigma_t^2\right\}$ are constant. The square roots of the diagonal of $\hat{\mathbf{V}}$ are the HCSEs above. When these are close to the OLS SEs, there is little evidence of distortion of inference from untreated heteroscedasticity.

All reported statistics depend on assumptions about how well the model describes the data, and until these are established as valid, the interpretation of output is unclear. In the previous chapter, we considered the many assumptions made to derive the distribution of 't'-tests : the assumptions for HCSEs are weaker, but nonetheless strong as just seen. As a first pass, we use Test, Graphical analysis to visually investigate the fit, the residuals, the residual correlogram, and the density of the residuals. The outcome is shown in Figure 12.1 and reveals a fair fit, but distinct residual autocorrelation, as well as a major group of 'outliers' in the residuals around 1973–4 (does this period ring any warning bells?).

More formal mis-specification tests are considered shortly, but the graph shows substantial residual autocorrelation. How to proceed now?

12.5.2 Specific-to-general

To test a specification, investigators often add extra variables, so we first include lagged INC to obtain:

```
EQ(2) Modelling CONS by OLS
The present sample is:  1953 (2) to 1992 (3)

Variable Coefficient Std.Error  t-value  t-prob    HCSE   PartRsq
Constant      2.5114    11.393    0.220  0.8258   11.555   0.0003
CONS_1       0.98587  0.027620   35.695  0.0000 0.029606   0.8922
INC          0.49584  0.037971   13.059  0.0000 0.033330   0.5255
INC_1       -0.48491  0.041031  -11.818  0.0000 0.038639   0.4756

Rsq = 0.988268 F(3,154) = 4324.2 [0.0000] s = 1.47998 DW = 1.35
RSS = 337.3133612 for 4 variables and 158 observations
```

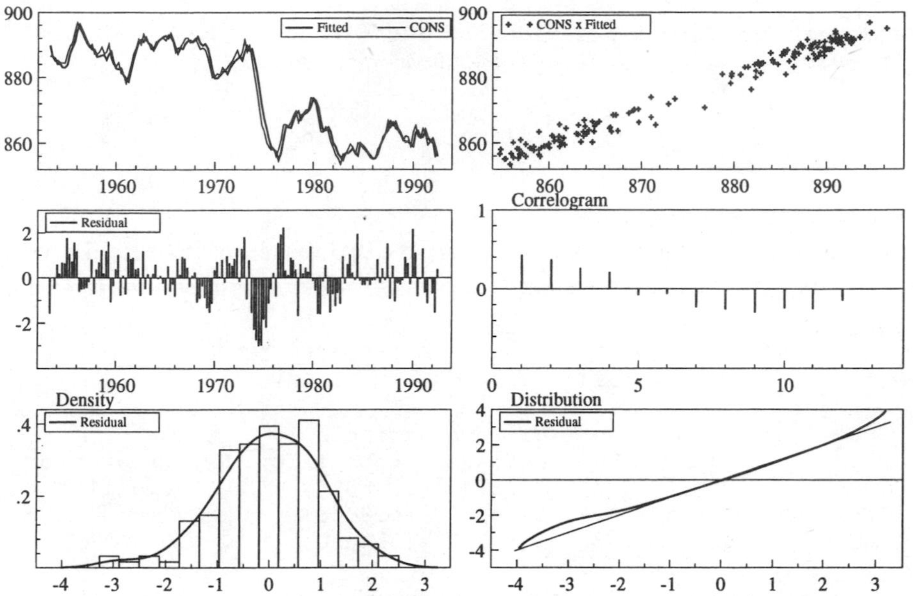

Figure 12.1 Goodness-of-fit measures for partial adjustment model.

The added variable is highly significant, and so invalidates the first partial adjustment model. The standard errors of both CONS and INC have fallen despite adding the collinear variable INC_1, mainly because *s* has fallen markedly. Consistent with that feature, the partial r^2 values have increased.

Unfortunately, the model appears to have a common factor of unity suggesting that CONS and INC are not cointegrated (the lagged dependent variable coefficient is near unity, and the coefficients on INC and INC lagged are equal magnitude opposite sign). Three formal tests are possible, assuming the model is a good data description. First, we test for a common factor to obtain:

```
Roots of the lag polynomials
CONS          lags 0 - 1
                   0.9859
INC           lags 0 - 1
                   0.9780

COMFAC WALD test statistic table
Order Chi2df     Value  p-value   Incr. Chi2df   Value  p-value
  1      1    0.030686 [0.8609]          1     0.030686 [0.8609]
```

The calculated values of the roots are close to unity and the test easily accepts. The model is now COMFAC rather than partial adjustment. Next, we test for a unit root by seeing if all the coefficients (other than the constant) add to unity: the linear restrictions test yields:

```
Wald test for linear restrictions (Rb = r)
LinRes F(1,154) =    0.064814 [0.7994]
       R matrix
   Constant      CONS_1         INC         INC_1
     0.0000       1.000       1.000         1.000
       r vector
      1.000
```

This too accepts with ease. Finally, we conduct the PcGive unit-root tests (see Banerjee and Hendry, 1992b) (from the Test menu, Dynamic analysis, reported only in part here):

```
Solved Static Long Run equation
       CONS =     +177.8                +0.7739 INC
(SE)          (     1022)            (    1.159)

Tests on the significance of each variable
variable    F(num,denom)      Value  Probability  Unit-root t-test
  CONS       F(1, 154) =     1274.1  [0.0000] **      -0.51143
  Constant   F(1, 154) =   0.048588  [0.8258]
  INC        F(2, 154) =     97.321  [0.0000] **       0.31073
```

The solved long run is badly determined and the unit-root test does not reject. All the evidence meshes: CONS and INC do not cointegrate.

Again one must ask: how valid are these tests? A glance at the graphical diagnostics (corresponding to Figure 12.1) shows that the residual autocorrelation has become worse, so none of the SEs is reliable. More formal mis-specification tests are provided in the Test summary, and yield:

```
AR 1- 5 F( 5,149) =      7.8187 [0.0000] **
ARCH 4   F( 4,146) =     6.1154 [0.0001] **
Normality Chi^2(2)=      7.6549 [0.0218] *
Xi^2     F( 6,147) =     1.0658 [0.3858]
Xi*Xj    F( 9,144) =     1.0443 [0.4080]
RESET    F( 1,153) =     2.6552 [0.1053]
```

There is indeed significant residual autocorrelation and apparently autoregressive conditional heteroscedasticity (ARCH) as well (see Engle, 1982). However, the latter could be caused by the former (see Engle, Hendry and Trumbull, 1985), and merely shows the difficulty of interpreting outcomes when several tests reject. If we test for the omission from the equation of the remaining two variables in the database, we obtain:

```
LM test for omitted variables
Add      F( 2,152) =     69.037 [0.0000] **

Added variables:
INFLAT INFLAT_1

LM test for omitted variables
Add      F( 2,152) =     11.188 [0.0000] **

Added variables:
```

```
OUTPUT OUTPUT_1
```

Both seem to matter! All previous results are invalidated: how to proceed now?

12.5.3 General-to-specific

It is precisely conundrums of the form just encountered that have led us to suggest an alternative approach to modelling. If at some stage you intend to investigate the relevance of a given phenomenon (for example, lagged INC, or INFLAT), include it in the model from the outset if sample size allows: this leads to general-to-specific modelling, discussed in greater detail in Chapter 15.

The initial general model should contain all the effects likely to be relevant, including sufficient lags to ensure no residual autocorrelation, then be tested for its validity. Once that has been established, further testing can proceed in confidence that conflicts will not arise. To illustrate, consider a model involving CONS, INC, and INFLAT, using one-period lags as an initial starting point:

```
EQ( 3) Modelling CONS by OLS
The present sample is:  1953 (2) to 1992 (3)
```

Variable	Coefficient	Std.Error	t-value	t-prob	HCSE	PartRsq
Constant	-20.270	8.5263	-2.377	0.0187	8.2398	0.0358
CONS_1	0.79831	0.027160	29.393	0.0000	0.026055	0.8504
INC	0.49894	0.028331	17.611	0.0000	0.026850	0.6711
INC_1	-0.27611	0.037876	-7.290	0.0000	0.037396	0.2590
INFLAT	-0.79309	0.18395	-4.311	0.0000	0.15872	0.1090
INFLAT_1	-0.25061	0.20310	-1.234	0.2191	0.18079	0.0099

```
Rsq = 0.993852 F(5,152) = 4914.6 [0.0000] s = 1.07836 DW = 1.95
RSS = 176.7534113 for 6 variables and 158 observations
```

The standard errors are much smaller than any previous results and PartRsqs are higher, although the correlations between the regressors are quite large:

Correlation matrix

	CONS	CONS_1	INC	INC_1	INFLAT
CONS	1.000				
CONS_1	0.9866	1.000			
INC	0.9422	0.9310	1.000		
INC_1	0.9144	0.9414	0.9510	1.000	
INFLAT	-0.3511	-0.2756	-0.1271	-0.07332	1.000
INFLAT_1	-0.4174	-0.3405	-0.1953	-0.1124	0.9266

Seven correlations exceed 0.9 yet every coefficient is well determined, although some are small. For example, the longest lag on INFLAT is irrelevant and could be eliminated. The goodness of fit as measured by s is 50% less than the first equation so the general model provides a usable baseline.

Next we test for a common factor:

```
Roots of the lag polynomials
CONS          lags 0 - 1
                  0.7983
INC           lags 0 - 1
                  0.5534
INFLAT        lags 0 - 1
                 -0.3160

COMFAC WALD test statistic table
Order Chi2df  Value  p-value     Incr. Chi2df  Value  p-value
  1      2   106.21 [0.0000] **        2       106.21 [0.0000] **
```

The roots are now well below unity in absolute value and the COMFAC test strongly rejects.[7] Correspondingly, the long run is well determined, and the unit-root test rejects the null, so cointegration is obtained between CONS, INC and INFLAT:

```
Solved Static Long Run equation
CONS =     -100.5             +1.105 INC            -5.175 INFLAT
(SE)   (    37.53)         (  0.04185)          (   0.5224)

Tests on the significance of each variable
variable     F(num,denom)     Value  Probability   Unit Root t-test
  CONS       F(1, 152) =     863.96 [0.0000] **       -7.4261**
  Constant   F(1, 152) =     5.6515 [0.0187] *
  INC        F(2, 152) =     159.04 [0.0000] **        6.8393
  INFLAT     F(2, 152) =     69.037 [0.0000] **        -11.1
```

The model satisfies all the statistics in the diagnostic test summary, and Figure 12.2 shows the improved graphical performance: with a little experience, a glance at Figure 12.1 shows a failed model, whereas Figure 12.2 is fine. Hopefully, your experience is growing rapidly.

12.5.4 Time series

PcGive allows all members of the typology to be estimated with ease, and as §12.3.1–§12.3.6 were considered in §12.5 above, we focus on §12.3.7 and §12.3.8 here, but in the opposite order.

12.5.5 Equilibrium correction

The concepts of I(1) behaviour and cointegration (or its absence) were briefly explained above, and were illustrated using the general unrestricted model option by formulating

[7] Neil Ericsson pointed out to us that, being a Wald test of non-linear restrictions, COMFAC is susceptible to how it is formulated (see e/g. Gregory and Veale, 1985): if the order of the variables was CONS, INFLAT, INC, the test statistic would have been $\chi^2(2) = 76.71$ [0.000]**. The test still strongly rejects here, but has a much smaller value.

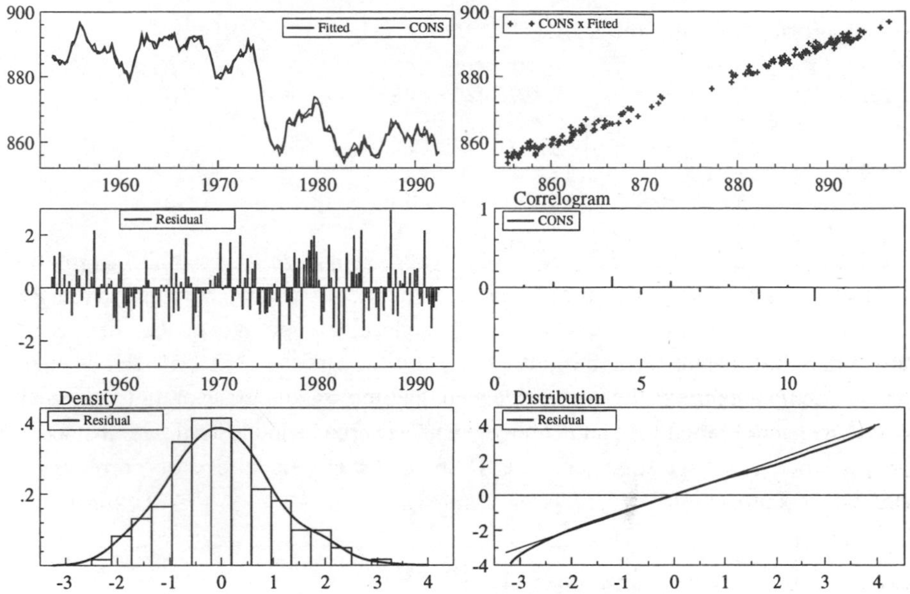

Figure 12.2 Goodness-of-fit measures for ADL.

a regression of y_t on $\mathbf{x}_t$ and setting the lag length of each variable at unity. After estimation, the long-run solution can be saved and graphed (called ECM by default). Above, we tested the model for a common factor by the COMFAC procedure and checked if the root was unity using the linear restrictions test. The unit-root tests were also applied. We now transform the preceding model to an ECM.

First, CONS, INC and INFLAT are transformed to differences, and the right-hand side levels to ECM form (denoted CI) using the rounded coefficients:

$$\mathrm{CI} = \mathrm{CONS} + 100 - \mathrm{INC} + 5 \times \mathrm{INFLAT},$$

where income homogeneity is imposed. Add CI lagged one period to the model in differences (the current value of CI must be deleted) and estimate as:

```
EQ( 4) Modelling DCONS by OLS
The present sample is:  1953 (2) to 1992 (3)

Variable Coefficient Std.Error t-value t-prob   HCSE   PartRsq
Constant    18.149    1.7257    10.517  0.0000  1.7414   0.4180
DINC        0.48943   0.027042  18.099  0.0000  0.02495  0.6802
DINFLAT    -0.70920   0.18258   -3.884  0.0002  0.15737  0.0892
CI_1       -0.19590   0.018481 -10.600  0.0000  0.01867  0.4218
Rsq = 0.758689 F(3,154) = 161.39 [0.0000] s = 1.0962 DW = 1.88
RSS = 185.0549866 for 4 variables and 158 observations
```

The outcome is a restricted, I(0), version of the ADL model, and all the coefficient estimates are well determined. The s value confirms that the restrictions are acceptable.

Testing using the test summary yields:

```
AR 1- 5F( 5,149) =      1.4037 [0.2262]
ARCH 4 F( 4,146) =      1.2801 [0.2805]
Normality Chi2(2)=     0.17211 [0.9175]
Xi2     F( 6,147) =     0.5359 [0.7803]
Xi*Xj   F( 9,144) =    0.76939 [0.6448]
RESET   F( 1,153) =      1.057 [0.3055]
```

Thus, there is no evidence of mis-specification against the historical sample information. Figure 12.3 shows the goodness of fit and graphical statistics: we have added a regression line to the cross plot both to show its 45° angle, and to remind you that these graphs can be modified as flexibly as desired..

This concludes the ECM analysis, except that the static regression in the next section both illustrates the Engle and Granger (1987) approach of OLS estimation of a cointegrating model (but see Banerjee *et al.*, 1986), and shows the effects of 'correcting for residual autocorrelation'.

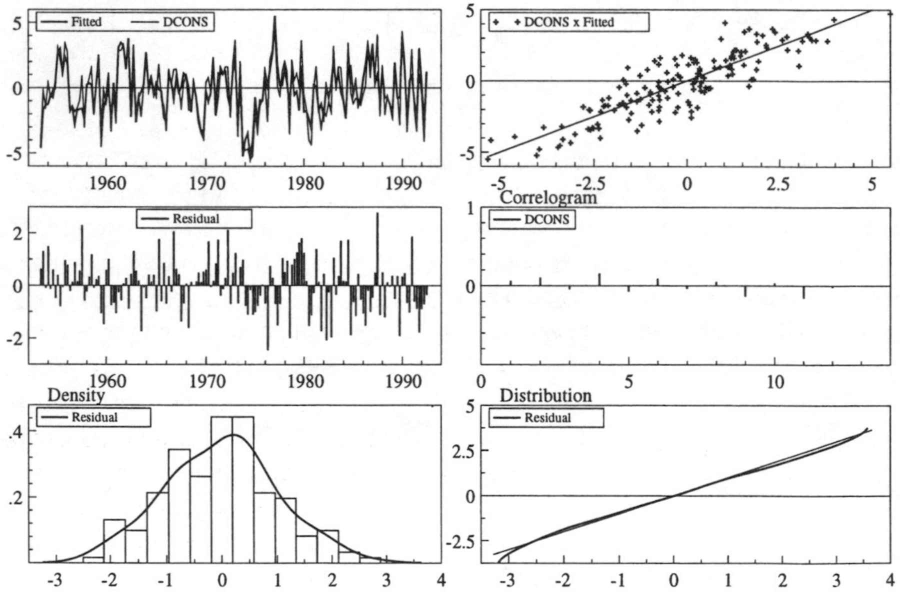

Figure 12.3 Goodness-of-fit measures for ECM.

12.5.6 Non-linear least squares, COMFAC, and RALS

As an alternative to ECM estimation, return to the model of §12.5.3, delete all the lagged variables and estimate the static regression from 1953(2). RALS denotes rth-order autoregressive least squares, and is for estimating equations with valid common factors, so that their dynamics can be validly simplified as an autoregressive error. The residual sum of squares function for RALS is non-linear in the parameters, so an analytic formula for the optimum does not exist, but numerical methods can be used to locate it. In fact, we could always use numerical methods, even for OLS, although it might be a little slow. To illustrate this principle, we first fit an OLS regression by numerical optimization and compare it with the result found by the analytical formula. Access the Non-linear choice on the Model menu and formulate the instructions as:

```
actual = CONS;
fitted = &0 + &1*INC + &2*INFLAT;
&0 = -147.3301;
&1 = 1.152563;
&2 = -2.475206;
```

Estimate from 1953 (2); convergence is fast and the outcomes are almost identical (even though standard errors are calculated numerically, not from the variance formula): in particular, the RSS values match precisely.

```
EQ( 5) Modelling actual by NLS  (using DATA.IN7)
The present sample is:  1953 (1) to 1992 (3)

Variable      Coefficient    Std.Error  t-value  t-prob PartR^2
&0                -147.33       21.897   -6.728  0.0000  0.2260
&1                 1.1526     0.024521   47.003  0.0000  0.9344
&2                -2.4752      0.20507  -12.070  0.0000  0.4845

Rsq = 0.942098  F(2,155) = 1261 [0.0000]   s = 3.27725  DW=0.601
RSS = 1664.754066 for 3 variables and 158 observations
```

Following the route at the end of the previous section, for the static model of CONS on INC and INFLAT, the value of the DW statistic suggests a very high degree of residual autocorrelation, not suggestive of cointegration. This ‘problem’ might be ‘corrected’ by removing the autocorrelation, so we consider that possibility next. Recall the static model, and estimate from 1953(2) using Autoregressive Least Squares (RALS). At the RALS estimation dialog, use Grid to graph the RSS (divided by T) as a function of the first-order autoregressive error parameter. Multiple optima are quite common and can be revealed by this procedure. Here, you will find that the optimum is on the boundary at unity – not an auspicious start. Use Estimate to start the numerical optimization.

```
EQ( 6) Modelling CONS by RALS
The present sample is:  1953 (2) to 1992 (3)

Variable      Coefficient    Std.Error  t-value  t-prob
Constant           403.49       34.868   11.572  0.0000
INC               0.51988     0.035482   14.652  0.0000
INFLAT           -0.72464      0.24489   -2.959  0.0036
Uhat_1            0.98835     0.014499   68.167  0.0000

Sy(t)sq = 28751.5   s = 1.43855
F = 318.6931763 for 3 vars and 158 obs (4 parameters)
```

```
Roots of the Error Polynomial
          0.9884
```

Consider these results in the light of §12.3.7, and use the *RSS* value to calculate a likelihood ratio test of COMFAC against the unrestricted dynamic model in §12.5. The evidence fits like a glove: no COMFAC, but ECM. Figure 12.4 shows the graphical output.

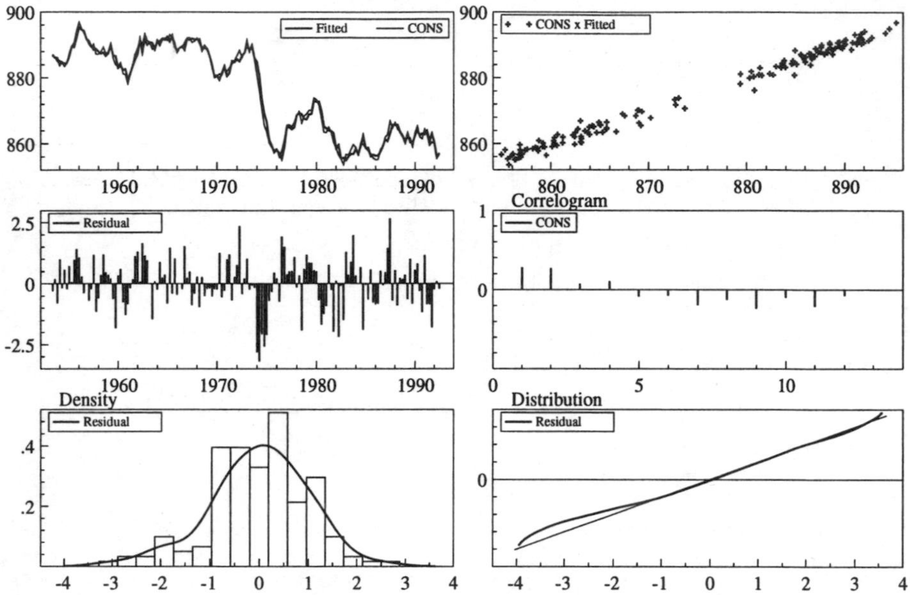

Figure 12.4 Goodness-of-fit measures for RALS.

12.6 Econometrics concepts

12.6.1 Innovations and white noise

It is possible to obtain a significant value on a COMFAC test, yet the residuals of the resulting RALS model be white noise according to the residual correlogram (Portmanteau) statistic; such an outcome illustrates a non-innovation white-noise process. The former (COMFAC rejects) entails that a better model can be developed on the same information (that is, one that does not impose COMFAC) so the error is not an innovation. The latter shows the same error to be white noise (not serially correlated).

An alternative illustration of that distinction can be created by dropping the ECM term from the model in §12.5. The correlogram statistic can be insignificant, but the omitted-variable test option shows that the ECM term still matters, so that the residuals are not an innovation against lagged levels information (see Davidson *et al.*, 1978, and Hendry and von Ungern-Sternberg, 1981, for empirical examples).

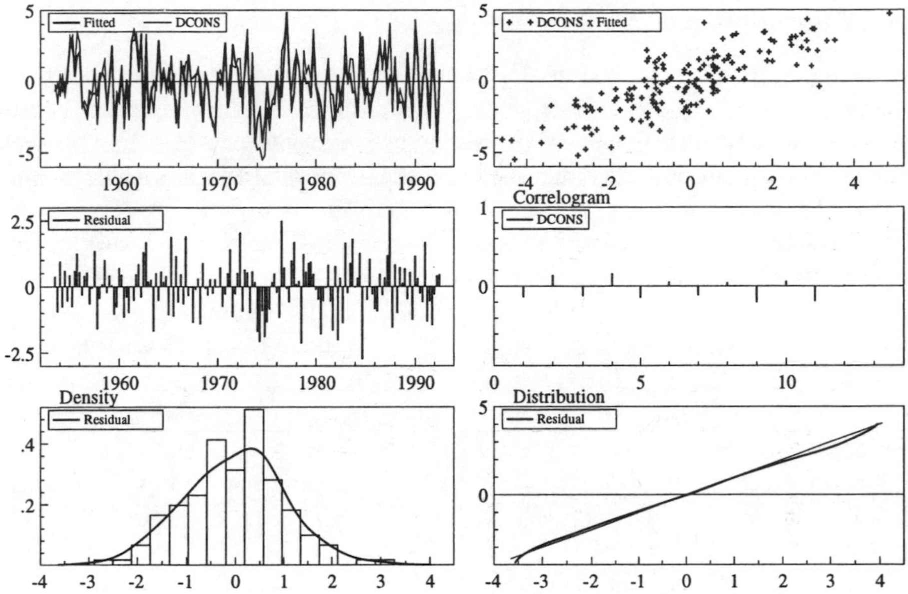

Figure 12.5 Mis-specified ECM with near white-noise residuals.

Delete the error correction term from the model in §12.5.5 and add in the 1-period lags of the three differences to produce:

```
EQ( 7) Modelling DCONS by OLS
The present sample is:  1953 (3) to 1992 (3)

Variable   Coefficient Std.Error  t-value t-prob     HCSE   PartRsq
Constant    -0.064451    0.10420   -0.619  0.5372  0.10447  0.0025
DINC          0.52735   0.032622   16.165  0.0000  0.02909  0.6338
DINFLAT      -0.52953    0.28833   -1.837  0.0682  0.29489  0.0218
DCONS_1       0.26043   0.073691    3.534  0.0005  0.08587  0.0764
DINC_1     -0.0078689   0.049626   -0.159  0.8742  0.05149  0.0002
DINFLAT_1    -0.74406    0.28221   -2.636  0.0093  0.27220  0.0440

Rsq = 0.66297 F(5,151) = 59.407 [0.0000] s = 1.29654 DW = 2.27
RSS = 253.8316094 for 6 variables and 157 observations
```

Figure 12.5 reports the corresponding graphical information: the correlogram is fairly flat and close to that of a white-noise process even though the errors contain the ECM, which would have a t-value of about 10 if entered directly in the model. An appropriate test for autocorrelated errors would reject. Also see the discussion in Hendry (1995a), and in §15.2 and §15.3.

12.6.2 Exogeneity

The analytic notion is described in §14.5.2 and recurs in §15.5: for a fuller treatment see Engle *et al.* (1983). To illustrate, in the present data set there is no valid consumption function with income weakly exogenous for invariant parameters of interest (CONS and INC are simultaneously determined); however, instrumental variables methods (discussed below) could be used to investigate such a difficulty.

The comparison of §12.4.3 and §12.4.4 is illuminating since $\mathbf{x}_t$ is not weakly exogenous for $\boldsymbol{\beta}$ in the latter. The required condition is that $\boldsymbol{\beta}$ can be learned from the conditional model alone, without loss of information. That this fails here is clear on the conventional notion of exogeneity since $\mathsf{E}[\mathbf{x}_t\epsilon_t] \neq \mathbf{0}$ in §12.4.4. Nevertheless, regressing y_t on $\mathbf{x}_t$ delivers a coefficient vector $\boldsymbol{\alpha}$ (say) such that $\mathsf{E}[y_t|\mathbf{x}_t] = \boldsymbol{\alpha}'\mathbf{x}_t$ and so $y_t = \boldsymbol{\alpha}'\mathbf{x}_t + \xi_t$ where $\mathsf{E}[\mathbf{x}_t\xi_t] = \mathbf{0}$. Indeed, $\mathbf{x}_t$ is weakly exogenous for $\boldsymbol{\alpha}$, but $\boldsymbol{\alpha}$ is, of course, not the parameter of interest. Let $\mathbf{x}_t = \boldsymbol{\Gamma}\mathbf{x}_{t-1} + \boldsymbol{\nu}_t$, so $x_t^e = \boldsymbol{\Gamma}\mathbf{x}_{t-1}$, and let $\mathsf{E}[\boldsymbol{\nu}_t\boldsymbol{\nu}_t'] = \boldsymbol{\Omega}$. In §12.4.4, $\mathsf{E}[\boldsymbol{\nu}_t\eta_s] = \mathbf{0}\,\forall t, s$ is not sufficient for $\mathbf{x}_t$ to be weakly exogenous for $\boldsymbol{\beta}$. Under stationarity, letting $\boldsymbol{\Phi} = \mathsf{E}[\mathbf{x}_t\mathbf{x}_t']$, then:

$$\boldsymbol{\alpha} = \left(\mathsf{E}[\mathbf{x}_t\mathbf{x}_t']\right)^{-1}\left(\mathsf{E}[\mathbf{x}_t y_t]\right) = \left(\mathbf{I}_k - \boldsymbol{\Phi}^{-1}\boldsymbol{\Omega}\right)\boldsymbol{\beta},$$

and so depends on $\boldsymbol{\Gamma}$ and $\boldsymbol{\Omega}$. Thus, $\boldsymbol{\beta}$ cannot be obtained from $\boldsymbol{\alpha}$ without knowledge of $(\boldsymbol{\Gamma},\ \boldsymbol{\Omega})$, which are the parameters of the $\{\mathbf{x}_t\}$ process, showing that the requirements for weak exogeneity are not satisfied. This case is most easily derived for a scalar x-process, where $\Phi = \Omega/\left(1 - \Gamma^2\right)$ and $\alpha = \Gamma^2\beta$. The outcome can also be related to errors-in-variables models, such as permanent income. Finally, to show that the presence or absence of $\mathbf{x}_t$ in the equation is not germane to its weak exogeneity status, §12.4.4 entails that $y_t = \boldsymbol{\beta}'\boldsymbol{\Gamma}\mathbf{x}_{t-1} + \epsilon_t + \boldsymbol{\beta}'\boldsymbol{\nu}_t$ and hence $\mathsf{E}[y_t|\mathbf{x}_{t-1}] = \boldsymbol{\beta}'\boldsymbol{\Gamma}\mathbf{x}_{t-1}$ is a valid specification for regression. However, $\boldsymbol{\beta}$ can be obtained from $\boldsymbol{\beta}'\boldsymbol{\Gamma}$ only if $\boldsymbol{\Gamma}$ is known, which necessitates estimating the marginal model for $\mathbf{x}_t$. That example reveals that $\mathbf{x}_t$ need not be weakly exogenous for the parameter of interest even when it is absent from the equation analysed.

12.6.3 Constancy and invariance

Recursive-estimation techniques are discussed formally in Chapter 13, but PcGive embodies graphical options which make parameter constancy, or its absence, easy to illustrate. The basic idea is straightforward. A tedious way to see if parameters are constant would be to fit the model to the first $M > k$ observations, then to fit it to $M+1$, $M+2$ etc. up to T, yielding $T-M+1$ estimates of each coefficient and its standard error over the sample. Plotting these would reveal any changes relative to the standard error measures. Fortunately, there are clever ways of doing so built into PcGive and we merely have to choose recursive estimation to obtain all the required statistics and associated tests. Use the same model as the final one for DCONS in §12.5.5, and estimate by RLS. Figure 12.6 illustrates the graphical output.

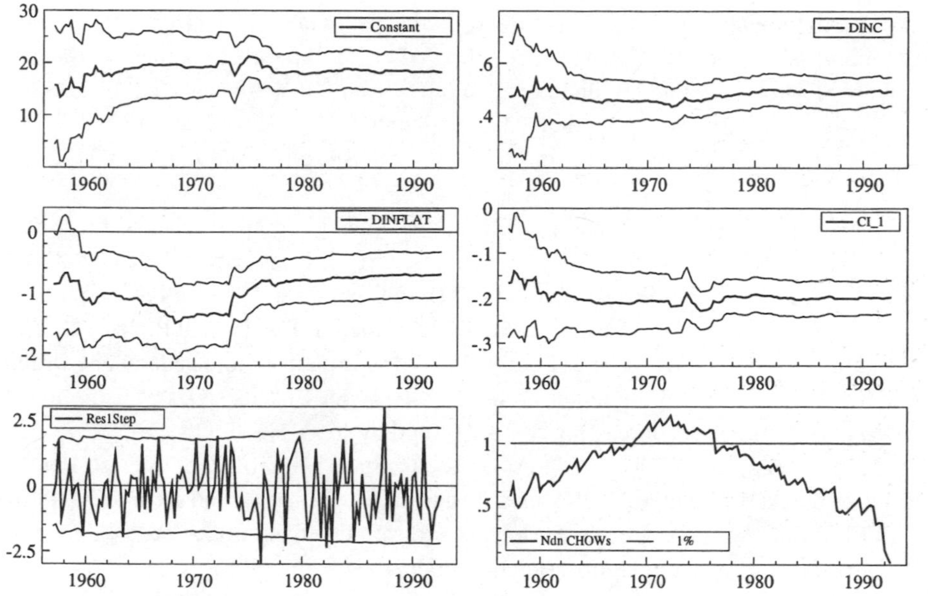

Figure 12.6 Recursive constancy statistics for ECM.

The first four plots are of the coefficient estimates at each point in the sample together with their approximate 95% confidence intervals ($\pm 2SE$ shown on either side); for most of the data set, the estimates are significantly different from zero, and are relatively constant over the sample. The fifth plot is of the 1-step ahead residuals (forecast errors) also with an approximate 95% confidence interval; the confidence bands are again reasonably constant, but increase somewhat around 1974. However, the final plot of the break-point Chow test (see Chow, 1960) shows that constancy is rejected at the 1% level over the oil-crisis period, and looking more carefully at the coefficient plots, the change in the coefficient of ΔINFLAT is just noticeable.

Invariance is more complex to illustrate, so the artificial data set is helpful. (The Appendix shows the DGP for the tutorial data set.) A model of INFLAT on OUTPUT and INFLAT_1 is non-constant at precisely the point at which an autoregression for OUTPUT shows a break, consistent with non-invariance of inflation to excess demand. A more realistic case of invariance analysis is described in Hendry (1988).

12.6.4 Encompassing rival models

Encompassing is easy to illustrate in PcGive, so we first explain the concept and its properties. Consider two rival explanations of a given variable denoted by M_1 and M_2. The question at issue is whether the M_2 model can explain features of the data which the M_1 model cannot. This is a test of M_1 with M_2 providing the alternative to see whether M_2 captures any specific information not embodied in M_1. The converse is whether M_1

can account for all the results found by M_2, and that idea is formalized in the notion of encompassing (see Hendry and Richard, 1982, 1989, Mizon, 1984, and Mizon and Richard, 1986). A congruent undominated model should encompass (that is, account for) previous empirical findings claimed to explain the given dependent variable(s). Encompassing is denoted by $\mathcal{E}$ so if the relevant models are M_1 and M_2, then $M_1 \mathcal{E} M_2$ reads as 'M_1 encompasses M_2'.

The ease of handling general models allows embedding approaches to be almost automatic in PcGive. Encompassing and non-nested hypothesis tests are offered for OLS and IV, based on Cox (1961), Pesaran (1974) and Ericsson (1983), allowing pairs of single equation models to be tested directly. As argued in Hendry and Richard (1989), encompassing essentially requires a simple model to explain a more general one within which it is nested (often the union of the simple model with its rivals); this notion is called parsimonious encompassing and is denoted by $\mathcal{E}_p$.

To apply encompassing procedures, we need to have two models of interest. For the first, use the ADL (1 lag) of CONS on INC and INFLAT, and for the second CONS on OUTPUT with two lags of each. Formulate and estimate them in that order, then from the Model menu, select Encompassing to produce:

```
Encompassing test statistics
The present sample is:  1953 (3) to 1992 (3)

M1 is:         CONS on
Constant    CONS_1    INC       INC_1     INFLAT     INFLAT_1

M2 is:         CONS on
Constant    CONS_1    CONS_2    OUTPUT    OUTPUT_1   OUTPUT_2

Instruments used:
Constant    CONS_1    INC       INC_1     INFLAT     INFLAT_1
CONS_2      OUTPUT    OUTPUT_1  OUTPUT_2

sigma[M1] = 1.08126  sigma[M2] = 2.03616  sigma[Joint] = 1.09367

Model1 v Model2  Form      Test          Form      Model2 v Model1
   0.196121      N(0,1)    Cox           N(0,1)     -46.1559
  -0.192866      N(0,1)    Ericsson IV   N(0,1)      24.6882
   0.607941     Chi^2(4)   Sargan       Chi^2(4)     108.59
   0.148708     F(4,147)   Joint Model  F(4,147)     94.0994
  [ 0.9633]                                        [ 0.0000]
```

The tests produced are those due to Cox (1961), (distributed asymptotically as $\mathsf{N}(0, 1)$ on the null of encompassing; Ericsson (1983) (an IV-based test with the same limiting distribution), another IV test owing to Sargan (1959) distributed as χ^2 with the degrees of freedom shown, and the F-test for each model being a valid simplification of the linear union of the two models under test. The second model clearly does not encompass the first on any of the tests whereas the first is not rejected by the second. We conclude that the second is inferentially redundant and the first remains undominated. Since empirical models can be designed to satisfy a range of criteria (see §12.9), encompassing tests against models designed by other investigators offer a useful check against spurious findings.

12.7 Instrumental variables

The method of instrumental variables was developed to handle endogenous regressors using limited information. It may happen that in the linear equation (12.14), $\mathsf{E}[y_t|\mathbf{x}_t] \neq \mathbf{x}_t'\boldsymbol{\beta}$ so that $\mathsf{E}[\mathbf{x}_t\epsilon_t] \neq \mathbf{0}$. Then OLS estimation is not consistent for $\boldsymbol{\beta}$. Assume there is a $k \times 1$ vector $\mathbf{z}_t$ such that:

$$\mathsf{E}[y_t \mid \mathbf{z}_t] = \mathsf{E}[\mathbf{x}_t \mid \mathbf{z}_t]' \boldsymbol{\beta} \tag{12.20}$$

so $\mathsf{E}[\mathbf{z}_t'\epsilon_t] = \mathbf{0}$. The role of $\mathbf{z}_t$ is purely instrumental in estimating $\boldsymbol{\beta}$ and its use leads to instrumental variables (IV) estimators as follows (the case of more than k instruments is handled by PcGive, but $\boldsymbol{\beta}$ is not estimable when there are fewer than k instruments).

We only consider the case where $\mathsf{E}[\mathbf{Z}'\boldsymbol{\epsilon}] = \mathbf{0}$ but in $\mathbf{y} = \mathbf{X}\boldsymbol{\beta} + \boldsymbol{\epsilon}$, $\mathsf{E}[\mathbf{X}'\boldsymbol{\epsilon}] \neq \mathbf{0}$. Premultiply (12.15) by $\mathbf{Z}'$:

$$\mathbf{Z}'\mathbf{y} = \mathbf{Z}'\mathbf{X}\boldsymbol{\beta} + \mathbf{Z}'\boldsymbol{\epsilon} \tag{12.21}$$

When $\text{rank}\left(T^{-1}\mathbf{Z}'\mathbf{X}\right) = k$, so that the matrix is invertible (which is also sufficient to identify $\boldsymbol{\beta}$: see White, 1984) then $\text{rank}\left(T^{-1}\mathbf{Z}'\mathbf{Z}\right) = k$. Thus, setting $\mathbf{Z}'\boldsymbol{\epsilon} = \mathbf{0}$:

$$\tilde{\boldsymbol{\beta}} = \left(\mathbf{Z}'\mathbf{X}\right)^{-1} \mathbf{Z}'\mathbf{y} \tag{12.22}$$

which is the instrumental variables estimator. In large samples, its variance matrix is estimated by:

$$\tilde{\sigma}_\epsilon^2 \left[\mathbf{X}'\mathbf{Z}\left(\mathbf{Z}'\mathbf{Z}\right)^{-1}\mathbf{Z}'\mathbf{X}\right]^{-1} \tag{12.23}$$

where:

$$\tilde{\boldsymbol{\epsilon}} = \mathbf{y} - \mathbf{X}\tilde{\boldsymbol{\beta}} \text{ and } \tilde{\sigma}_\epsilon^2 = \frac{\tilde{\boldsymbol{\epsilon}}'\tilde{\boldsymbol{\epsilon}}}{T-k}. \tag{12.24}$$

Check that the formulae collapse to the OLS outcomes when $\mathbf{Z} = \mathbf{X}$. However, statistics like R^2 are not so easily defined.

The fourth case of §12.4 can be compared to the third when the IVs are variables in $\mathcal{I}_{t-1}$. When §12.4.3 holds with ϵ_t being an innovation against $\mathcal{I}_{t-1}$ then $\mathsf{E}[y_t|\mathbf{x}_t] = \mathbf{x}_t'\boldsymbol{\beta}$ implies that $\mathsf{E}[y_t|\mathcal{I}_{t-1}] = \boldsymbol{\beta}'\mathsf{E}[\mathbf{x}_t|\mathcal{I}_{t-1}]$ also. The converse does not hold, however, otherwise types §12.4.3 and §12.4.4 would coincide. Check that you can prove this claim. Since the failure of OLS is owing to the $\{\mathbf{x}_t\}$ process being informative about the parameter of interest, the analysis of exogeneity above is directly relevant to clarifying when regression can be used.

The ECM model of CONS in fact has INC endogenous owing to contemporaneous feedback, so we now estimate it by recursive IV, using 1-lagged values of ΔCONS and

ΔINC as instruments, as well as the other regressors (ΔINFLAT and the CI_1). The full sample estimates and test statistics are:

```
EQ( 9) Modelling DCONS by IVE
The present sample is:  1953 (3) to 1992 (3)

Variable       Coefficient     Std.Error  t-value  t-prob
DINC               0.44045      0.13227     3.330  0.0011
DINFLAT           -0.61811      0.27140    -2.278  0.0241
CI_1              -0.20016      0.020261   -9.879  0.0000
Constant          18.535        1.8843      9.837  0.0000

Additional Instruments used:
  DCONS_1     DINC_1

s = 1.11086  DW = 1.9
RSS = 188.804732 for 4 variables and 157 observations
2 endogenous and 3 exogenous variables with 5 instruments
Reduced Form s = 1.92016
Specification  Chisq(1) =       0.5315 [0.4660]
Testing b = 0: Chisq(3) =       155.66 [0.0000] **
```

As can be seen by comparing with the earlier OLS results, the coefficients of INC and INFLAT are smaller, and their standard errors much larger. The ECM coefficient is somewhat larger. The value of s is not much altered, but the much larger value of the 'reduced form' s (which measures the fit from regressing CONS on the instruments) shows the importance of contemporaneous information. The specification χ^2 tests for the independence of the instruments and the errors (see §17.2.3 and Sargan, 1958) does not reject, and the diagnostic tests yield similar outcomes to OLS. The goodness-of-fit plots are also similar to those for OLS and we conclude this section with the recursive statistics graphs (no equivalent of the Chow tests is provided for IV) shown in Figure 12.7. The parameters are reasonably constant, although that for INFLAT still shows signs of changing around the oil crisis.

12.8 Inference and diagnostic testing

Many aspects of inference and testing have occurred above, so a preliminary knowledge was implicitly assumed throughout. Formal derivations will not be presented (see Godfrey, 1988) but the intuition behind the Lagrange Multiplier (LM)-test for residual autocorrelation, ARCH etc. is useful. These statistics are essentially extrapolating from the likelihood function value when a parameter has been restricted (usually to zero) to what the likelihood value would be when the parameter was estimated. When the likelihood is quadratic, the score is linear and the extrapolation is completely successful (that is, the outcome is the same as a likelihood-ratio test). Asymptotically, as likelihoods are quadratic, LM-tests become fully powerful.

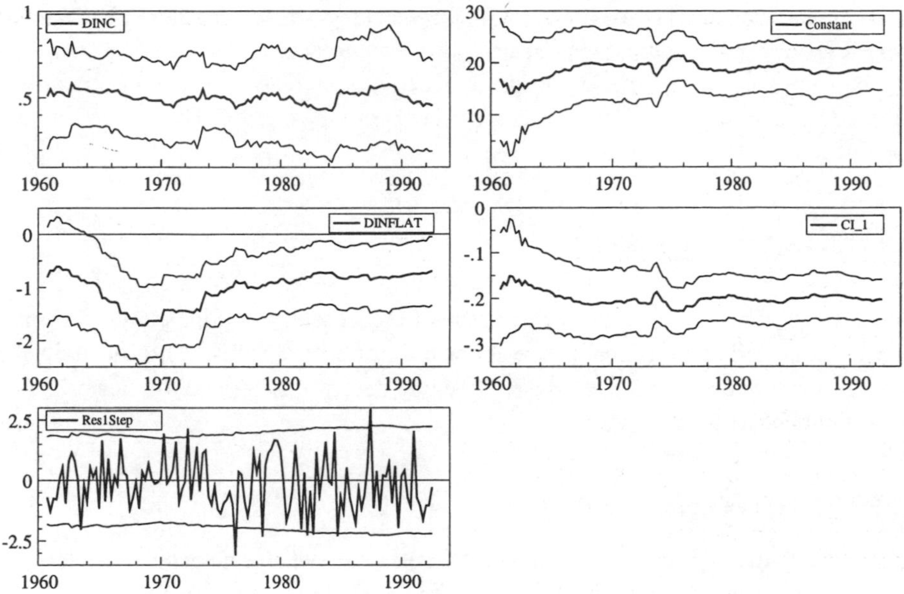

Figure 12.7 Recursive constancy statistics for IV estimation.

However, some statistics are LM-tests only under restrictive assumptions: for example, the Durbin–Watson test is an LM-test when the regressors are fixed, but ceases to be correct for lagged endogenous variables. An issue worth showing empirically is the flattening of the residual correlogram in models with lagged dependent variables. To do so, we contrast the residual autoregression coefficients and the associated F-test with those entailed in the equivalent length LM-test. When the model is mis-specified as a partial adjustment of CONS on INC and INFLAT, we find:

```
Autoregression  for Residual: 2 lags from 1 to 2
The present sample is:  1953 (4) to 1992 (3)
          Constant      Lag  1      Lag  2
Coeff.   -0.004131      0.1697      0.1127
Std.Err     0.1027        0.08     0.08067

RSS = 231.5868661     s = 1.20233     R2 = 0.0486202
F(2,153) = 3.90953 [0.0221] *

Testing for Error Autocorrelation from lags 1 to 2
Chi2(2) = 9.118 [0.0105] * and F-Form(2,152) = 4.6545 [0.0109] *

Error Autocorrelation Coefficients:
            Lag  1      Lag  2
Coeff.      0.2009      0.1467
```

Both tests happen to reject the null, but the LM F-test is about 20% larger, and its first-order autoregressive coefficient is about 25% larger.

A similar bias occurs even if there is no lagged dependent variable but $\mathbf{x}_t$ is Granger-caused by y (see Granger, 1969): again this is easy to demonstrate. Many other tests can be computed using PcGive, but more generally, inference is better illustrated via Monte Carlo, so we turn to considering the methodology of modelling, of which mis-specification tests are one aspect.

12.9 Model selection

Some discussion and illustration of the issue of model selection is imperative if econometrics is to find any practical use, even as a set of critical skills. Unfortunately, the topic is a vast one and prone to disaster. We first describe the general framework, then consider model design.

12.9.1 Three levels of knowledge

It is useful to distinguish between the three levels of knowledge potentially available in a theoretical analysis. Write the data set as $\mathbf{X}_T^1 = (\mathbf{x}_1 \ldots \mathbf{x}_T)$ and denote the DGP by $\mathsf{D_X}\left(\mathbf{X}_T^1|\boldsymbol{\theta}\right)$. Then:

(1) Both $\mathsf{D_X}(\cdot)$ and $\boldsymbol{\theta}$ known corresponds to a probability theory course: that is, given $\mathsf{D_X}(\cdot|\boldsymbol{\theta})$, what xs will be observed and with what probabilities of lying in various intervals or regions? The analyses in the first two sections above are examples of this level of knowledge.

(2) $\mathsf{D_X}(\cdot)$ known and $\boldsymbol{\theta}$ unknown corresponds to an estimation and inference course, that is, given $\mathbf{X}_T^1$ and knowledge of $\mathsf{D_X}(\cdot)$, how should one estimate $\boldsymbol{\theta}$? This route leads on to likelihood, maximum likelihood estimation etc. and characterizes the state of knowledge of Chapter 13.

(3) Both $\mathsf{D_X}(\cdot)$ and $\boldsymbol{\theta}$ unknown corresponds to a modelling course: that is, given only $\mathbf{X}_T^1$ how do we discover, design or develop useful models of the observables, and what criteria characterize useful etc.?

Since (3) is the realistic situation in empirical econometrics, §12.5 discussed a number of the background issues. The illustrations fell in an intermediate state, as we knew the DGP but did not use that knowledge – but the reader did not know the DGP.

Two important issues arise once the limited knowledge of (3) is granted: first, the postulated likelihood function for an empirical model will not coincide with the actual density function of the observables; and secondly, models will inevitably be simplifications, not facsimilies of the economic mechanism. Consequently, it is crucial to test empirical claims rigorously and that feature is built into PcGive. Even so, we now examine the problems deriving from the ability to design empirical models to achieve prespecified criteria, despite the DGP not satisfying those criteria.

12.9.2 Modelling criteria

Sections 14.4 and 14.5 will propose a range of relevant criteria for model selection in terms of necessary conditions for congruence. A model is congruent when it matches the available evidence in all the dimensions examined (for example, has innovation, homoscedastic errors, constant parameters etc.). This destructive or evaluation aspect has been covered (in part) already in §12.5 above (see Baba, Hendry and Starr, 1992, for an example analyzing US M1 demand).

Information criteria, which penalize for additional parameters more than the degrees of freedom adjustment to $\hat{\sigma}$, are often used but assume that many of the necessary criteria are satisfied. They are related to the use of R^2, $\bar{\mathsf{R}}^2$ and $\hat{\sigma}^2$ as model-selection criteria, and in finite samples seem preferable to those. PcGive provides three, namely the Schwarz, Hannan–Quinn, and final prediction error criteria (see Chapter 17), and uses the Schwarz criterion in general-to-specific modelling for selecting between congruent simplifications.

12.9.3 Implicit model design

The reinterpretation of RALS estimation, following a significant residual autocorrelation test, as covert or implicit design should now be clear. Irrespective of the cause of the residual autocorrelation, a high enough order process fitted to the residuals can remove it – and hence designs the model according to a white-noise selection criterion. In the discussion of COMFAC, we noted that the order of hypothesis testing was incorrect. More generally, we saw the problems with unstructured searches such as simple-to-general at the start of this chapter. A simple model of a complicated process can be made to 'work' by selecting a particular criterion (for example, white-noise residuals) and an associated test statistic, then successively correcting the problem until the test is insignificant. However, a second test (for example, COMFAC, or constancy) may reject, forcing the entire exercise up to that point to be discarded, or lead to an unfounded strategy of patching the next mistake. Rejection means that all previous inferences were invalid, including even the existence of the initial problem. The apparent residual autocorrelation (say) could derive from the wrong functional form (linear instead of log), or parameter change. Also, alternative routes begin to multiply because simple-to-general is a divergent branching process. There are many possible solutions to each rejection, but the model evolves differently depending on which are selected and in what order. Moreover, when do you stop testing or correcting previous rejections? There are obvious dangers in stopping at the first non-rejection (see the analysis of selecting the order of an autoregressive process in Anderson, 1971).

Conversely, with a predefined stopping point (that is, a general model in the background), a more coherent strategy is possible. The ordering of hypothesis tests is often clearer, rejections do not lead to a loss of previous work, and the tests are nested. Once the initial general model is rigorously tested for congruence, later tests are of reductions, not of model validity. Further, it is clear when to stop: when the selected model parsimoniously encompasses the initial general model but fails to do so on further simplification. Of course, if the initial model is non-congruent, there is no alternative to a generalization, but that is not a telling argument: a simpler starting point would fare even less well.

12.9.4 Explicit model design

Consequently, PcGive is easiest to use for sequential simplification following the testing for congruence of the initial general model (often called the statistical model: see Spanos, 1986). Why simplify? We consider that parsimony is essential for test power and for interpretability, and is often found to sustain parameter constancy. Collinearity is not the driving force: we saw above that models can be designed to have orthogonal parameters, however many regressors there are. On the other hand, orthogonality is useful for robustness and for testing for the marginal significance of each variable in isolation (that is, without strong *ceteris paribus* assumptions) as well as for interpretability. Thus, we aim to conclude with parsimonious models which have orthogonal regressors as well as satisfying the necessary conditions for both congruence and encompassing.

Models can also be designed to be consistent with the available economic theory, which leads to the concept of an econometric model (which again must be congruent and should parsimoniously encompass the statistical model). Section 14.5.7 discusses sequential simplification in the theory of reduction (the Progressmenu tracks explicit design). It can be useful to retain a subset of data throughout (for example, by initially loading only a time subset of the available data), since Neyman–Pearson testing for quality control can then be undertaken at the end of the analysis (and what would you do next if this led to rejection after six months' work?).

A vast number of other aspects could be illustrated but we hope that the flavour of econometric modelling is both well established and has proved interesting. Chapter 14 discusses the theory of reduction, model concepts, the information taxonomy, and modelling more formally, building on Hendry (1987). An overview is presented in Hendry and Richard (1983), and Hendry (1993) provides a collection of papers on modelling methodology. Hendry and Doornik (1994) and Hendry, Neale and Srba (1988) extend the analysis to linear systems modelling, including recursive estimation of simultaneous systems and VARs. Hendry (1988) considers the refutability of the Lucas critique for models with current-dated expectations variables using such techniques. On the rapidly developing subject of cointegration, many of the currently proposed estimators and tests are easily calculated (see Engle and Granger, 1987, and Phillips, 1987 among others). The Johansen (1988) procedure is implemented in PcFiml. Monte Carlo is also useful as an illustrative tool, given the difficulty of analytical derivations of sampling distributions; but that is the subject of a separate program (see the companion book on Ox as well as Hendry *et al.*, 1991).

Chapter 13

Statistical Theory

13.1 Introduction

We will review three main statistical tools: regression, maximum likelihood, and least squares. To explain these closely related methods of estimating unknown parameters, we first introduce the normal distribution for one variable, then the bivariate normal distribution, and finally a multivariate normal. A regression is a conditional relation and arises when looking at the conditional distribution of one random variable, denoted Y, given values of another, denoted Z. In a bivariate normal, the regression is linear, so has the form $\mathsf{E}[Y] = \alpha + \beta z$ when $Z = z$, which provides an introductory case. In a multivariate normal, the regression remains linear but involves several given variables, denoted by a vector $\mathbf{z}$.

Such regressions are defined in terms of unknown parameters like α and β, and these require estimation from sample data. When samples are randomly drawn from a common population, and the linear regression holds for that population, then maximum likelihood or least squares will deliver 'good' estimates in general. These methods are described in §13.5 and §13.7.

13.2 Normal distribution

The normal, or Gaussian, density $f_{\mathsf{X}}\left(x|\mu_x, \sigma_x^2\right)$ of a random variable X is defined by:

$$f_{\mathsf{X}}\left(x \mid \mu_x, \sigma_x^2\right) = \left(2\pi\sigma_x^2\right)^{-\frac{1}{2}} \exp\left[-\frac{\left(x-\mu_x\right)^2}{2\sigma_x^2}\right] \qquad (13.1)$$

where $|\mu_x| < \infty$ and $0 < \sigma_x^2 < \infty$ for $x \in \mathbb{R}$. The normal density function reaches a maximum at $x = \mu_x$ and is symmetric about μ_x which is the mean: $\mathsf{E}[X] = \mu_x$. Its spread increases with σ_x^2 which is the variance: $\mathsf{E}[(X-\mu_x)^2] = \sigma_x^2$; the square root $\sigma_x = \sqrt{\sigma_x^2}$ is the standard deviation. The normal distribution is denoted by $X \sim \mathsf{N}\left(\mu_x, \sigma_x^2\right)$, and read as: X is distributed as a normal random variable with mean μ_x and variance σ_x^2.

Let $Y = (X - \mu_x)/\sigma_x$ so that $X = \sigma_x Y + \mu_x$. This linear transform from X to Y alters the density to:

$$f_{\mathsf{y}}(y \mid \cdot) = \left(2\pi\sigma_x^2\right)^{-\frac{1}{2}} \exp\left[-\tfrac{1}{2}\, y^2\right]\sigma_x = (2\pi)^{-\frac{1}{2}} \exp\left[-\tfrac{1}{2}\, y^2\right]. \qquad (13.2)$$

This is the standardized form of the density, denoted by $Y \sim \mathsf{N}(0,1)$. Note that $f_{\mathsf{x}}(x) \geq 0$ since the exponential function is always positive, and that the density integrates to unity:

$$\int_{-\infty}^{\infty} (2\pi)^{-\frac{1}{2}} \exp\left[-\tfrac{1}{2}\, y^2\right] \mathrm{d}y = 1.$$

13.3 The bivariate normal density

Consider two random variables denoted X and W. The correlation $\mathsf{corr}[X, W] = \rho$ between X and W is defined by:

$$\rho = \frac{\mathsf{E}\left[(X-\mu_x)(W-\mu_w)\right]}{\sqrt{\mathsf{E}\left[(X-\mu_x)^2\right]\mathsf{E}\left[(W-\mu_w)^2\right]}} = \frac{\sigma_{xw}}{\sigma_x\sigma_w}$$

where σ_{xw} is the covariance. It can be shown that $-1 \leq \rho \leq 1$. When X and W are distributed according to a standardized bivariate normal distribution, the formula for $f_{\mathsf{x,w}}(x, w \mid \rho)$ is:

$$f_{\mathsf{x,w}}(x, w \mid \rho) = \left(2\pi\sqrt{(1-\rho^2)}\right)^{-1} \exp\left[-\frac{(x^2 - 2\rho x w + w^2)}{2(1-\rho^2)}\right]. \qquad (13.3)$$

Since $\exp[\cdot]$ has a non-positive argument, its value is positive but less than unity, and hence:

$$\left(2\pi\sqrt{(1-\rho^2)}\right)^{-1} \geq f_{\mathsf{x,w}}(x, w) \geq 0. \qquad (13.4)$$

For the standardized bivariate normal distribution, the covariance $\mathsf{E}[XW] = \sigma_{xw} = \rho$, and $\rho = 0$ is necessary and sufficient to ensure independence between X and W.

Linear combinations of jointly normal variables are also normal. The proof is based on deriving the distribution of the random variables $(aX + bW : W)$ where $(X : W)$ is bivariate normal and $a \neq 0$.

13.3.1 Conditional normal

The marginal distribution of W is normal, and from it we can obtain the conditional distribution of X given W denoted $f_{\mathsf{x|w}}(x|w)$. By definition, the marginal density of W is:

$$f_{\mathsf{w}}(w) = \int_{-\infty}^{\infty} f_{\mathsf{x,w}}(x, w)\, \mathrm{d}x. \qquad (13.5)$$

Calculating that expression for the standardized bivariate normal yields:

$$\int_{-\infty}^{\infty} \left(2\pi\sqrt{(1-\rho^2)}\right)^{-1} \exp\left[-\frac{\left(x^2-2\rho xw+w^2\right)}{2\left(1-\rho^2\right)}\right] \mathrm{d}x. \tag{13.6}$$

The term in $[\cdot]$ can be rewritten as $\left[(x-\rho w)^2 + \left(1-\rho^2\right) w^2\right]$ (a result of use below). Since $\exp(a+b) = \exp(a)\exp(b)$, then $\int_{-\infty}^{\infty} f_{\mathsf{x,w}}(x,w)\mathrm{d}x$ is:

$$\begin{aligned} &\left(2\pi\sqrt{(1-\rho^2)}\right)^{-1} \int_{-\infty}^{\infty} \exp\left[-\frac{(x-\rho w)^2}{2\left(1-\rho^2\right)}\right] \cdot \exp\left[-\frac{\left(1-\rho^2\right) w^2}{2\left(1-\rho^2\right)}\right] \mathrm{d}x \\ &= (2\pi)^{-\frac{1}{2}} \exp\left(-\tfrac{1}{2}w^2\right) \int_{-\infty}^{\infty} \left(2\pi\left(1-\rho^2\right)\right)^{-\frac{1}{2}} \cdot \exp\left[-\frac{(x-\rho w)^2}{2\left(1-\rho^2\right)}\right] \mathrm{d}x. \end{aligned} \tag{13.7}$$

The term inside the integral is the density of a normal random variable with mean ρw and standard deviation $\sqrt{(1-\rho^2)}$ and hence the integral is unity. Thus, the marginal distribution of W is the term before the integral, and so is $\mathsf{N}(0,1)$. Note that $(X-\rho W)/\sqrt{(1-\rho^2)}$ and W are independent standardized normal random variables since they have zero means, unit variances, are jointly normal, and have a covariance of:

$$\mathsf{E}\left[\frac{W(X-\rho W)}{\sqrt{(1-\rho^2)}}\right] = 0 \tag{13.8}$$

which checks the density factorization.

13.3.2 Regression

The term inside the integral in (13.7) is the conditional density since it is also true that:

$$f_{\mathsf{x,w}}(x,w) = f_{\mathsf{x|w}}(x \mid w)\, f_{\mathsf{w}}(w) \tag{13.9}$$

Thus:

$$(X \mid W = w) \sim \mathsf{N}\left(\rho w, \left(1-\rho^2\right)\right).$$

The conditional expectation, $\mathsf{E}[X|W=w] = \rho w$, considered as a function of w, is the regression function, and ρ is the regression coefficient. The conditional mean is a linear function of w. Because the random variables are standardized, ρ is also the correlation coefficient (matching the requirement $|\rho| \leq 1$) but in general, the regression coefficient will not be ρ itself as shown below. The other conditional moments can be defined in a similar way, so that $\mathsf{V}[X|W=w]$ is the conditional variance function. For the normal distribution, $\mathsf{V}[X|W=w] = \left(1-\rho^2\right)$ does not depend on w, so the conditional variance is said to be homoscedastic (literally, constant variance).

Reverting to the unstandardized variables, $f_{\mathsf{y,z}}(y,z)$ is:

$$\frac{1}{2\pi\sigma_y\sigma_z\sqrt{1-\rho^2}}\exp\left[-\frac{(y-\mu_y)^2}{2(1-\rho^2)\sigma_y^2}+\frac{\rho(y-\mu_y)(z-\mu_z)}{(1-\rho^2)\sigma_y\sigma_z}-\frac{(z-\mu_z)^2}{2(1-\rho^2)\sigma_z^2}\right] \tag{13.10}$$

The marginal distribution of Z is $\mathsf{N}[\mu_z,\sigma_z^2]$, and by an equivalent factorization to (13.7) since $\rho=\sigma_{yz}/\sigma_y\sigma_z$ and $\sigma_y^2\left[1-\rho^2\right]=\sigma_y^2-(\sigma_{yz})^2/\sigma_z^2$:

$$(Y \mid Z=z)\sim\mathsf{N}\left(\alpha+\beta z,\omega^2\right) \tag{13.11}$$

where:

$$\alpha=(\mu_y-\beta\mu_z),\quad \beta=\left[\frac{\sigma_{zy}}{\sigma_z^2}\right]\quad\text{and } \omega^2=\left[\sigma_y^2-\frac{\sigma_{yz}^2}{\sigma_z^2}\right].$$

In general, therefore, $\beta=\rho\sigma_y/\sigma_z$. There are four important aspects of (13.11). First, for the normal distribution $\mathsf{E}[Y|Z=z]$ is a linear function of z. Unlike the normal distribution, many other distributions do not have linear regression functions, so $\mathsf{E}[Y|Z=z]$ may depend on higher powers of z. Secondly, the parameters of the conditional distribution, namely $\left(\alpha,\beta,\omega^2\right)$ depend on all the moments μ_y, μ_z, σ_y^2, σ_{zy} and σ_z^2 of $f_{\mathsf{y,z}}(y,z)$. However, the parameter sets $\left(\alpha,\beta,\omega^2\right)$ and $\left(\mu_z,\sigma_z^2\right)$ are variation free, in that for any given values of the second, the first set can freely take any values. Further, since σ_{yz}^2/σ_z^2 is non-negative, the variance of the conditional distribution is smaller than that of the unconditional distribution: that is, $\omega^2\le\sigma_y^2$. Finally, we have already commented on homoscedasticity which still holds.

13.4 Multivariate normal

13.4.1 Multivariate normal density

Going beyond the bivariate distribution necessitates matrix formulations, but in many respects these simplify the formulae. Denote the k-dimensional multivariate normal density of a random vector $\mathbf{V}$ of length k by $\mathbf{V}\sim\mathsf{N}_k(\boldsymbol{\mu},\boldsymbol{\Sigma})$ where $\mathsf{E}[\mathbf{V}]=\boldsymbol{\mu}$ is the vector of means (that is, for the ith element $\mathsf{E}[V_i]=\mu_i$), and $\boldsymbol{\Sigma}$ is the variance-covariance matrix of rank k:

$$\mathsf{E}\left[(\mathbf{V}-\boldsymbol{\mu})(\mathbf{V}-\boldsymbol{\mu})'\right]=\boldsymbol{\Sigma} \tag{13.12}$$

(that is, for the $(i,j)^{th}$ element $\mathsf{E}[(V_i-\mu_i)(V_j-\mu_j)]=\sigma_{ij}$). The multivariate normal density function is:

$$f_{\mathsf{v}}(\mathbf{v})=\left[(2\pi)^k|\boldsymbol{\Sigma}|\right]^{-\frac{1}{2}}\exp\left[-\tfrac{1}{2}(\mathbf{v}-\boldsymbol{\mu})'\boldsymbol{\Sigma}^{-1}(\mathbf{v}-\boldsymbol{\mu})\right] \tag{13.13}$$

where $|\boldsymbol{\Sigma}|$ is the determinant of $\boldsymbol{\Sigma}$. When $k=2$, (13.13) specializes to the bivariate case. If all elements of $\mathbf{V}$ are independently and identically distributed (IID), having a normal distribution with mean μ and variance σ^2, we can write this as $\mathbf{V} \sim \mathsf{N}_k\left(\mu\iota, \sigma^2\mathbf{I}\right)$, in which ι is the $k \times 1$ vector of ones, and $\mathbf{I}$ is the $k \times k$ identity matrix. An alternative way of writing this is: $V_i \sim \mathsf{IN}\left(\mu, \sigma^2\right), i = 1, \ldots, k$.

13.4.2 Multiple regression

To obtain multiple regression, partition $\mathbf{v}$, $\boldsymbol{\mu}$ and $\boldsymbol{\Sigma}$ conformably into:

$$\mathbf{v} = \begin{pmatrix} y \\ \mathbf{z} \end{pmatrix}, \ \boldsymbol{\mu} = \begin{pmatrix} \mu_y \\ \boldsymbol{\mu}_z \end{pmatrix} \text{ and } \boldsymbol{\Sigma} = \begin{pmatrix} \sigma_{yy} & \boldsymbol{\sigma}_{zy} \\ \boldsymbol{\sigma}_{yz} & \boldsymbol{\Sigma}_{zz} \end{pmatrix} \tag{13.14}$$

where the sub-vector $\mathbf{z}$ is $(k-1)\times 1$, and $\boldsymbol{\sigma}_{zy} = \boldsymbol{\sigma}'_{yz}$. The conditional distribution of Y given $\mathbf{Z} = \mathbf{z}$ is derived by factorizing the joint distribution. It is common in econometrics to adopt a shorthand where the lower-case letters denote both the outcome and the random variable (when no confusion is likely – but does sometimes ensue), and we will do so henceforth. The marginal distribution of $\mathbf{z}$ is a special case of the general formula in (13.13):

$$f_{\mathsf{z}}(\mathbf{z}) = \left[(2\pi)^{(k-1)} \left|\boldsymbol{\Sigma}_{zz}\right|\right]^{-\frac{1}{2}} \exp\left[-\ \tfrac{1}{2}\ \left(\mathbf{z} - \boldsymbol{\mu}_z\right)' \boldsymbol{\Sigma}_{zz}^{-1} \left(\mathbf{z} - \boldsymbol{\mu}_z\right)\right]. \tag{13.15}$$

To derive the conditional distribution $f_{\mathsf{y}|\mathsf{z}}(y|\mathbf{z})$ of y given $\mathbf{z}$, express $f_{\mathsf{v}}(\cdot)$ in the transformed space of $(y|\mathbf{z})$ and $\mathbf{z}$. From §13.7.5, using partitioned inversion (see §13.7.5 below, or e.g. Hendry, 1995a, if this idea is unfamiliar):

$$\boldsymbol{\Sigma}^{-1} = \begin{pmatrix} \sigma_{yy\cdot z}^{-1} & -\sigma_{yy\cdot z}^{-1}\boldsymbol{\sigma}_{yz}\boldsymbol{\Sigma}_{zz}^{-1} \\ -\boldsymbol{\Sigma}_{zz}^{-1}\boldsymbol{\sigma}_{zy}\sigma_{yy\cdot z}^{-1} & \boldsymbol{\Sigma}_{zz}^{-1}\left(\mathbf{I} + \boldsymbol{\sigma}_{zy}\sigma_{yy\cdot z}^{-1}\boldsymbol{\sigma}_{yz}\boldsymbol{\Sigma}_{zz}^{-1}\right) \end{pmatrix}$$

where $\sigma_{yy\cdot z} = (\sigma_{yy} - \boldsymbol{\sigma}_{yz}\boldsymbol{\Sigma}_{zz}^{-1}\boldsymbol{\sigma}_{zy})$ and:

$$|\boldsymbol{\Sigma}| = |\boldsymbol{\Sigma}_{zz}| \left|\sigma_{yy} - \boldsymbol{\sigma}_{yz}\boldsymbol{\Sigma}_{zz}^{-1}\boldsymbol{\sigma}_{zy}\right| = |\boldsymbol{\Sigma}_{zz}| \left|\sigma_{yy\cdot z}\right|.$$

Letting $\boldsymbol{\beta}' = \boldsymbol{\sigma}_{yz}\boldsymbol{\Sigma}_{zz}^{-1}$, then $(\mathbf{v} - \boldsymbol{\mu})' \boldsymbol{\Sigma}^{-1} (\mathbf{v} - \boldsymbol{\mu})$ can be factorized as:

$$\begin{aligned} &\left(y - \mu_y\right)^2 \sigma_{yy\cdot z}^{-1} - 2\left(\mathbf{z} - \boldsymbol{\mu}_z\right)' \boldsymbol{\beta}\sigma_{yy\cdot z}^{-1}\left(y - \mu_y\right) \\ &+ \left(\mathbf{z} - \boldsymbol{\mu}_z\right)' \boldsymbol{\beta}\sigma_{yy\cdot z}^{-1}\boldsymbol{\beta}'\left(\mathbf{z} - \boldsymbol{\mu}_z\right) + \left(\mathbf{z} - \boldsymbol{\mu}_z\right)' \boldsymbol{\Sigma}_{zz}^{-1}\left(\mathbf{z} - \boldsymbol{\mu}_z\right), \end{aligned}$$

since $(y - \mu_y)\sigma_{yy\cdot z}^{-1}\boldsymbol{\beta}'(\mathbf{z} - \boldsymbol{\mu}_z)$ is a scalar and so equals its transpose; or on rearranging:

$$\left(y - \mu_y - \boldsymbol{\beta}'\left(\mathbf{z} - \boldsymbol{\mu}_z\right)\right)^2 \sigma_{yy\cdot z}^{-1} + \left(\mathbf{z} - \boldsymbol{\mu}_z\right)' \boldsymbol{\Sigma}_{zz}^{-1}\left(\mathbf{z} - \boldsymbol{\mu}_z\right)$$

Substituting these results in $f_{\mathsf{v}}(\cdot)$, then $f_{\mathsf{y}|\mathsf{z}}(y|\mathbf{z})$ is:

$$\left[2\pi\sigma_{yy\cdot z}\right]^{-\frac{1}{2}} \exp\left[-\ \tfrac{1}{2}\ \frac{\left(y - \alpha - \boldsymbol{\beta}'\mathbf{z}\right)^2}{\sigma_{yy\cdot z}}\right] \tag{13.16}$$

where $\alpha = \mu_y - \boldsymbol{\beta}'\boldsymbol{\mu}_z$, or:

$$(Y \mid \mathbf{Z} = \mathbf{z}) \sim \mathsf{N}\left(\alpha + \boldsymbol{\beta}'\mathbf{z}, \sigma_{yy\cdot z}\right). \quad (13.17)$$

The same four important points noted above hold for (13.17). Now, however, $\mathsf{E}[Y|\mathbf{Z} = \mathbf{z}]$ is a linear function of the vector $\mathbf{z}$, $(\alpha, \boldsymbol{\beta}, \sigma_{yy\cdot z})$ depend on all the moments of $f_{\mathsf{v}}(\cdot)$, and as $\boldsymbol{\sigma}_{yz}\boldsymbol{\Sigma}_{zz}^{-1}\boldsymbol{\sigma}_{zy}$ is non-negative, $\sigma_{yy\cdot z} \leq \sigma_{yy}$.

13.4.3 Functions of normal variables: χ^2, t and F distributions

Three important functions of normally distributed random variables are distributed as the χ^2, t, and F distributions. First we define these three distributions then consider generalizations. Let $Z \sim \mathsf{N}(0,1)$ then:

$$Z^2 \sim \chi^2(1),$$

where $\chi^2(1)$ is the chi-squared distribution with one degree of freedom. For a set of k independent random variables $Z_i \sim \mathsf{IN}(0,1)$:

$$\sum_{i=1}^{k} Z_i^2 \sim \chi^2(k), \quad (13.18)$$

where $\chi^2(k)$ is the χ^2-distribution with k degrees of freedom.

Next, let $X \sim \mathsf{N}\left(\mu_x, \sigma_x^2\right)$ and let $\eta(k)$ be a $\chi^2(k)$ independently distributed from X then:

$$\tau = \frac{(X - \mu_x)\sqrt{k}}{\sigma_x\sqrt{\eta(k)}} \sim \mathsf{t}(k)$$

where $\mathsf{t}(k)$ is Student's t-distribution with k degrees of freedom.

Thirdly, let $\eta_1(k_1)$ and $\eta_2(k_2)$ be two independent chi-squareds of k_1 and k_2 degrees of freedom, then:

$$\phi = \frac{[\eta_1(k_1)/k_1]}{[\eta_2(k_2)/k_2]} \sim \mathsf{F}(k_1, k_2)$$

where $\mathsf{F}(k_1, k_2)$ is the F-distribution with k_1 and k_2 degrees of freedom. Note that $\mathsf{t}(k)^2 \sim \mathsf{F}(1, k)$ by using these three results. All of these distributions have been tabulated (in more modern terms, programmed into computer packages) and occur frequently in empirical research, in the sense that an underlying normal distribution is often assumed.

In the context of the multivariate normal, let $\mathbf{V} \sim \mathsf{N}_k(\boldsymbol{\mu}, \boldsymbol{\Sigma})$, then:

$$\eta(k) = (\mathbf{V} - \boldsymbol{\mu})'\boldsymbol{\Sigma}^{-1}(\mathbf{V} - \boldsymbol{\mu}) \sim \chi^2(k). \quad (13.19)$$

This result follows from the definition of a χ^2 by noting that any positive definite matrix $\boldsymbol{\Sigma}$ can be written as $\boldsymbol{\Sigma} = \mathbf{H}\mathbf{H}'$ where $\mathbf{H}$ is a non-singular lower triangular matrix, so that:

$$\mathbf{H}^{-1}(\mathbf{V} - \boldsymbol{\mu}) = \boldsymbol{\zeta} \sim \mathsf{N}_k(\mathbf{0}, \mathbf{I}), \quad (13.20)$$

and hence from (13.19):

$$\eta(k) = \zeta'\zeta = \sum_{i=1}^{k} \zeta_i^2 \sim \chi^2(k). \tag{13.21}$$

Partition ζ' into the k_1 and k_2 independent components $(\zeta_1' : \zeta_2')$, each of which is normal, then for $k_1 + k_2 = k$:

$$\eta_1(k_1) = \zeta_1'\zeta_1 \sim \chi^2(k_1) \text{ and } \eta_2(k_2) = \zeta_2'\zeta_2 \sim \chi^2(k_2) \tag{13.22}$$

are also independent.

13.5 Likelihood

Assume we have a sample $x_1 \dots x_T$, generated by a sequence of scalar random variables $X_1 \dots X_T$ distributed with multivariate density $f_X(x_1 \dots x_T|\theta)$ which is indexed by one unknown parameter $\theta \in \Theta \subseteq \mathbb{R}$. In empirical research, the underlying parameter(s) are unknown and need to be estimated from the observed outcomes of the random processes. A major tool for accomplishing this is the likelihood function $\mathsf{L}(\cdot)$ defined in terms of the density function of the sample but exchanging the roles of variables and parameters:

$$f_X(x_1 \dots x_T \mid \theta) \propto \mathsf{L}(\theta \mid x_1 \dots x_T) \text{ for } \theta \in \Theta. \tag{13.23}$$

$f_X(\cdot|\theta)$ maps from $\mathbb{R}^T$ to $\mathbb{R}_+$, whereas $\mathsf{L}(\theta|x_1 \dots x_T)$ maps from $\mathbb{R}$ to $\mathbb{R}_+$, so they are linked by a function $\varphi(x)$ which does not depend on θ. Any monotonic transformation of $\mathsf{L}(\cdot)$ is also admissible, and this feature is useful when working with the log-likelihood function, and its first derivative. We set $\varphi(x)$ to unity so that the integral of the likelihood function is unity for a single random variable x:

$$\int_{-\infty}^{\infty} \mathsf{L}(\theta \mid x)\, dx = 1. \tag{13.24}$$

The density function $f_X(\cdot|\theta)$ describes the mechanism generating observations on the random variables. (In other chapters this mechanism is called the data generation process (DGP), and the joint density is then written as $\mathsf{D}_X(\cdot)$.) For an independent sample $x_1 \dots x_T$ of T observations on the random variable X, since the joint probability is then the product of the individual probabilities:

$$f_X(x_1 \dots x_T \mid \theta) = \prod_{t=1}^{T} f_x(x_t \mid \theta). \tag{13.25}$$

For a given value of θ, the outcomes differ owing to random variation which is characterized by the form of $f_x(\cdot)$: for example, the location, spread, and shape of the distribution of a random sample $(x_1 \dots x_T)$ are determined by $f_{\mathsf{x}}(\cdot)$. At different points in the parameter space, the distribution also differs, so when the impact of distinct values of θ on $f_{\mathsf{x}}(\cdot)$ is sufficiently marked, we might hope to infer what the value of θ is, taking into account the randomness arising from $f_{\mathsf{x}}(\cdot)$.

For example, when $X \sim \mathsf{IN}(\mu_x, 1)$ and $\mu_x = 0$, then $|x_t| < 2$ will occur roughly 95% of the time, whereas when $\mu_x = 5$, almost every observed x-value will exceed 2. Thus, the data on X yield information on μ_x, and from a sufficiently large sample we may be able to determine the unknown parameter value precisely.

Since $f_{\mathsf{X}}(\mathbf{x}) \geq 0$ for all $\mathbf{x} = (x_1 \dots x_T)$, we can take the logarithm of $f_{\mathsf{X}}(\mathbf{x}|\theta)$ and hence of $\mathsf{L}(\theta|\cdot)$, which is denoted by $\ell(\theta|\cdot)$:

$$\ell(\theta \mid x_1 \dots x_T) = \log \mathsf{L}(\theta \mid x_1 \dots x_T). \tag{13.26}$$

For an independent sample of T observations on X, using (13.25):

$$\ell(\theta \mid x_1 \dots x_T) = \log \prod_{t=1}^{T} f_{\mathsf{x}}(x_t \mid \theta) = \sum_{t=1}^{T} \ell(\theta \mid x_t). \tag{13.27}$$

Thus, the log-likelihood of an independent sample is the sum of the individual log-likelihoods.

13.6 Estimation

Maximum likelihood estimation (MLE) locates the value $\hat{\theta}$ of θ which produces the highest value of the log-likelihood:

$$\hat{\theta} = \underset{\theta \in \Theta}{\operatorname{argmax}}\, \ell(\theta \mid \mathbf{x}) = \underset{\theta \in \Theta}{\operatorname{argmax}} \sum_{t=1}^{T} \ell(\theta \mid x_t) \tag{13.28}$$

where the second equality holds for independent Xs. Since we are considering the sample realization $\mathbf{X} = \mathbf{x}$, $\ell(\theta|\mathbf{x})$ is written with the realization as an argument, but is thought of as a function of the random variable X as in (13.29) below. Thus, it makes sense to take the expectation of $\ell(\theta|\mathbf{x})$, to consider the large sample distribution of functions of $\ell(\theta|\mathbf{x})$ etc.

The form of any MLE depends on $f_{\mathsf{X}}(\cdot)$. If the X_t are IID with a univariate normal distribution, θ is a two dimensional vector denoted by $\boldsymbol{\theta}' = (\mu_x, \sigma_x^2)$ and so:

$$\ell(\boldsymbol{\theta} \mid x_t) = -\tfrac{1}{2} \log(2\pi) - \log(\sigma_x) - \frac{(x_t - \mu_x)^2}{2\sigma_x^2} = \ell_t. \tag{13.29}$$

Hence, for an independent sample $(x_1 \dots x_T)$:

$$\begin{aligned} \ell(\boldsymbol{\theta} \mid \mathbf{x}) &= -\tfrac{T}{2} \log(2\pi) - T\log(\sigma_x) - 2\sigma_x^{-2} \textstyle\sum_{t=1}^{T} (x_t - \mu_x)^2 \\ &= -\tfrac{T}{2} \left(\log(2\pi) + \log(\sigma_x^2) + \sigma_x^{-2} \left[\hat{\sigma}_x^2 + (\mu_x - \hat{\mu}_x)^2 \right] \right) \end{aligned} \tag{13.30}$$

where $\hat{\mu}_x = T^{-1}\sum_{t=1}^{T} x_t$ and $\hat{\sigma}_x^2 = T^{-1}\sum_{t=1}^{T}(x_t - \hat{\mu}_x)^2$. All the sample information is 'concentrated' in $(\hat{\mu}_x, \hat{\sigma}_x^2)$, so these statistics are sufficient for (μ_x, σ_x^2), in that the second line of (13.30) no longer depends explicitly on the $\{x_t\}$. From (13.30), $\ell(\boldsymbol{\theta}|\mathbf{x})$ is maximized by minimizing $[\hat{\sigma}_x^2 + (\mu_x - \hat{\mu}_x)^2]/\sigma_x^2$. Setting $\mu_x = \hat{\mu}_x$ achieves the smallest value of the second component, and as $\hat{\sigma}_x^2$ corresponds to the smallest value of the sum of squares, $\hat{\sigma}_x^2 = \sigma_x^2$ lowers the remaining term to unity. The next section derives the MLE more formally.

13.6.1 The score and the Hessian

When the log-likelihood is differentiable, $\ell(\theta|x)$ can be maximized by differentiating with respect to θ and equating to zero (a necessary condition for a maximum). The first derivative of $\ell(\cdot)$ with respect to θ is the score, denoted by:

$$q(\theta \mid \mathbf{x}) = \frac{\partial \ell(\theta|\mathbf{x})}{\partial \theta} = \sum_{t=1}^{T} \frac{\partial \ell_t(\theta|\mathbf{x})}{\partial \theta} = \sum_{t=1}^{T} q_t(\theta \mid \mathbf{x}) \tag{13.31}$$

where the second and third equalities hold for independent Xs. Solving for $\hat{\theta}$ such that $q(\hat{\theta}) = 0$ yields the MLE (when the second derivative is negative). In the case of the normal distribution illustration (remember that we differentiate with respect to σ^2, not σ):

$$\mathbf{q}(\boldsymbol{\theta} \mid \mathbf{x}) = \begin{pmatrix} q(\mu_x|\mathbf{x}) \\ q(\sigma_x^2|\mathbf{x}) \end{pmatrix} = \begin{pmatrix} T(\hat{\mu}_x - \mu_x)/\sigma_x^2 \\ -\frac{1}{2}T\sigma_x^{-2}\left[1 - \left\{\hat{\sigma}_x^2 + (\hat{\mu}_x - \mu_x)^2\right\}/\sigma_x^2\right] \end{pmatrix} \tag{13.32}$$

Then $\mathbf{q}(\hat{\boldsymbol{\theta}|\mathbf{x}}) = \mathbf{0}$ occurs at $\hat{\boldsymbol{\theta}}' = (\hat{\mu}_x, \hat{\sigma}_x^2)$, where, as before:

$$\hat{\mu}_x = T^{-1}\sum_{t=1}^{T} X_t \ \text{ and } \hat{\sigma}_x^2 = T^{-1}\sum_{t=1}^{T}(X_t - \hat{\mu}_x)^2 \tag{13.33}$$

which are the sample mean and (unadjusted) variance. At the maximum $\hat{\boldsymbol{\theta}}$:

$$\ell\left(\hat{\boldsymbol{\theta}} \mid x\right) = -\tfrac{1}{2}T\left(\log(2\pi) + \log\left(\hat{\sigma}_x^2\right) + 1\right). \tag{13.34}$$

The second derivative of $\ell(\theta|\mathbf{x})$ with respect to θ is the Hessian of the likelihood, and evaluated at $\hat{\theta}$ can be shown to be negative. Differentiate $q(\theta|\mathbf{x})$ with respect to θ once more:

$$H(\theta \mid \mathbf{x}) = \frac{\partial^2 \ell(\theta|\mathbf{x})}{\partial \theta^2} = \sum_{t=1}^{T} \frac{\partial^2 \ell_t(\theta|\mathbf{x})}{\partial \theta^2} = \sum_{t=1}^{T} H_t(\theta \mid \mathbf{x}) \tag{13.35}$$

where the last two equalities hold for independent Xs. Thus, for the example from (13.32):

$$\mathbf{H}(\theta \mid \mathbf{x}) = \begin{pmatrix} -T/\sigma_x^2 & -T(\hat{\mu}_x - \mu_x)/\sigma_x^4 \\ -T(\hat{\mu}_x - \mu_x)/\sigma_x^4 & -T\sigma_x^{-6}\{\hat{\sigma}_x^2 + (\hat{\mu}_x - \mu_x)^2\} + \frac{1}{2}T\sigma_x^{-4} \end{pmatrix} \tag{13.36}$$

and when evaluated at $\hat{\theta}$:

$$\mathbf{H}\left(\hat{\theta} \mid \mathbf{x}\right) = \begin{pmatrix} -T\hat{\sigma}_x^{-2} & 0 \\ 0 & -\frac{1}{2}T\hat{\sigma}_x^{-4} \end{pmatrix},$$

which is negative definite and shows that the parameter estimates are uncorrelated.

13.6.2 Maximum likelihood estimation

The justification for maximum likelihood is that the principle is general, and when the form of the data density is known and the sample size is sufficiently large, MLE usually yields estimators of θ that are as good as can be obtained. We now demonstrate that claim in a simple setting.

13.6.3 Efficiency and Fisher's information

Subject to reasonable regularity conditions, which ensure the required derivatives exist etc., maximum likelihood estimators are consistent, and also tend to be efficient in large samples such that no other method dominates MLE. This last claim can be proved to hold in finite samples for the special class of unbiased estimators defined by $\mathsf{E}[\hat{\theta}] = \theta \; \forall \theta \in \Theta$, and this section outlines the proof. To simplify notation, we drop the reference to x in the arguments. The population value of the parameter is denoted by θ_p.

Five steps are required in the proof when $\ell(\theta)$ is a quadratic function of θ so that $q(\theta)$ is linear in θ. Hence $\mathsf{E}[q(\theta_p)^2] = H(\theta_p) = H$ is constant, and higher-order derivatives vanish: such a condition provides a good approximation in large samples.

(1) Expand $q(\theta_p)$ around $q(\hat{\theta})$ in a Taylor series:

$$q(\theta_p) = q\left(\hat{\theta}\right) + \left.\frac{\mathrm{d}q(\theta)}{\mathrm{d}\theta}\right\rfloor_{\hat{\theta}} \left(\theta_p - \hat{\theta}\right) + \frac{1}{2}\left.\frac{\mathrm{d}^2 q(\theta)}{\mathrm{d}\theta^2}\right\rfloor_{\hat{\theta}} \left(\theta_p - \hat{\theta}\right)^2. \tag{13.37}$$

Since $q(\hat{\theta}) = 0$ and $\mathrm{d}^2 q(\theta)/\mathrm{d}\theta^2 = 0$ as H is constant:

$$q(\theta_p) = H \cdot \left(\theta_p - \hat{\theta}\right) \tag{13.38}$$

so that:

$$\left(\hat{\theta} - \theta_p\right) = -H^{-1} q(\theta_p). \tag{13.39}$$

Consequently, the MLE $\hat{\theta}$ differs from θ_p by a linear function of $q(\theta_p)$. The last expression holds generally but as an approximation when $H(\theta)$ is not constant, needing iterative solution.

(2) Next, $\mathsf{E}[q(\theta_p)] = 0$. Since we solve $q(\hat{\theta}) = 0$ to obtain $\hat{\theta}$, it is important that on average $\mathsf{E}[q(\theta_p)]$ is indeed zero. Taking expectations in (13.38), for linear score functions $q(\theta_p)$, $\mathsf{E}[\hat{\theta}] = \theta_p$, so the MLE is unbiased under our assumptions.

(3) Since $\mathsf{E}[q(\theta_p)] = 0$, the variance of $q(\theta_p)$ is $\mathsf{E}[q(\theta_p)^2] = \mathcal{I}(\theta_p)$ which is Fisher's information. The key result is that:

$$\mathsf{E}\left[q(\theta_p)^2\right] = \mathcal{I}(\theta_p) = -\mathsf{E}\left[H(\theta_p)\right]$$

and hence Fisher's information is the negative of the Hessian ($\ell(\theta|x)$ must be equated with $\mathsf{D}_{\mathsf{X}}(x|\theta)$ in such derivations, although $\ell(\theta|x)$ is specified by the investigator and $\mathsf{D}_{\mathsf{X}}(x|\theta)$ by nature, so take care in practice).

(4) The variance of $\hat{\theta}$ can be obtained from its definition as $\mathsf{E}[(\hat{\theta}-\theta_p)^2]$ and the Taylor-series expansion of $q(\theta_p)$ around $q(\hat{\theta})$. With constant H, from (13.39):

$$\mathsf{E}\left[\left(\hat{\theta}-\theta_p\right)^2\right] = \mathsf{E}\left[H(\theta_p)^{-1} q(\theta_p)^2 H(\theta_p)^{-1}\right] = H^{-1}\mathcal{I}H^{-1} = \mathcal{I}^{-1} \tag{13.40}$$

using (1) and (3). Thus, $\mathsf{V}[\hat{\theta}]$ is the inverse of Fisher's information. This result is of sufficient importance to merit a separate section, which then solves the fifth step.

13.6.4 Cramér–Rao bound

(5) Let $\hat{\alpha}$ be any other unbiased estimator of θ so that $\mathsf{E}[\hat{\alpha}] = \theta_p$ with variance $\mathsf{E}[(\hat{\alpha}-\theta_p)^2] = V$. We now show that $V \geq \mathcal{I}^{-1}$ and hence prove that the MLE is the minimum-variance unbiased estimator here. First, a surprising intermediate result: $\mathsf{E}[q(\theta_p)\hat{\alpha}] = 1\ \forall\hat{\alpha}$ such that $\mathsf{E}[\hat{\alpha}] = \theta_p$. All unbiased estimators have a covariance of unity with the score. This is most easily seen with $\hat{\theta}$ as the unbiased estimator using the results in (1), (2) and (4). Now the squared correlation between $q(\theta_p)$ and $\hat{\alpha}$ is:

$$\mathsf{r}^2 = \frac{\left(\mathsf{E}\left[q(\theta_p)\hat{\alpha}\right]\right)^2}{V\cdot\mathcal{I}} = \frac{1}{V\mathcal{I}}. \tag{13.41}$$

Since a squared correlation must be between 0 and 1, $V\cdot\mathcal{I} \geq 1$ so that $V \geq \mathcal{I}^{-1}$. This result is the Cramér–Rao bound and shows that no unbiased estimator $\hat{\alpha}$ can have a smaller variance than $\mathcal{I}(\theta_p)^{-1}$; since the unbiased MLE had that variance, it is not dominated by any other $\hat{\alpha}$. More generally, the Cramér–Rao bound holds for most MLEs as $T \to \infty$.

13.6.5 Properties of Fisher's information

Several other properties of Fisher's information merit note. First, since under independence $q(\theta_p) = \sum_{t=1}^{T} q_t(\theta_p)$:

$$\begin{aligned}\mathsf{E}\left[q(\theta_p)^2\right] &= \mathsf{E}\left[\left(\sum_{t=1}^{T} q_t(\theta_p)\right)^2\right] = \mathsf{E}\left[\sum_{s=1}^{T}\sum_{t=1}^{T} q_t(\theta_p)\, q_s(\theta_p)\right] \\ &= \sum_{s=1}^{T}\sum_{t=1}^{T} \mathsf{E}\left[q_t(\theta_p)\, q_s(\theta_p)\right].\end{aligned} \tag{13.42}$$

Under independence, $\mathsf{E}[q_t(\theta_p)q_s(\theta_p)] = 0$, but otherwise is non-zero which will pose problems for estimation and inference. Secondly, when $\mathsf{E}[q_t(\theta_p)q_s(\theta_p)] = 0$, (13.42) becomes:

$$\mathsf{E}\left[q(\theta_p)^2\right] = \sum_{t=1}^{T} \mathsf{E}\left[q_t(\theta_p)^2\right] = \sum_{t=1}^{T} \mathcal{I}_t(\theta_p) = \mathcal{I}_{(T)}(\theta_p). \tag{13.43}$$

Thus, Fisher's information is additive for independent random variables. When $\mathsf{E}[q_t(\theta_p)^2]$ is constant over t, then $\mathcal{I}_{(T)}(\theta_p) = T\mathcal{I}_0(\theta_p)$ where $\mathcal{I}_0(\theta_p)$ is Fisher's information for a single sample point. From the fact that $\mathcal{I}_{(T)}(\theta_p)$ is $T\mathcal{I}_0(\theta_p)$, we see that information increases linearly with sample size in this setting. Conversely, when $\mathcal{I}_t(\theta_p)$ is not constant, inference difficulties may again ensue: see the discussion of HCSEs in Chapter 12.

When $\mathcal{I}_t(\theta_p)$ is constant over t, $\mathsf{V}[q(\theta_p)] = T\mathcal{I}_0(\theta_p)$, so when $q(\theta_p)$ is a linear function of θ_p for a normally distributed random variable (as in (13.30) when σ_x^2 is known):

$$q(\theta_p) \sim \mathsf{N}\left(0, T\mathcal{I}_0(\theta_p)\right) \text{ so that } \sqrt{T}q(\theta_p) \sim \mathsf{N}\left(0, \mathcal{I}_0(\theta_p)\right). \tag{13.44}$$

From (13.39), $(\hat{\theta} - \theta_p)$ is a linear function of $q(\theta_p)$, so:

$$\sqrt{T}\left(\hat{\theta} - \theta_p\right) \sim \mathsf{N}\left(0, \mathcal{I}_0(\theta_p)^{-1}\right). \tag{13.45}$$

This result is dependent on many strong assumptions which can be weakened.

Finally, when there is a set of sufficient statistics $g(\mathbf{X})$, since $h(\mathbf{x})$ does not depend on θ, $q(\theta; \mathbf{x})$ is a function of $g(\mathbf{x})$, and hence so is $\mathcal{I}(\cdot)$. Thus, the MLE retains all of the available information.

13.6.6 Estimating Fisher's information

Having established the MLE $\hat{\theta}$ of θ and how to solve for it from $q(\hat{\theta}) = 0$, we now consider how to estimate $\mathsf{V}[\hat{\theta}] = T\mathcal{I}_0(\theta_p)^{-1}$. The first way uses the result that $T\mathcal{I}_0(\theta_p) = -\mathsf{E}[H(\theta_p)]$, which holds more generally than the quadratic log-likelihood considered above. On replacing θ_p by $\hat{\theta}$:

$$\widehat{\mathsf{V}\left[\hat{\theta}\right]} = -H\left(\hat{\theta}\right)^{-1}. \tag{13.46}$$

Since $\hat{\theta}$ converges on θ_p as $T \to \infty$ owing to consistency, whereas from (13.45), $\sqrt{T}(\hat{\theta}-\theta_p)$ has a well-defined distribution, then $-T[H(\hat{\theta})^{-1}]$ tends to $\mathcal{I}_0(\theta_p)^{-1}$.

However, $q(\hat{\theta})^2$ cannot be used as an estimator of $\mathsf{V}[\hat{\theta}]$ since $q(\hat{\theta}) = 0$. Nevertheless, since $q(\hat{\theta}) = \sum_{t=1}^{T} q_t(\hat{\theta})$, and $q_t(\hat{\theta}) \neq 0 \;\forall t$, the estimator:

$$\widehat{\mathsf{V}\left[\hat{\theta}\right]} = \sum_{t=1}^{T} q_t\left(\hat{\theta}\right)^2 \tag{13.47}$$

is feasible. Later, we confront the issues which arise when modelling data, since in any realistic application, the form of $f_{\mathsf{X}}(\mathbf{x}|\theta)$ is unknown and we cannot be sure that the postulated likelihood function is proportional to the actual data density. Many of the above results depend on that identity, and important practical issues arise when its validity is uncertain.

13.7 Multiple regression

Since linear models play a major role in econometrics, we consider the empirical counterpart of regression. This section formulates the conditional multiple regression model in §13.7.1, and the least squares estimator of its parameters in §13.7.2, followed by distributional results in §13.7.3. Parameter subset estimation is developed in §13.7.4, and partitioned inversion in §13.7.5. Finally, multiple and partial correlation are discussed in §13.7.6 and §13.7.7.

13.7.1 The multiple regression model

The notation adopted for the linear regression model, viewed as the mechanism which generated the observed data, is:

$$y_t = \boldsymbol{\beta}'\mathbf{x}_t + u_t \text{ with } u_t \sim \mathsf{IN}\left(0, \sigma_u^2\right) \tag{13.48}$$

where $\boldsymbol{\beta} = (\beta_1 \ldots \beta_k)' \in \mathbb{R}^k$ is the $k \times 1$ parameter vector of interest and $\mathbf{x}_t = (x_{1t} \ldots x_{kt})'$. Then $\boldsymbol{\beta}'\mathbf{x}_t = \sum_{i=1}^{k} \beta_i x_{it}$. One of the elements in $\mathbf{x}_t$ is unity with the corresponding parameter being the intercept in (13.48). We interpret (13.48) as a regression equation, based on a joint normal distribution for $(y_t : \mathbf{x}_t')$ conditional on $\mathbf{x}_t$ so that from above:

$$\mathsf{E}\left[y_t \mid \mathbf{x}_t\right] = \boldsymbol{\beta}'\mathbf{x}_t \text{ with } \mathsf{E}\left[\mathbf{x}_t u_t\right] = \mathbf{0}.$$

Hence $\mathsf{E}[(y_t - \boldsymbol{\gamma}'\mathbf{x}_t)^2]$ is minimized at σ_u^2 by the choice of $\boldsymbol{\gamma} = \boldsymbol{\beta}$. Chapter 14 considers the conditions necessary to sustain a factorization of a joint density into a conditional model of y_t given $\mathbf{x}_t$, and a marginal model for $\mathbf{x}_t$ which is then ignored, and Chapter 12 considers other interpretations of linear equations like (13.48) and their implications.

Grouping the observations so that $\mathbf{y}' = (y_1 \dots y_T)$ and $\mathbf{X}' = (\mathbf{x}_1 \dots \mathbf{x}_T)$, which is a $T \times k$ matrix with rank($\mathbf{X}$) $= k$ and $\mathbf{u}' = (u_1 \dots u_T)$:

$$\mathbf{y} = \mathbf{X}\boldsymbol{\beta} + \mathbf{u} \;\text{ with }\; \mathbf{u} \sim \mathsf{N}_T\left(\mathbf{0}, \sigma_u^2 \mathbf{I}\right). \tag{13.49}$$

To simplify the derivations, we assume that $\mathsf{E}[\mathbf{y}|\mathbf{X}] = \mathbf{X}\boldsymbol{\beta}$, and hence $\mathsf{E}[\mathbf{X}'\mathbf{u}] = \mathbf{0}$. Although conditioning on $\mathbf{X}$ is too strong to be justifiable in economics, and essentially entails an experimental setting, most of the results hold in large samples under weaker assumptions. The assumptions about $\mathbf{u}$ are almost equally strong, but less objectionable in practice given the discussion in Chapter 14.

13.7.2 Ordinary least squares

The algebra of what is conventionally called ordinary least squares (OLS) estimation can now be established: these algebraic results do not depend on the actual statistical status of $\mathbf{X}$, and hold even when conditioning is invalid. The OLS estimator is also the MLE under our present assumptions (see §13.6.2). OLS estimation seeks to find the value $\widehat{\boldsymbol{\beta}}$ of $\boldsymbol{\beta}$ which minimizes the quadratic function:

$$h(\boldsymbol{\beta}) = (\mathbf{y} - \mathbf{X}\boldsymbol{\beta})'(\mathbf{y} - \mathbf{X}\boldsymbol{\beta}). \tag{13.50}$$

Either by differentiating $h(\boldsymbol{\beta})$ with respect to $\boldsymbol{\beta}$ and solving the resulting expression equated to zero, or using the sample analogue of $\mathsf{E}[\mathbf{X}'\mathbf{u}] = \mathbf{0}$, namely $\mathbf{X}'(\mathbf{y} - \mathbf{X}\widehat{\boldsymbol{\beta}}) = \mathbf{0}$, the best value is given by:

$$\widehat{\boldsymbol{\beta}} = (\mathbf{X}'\mathbf{X})^{-1}\mathbf{X}'\mathbf{y}. \tag{13.51}$$

It can be verified that the value $\widehat{\boldsymbol{\beta}}$ of $\boldsymbol{\beta}$ in (13.51) minimizes $h(\boldsymbol{\beta})$ in (13.50).

To determine the properties of $\widehat{\boldsymbol{\beta}}$ as an estimator of $\boldsymbol{\beta}$ substitute for $\mathbf{y}$ from (13.49):

$$\widehat{\boldsymbol{\beta}} = \boldsymbol{\beta} + (\mathbf{X}'\mathbf{X})^{-1}\mathbf{X}'\mathbf{u} \tag{13.52}$$

then taking expectations conditional on $\mathbf{X}$:

$$\mathsf{E}\left[\left(\widehat{\boldsymbol{\beta}} - \boldsymbol{\beta}\right) \mid \mathbf{X}\right] = \mathsf{E}\left[(\mathbf{X}'\mathbf{X})^{-1}\mathbf{X}'\mathbf{u} \mid \mathbf{X}\right] = (\mathbf{X}'\mathbf{X})^{-1}\mathbf{X}'\mathsf{E}[\mathbf{u}] = \mathbf{0}. \tag{13.53}$$

Next, $\mathsf{V}[\widehat{\boldsymbol{\beta}}]$ is given by:

$$\begin{aligned} \mathsf{E}\left[\left(\widehat{\boldsymbol{\beta}} - \boldsymbol{\beta}\right)\left(\widehat{\boldsymbol{\beta}} - \boldsymbol{\beta}\right)' \mid \mathbf{X}\right] &= \mathsf{E}\left[(\mathbf{X}'\mathbf{X})^{-1}\mathbf{X}'\mathbf{u}\mathbf{u}'\mathbf{X}(\mathbf{X}'\mathbf{X})^{-1} \mid \mathbf{X}\right] \\ &= (\mathbf{X}'\mathbf{X})^{-1}\mathbf{X}'\mathsf{E}[\mathbf{u}\mathbf{u}']\mathbf{X}(\mathbf{X}'\mathbf{X})^{-1} \\ &= \sigma_u^2(\mathbf{X}'\mathbf{X})^{-1}. \end{aligned} \tag{13.54}$$

Further, letting $\widehat{\mathbf{u}} = (\mathbf{y} - \mathbf{X}\widehat{\boldsymbol{\beta}})$, σ_u^2 can be estimated by (note that the least-squares estimate of the variance is scaled by $T - k$, whereas the maximum-likelihood estimate of (13.33) is scaled by T):

$$\widehat{\sigma}_u^2 = \frac{\widehat{\mathbf{u}}'\widehat{\mathbf{u}}}{(T - k)} \tag{13.55}$$

when $\hat{\mathbf{u}}'\hat{\mathbf{u}} = RSS$ (an acronym for residual sum of squares). In turn, $\mathsf{V}[\hat{\beta}]$ can be estimated by:

$$\widehat{\mathsf{V}\left[\hat{\beta}\right]} = \hat{\sigma}_u^2 \left(\mathbf{X}'\mathbf{X}\right)^{-1}. \tag{13.56}$$

From (13.49)–(13.54), since $\hat{\beta}$ is a linear function of the normally distributed vector $\mathbf{u}$:

$$\hat{\beta} \sim \mathsf{N}_k\left(\beta, \sigma_u^2 \left(\mathbf{X}'\mathbf{X}\right)^{-1}\right). \tag{13.57}$$

Consequently, from (13.57):

$$\eta_1 = \frac{\left(\hat{\beta}-\beta\right)' \left(\mathbf{X}'\mathbf{X}\right)\left(\hat{\beta}-\beta\right)}{\sigma_u^2} \sim \chi^2(k). \tag{13.58}$$

Let $\mathbf{M} = \mathbf{I}_T - \mathbf{X}\left(\mathbf{X}'\mathbf{X}\right)^{-1}\mathbf{X}'$, which is a symmetric and idempotent $T \times T$ matrix, such that $\mathbf{M} = \mathbf{M}'$, $\mathbf{M} = \mathbf{M}^2$ and $\mathbf{M}\left(\mathbf{I}_T - \mathbf{M}\right) = \mathbf{0}$. From (13.58) and (13.51):

$$\begin{aligned} \sigma_u^2\eta_1 &= \left[\mathbf{u}'\mathbf{X}\left(\mathbf{X}'\mathbf{X}\right)^{-1}\right]\left(\mathbf{X}'\mathbf{X}\right)\left[\left(\mathbf{X}'\mathbf{X}\right)^{-1}\mathbf{X}'\mathbf{u}\right] \\ &= \mathbf{u}'\mathbf{X}\left(\mathbf{X}'\mathbf{X}\right)^{-1}\mathbf{X}'\mathbf{u} \\ &= \mathbf{u}'\left(\mathbf{I}-\mathbf{M}\right)\mathbf{u}. \end{aligned} \tag{13.59}$$

Further, $\mathbf{M}$ annihilates $\mathbf{X}$ since $\mathbf{MX} = \mathbf{0}$, so that:

$$\mathbf{My} = \mathbf{y} - \mathbf{X}\left(\mathbf{X}'\mathbf{X}\right)^{-1}\mathbf{X}'\mathbf{y} = \mathbf{y} - \mathbf{X}\hat{\beta} = \hat{\mathbf{u}} = \mathbf{Mu}, \tag{13.60}$$

where the last equality follows from premultiplying (13.49) by $\mathbf{M}$. Consequently:

$$RSS = \mathbf{y}'\mathbf{My} = \mathbf{u}'\mathbf{Mu}. \tag{13.61}$$

Since $\mathbf{M}$ is real and symmetric, let $\mathbf{M} = \mathbf{H\Lambda H}'$ where $\mathbf{\Lambda}$ is the diagonal matrix of eigenvalues and $\mathbf{H}$ is the non-singular matrix of eigenvectors with $\mathbf{H}'\mathbf{H} = \mathbf{I}_T$. By idempotency:

$$\mathbf{M}^2 = \mathbf{H\Lambda H}'\mathbf{H\Lambda H}' = \mathbf{H\Lambda}^2\mathbf{H}' = \mathbf{M} = \mathbf{H\Lambda H}'$$

so $\mathbf{\Lambda}^2 = \mathbf{\Lambda}$ and all the eigenvalues of $\mathbf{M}$ are either zero or unity. Thus, $\text{rank}(\mathbf{M}) = tr\left(\mathbf{M}\right)$ so:

$$\text{rank}\left(\mathbf{M}\right) = tr\left(\mathbf{I}_T - \mathbf{X}\left(\mathbf{X}'\mathbf{X}\right)^{-1}\mathbf{X}'\right) = tr\left(\mathbf{I}_T\right) - tr\left(\left(\mathbf{X}'\mathbf{X}\right)^{-1}\mathbf{X}'\mathbf{X}\right) = (T-k) \tag{13.62}$$

There are $(T-k)$ unit and k zero eigenvalues and $\mathbf{M}$ is singular of rank $(T-k)$.

13.7.3 Distributional results

Since $\mathbf{u} \sim \mathsf{N}_T(\mathbf{0}, \sigma_u^2\mathbf{I})$, then $\mathbf{u}'\mathbf{u}/\sigma_u^2 \sim \chi^2(T)$. Because $\mathbf{M}$ is singular, we cannot apply the theorems of §13.4.3 on the distributions of functions of normal variables to $\mathbf{Mu}$ or $\mathbf{u}'\mathbf{Mu}$. An alternative route is nevertheless feasible. Collect all of the unit eigenvalues of $\mathbf{M}$ in the first $(T-k)$ diagonal elements of $\mathbf{\Lambda}$, with the last k diagonal elements being zeros. Let:

$$\boldsymbol{\nu} = \mathbf{H}'\mathbf{u} \sim \mathsf{N}_T\left(\mathbf{0}, \sigma_u^2\mathbf{H}'\mathbf{H}\right) = \mathsf{N}_T\left(\mathbf{0}, \sigma_u^2\mathbf{I}\right)$$

and consider the quadratic form:

$$\mathbf{u}'\mathbf{Mu} = \mathbf{u}'\mathbf{H\Lambda H}'\mathbf{u} = \boldsymbol{\nu}'\mathbf{\Lambda}\boldsymbol{\nu} = \boldsymbol{\nu}_1'\boldsymbol{\nu}_1, \tag{13.63}$$

where $\boldsymbol{\nu}' = (\boldsymbol{\nu}_1' : \boldsymbol{\nu}_2')$ and $\boldsymbol{\nu}_1$ and $\boldsymbol{\nu}_2$ correspond to the unit and zero roots respectively in $\mathbf{\Lambda}$, so that $\boldsymbol{\nu}_1$ denotes the first $(T-k)$ elements of $\boldsymbol{\nu}$ corresponding to the unit eigenvalues of $\mathbf{M}$. Then $\boldsymbol{\nu}_1 \sim \mathsf{N}_{T-k}(\mathbf{0}, \sigma_u^2\mathbf{I})$, and since $\boldsymbol{\nu} \sim \mathsf{N}_T\left(\mathbf{0}, \sigma_u^2\mathbf{I}\right)$, $\boldsymbol{\nu}_1$ and $\boldsymbol{\nu}_2$ are distributed independently. Hence:

$$\eta_2 = \frac{\mathbf{u}'\mathbf{Mu}}{\sigma_u^2} = \frac{\boldsymbol{\nu}_1'\boldsymbol{\nu}_1}{\sigma_u^2} \sim \chi^2(T-k). \tag{13.64}$$

This result shows that an idempotent quadratic form in standardized normal variables is distributed as a χ^2 with degrees of freedom equal to the rank of the idempotent matrix. Also:

$$\eta_2 = \frac{(T-k)\,\hat{\sigma}_u^2}{\sigma_u^2} \quad \text{so that } \hat{\sigma}_u^2 \sim \frac{\sigma_u^2}{(T-k)}\chi^2(T-k). \tag{13.65}$$

The properties of $\hat{\sigma}_u^2$ can be calculated from this last result using the χ^2-distribution. Let $\eta_2 \sim \chi^2(T-k)$, then $\mathsf{E}[\eta_2] = T-k$ and $\mathsf{V}[\eta_2] = 2(T-k)$.

Since $(\mathbf{I}_T - \mathbf{M}) = \mathbf{H}(\mathbf{I}_T - \mathbf{\Lambda})\mathbf{H}'$:

$$\mathbf{u}'(\mathbf{I}_T - \mathbf{M})\mathbf{u} = \boldsymbol{\nu}'(\mathbf{I}_T - \mathbf{\Lambda})\boldsymbol{\nu} = \boldsymbol{\nu}_2'\boldsymbol{\nu}_2,$$

so $\eta_1 = \boldsymbol{\nu}_2'\boldsymbol{\nu}_2/\sigma_u^2$. As $\boldsymbol{\nu}_1$ and $\boldsymbol{\nu}_2$ are distributed independently, η_1 and η_2 are also independent, matching their being $\chi^2(k)$ and $\chi^2(T-k)$ respectively. Tests of H_0: $\boldsymbol{\beta} = \mathbf{0}$ (or components thereof) follow from these results using the F-distribution, since $\mathbf{y} = \mathbf{u}$ when $\boldsymbol{\beta} = \mathbf{0}$, so that on H_0:

$$\mathbf{u}'(\mathbf{I}_T - \mathbf{M})\mathbf{u} = \mathbf{y}'(\mathbf{I}_T - \mathbf{M})\mathbf{y} = \hat{\boldsymbol{\beta}}'(\mathbf{X}'\mathbf{X})\hat{\boldsymbol{\beta}}, \tag{13.66}$$

and hence:

$$\eta_{\beta} = \frac{(T-k)\,\eta_1}{k\eta_2} = \frac{(T-k)\,\mathbf{y}'(\mathbf{I}-\mathbf{M})\mathbf{y}}{k\mathbf{y}'\mathbf{My}} = \frac{(T-k)\,\hat{\boldsymbol{\beta}}'(\mathbf{X}'\mathbf{X})\hat{\boldsymbol{\beta}}}{kRSS} \underset{\mathsf{H}_0}{\sim} \mathsf{F}(k, T-k). \tag{13.67}$$

The last expression for η_β is the statistic which is actually computed. If $\boldsymbol{\beta} \neq \mathbf{0}$, then from (13.57) the numerator of η_β becomes a non-central χ^2 with non-centrality parameter

$\boldsymbol{\beta}'\mathbf{X}'\mathbf{X}\boldsymbol{\beta} \geq 0$, whereas the denominator is unchanged. Thus, the statistic η_β will on average lead to values larger than the $\mathsf{F}(k, T-k)$ anticipated under the null.

Finally, from (13.57) each element $\hat{\beta}_i$ of $\hat{\boldsymbol{\beta}}$ is normally distributed with variance given by σ_u^2 times the ith diagonal element d_{ii} of $(\mathbf{X}'\mathbf{X})^{-1}$ and is independent of η_2. Thus:

$$\frac{\left(\hat{\beta}_i - \beta_i\right)}{\hat{\sigma}_u \sqrt{d_{ii}}} \sim \mathsf{t}(T-k), \tag{13.68}$$

where $\mathsf{t}(T-k)$ denotes Student's t-distribution with $(T-k)$ degrees of freedom and:

$$\hat{\sigma}_u \sqrt{d_{ii}} = \mathsf{SE}\left(\hat{\beta}_i\right) \tag{13.69}$$

is the standard error of $\hat{\beta}_i$. On the hypothesis H_0: $\beta_i = 0$:

$$\tau_i = \frac{\hat{\beta}_i}{\mathsf{SE}\left(\hat{\beta}_i\right)} \underset{\mathsf{H}_0}{\sim} \mathsf{t}(T-k) \tag{13.70}$$

which is a computable statistic from sample evidence alone.

13.7.4 Subsets of parameters

Consider estimating a subset of k_b parameters $\boldsymbol{\beta}_b$ of $\boldsymbol{\beta}$ where $k_a + k_b = k$. Partition $\mathbf{X} = (\mathbf{X}_a : \mathbf{X}_b)$ and $\boldsymbol{\beta}' = (\boldsymbol{\beta}'_a : \boldsymbol{\beta}'_b)$ so that:

$$\mathbf{y} = \mathbf{X}_a\boldsymbol{\beta}_a + \mathbf{X}_b\boldsymbol{\beta}_b + \mathbf{u}. \tag{13.71}$$

Let $\mathbf{M}_a = \mathbf{I}_T - \mathbf{X}_a\left(\mathbf{X}'_a\mathbf{X}_a\right)^{-1}\mathbf{X}'_a$ which implies that $\mathbf{M}_a\mathbf{X}_a = \mathbf{0}$ then:

$$\mathbf{M}_a\mathbf{y} = \mathbf{M}_a\mathbf{X}_b\boldsymbol{\beta}_b + \mathbf{M}_a\mathbf{u} \tag{13.72}$$

and hence:

$$\hat{\boldsymbol{\beta}}_b = \left(\mathbf{X}'_b\mathbf{M}_a\mathbf{X}_b\right)^{-1}\mathbf{X}'_b\mathbf{M}_a\mathbf{y}. \tag{13.73}$$

From (13.72) and (13.73):

$$\hat{\boldsymbol{\beta}}_b = \boldsymbol{\beta}_b + \left(\mathbf{X}'_b\mathbf{M}_a\mathbf{X}_b\right)^{-1}\mathbf{X}'_b\mathbf{M}_a\mathbf{u} \tag{13.74}$$

so that

$$\mathsf{V}\left[\hat{\boldsymbol{\beta}}_b\right] = \sigma_u^2\left(\mathbf{X}'_b\mathbf{M}_a\mathbf{X}_b\right)^{-1}. \tag{13.75}$$

Thus:

$$\hat{\boldsymbol{\beta}}_b \sim \mathsf{N}_{k_b}\left(\boldsymbol{\beta}_b, \sigma_u^2\left(\mathbf{X}'_b\mathbf{M}_a\mathbf{X}_b\right)^{-1}\right). \tag{13.76}$$

Hypothesis tests about β_b follow analogously to the previous section. In particular, from §13.7.3 and (13.76):

$$\eta_b = \frac{\left(\hat{\beta}_b - \beta_b\right)' \left(\mathbf{X}_b' \mathbf{M}_a \mathbf{X}_b\right) \left(\hat{\beta}_b - \beta_b\right)}{k_b \hat{\sigma}_u^2} \sim \mathsf{F}\left(k_b, T - k\right). \tag{13.77}$$

When $k_b = 1$, this matches (13.70) under H_0: $\beta_b = 0$, and when $k_b = k$, (13.77) reproduces (13.67) under H_0: $\boldsymbol{\beta} = \mathbf{0}$. A useful case of (13.77) is $k_b = (k-1)$ and $\mathbf{X}_a = \boldsymbol{\iota}$ (a $T \times 1$ vector of ones), so all coefficients other than the intercept are tested.

If, instead of estimating (13.71), $\mathbf{X}_a$ is omitted from the model in the incorrect belief that $\boldsymbol{\beta}_a = \mathbf{0}$, the equation to be estimated becomes:

$$\mathbf{y} = \mathbf{X}_b \boldsymbol{\beta}_b + \mathbf{e} \tag{13.78}$$

The resulting estimator of $\boldsymbol{\beta}_b$, denoted by $\tilde{\boldsymbol{\beta}}_b = \left(\mathbf{X}_b'\mathbf{X}_b\right)^{-1} \mathbf{X}_b'\mathbf{y}$, confounds the effects of $\mathbf{X}_a$ and $\mathbf{X}_b$:

$$\begin{aligned} \tilde{\boldsymbol{\beta}}_b &= \left(\mathbf{X}_b'\mathbf{X}_b\right)^{-1} \mathbf{X}_b' \left(\mathbf{X}_a \boldsymbol{\beta}_a + \mathbf{X}_b \boldsymbol{\beta}_b + \mathbf{u}\right) \\ &= \mathbf{B}_{ba} \boldsymbol{\beta}_a + \boldsymbol{\beta}_b + \left(\mathbf{X}_b'\mathbf{X}_b\right)^{-1} \mathbf{X}_b'\mathbf{u} \end{aligned} \tag{13.79}$$

where $\mathbf{B}_{ba} = \left(\mathbf{X}_b'\mathbf{X}_b\right)^{-1} \mathbf{X}_b'\mathbf{X}_a$. Thus:

$$\mathsf{E}\left[\tilde{\boldsymbol{\beta}}_b\right] = \mathbf{B}_{ba} \boldsymbol{\beta}_a + \boldsymbol{\beta}_b, \tag{13.80}$$

which equals $\boldsymbol{\beta}_b$ if and only if $\mathbf{B}_{ba} \boldsymbol{\beta}_a = \mathbf{0}$. Moreover, let $\mathbf{M}_b$ have the same form as $\mathbf{M}_a$ but using $\mathbf{X}_b$ then:

$$\widehat{\mathsf{V}\left[\tilde{\boldsymbol{\beta}}_b\right]} = \tilde{\sigma}_u^2 \left(\mathbf{X}_b'\mathbf{X}_b\right)^{-1} \text{ where } \tilde{\sigma}_u^2 = \frac{\mathbf{y}'\mathbf{M}_b\mathbf{y}}{(T - k_b)} = \frac{\tilde{\mathbf{u}}'\tilde{\mathbf{u}}}{(T - k_b)} \tag{13.81}$$

when $\mathbf{u} \triangleq \mathbf{y} - \mathbf{X}_b \tilde{\boldsymbol{\beta}}_b$ and:

$$\mathsf{E}\left[\tilde{\sigma}_u^2\right] = \sigma_u^2 + \frac{\boldsymbol{\beta}_a' \mathbf{X}_a' \mathbf{M}_b \mathbf{X}_a \boldsymbol{\beta}_a}{(T - k_b)} \geq \sigma_u^2. \tag{13.82}$$

Conventionally, $\tilde{\boldsymbol{\beta}}_b$ is interpreted as a biased estimator of $\boldsymbol{\beta}_b$ with bias given by $\mathbf{B}_{ba}\boldsymbol{\beta}_a$. The estimated variance matrix in (13.81) may exceed or be less than that given by the relevant sub-matrix of (13.56), in the sense that the difference could be positive or negative semi-definite.

The sign of an estimated coefficient from (13.78) can be the same as, or the opposite to, that expected from prior theoretical reasoning, and the latter is sometimes called a 'wrong sign'. We interpret the outcome in (13.80) as delivering a different coefficient $\boldsymbol{\gamma}_b = \mathbf{B}_{ba}\boldsymbol{\beta}_a + \boldsymbol{\beta}_b$ than $\boldsymbol{\beta}_b$, consonant with the following argument. First:

$$\mathbf{X}_a \equiv \mathbf{M}_b \mathbf{X}_a + \left(\mathbf{I}_T - \mathbf{M}_b\right) \mathbf{X}_a = \mathbf{M}_b \mathbf{X}_a + \mathbf{X}_b \mathbf{B}_{ba}. \tag{13.83}$$

Consequently, from (13.71):

$$\begin{aligned} \mathbf{y} &= (\mathbf{M}_b\mathbf{X}_a + \mathbf{X}_b\mathbf{B}_{ba})\,\boldsymbol{\beta}_a + \mathbf{X}_b\boldsymbol{\beta}_b + \mathbf{u} \\ &= \mathbf{X}_b\boldsymbol{\gamma}_b + (\mathbf{u} + \mathbf{M}_b\mathbf{X}_a\boldsymbol{\beta}_a) \\ &= \mathbf{X}_b\boldsymbol{\gamma}_b + \mathbf{v} \end{aligned} \tag{13.84}$$

where $\mathsf{E}[\mathbf{v}] = \mathbf{M}_b\mathbf{X}_a\boldsymbol{\beta}_a \neq \mathbf{0}$, but since $\mathbf{M}_b\mathbf{X}_b = \mathbf{0}$:

$$\mathsf{E}[\mathbf{X}_b'\mathbf{v}] = \mathsf{E}[\mathbf{X}_b'\mathbf{u}] + \mathbf{X}_b'\mathbf{M}_b\mathbf{X}_a\boldsymbol{\beta}_a = \mathbf{0}. \tag{13.85}$$

Thus, the model is implicitly reparameterized by omitting $\mathbf{X}_a$, and OLS is an unbiased estimator of $\boldsymbol{\gamma}_b$ despite $\mathsf{E}[\mathbf{v}] \neq \mathbf{0}$. Under more general assumptions, a related large-sample result holds.

13.7.5 Partitioned inversion

The results on estimating subsets of parameters can be obtained by partitioned inversion of $(\mathbf{X}'\mathbf{X})$. Consider the matrix $(\mathbf{X}'\mathbf{X})^{-1}$. Let $\mathbf{H} = (\mathbf{X}_b'\mathbf{M}_a\mathbf{X}_b)$ and $\mathbf{G} = (\mathbf{X}_a'\mathbf{M}_b\mathbf{X}_a)$, then:

$$\begin{pmatrix} \mathbf{X}_a'\mathbf{X}_a & \mathbf{X}_a'\mathbf{X}_b \\ \mathbf{X}_b'\mathbf{X}_a & \mathbf{X}_b'\mathbf{X}_b \end{pmatrix}^{-1} = \begin{pmatrix} (\mathbf{X}_a'\mathbf{M}_b\mathbf{X}_a)^{-1} & -(\mathbf{X}_a'\mathbf{M}_b\mathbf{X}_a)^{-1}\,\mathbf{B}_{ba}' \\ -\mathbf{B}_{ab}\,(\mathbf{X}_b'\mathbf{M}_a\mathbf{X}_b)^{-1} & (\mathbf{X}_b'\mathbf{M}_a\mathbf{X}_b)^{-1} \end{pmatrix} \tag{13.86}$$

where $\mathbf{B}_{ab} = (\mathbf{X}_a'\mathbf{X}_a)^{-1}\,\mathbf{X}_a'\mathbf{X}_b$. Further, $\mathbf{X}'\mathbf{y}$ can be partitioned conformably as:

$$\begin{pmatrix} \mathbf{X}_a'\mathbf{y} \\ \mathbf{X}_b'\mathbf{y} \end{pmatrix} \tag{13.87}$$

and multiplication of (13.87) by (13.86) delivers (13.73) together with corresponding expressions for estimating $\boldsymbol{\beta}_a$; the coefficient variance matrix follows from (13.86).

Alternatively, when $(\mathbf{X}'\mathbf{X})^{-1}$ is given by:

$$\begin{pmatrix} (\mathbf{X}_a'\mathbf{M}_b\mathbf{X}_a)^{-1} & -(\mathbf{X}_a'\mathbf{M}_b\mathbf{X}_a)^{-1}\,\mathbf{B}_{ba}' \\ -\mathbf{B}_{ba}\,(\mathbf{X}_a'\mathbf{M}_b\mathbf{X}_a)^{-1} & (\mathbf{X}_b'\mathbf{X}_b)^{-1} + \mathbf{B}_{ba}\,(\mathbf{X}_a'\mathbf{M}_b\mathbf{X}_a)^{-1}\,\mathbf{B}_{ba}' \end{pmatrix} \tag{13.88}$$

then multiplication of (13.87) by (13.88) delivers for the second row:

$$\begin{aligned} \widehat{\boldsymbol{\beta}}_b &= -\mathbf{B}_{ba}\,(\mathbf{X}_a'\mathbf{M}_b\mathbf{X}_a)^{-1}\,\mathbf{X}_a'\mathbf{y} + (\mathbf{X}_b'\mathbf{X}_b)^{-1}\,\mathbf{X}_b'\mathbf{y} + \mathbf{B}_{ba}\,(\mathbf{X}_a'\mathbf{M}_b\mathbf{X}_a)^{-1}\,\mathbf{B}_{ba}'\mathbf{X}_b'\mathbf{y} \\ &= \tilde{\boldsymbol{\beta}}_b - \mathbf{B}_{ba}\,(\mathbf{X}_a'\mathbf{M}_b\mathbf{X}_a)^{-1}\,\mathbf{X}_a'\left(\mathbf{I}_T - \mathbf{X}_b\,(\mathbf{X}_b'\mathbf{X}_b)^{-1}\,\mathbf{X}_b'\right)\mathbf{y} \\ &= \tilde{\boldsymbol{\beta}}_b - \mathbf{B}_{ba}\widehat{\boldsymbol{\beta}}_a \end{aligned} \tag{13.89}$$

from which it follows that:

$$\tilde{\boldsymbol{\beta}}_b = \widehat{\boldsymbol{\beta}}_b + \mathbf{B}_{ba}\widehat{\boldsymbol{\beta}}_a. \tag{13.90}$$

Then (13.90) is the exact estimation analogue of (13.80): the simple regression estimate of $\boldsymbol{\beta}_b$ equals the corresponding multiple regression estimate of $\boldsymbol{\beta}_b$ plus the auxiliary regression matrix multiplied by the multiple regression estimate of the omitted effect. Consequently, a regression coefficient is interpretable as a partial derivative of y with respect to the relevant x only to the extent that all other effects have either been included in the regression, or are orthogonal to the variables under study.

13.7.6 Multiple correlation

Let $\hat{\mathbf{y}} = \mathbf{X}\hat{\boldsymbol{\beta}}$, then $\mathbf{y} = \hat{\mathbf{y}} + \hat{\mathbf{u}}$ and $\mathbf{X}'\hat{\mathbf{u}} = \mathbf{0}$ since $\mathbf{MX} = \mathbf{0}$. Thus, $\hat{\mathbf{y}}'\hat{\mathbf{u}} = 0$ implying that:

$$\mathbf{y}'\hat{\mathbf{y}} = \hat{\mathbf{y}}'\hat{\mathbf{y}} \text{ and } \mathbf{y}'\mathbf{y} = \hat{\mathbf{y}}'\hat{\mathbf{y}} + \hat{\mathbf{u}}'\hat{\mathbf{u}}. \tag{13.91}$$

A natural choice to measure the 'goodness of fit' between $\mathbf{y}$ and $\hat{\mathbf{y}} = \mathbf{X}\hat{\boldsymbol{\beta}}$ is their correlation coefficient. When a constant is present in $\mathbf{X}$ as the vector of ones $\boldsymbol{\iota}$, since $\mathbf{MX} = \mathbf{0}$, then $\boldsymbol{\iota}'\hat{\mathbf{u}} = \boldsymbol{\iota}'\mathbf{M}\hat{\mathbf{u}} = 0$ and $T^{-1}\boldsymbol{\iota}'\mathbf{y} = T^{-1}\boldsymbol{\iota}'\hat{\mathbf{y}} = \bar{y}$ (the sample mean). Consequently, the squared correlation between $\mathbf{y}$ and $\hat{\mathbf{y}}$ is given by:

$$\mathsf{R}^2(\mathbf{y}, \hat{\mathbf{y}}) = \frac{\left[(\mathbf{y} - \boldsymbol{\iota}\bar{y})'(\hat{\mathbf{y}} - \boldsymbol{\iota}\bar{y})\right]^2}{\left[(\mathbf{y} - \boldsymbol{\iota}\bar{y})'(\mathbf{y} - \boldsymbol{\iota}\bar{y})\right]\left[(\hat{\mathbf{y}} - \boldsymbol{\iota}\bar{y})'(\hat{\mathbf{y}} - \boldsymbol{\iota}\bar{y})\right]}. \tag{13.92}$$

Substituting $(\mathbf{y} - \boldsymbol{\iota}\bar{y}) = (\hat{\mathbf{y}} - \boldsymbol{\iota}\bar{y}) + \hat{\mathbf{u}}$ takes deviations about means in $\mathbf{y} = \hat{\mathbf{y}} + \hat{\mathbf{u}}$, so using the results that $\hat{\mathbf{y}}'\hat{\mathbf{u}} = 0$ and $\boldsymbol{\iota}'\hat{\mathbf{u}} = 0$:

$$\mathsf{R}^2 = \frac{(\hat{\mathbf{y}} - \boldsymbol{\iota}\bar{y})'(\hat{\mathbf{y}} - \boldsymbol{\iota}\bar{y})}{(\mathbf{y} - \boldsymbol{\iota}\bar{y})'(\mathbf{y} - \boldsymbol{\iota}\bar{y})}, \tag{13.93}$$

and hence:

$$\left(1 - \mathsf{R}^2\right) = \frac{\hat{\mathbf{u}}'\hat{\mathbf{u}}}{(\mathbf{y} - \boldsymbol{\iota}\bar{y})'(\mathbf{y} - \boldsymbol{\iota}\bar{y})}.$$

R^2 is the squared multiple correlation between y and $\mathbf{x}$. The statistic η_b in (13.77) for testing the hypothesis that all coefficients other than the intercept are zero can be written as a function of $\mathsf{R}^2/\left(1 - \mathsf{R}^2\right)$. On H_0: $\boldsymbol{\beta}_b = \mathbf{0}$, since $\hat{\mathbf{y}} = \boldsymbol{\iota}\hat{\beta}_a + \mathbf{X}_b\hat{\boldsymbol{\beta}}_b$ and:

$$\hat{\beta}_a = \bar{y} - \bar{\mathbf{x}}_b'\hat{\boldsymbol{\beta}}_b = \bar{y} - T^{-1}\boldsymbol{\iota}'\mathbf{X}_b\hat{\boldsymbol{\beta}}_b$$

then:

$$\hat{\mathbf{y}} = \boldsymbol{\iota}\bar{y} - T^{-1}\boldsymbol{\iota}\boldsymbol{\iota}'\mathbf{X}_b\hat{\boldsymbol{\beta}}_b + \mathbf{X}_b\hat{\boldsymbol{\beta}}_b = \boldsymbol{\iota}\bar{y} + \mathbf{M}_a\mathbf{X}_b\hat{\boldsymbol{\beta}}_b$$

as $\mathbf{M}_a = \left(\mathbf{I}_T - \boldsymbol{\iota}\left(\boldsymbol{\iota}'\boldsymbol{\iota}\right)^{-1}\boldsymbol{\iota}'\right) = \left(\mathbf{I}_T - T^{-1}\boldsymbol{\iota}\boldsymbol{\iota}'\right)$, so that:

$$\eta_b = \frac{(T-k)\,\hat{\boldsymbol{\beta}}_b'\mathbf{X}_b'\mathbf{M}_a\mathbf{X}_b\hat{\boldsymbol{\beta}}_b}{(k-1)\,\hat{\mathbf{u}}'\hat{\mathbf{u}}} = \frac{(T-k)\,(\hat{\mathbf{y}} - \boldsymbol{\iota}\bar{y})'(\hat{\mathbf{y}} - \boldsymbol{\iota}\bar{y})}{(k-1)\,\hat{\mathbf{u}}'\hat{\mathbf{u}}} = \frac{(T-k)\,\mathsf{R}^2}{(k-1)\,(1-\mathsf{R}^2)}. \tag{13.94}$$

As $\mathsf{R}^2 \to 1$, highly 'significant' results are bound to occur independently of their substance.

13.7.7 Partial correlation

The notion of a partial correlation, or a partial regression coefficient, is fundamental to interpreting econometric evidence. For empirical modelling, equations like (13.48) are usually formulated with the implicit assumption that:

$$\frac{\partial y_t}{\partial x_{it}} = \beta_i \text{ for } i = 1, \ldots, k. \tag{13.95}$$

OLS estimates $\hat{\beta}_i$ are then interpreted as if they have the same properties. When $i = b$, β_b is a scalar so that $\mathbf{X}_b$ is a vector $\mathbf{x}_b$, and the marginal distribution of $\hat{\beta}_b$ is given in (13.76). Then the partial correlation $\mathsf{r}_{by \cdot a}$ between y and x_b having removed the linear influence of $\mathbf{X}_a$ (assumed to contain ι) is the correlation between $\mathbf{M}_a\mathbf{y}$ and $\mathbf{M}_a\mathbf{x}_b$:

$$\mathsf{r}_{by \cdot a} = \frac{\mathbf{y}'\mathbf{M}_a\mathbf{x}_b}{\sqrt{(\mathbf{y}'\mathbf{M}_a\mathbf{y})\,(\mathbf{x}_b'\mathbf{M}_a\mathbf{x}_b)}} = \frac{\hat{\beta}_b\sqrt{(\mathbf{x}_b'\mathbf{M}_a\mathbf{x}_b)}}{\sqrt{(\mathbf{y}'\mathbf{M}_a\mathbf{y})}} \tag{13.96}$$

Note that $\mathbf{M}_a\mathbf{y}$ and $\mathbf{M}_a\mathbf{x}_b$ have zero means and that:

$$\mathsf{r}^2_{by \cdot a} = \frac{\hat{\beta}_b\,(\mathbf{x}_b'\mathbf{M}_a\mathbf{x}_b)\,\hat{\beta}_b}{\mathbf{y}'\mathbf{M}_a\mathbf{y}}. \tag{13.97}$$

The numerator of $(1 - \mathsf{r}^2_{by \cdot a})$ is $\mathbf{y}'\mathbf{M}_a\mathbf{y} - \hat{\beta}_b\,(\mathbf{x}_b'\mathbf{M}_a\mathbf{x}_b)\,\hat{\beta}_b = \mathbf{y}'\mathbf{M}^*\mathbf{y}$ where:

$$\begin{aligned} \mathbf{M}^* &= \mathbf{M}_a - \mathbf{M}_a\mathbf{x}_b\,(\mathbf{x}_b'\mathbf{M}_a\mathbf{x}_b)^{-1}\,\mathbf{x}_b'\mathbf{M}_a \\ &= \mathbf{M}_a\left[\mathbf{I}_T - \mathbf{M}_a\mathbf{x}_b\,(\mathbf{x}_b'\mathbf{M}_a\mathbf{x}_b)^{-1}\,\mathbf{x}_b'\mathbf{M}_a\right]\mathbf{M}_a \end{aligned} \tag{13.98}$$

so $\mathbf{M}^* = \mathbf{M}$. This last equality follows from applying (13.86) since $[\cdot]$ annihilates $\mathbf{M}_a\mathbf{x}_b$. As a check, by suitable rearrangement of the order of regressors, $\mathbf{M}^*\mathbf{X} = \mathbf{M}^*\,(\mathbf{X}_a : \mathbf{x}_b) = \mathbf{0} = \mathbf{M}\mathbf{X}$. From the earlier formula for τ_i when $i = b$:

$$\tau_b^2 = \frac{(T-k)\,\mathsf{r}^2_{by \cdot a}}{\left(1 - \mathsf{r}^2_{by \cdot a}\right)}, \tag{13.99}$$

In the special case that $k = 2$ and $\mathbf{x}_a = \iota$, (13.94) coincides with (13.99).

When $\mathbf{X}_a$ includes ι and $k_b > 1$, (13.98) holds in the form:

$$\mathbf{M} = \mathbf{M}_a - \mathbf{M}_a\mathbf{X}_b\,(\mathbf{X}_b'\mathbf{M}_a\mathbf{X}_b)^{-1}\,\mathbf{X}_b'\mathbf{M}_a$$

so that:

$$\mathbf{y}'\mathbf{M}\mathbf{y} = \mathbf{y}'\mathbf{M}_a\mathbf{y} - \mathbf{y}'\mathbf{M}_a\mathbf{X}_b\,(\mathbf{X}_b'\mathbf{M}_a\mathbf{X}_b)^{-1}\,\mathbf{X}_b'\mathbf{M}_a\mathbf{y} = \mathbf{y}'\mathbf{M}_a\mathbf{y} - \hat{\beta}_b'\mathbf{X}_b'\mathbf{M}_a\mathbf{X}_b\hat{\beta}_b. \tag{13.100}$$

Substituting (13.100) in (13.77):

$$\eta_b = \frac{(T-k)\left[\mathbf{y}'\mathbf{M}_a\mathbf{y} - \mathbf{y}'\mathbf{M}\mathbf{y}\right]}{k_b\hat{\mathbf{u}}'\hat{\mathbf{u}}} = \frac{(T-k)\left[\tilde{\mathbf{u}}'\tilde{\mathbf{u}} - \hat{\mathbf{u}}'\hat{\mathbf{u}}\right]}{k_b\hat{\mathbf{u}}'\hat{\mathbf{u}}} = \frac{(T-k)}{k_b}\left[d\frac{\tilde{\sigma}_u^2}{\hat{\sigma}_u^2} - 1\right] \tag{13.101}$$

where $d = (T-k_a)\,/\,(T-k)$. Thus, when $\hat{\sigma}_u^2 = \tilde{\sigma}_u^2$, $\eta_b = 1$ and when $\hat{\sigma}_u^2 > \tilde{\sigma}_u^2$, $\eta_b < 1$. Deleting k_b regressors when the F-test for the significance of their coefficients is less than unity will lower the estimated residual standard error. For $k_b = 1$, deleting a single variable with $\tau_b^2 < 1$ will lower the estimated residual standard error.

13.7.8 Maximum likelihood estimation

As noted, OLS is also the MLE here. When $\mathbf{u} \sim \mathsf{N}_T\left(\mathbf{0}, \sigma_u^2\mathbf{I}\right)$, the conditional log-likelihood function is:

$$\ell\left(\boldsymbol{\beta},\sigma_u^2 \mid \mathbf{X};\mathbf{y}\right) = -\frac{T}{2}\log(2\pi) - \frac{T}{2}\log\left(\sigma_u^2\right) - \frac{(\mathbf{y}-\mathbf{X}\boldsymbol{\beta})'(\mathbf{y}-\mathbf{X}\boldsymbol{\beta})}{2\sigma_u^2} \tag{13.102}$$

so the MLE minimizes the last term, which yields OLS. From above:

$$\ell\left(\boldsymbol{\beta},\sigma_u^2 \mid \mathbf{X};\mathbf{y}\right) = -\frac{T}{2}\log(2\pi) - \frac{T}{2}\log\left(\sigma_u^2\right) - \frac{\left(\hat{\boldsymbol{\beta}}-\boldsymbol{\beta}\right)'\mathbf{X}'\mathbf{X}\left(\hat{\boldsymbol{\beta}}-\boldsymbol{\beta}\right)}{2\sigma_u^2} - \frac{\hat{\mathbf{u}}'\hat{\mathbf{u}}}{2\sigma_u^2} \tag{13.103}$$

From (13.103), $(\hat{\boldsymbol{\beta}}, \hat{\sigma}_u^2)$ are jointly sufficient for $\left(\boldsymbol{\beta},\sigma_u^2\right)$, and by independence, the joint distribution of $\hat{\boldsymbol{\beta}}$ and $\hat{\sigma}_u^2$ factorizes into the products of their marginals.

13.7.9 Recursive estimation

To understand the basis of recursive estimation, denote the specified equation by:

$$y_t = \boldsymbol{\beta}'\mathbf{x}_t + u_t \tag{13.104}$$

where $\boldsymbol{\beta}$ is asserted to be constant, $\mathsf{E}\left[\mathbf{x}_t u_t\right] = \mathbf{0}\,\forall t$, $\mathsf{E}\left(u_t^2\right) = \sigma_u^2$, and $\mathsf{E}\left(u_t u_s\right) = 0$ if $t \neq s$. Let the complete sample period be $(1, \ldots, T)$, and consider the least-squares outcome on a subsample up to $t-1$ (for $t > k$ when there are k regressors in $\mathbf{x}_{t-1}$):

$$\hat{\boldsymbol{\beta}}_{t-1} = \left(\mathbf{X}_{t-1}'\mathbf{X}_{t-1}\right)^{-1}\mathbf{X}_{t-1}'\mathbf{y}_{t-1}, \tag{13.105}$$

with $\mathbf{X}_{t-1} = (\mathbf{x}_1 \ldots \mathbf{x}_{t-1})'$ and $\mathbf{y}_{t-1} = (y_1 \ldots y_{t-1})'$. If the sample were increased by one observation, then:

$$\mathbf{X}_t'\mathbf{X}_t = \mathbf{X}_{t-1}'\mathbf{X}_{t-1} + \mathbf{x}_t\mathbf{x}_t' \tag{13.106}$$

and:

$$\mathbf{X}_t'\mathbf{y}_t = \mathbf{X}_{t-1}'\mathbf{y}_{t-1} + \mathbf{x}_t y_t. \tag{13.107}$$

However, given $\left(\mathbf{X}_{t-1}'\mathbf{X}_{t-1}\right)^{-1}$, one does not need to invert $(\mathbf{X}_t'\mathbf{X}_t)$ to calculate $\hat{\beta}_t$. Rather:

$$\left(\mathbf{X}_t'\mathbf{X}_t\right)^{-1} = \left(\mathbf{X}_{t-1}'\mathbf{X}_{t-1}\right)^{-1} - \frac{\boldsymbol{\lambda}_t\boldsymbol{\lambda}_t'}{1+\boldsymbol{\lambda}_t'\mathbf{x}_t}, \tag{13.108}$$

where

$$\boldsymbol{\lambda}_t = \left(\mathbf{X}_{t-1}'\mathbf{X}_{t-1}\right)^{-1}\mathbf{x}_t. \tag{13.109}$$

Thus, the inverse can be sequentially updated and $\hat{\beta}_t$ follows directly. A similar updating formula is available for updating the residual sum of squares (RSS) from the innovations given by:

$$RSS_t = RSS_{t-1} + \frac{\nu_t^2}{1+\boldsymbol{\lambda}_t'\mathbf{x}_t} \tag{13.110}$$

where the innovations are the one-step ahead forecast errors:

$$\nu_t = y_t - \mathbf{x}_t'\hat{\beta}_t. \tag{13.111}$$

These are mean zero independent random variables, with variance

$$\mathsf{E}\left[\nu_t^2\right] = \sigma_u^2\left(1+\lambda_t'x_t\right) = \sigma_u^2\omega_t.$$

The standardized innovations are:

$$\frac{\nu_t}{\left(1+\lambda_t'x_t\right)^{1/2}}.$$

From this, equation and parameter standard errors are readily calculated:

$$\hat{\sigma}_t^2 = RSS_t/\left(t-k\right) \tag{13.112}$$

and:

$$\mathsf{V}\left[\hat{\beta}_t\right] = \hat{\sigma}_t^2\left(\mathbf{X}_t'\mathbf{X}_t\right)^{-1} \tag{13.113}$$

where $\mathsf{V}[\cdot]$ denotes variance.

Finally, from the sequence of $\{RSS_{t-1}\}$, sequences of tests (for example, for parameter constancy) can be calculated, based on Chow (1960).

If instrumental variables estimators are used, the recursive formulae are similar but more cumbersome (see Hendry and Neale, 1987).

Chapter 14

Advanced Econometrics

14.1 Introduction

This chapter offers an overall description of the class of dynamic models handled by PcGive, the most frequently used concepts and modelling strategies, and the estimation and evaluation procedures available. The class of single-equation dynamic linear models analysed by PcGive, including a model typology and distinctions between interpretations of linear models, were described in Chapter 12. Here we discuss dynamic systems in §14.2. The crucial concept of weak exogeneity is described in §14.3.2 as the basis for valid inference in single-equation conditional models which are nevertheless part of a dynamic economic system. That section also introduces several factorizations of data density functions, and relates these to such concepts as white noise and innovations. The discussion then turns to model evaluation in §14.4, an information taxonomy for model evaluation and design in §14.5, and the types of test used in §14.6. Section 14.7 considers modelling strategies, and the chapter concludes with a brief discussion of estimation techniques in §14.8.

14.2 Dynamic systems

The class of models basic to PcGive is that of linear dynamic single equations. Chapter 12 discussed the formulation and properties of such equations, their forms (in the typology), and their different interpretations. In economics, however, equations cannot be viewed in isolation: they are inherently part of a system. Here we note the structure of such systems and lay the ground for determining when a single-equation analysis is likely to be valid despite the system context. PcFiml analyses linear dynamic systems *qua* systems, but PcGive provides methods that are applicable when one equation is the focus of interest from a system that otherwise is rather loosely specified. Dynamic systems are more extensively described in the book on PcFiml. For completeness, we give a brief overview here.

As in Chapter 12, dynamic linear equation analysis follows from the use of lag operators (denoted by L) such that $L^r x_t = x_{t-r}$ for a variable x_t. When $\mathbf{y}_t$ and $\mathbf{z}_t$ are $n \times 1$ and $k \times 1$ vectors of variables of modelled and non-modelled variables respectively, an expression like (12.3) constitutes a dynamic linear system. Since $L^r \mathbf{x}_t = \mathbf{x}_{t-r}$ for vectors as well, this enables us to describe the formulation of a dynamic system rather compactly.

The data sets of observations on $\{\mathbf{y}_t\}$ and $\{\mathbf{z}_t\}$ are denoted by $\mathbf{Y}_T^1 = (\mathbf{y}_1 \dots \mathbf{y}_T)$ and $\mathbf{Z}_T^1$ respectively where:

$$\mathbf{y}_t = \begin{pmatrix} y_{1t} \\ y_{2t} \\ \vdots \\ y_{nt} \end{pmatrix} \text{ and } \mathbf{z}_t = \begin{pmatrix} z_{1t} \\ z_{2t} \\ \vdots \\ z_{kt} \end{pmatrix}.$$

Formally, a dynamic system can be written as:

$$\mathbf{y}_t = \sum_{i=1}^{m} \pi_{1i} \mathbf{y}_{t-i} + \sum_{j=0}^{r} \pi_{2j} \mathbf{z}_{t-j} + \mathbf{v}_t \tag{14.1}$$

where $\mathbf{v}_t \sim \mathsf{N}_n(\mathbf{0}, \mathbf{\Omega})$ for $t = 1, \dots, T$. Section 14.3.2 describes when $\mathbf{z}_t$ can be treated as weakly exogenous for the parameters of interest in the system so that it is legitimate to treat $\{\mathbf{z}_t\}$ as determined outside the system in (14.1). Note that x_t in (12.3) may be endogenous in the system context (14.1) even though it is not jointly determined with y_t in (12.3). Also, m and r in (14.1) may differ between $\mathbf{y}_t$ and $\mathbf{z}_t$ as well as between variables within that partition.

Introducing matrix lag polynomials:

$$\pi_1(L) = \sum_{i=0}^{m} \pi_{1i} L^i \text{ and } \pi_2(L) = \sum_{j=0}^{r} \pi_{2j} L^j,$$

write (14.1) as:

$$\pi_1(L)\mathbf{y}_t = \pi_2(L)\mathbf{z}_t + \mathbf{v}_t,$$

where it is assumed that $\pi_{10} = \mathbf{I}_n$ (the $n \times n$ identity matrix), and that $\pi_1(1) \neq \mathbf{0}$ and $\pi_2(1) \neq \mathbf{0}$, so that $\mathbf{y}$ and $\mathbf{z}$ are cointegrated. In conventional parlance, (14.1) is a reduced form, but since no structural model has been specified from which it can have been reduced, we refer to (14.1) as the system (see Hendry, Neale and Srba, 1988). When $\mathbf{z}_t$ is deterministic, (14.1) is closed and is a vector autoregression (VAR). However, at least conceptually, one could imagine extending the system to endogenize $\mathbf{z}_t$ and make a bigger VAR, so if $\pi_{20} = \mathbf{0}$, (14.1) is part of a VAR (cut across equations), and if $\pi_{20} \neq \mathbf{0}$ it is a VAR conditional on $\mathbf{z}_t$.

A model of the system is created by premultiplying (14.1) by a non-singular $n \times n$ matrix $\mathbf{B}$:

$$\mathbf{B}\mathbf{y}_t = \sum_{i=1}^{m} \mathbf{B}\boldsymbol{\pi}_{1i}\mathbf{y}_{t-i} + \sum_{j=0}^{r} \mathbf{B}\boldsymbol{\pi}_{2j}\mathbf{z}_{t-j} + \mathbf{B}\mathbf{v}_t, \tag{14.2}$$

or switching notation:

$$\mathbf{B}(L)\,\mathbf{y}_t = \mathbf{C}(L)\,\mathbf{z}_t + \mathbf{u}_t \ \text{ with } \ \mathbf{u}_t \sim \mathsf{IN}_n(\mathbf{0}, \boldsymbol{\Sigma}). \tag{14.3}$$

The system is said to be complete if $\mathbf{B}$ is non-singular. Let $\mathbf{A}$ be the matrix of all the coefficients:

$$\mathbf{A} = (\mathbf{B}_0 : \mathbf{B}_1 : \cdots : \mathbf{B}_m : -\mathbf{C}_0 : \cdots : -\mathbf{C}_r)$$

and $\mathbf{x}_t$ the column vector of all the variables $(\mathbf{y}_t \ldots \mathbf{y}_{t-m} : \mathbf{z}_t \ldots \mathbf{z}_{t-r})$ then (14.3) can be written neatly as:

$$\mathbf{A}\mathbf{x}_t = \mathbf{u}_t \sim \mathsf{IN}_n(\mathbf{0}, \boldsymbol{\Sigma}).$$

The matrix $\mathbf{A}$ must be restricted if the $\{\mathbf{B}_i, \mathbf{C}_i\}$ are to be unique: otherwise, a further non-singular multiplication of (14.2) would produce a different model, yet one which looked exactly like (14.3), thereby destroying uniqueness. The rank and order conditions for identification apply: both are fully discussed and implemented in PcFiml. The main issue of relevance to PcGive is that in any equation containing p right-hand side endogenous variables, the system of which it is part must contain at least p non-modelled variables not included in that equation: this is the order condition. When the sample of T observations on these p endogenous variables is just denoted by $\mathbf{Y}$ and the sample on the excluded but available non-modelled variables is $\mathbf{Z}$, then:

$$\text{rank}\,(\mathbf{Y}'\mathbf{Z}) = p$$

is both necessary and sufficient for identification: this is the rank condition (see White, 1984).

All of the model types of §12.3 could occur within (14.3), and if $\mathbf{A}$ is over-identified, the imposed restrictions are testable. When developing a model of a system, it is sensible to commence from the unrestricted representation (14.1), test its validity, and then reduce the system to the model. All of the attributes needed for the model to match the evidence are called congruency (see §14.5) and these can be tested, but care is required in modelling integrated data. As a first step, cointegration tests can be conducted to establish the dimension of the cointegrating space, and the relevant set of cointegration restrictions and differences can be imposed to reduce the data to I(0). This order will facilitate later testing since conventional limiting distributions can be used: see Phillips (1991) and Hendry and Mizon (1993) for discussions of modelling cointegrated processes, Johansen (1988) and Johansen and Juselius (1990) for analyses of the maximum likelihood estimator, and Hendry *et al.* (1988) for an approach to structural system modelling in I(0) processes. Such a methodology implements the general-to-specific notion in the system context, and contrasts with the alternative of specifying a structural model at the outset and testing its restrictions against the (derived) reduced form. Since the latter may be invalid, it provides an unreliable benchmark for any tests. Techniques for estimating models, as well as general derivations of standard errors etc., are considered in §14.8 below; further detail on systems and models thereof is provided in the PcFiml documentation which includes the implementation of a complete modelling exercise on a dynamic cointegrated system.

Prior to proceeding, we note that since (14.1) is a model of itself, and there are likely to be valid parsimonious representations of the system (14.1), the critique in Sims (1980) lacks force. Specifying a model in structural form corresponds to imposing non-linear restrictions across functions of the πs in (14.1), and there are no *a priori* grounds for claiming that all possible restrictions are invalid. For example, if the response of y_{1t} to y_{2t} is very rapid compared to that of y_{2t} to y_{1t} in a second equation, a structural model of their joint representation can impose valid restrictions on the VAR. The application of encompassing discussed in §14.5 will clarify this issue further. At the heart of the issue of conditional estimation is the role of weak exogeneity in modelling single equations, so we now discuss that issue (see Engle, Hendry and Richard, 1983).

14.3 Data density factorizations

To undertake valid inference using a single-equation approach, some conditions must be fulfilled such that the system dependence of conditioning variables can be neglected without losing relevant information. These conditions are encapsulated in the concept of weak exogeneity. First, we introduce joint data density functions, and extend the notion of factorization introduced in Chapter 13.

14.3.1 Innovations and white noise

The data set of observations on $\{\mathbf{y}_t\}$ and $\{\mathbf{z}_t\}$ in (14.1) is denoted by $\mathbf{X}_T^1 = (\mathbf{x}_1 \ldots \mathbf{x}_T)$ where $\mathbf{x}_t' = (\mathbf{y}_t' : \mathbf{z}_t')$. Thus:

$$\mathbf{X}_T^1 = \begin{pmatrix} \mathbf{y}_1 & \mathbf{y}_2 & \cdots & \mathbf{y}_T \\ \mathbf{z}_1 & \mathbf{z}_2 & \cdots & \mathbf{z}_T \end{pmatrix}.$$

Denote the process generating $\mathbf{X}_T^1$ by $\mathsf{D}_\mathsf{X}\left(\mathbf{X}_T^1|\boldsymbol{\theta}_T^1, \mathbf{X}_0\right)$ where $\mathbf{X}_0$ are the initial conditions and $\boldsymbol{\theta}_T^1 \in \Theta$ are the 'parameters' of the process, which may depend on the historical time (hence the indexing by $1, \ldots, T$). Since $\mathbf{X}_T^1 = (\mathbf{x}_1 \ldots \mathbf{x}_T)$, the whole sample data density $\mathsf{D}_\mathsf{X}(\cdot)$ can be sequentially factorized as the product of terms like $\mathsf{D}_\mathsf{x}\left(\mathbf{x}_t|\mathbf{X}_{t-1}^1, \boldsymbol{\theta}_t, \mathbf{X}_0\right)$ which is each time period's density. This exploits the fact that if $\mathsf{P}(a)$ denotes the probability of an event a, then $\mathsf{P}(ab) = \mathsf{P}(a|b)\,\mathsf{P}(b)$, and this can be repeated starting at $t, t-1, \ldots, 1$. Assume $\boldsymbol{\theta}_t = \boldsymbol{\theta}\,\forall t$ (constancy is the topic of §14.5.3), and let $\mathbf{X}_{t-1} = \left(\mathbf{X}_{t-1}^{1}, \mathbf{X}_0\right)$ so that $\mathsf{D_X}(\cdot)$ at every t is $\mathsf{D_x}\left(\mathbf{x}_t|\boldsymbol{\theta}, \mathbf{X}_{t-1}\right)$. Then:

$$\mathsf{D_X}\left(\mathbf{X}_T^1 \mid \boldsymbol{\theta}, \mathbf{X}_0\right) = \prod_{t=1}^{T} \mathsf{D_x}\left(\mathbf{x}_t \mid \boldsymbol{\theta}, \mathbf{X}_{t-1}\right). \tag{14.4}$$

Let:

$$\boldsymbol{\nu}_t = \mathbf{x}_t - \mathsf{E}\left[\mathbf{x}_t \mid \mathbf{X}_{t-1}\right],$$

then by construction, $\{\boldsymbol{\nu}_t\}$ is a mean innovation process since:

$$\mathsf{E}\left[\boldsymbol{\nu}_t \mid \mathbf{X}_{t-1}\right] = \mathsf{E}\left[\left(\mathbf{x}_t - \mathsf{E}\left[\mathbf{x}_t \mid \mathbf{X}_{t-1}\right]\right) \mid \mathbf{X}_{t-1}\right] = \mathbf{0}. \tag{14.5}$$

Moreover, since lagged $\boldsymbol{\nu}s$, denoted by $\mathbf{V}_{t-1}$, can be derived from $\mathbf{X}_{t-1}$ (by lagging their definition), they are also white noise:

$$\mathsf{E}\left[\boldsymbol{\nu}_t \mid \mathbf{V}_{t-1}\right] = \mathbf{0}. \tag{14.6}$$

Thus, the DGP can be expressed without loss in an innovation-error representation.

A well-known example is provided by the stationary first-order autoregressive process:

$$y_t = \mu y_{t-1} + e_t,$$

when $\{e_t\}$ is jointly normal and $\mathsf{E}\left[e_t e_s\right] = 0 \; \forall t \neq s$. Then, $\mathsf{D_Y}\left(y_1 \ldots y_T | \mu, \sigma_e^2, y_0\right)$ is the multivariate normal density $\mathsf{N}_T\left(\mathbf{0}, \sigma_e^2 \boldsymbol{\Omega}\right)$ where $\boldsymbol{\Omega}$ is a $T \times T$ symmetric matrix with $(i,j)^{th}$ element:

$$\frac{\mu^{|i-j|}}{(1-\mu^2)}.$$

The factorization of the joint density of $(y_1 \ldots y_T)$ is:

$$\mathsf{D_Y}\left(y_1 \ldots y_T \mid \mu, \sigma_e^2, y_0\right) = \prod_{t=1}^{T} \mathsf{D_y}\left(y_t \mid \mathbf{Y}_{t-1}; \mu, \sigma_e^2\right)$$

which yields a product of individual density terms like $\mathsf{N}\left(\mu y_{t-1}, \sigma_e^2\right)$. Since $\nu_t = y_t - \mathsf{E}\left(y_t | \mathbf{Y}_{t-1}\right)$, then:

$$\nu_t = y_t - \mathsf{E}\left[y_t \mid y_{t-1}\right] = y_t - \mu y_{t-1} = e_t$$

is indeed the (mean) innovation (see e.g., Judge, Griffiths, Hill, Lütkepohl and Lee, 1985, Chapter 8).

14.3.2 Weak exogeneity

We can now formalize weak exogeneity. Its importance is that all current-dated regressors treated as conditioning variables must be weakly exogenous to sustain valid and efficient inferences (see Engle *et al.*, 1983). To relate the analysis more closely to that in Chapter 12, we only consider a bivariate system, where the two variables are $(y_t : z_t)$: the analysis generalizes by interpreting these as vectors.

First, note that the joint density $\mathsf{D_x}(\mathbf{x}_t|\boldsymbol{\theta}, \mathbf{X}_{t-1})$ is unaffected by 1-1 transformations of its parameters $\boldsymbol{\theta}$ to $\boldsymbol{\phi}$ (say) where:

$$\boldsymbol{\phi} = \mathbf{f}(\boldsymbol{\theta}) \text{ and } \boldsymbol{\phi} \in \boldsymbol{\Phi},$$

so that:

$$\mathsf{D_x}(\mathbf{x}_t \mid \boldsymbol{\theta}, \mathbf{X}_{t-1}) = \mathsf{D_x}(\mathbf{x}_t \mid \boldsymbol{\phi}, \mathbf{X}_{t-1}).$$

Secondly, we can partition into $\boldsymbol{\phi} = (\boldsymbol{\phi}_1 : \boldsymbol{\phi}_2)$ to match the partition of $\mathbf{x}_t$ into $(y_t : z_t)$. Then, using the factorization in (14.4), if y_t is to be conditioned on z_t, we can factorize $\mathsf{D_x}(\cdot)$ into a conditional and a marginal distribution:

$$\mathsf{D_x}(\mathbf{x}_t \mid \boldsymbol{\theta}, \mathbf{X}_{t-1}) = \mathsf{D_{y|z}}(y_t \mid z_t, \mathbf{X}_{t-1}, \boldsymbol{\phi}_1)\, \mathsf{D_z}(z_t \mid \mathbf{X}_{t-1}, \boldsymbol{\phi}_2). \qquad (14.7)$$

This does not impose any restrictions and hence loses no information.

Thirdly, some parameters, denoted $\boldsymbol{\mu}$, will be the focus of the econometric modelling exercise, and these are called parameters of interest. To avoid information loss from only modelling the conditional relation in (14.7), it must be possible to learn about $\boldsymbol{\mu}$ from the factor:

$$\mathsf{D_{y|z}}(y_t \mid z_t, \mathbf{X}_{t-1}, \boldsymbol{\phi}_1) \qquad (14.8)$$

alone. Moreover, the resulting knowledge about $\boldsymbol{\mu}$ must be equivalent to that which could have been gleaned from analysing the joint density $\mathsf{D_x}(\cdot)$. Two conditions ensure that equivalence. First:

(1) all the parameters of interest $\boldsymbol{\mu}$ can be obtained from $\boldsymbol{\phi}_1$ alone; and
(2) $\boldsymbol{\phi}_1$ and $\boldsymbol{\phi}_2$ must be variation free (that is, impose no restrictions on each other), so:

$$(\boldsymbol{\phi}_1 : \boldsymbol{\phi}_2) \in \boldsymbol{\Phi}_1 \times \boldsymbol{\Phi}_2 \text{ where } \boldsymbol{\phi}_1 \in \boldsymbol{\Phi}_1 \text{ and } \boldsymbol{\phi}_2 \in \boldsymbol{\Phi}_2.$$

If so, z_t is said to be weakly exogenous for $\boldsymbol{\mu}$, and only the conditional model $\mathsf{D_{y|z}}(y_t|z_t, \mathbf{X}_{t-1}, \boldsymbol{\phi}_1)$ needs to be estimated to determine $\boldsymbol{\mu}$, since the marginal model $\mathsf{D_z}(z_t|\mathbf{X}_{t-1}, \boldsymbol{\phi}_2)$ contains no information about $\boldsymbol{\mu}$. For more extensive and expository discussions, see Ericsson (1992) and Hendry (1995a).

14.4 Model evaluation

In Chapter 12, the basic single-equation dynamic model was written as:

$$b_0(L)\, y_t = \sum_{i=1}^{k} b_i(L)\, z_{it} + \epsilon_t \tag{14.9}$$

where there are k explanatory variables $(z_{1t} \ldots z_{kt})$, $b_i(L)$ denotes a lag polynomial, and we have changed notation for the non-modelled variables from x to z to match the system notation above.

It is relatively easy to specify and analyse models such as those in (14.9), or any generalizations thereof, when they are regarded as mathematical formulations. Unfortunately, it is far more difficult to develop useful empirical relationships corresponding to these for a given time series on a set of variables. In particular, the orders of the lag lengths of every polynomial $b_0(L)$, $b_1(L)$ etc. must be established, as must the revelance of any given variable, the constancy of the entities called parameters, the validity of conditioning, the required functional form, and the properties of the unmodelled term. Indeed, this description begs the very issue of what defines the usefulness of an econometric relationship.

At a general level, the utility of anything depends on the purposes for which it is being developed. Hence if a completely specified loss function existed for judging a particular modelling exercise, it would seem natural to develop a model to optimize that criterion. Two problems arise, however, neither of which can be sidestepped. First, it is rare in econometrics to be able to fully specify the loss function. Models are wanted for prediction, for scenario or policy analyses, for testing economic hypotheses, and for understanding how the economy functions. Empirically, there often exist conflicts in criteria in selecting models to achieve such multiple objectives. For example, a model which predicts well historically may yield no insight into how a market will behave under some change in regulations, the implementation of which will cause that model to mispredict. Secondly, even assuming that a fully specified loss function did exist and that the optimal model could be selected, there remains the difficulty of establishing how 'good' that best model is. For example, the best model that could be found may still suffer from non-constant parameters and hence yield a low level of utility; worse still, by not knowing this weakness, serious losses may accrue in the future. Thus, whatever the basis on which a model has been formulated or developed, there remains an issue of assessment or evaluation.

The program PcGive operates easily and efficiently to implement this aspect. Since we do not know how the economy works, we do not know the best way of studying it. Consequently, any model might correspond to reality, however unlikely its mode of creation; or unfortunately, it might transpire to be invalid, however clever and thorough its development. Nevertheless, taking a model as stated by its proprietor, a vast range of states of the world will be excluded by that model, and thus it is open to evaluation against the available information (see Hendry, 1987, for a more extensive analysis). For example, because its residual process is white noise, a particular model may claim to explain a given data set adequately; yet the residuals may not be an innovation process, so testing that latter hypothesis might reveal an important model weakness (as in the COMFAC procedure discussed in §12.3). This is the destructive testing aspect of PcGive, and accounts for its wide range of preprogrammed statistics for model evaluation.

Testing focuses on the empirical validity of assertions about a given model. Tests are statistics with a known distribution under a null hypothesis and some power against a specific alternative. The tests below are designed to have (central) t, F or χ^2 distributions under the null, and corresponding non-central distributions against some alternative. Usually, they are invariant to the direction of the departure from the null for a given class of alternatives, and only depend on the distance (that is, the overall extent of the departure: this holds for t^2, F and χ^2 statistics). However, most tests also have some power to detect other alternatives, so rejecting the null does not entail accepting the alternative, and in many instances, accepting the alternative would be a *non sequitur*. Rejection reveals model invalidity, albeit with some chance of a type-I error of incorrectly rejecting a valid null.

First, however, we need to delineate the relevant class of null hypotheses, and then derive associated test statistics for reasonable alternatives. The former task is considered in §14.5 in terms of a taxonomy of available information, and the latter in §14.6 where the main test principles are briefly described.

14.5 An information taxonomy

A further division of the data set $\mathbf{X}_t^1 = (\mathbf{x}_1 \ldots \mathbf{x}_t)$ into:

$$\mathbf{X}_T^1 = \left(\mathbf{X}_{t-1}^1 : \mathbf{x}_t : \mathbf{X}_T^{t+1}\right)$$

yields the trichotomy of the (past : present : future) relative to t. In addition, we allow for theory information, measurement information, and the information in rival models (see Hendry and Richard, 1982, 1983, and Gilbert, 1986, for expositions). Statistical tests can be constructed to evaluate a model against each element of this six-fold taxonomy. Such tests require formulating both the appropriate null hypothesis for the relevant information set, and devising a reasonable class of alternatives against which the test should have power. The taxonomy clarifies the relevant null hypotheses, and generally points up interesting alternatives against which to test model validity.

The six major aspects of model evaluation are discussed next, followed by a brief analysis of their relation to the theory of reduction.

14.5.1 The relative past

The residuals should be white noise and hence unpredictable from their own past as in (14.6). This entails that they should not be significantly autocorrelated. If they are autocorrelated, a better-fitting model can be developed by removing the autocorrelation, although this is not a recommended practice since it may impose invalid common factors. PcGive provides valid tests and diagnostic information for residual autocorrelation, including Lagrange-multiplier tests for a wide range of orders of autoregressive errors, as well as residual correlograms and autoregressions.

Further, the errors should not be explainable from the information set being used. Alternatively expressed, the errors should be an innovation process which is unpredictable from lagged functions of the available data as in (14.5). Being white noise is a necessary, but not sufficient, condition for being an innovation, as shown above. A good example arises when removing autocorrelation by fitting, say, autoregressive error processes, since that automatically ensures the white noise, but may impose invalid common-factor restrictions and hence does not entail an innovation error (see Sargan, 1964, 1980a). This problem can be avoided by beginning with a general specification like (14.9) and testing for valid common factors prior to imposing them. In PcGive, the COMFAC tests to check such restrictions are based on Sargan's algorithms.

Neither white-noise errors nor innovations need be homoscedastic, so that the standard errors of OLS estimators in PcGive can allow for residual heteroscedasticity (the HCSEs in Chapter 12: see White, 1980, and MacKinnon and White, 1985). Tests of both autoregressive conditional heteroscedasticity (ARCH: see Engle, 1982) and unconditional heteroscedasticity are also provided. Similarly, tests for normality are included to check on the distributional assumptions underlying finite-sample inference.

To summarize these aspects relating to the (relative) past of the process, namely $\mathbf{X}_{t-1}^{1}$, a reasonable null is that the unexplained component of a behavioural model should be a homoscedastic innovation.

14.5.2 The relative present

As noted above, all current-dated conditioning variables should be at least weakly exogenous (see Engle *et al.*, 1983) to sustain valid and efficient inferences. While weak exogeneity is not easy to test directly, tests of estimation consistency based on Engle (1984) can be calculated from stored regression predictions, using the fact that lagged variables are predetermined once the errors are innovations. These statistics test for the overall model specification and need not detect all forms of weak exogeneity failure: see Hendry (1995b). However, valid conditioning in conjunction with other hypotheses may entail many testable hypotheses: for example, parameter constancy in a structural equation, despite non-constancy in a reduced form or marginal processes, strongly supports weak exogeneity (see Favero and Hendry, 1992). Conversely, parameters of current endogenous variables (other than the dependent variable) should be estimated using instrumental variables (IV) in PcGive, or full-information maximum likelihood (FIML) techniques in PcFiml. Any instruments chosen must themselves be weakly exogenous for the parameters of interest (see §12.7 for the algebra of IV estimation).

Thus, for the (relative) present, namely $\mathbf{x}_t$ above, the crucial null hypothesis is that the conditioning variables (regressors or instruments) are valid.

14.5.3 The relative future

The parameters should be constant over time, where such 'parameters' are those entities which are anticipated on *a priori* grounds to be the basic invariants of the model. Here, an invariant is a parameter which remains constant over a range of interventions or regime shifts in policy (or marginal) variables. If z_t in (14.8) is weakly exogenous for the parameters of interest μ, and ϕ_1 is invariant to changes in the distribution of $\{z_t\}$, then z_t is super exogenous for μ. In this formulation, constancy is necessary for invariance.

PcGive calculates tests for parameter constancy based on Hansen (1992), and *ex post* 1-step forecast confidence bands, as well as offering comprehensive recursive estimation routines including recursive least squares (RLS) and recursive instrumental variables (RIV) (see Hendry and Neale, 1987). Various types of constancy tests based on Chow (1960) are available with the first.

Much of the power of PcGive resides in its recursive procedures. These are a useful tool for investigating issues of invariance and super exogeneity by showing that the behaviour of the z_t process did actually alter without changing the parameters of interest. This is one way of testing assertions that parameters are liable to suffer from the Lucas critique (see Hendry, 1988, and Favero and Hendry, 1992). The algebra of recursive estimation is described in Chapter 13. For both types of recursive estimator, a large volume of output is generated, which can be analysed graphically by plotting the recursive errors or coefficients etc. against t. The systems estimator is similar in structure, except that y_t becomes a vector of endogenous variables at time t.

Thus, in this group of tests about the (relative) future, denoted above by $\mathbf{X}_T^{t+1}$, the crucial null is parameter constancy.

14.5.4 Theory information

Econometrics is essentially concerned with the mutual interplay of economic theory and empirical evidence. Neither has precedence, and both are essential. It is difficult to characterize this information source in the abstract, partly because it is so pervasive, and partly because it is itself under scrutiny. The role that theory information plays depends on the precise context, as is easily seen by contrasting exercises modelling the demand for cheese with modelling either the supply of money or the determination of an international exchange rate. Through national income accounts concepts, economics affects the measurement of the data variables, and theory models influence the choice of the data to examine, and the classes of models and functional forms to use, as well as suggesting the parameterizations of interest. Conversely, a major objective of a study in economics may be to test the validity of some theoretical propositions.

Not all theories are equal, and indeed theories differ greatly in their level, some being very low-level and well established (for example, those concerned with measuring the output of apples or the volume of visible imports); some being medium level and widely used but potentially open to revision as knowledge improves (for example, price indices, or concepts of the capital stock), and yet others being high level and under test (for example, a rational expectations, inter-temporal substitution theory of labour supply; or a surplus-rent theory of house price determination). Thus, that all observations are theory laden does not entail that data-based studies are impossible or even misguided; rather, the respective roles of evidence and theory will vary with the reliability of each in the given context (for a more extensive discussion, see Hendry, 1995a).

To test any theory requires a baseline, so first one must determine the extent to which that baseline satisfies the evaluation criteria. Thus, we are led to distinguish between the statistical model and the econometric model, where the former is the baseline and is judged on statistical criteria, and the latter is interpreted in the light of the economic theory, but tested against the former (see, for example, Spanos, 1986). This distinction is at its clearest for the system and the model thereof in the PcFiml module, where a test of over-identifying restrictions is automatically calculated to check the coherence between the two.

Overall, one can do little better than state the need for an econometric model to be theory consistent.

14.5.5 Measurement information

This too is not open to a general discussion, but relates to the issue of data admissibility: could a given model logically have generated the observed and future potential data? For example, the unemployment rate must lie between zero and unity; a logit transformation ensures that, but a linear model could generate negative unemployment (see White, 1990, for a critique). The relevance of such considerations depends on the problem under study, but since (for example) cointegration between the logarithms of any given set of I(1) variables need not entail cointegration between the levels, choosing the appropriate functional form can be vitally important.

The other key aspect is data measurement accuracy, and like apple pie, almost everyone favours more accurate data. Again we can only reiterate the obvious point that effort must be devoted to preparing the best available data, and to taking account of any known inaccuracies as well as the average level of their imprecision. Modelling the mismeasurement is sometimes possible (see Hendry, 1995a), and the use of instrumental variables rather than OLS is an example of doing so.

14.5.6 Rival models

The final necessary condition to ensure that an empirical model is in the set of useful contenders is that it is not dominated by any other model. More stringently, one might desire that no other model (M_2 say) explained features of the data which one's own model (M_1) could not. This idea was formalized in Chapter 12 by encompassing, and testing whether other models captured specific information not embodied in the model under test (see Hendry and Richard, 1982, 1989, Mizon, 1984, and Mizon and Richard, 1986). The contending model must encompass (denoted by $\mathcal{E}$) previous empirical models of the dependent variable (in symbols $\mathsf{M}_1 \, \mathcal{E} \, \mathsf{M}_2$).

Parsimonious encompassing (which is reflexive, antisymmetric and transitive) requires a model to explain the results of a larger model within which it is nested. Let $\subset$ denote nesting when parsimonious encompassing is denoted by $\mathcal{E}_p$: if $\mathsf{M}_1 \subset \mathsf{M}_2$ then $\mathsf{M}_1 \, \mathcal{E}_p \, \mathsf{M}_2$ is that requirement. Consider a sequence of models:

$$\mathsf{M}_1 \subset \mathsf{M}_2 \subset \mathsf{M}_3.$$

When $\mathsf{M}_1 \, \mathcal{E}_p \, \mathsf{M}_2$ and $\mathsf{M}_2 \, \mathcal{E}_p \, \mathsf{M}_3$, then $\mathsf{M}_1 \, \mathcal{E}_p \, \mathsf{M}_3$. This follows because when $\mathsf{M}_1 \, \mathcal{E}_p \, \mathsf{M}_2$ and $\mathsf{M}_2 \, \mathcal{E} \, \mathsf{M}_1$ (by virtue of nesting it), then M_1 represents a limit to which M_2 can be validly reduced (although further reduction may be feasible as is entailed by the sequence $\mathsf{M}_3 \rightarrow \mathsf{M}_2 \rightarrow \mathsf{M}_1$). Since M_2 is a valid reduction of M_3 by hypothesis, then M_1 must also be a valid reduction of M_3. Indeed, despite encompassing initially arising as a distinct concept in a different research area, it is an intimate component of the theory of reduction discussed in §14.5.7 and a further major reason for adopting a general-to-specific approach.

Let M^m be the minimal nesting model of two non-nested models M_1 and M_4 (so that neither M_1 nor M_4 is a special case of the other). M^m may be hard to synthesize, and may not be unique without arbitrary restrictions, but this difficulty reflects the inherent problems of any specific-to-general approach, and is not a difficulty for encompassing *per se*: the relevant issue of interest here is when M_1 does or does not encompass M_4, not the route by which the problem arose. If $\mathsf{M}_1 \, \mathcal{E}_p \, \mathsf{M}^m$, then M_4 can contain no specific information not already embodied in M_1 (since otherwise M^m would reflect that information and M_1 could not be a valid reduction). Conversely, if $\mathsf{M}_1 \, \mathcal{E} \, \mathsf{M}_4$ then $\mathsf{M}_1 \, \mathcal{E}_p \, \mathsf{M}^m$. Thus, it should not matter whether M_1 is tested against M_4, $\mathsf{M}_1 \cup \mathsf{M}_4 = \mathsf{M}^m$ or any combination thereof (including the orthogonal complement of M^m relative to M_1). Tests which are invariant to such common variables consequently seem essential, and the F-test for model simplification has that property for linear models. Chapter 12 provided an empirical illustration.

In the multi-equation context, the econometric model should encompass the statistical system (usually a VAR or unrestricted reduced form), and this is the test for overidentifying restrictions noted above (see Hendry and Mizon, 1993).

Consequently, the crucial null hypothesis in this information set is that the econometric model should parsimoniously encompass the statistical system.

14.5.7 The theory of reduction

The key concept underpinning the above analysis is that models are reductions of the DGP, obtained by transforming the initial variables to those which are to be investigated; marginalizing with respect to the many variables deemed irrelevant (but perhaps incorrectly treated as such); sequentially factorizing as in §14.5.1; and conditioning on other variables deemed to be weakly exogenous (as in §14.5.2): see Hendry and Richard (1982) and Hendry (1987). Every reduction induces a transformation of the original parameters $\boldsymbol{\lambda}$ of the DGP; consequently, invalid reductions may lead to the coefficients of the resulting model not being constant or invariant or even interpretable (as in so-called wrong signs). Thus, implicitly the analysis really begins with a far bigger set of variables $\mathbf{W}_T^1$ (say) than the set $\mathbf{X}_T^1$ considered by the current group of investigators, so, for example, $\mathbf{W}$ includes all the disaggregated variables which were eliminated when only aggregate time series were retained for analysis. The process of elimination or reduction then transforms $\boldsymbol{\lambda}$ into the $\boldsymbol{\theta}_T^1$ used above, although nothing guarantees that $\boldsymbol{\lambda}$ itself is constant.

The taxonomy of information sets §14.5.1–§14.5.6 arises naturally when considering each possible reduction step, so that reduction theory is invaluable in the context of model evaluation for delineating null hypotheses and in the context of discovery for specifying the relevant design criteria. It also offers insights into many of the central concepts of econometrics in terms of whether a reduction does or does not involve a loss of information. Thus, we can consider the reverse of the taxonomy by relating extant concepts to associated reduction steps:

(1) the theory of sufficient statistics concerns when reduction by marginalizing with respect to a subset of observations retains all of the information relevant to the parameters of interest, as in aggregation;
(2) the concept of Granger non-causality concerns when there is no loss of information from marginalizing with respect to the entire history of a subset of variables (for example, the elements of $\mathbf{W}_{t-1}$ which are not included in $\mathbf{X}_{t-1}$): this concept is germane to marginalizing and not to conditioning (contrast Sims, 1980, with Engle *et al.*, 1983);
(3) the concept of an innovation concerns when there is no information remaining in lagged data: as shown above, all models can be expressed with innovation errors via sequential factorization; thus, all forms of autocorrelated-error representation are at best 'convenient simplifications';
(4) the concept of weak exogeneity concerns when there is no loss from ignoring information in the marginal distributions of the conditioning variables;
(5) the concept of invariance (or autonomy) concerns when the reduction sequence has successfully isolated constant parameters of the DGP;
(6) the concept of encompassing concerns when alternative models contain no additional information about the variables being modelled, so that an encompassing

model represents a limit (though not necessarily the final limit) to the set of feasible reductions.

The theory of reduction also clarifies and extends the theory of encompassing by revealing that all models are comparable via the DGP. Indeed, the concept of reduction points up that model design is endemic, but because all models must arise as reductions of the DGP, the pertinent issue is their validity, not how they were designed. Some designs are inadvertent (as when residual autocorrelation is removed), whereas others are deliberate (as in general-to-specific). Thus, reduction theory even explains why the 'problems approach' to econometric modelling arises: overly reduced empirical representations of the DGP will usually manifest all sorts of symptoms of mis-specification. However, badly-designed models will often result from sequentially correcting such symptoms by adopting the alternative hypothesis corresponding to every null hypothesis that is rejected (see Hendry, 1979).

Models that are satisfactory against all six of the above information sets are called congruent and undominated (given the available information). Succinctly, PcGive is designed for efficiently developing congruent encompassing models and for evaluating existing models for potential departures from congruency.

14.6 Test types

Various test principles are commonly used in econometrics and the three main ones are Wald (W), Lagrange-multiplier (LM) and Likelihood-ratio (LR) tests (see Breusch and Pagan, 1980, and Engle, 1984). For example, the Chow (1960) test for parameter constancy is derivable from all three principles, whereas the test of over-identifying restrictions is LR, the portmanteau tests for autocorrelation in OLS are based on LM, and the COMFAC tests are Wald tests. In each instance, the choice of test type tends to reflect computational ease. Under the relevant null hypothesis and for local alternatives, the three test types are asymptotically equivalent; however, if equations are mis-specified in other ways than that under test, or the sample size is small, different inferences can result.

Although LM tests conventionally come in the form $T\mathsf{R}^2$ (being distributed as χ^2), research indicates that F-forms have more appropriate significance levels and that χ^2 versions reject acceptable models too often (see Kiviet, 1987). (Incidentally, Kiviet's results also show that the Chow test and LM tests for autocorrelated residuals are approximately independently distributed.) Thus, PcGive tends to report F-forms when possible. Pagan (1984) exposits testing in terms of residual diagnostic procedures. Further details on econometric testing can be found in Harvey (1981, 1990), Spanos (1986), Godfrey (1988), Hendry (1995a) or in relevant chapters of Griliches and Intriligator (1984).

While a basic feature of PcGive is that most of the test statistics are calculated by a simple choice from a menu, others are inbuilt. For example, parameter constancy tests based on Hansen (1992) are automatically undertaken with OLS estimation; alternatively, if the user initially specifies some post-sample observations, forecast-based tests are computed. Similar considerations apply to tests for the validity of any given choice of instrumental variables (automatic), and to the significance of lagged variables (computed by selecting Dynamic analysis). Note that the options in the Profile dialog can be set to ensure automatic computation of the test summary.

14.7 Modelling strategies

Turning now to constructive aspects of empirical research, since the DGP is unknown, any method of discovery might produce a Nobel-prize winning model, as illustrated by the apocryphal tale of Archimedes' 'Eureka' or Poincaré's memoirs. Nevertheless, different research strategies are likely to have different efficiencies. If one needs to estimate 'literally hundreds of regressions' (as in Friedman and Schwartz, 1982) to develop a single linear relationship between four or five variables, that strategy would seem to have a low level of efficiency relative to an approach which could locate at least as good a model in a couple of steps. This is the second aspect of PcGive, whereby it facilitates general-to-specific model simplification approaches (see, for example, Mizon, 1977, and Hendry and Mizon, 1978). Unsurprisingly, these mimic the theory of reduction in §14.5.7. Thus, PcGive provides easy ways of formulating polynomials like $b_i(L)$; solves for $b_0(1)$, $b_1(1)$ etc. (where the lag length n might be 8 for quarterly data), and provides associated standard errors; and tests for whether $(z_{t-m} \ldots z_{t-n})$ as a group contribute to the model's explanatory power. For single equations, common factor (COMFAC) simplifications are checked, and long-run coefficients such as K in (12.6) are derived together with standard errors. Finally, all of the necessary conditions for model validity which were discussed in §14.5 above can be checked.

Naturally, a premium rests on a sensible specification of the initial general model and that is where both economic theory and previous studies (to be encompassed in due course) play a major guiding role. Economic theories are powerful at specifying long-run equilibria (such as (12.6) above) which delineate the menu of variables, and earlier work often indicates at least minimal lag-length requirements. Once formulated, the general model should be transformed to an interpretable (probably orthogonal) parameterization and then simplified before rigorous testing. More detailed discussions are provided in Hendry (1986c, 1987, 1995a).

14.8 Model estimation

Like many of the other aspects considered above, appropriate estimation is a necessary rather than a sufficient condition for developing useful models. Given a particular model form and a distributional assumption about the data, the log-likelihood function can be formulated and is denoted $\ell(\boldsymbol{\theta})$ where $\boldsymbol{\theta}$ is the vector of unknown parameters of interest. Maximum likelihood (MLE) and least squares estimators are described in Chapter 13. In some cases, the set of first-order conditions defining the MLE may be non-linear and require iterative solution methods: this holds for any non-linear regression model. In large samples, for correctly specified problems, MLEs have many excellent statistical properties. Moreover, for models linear in both variables and parameters, almost all other estimation methods can be obtained as approximate solutions of the score equation based on choosing different initial values and selecting different numbers of iterative steps in alternative numerical methods. For example, estimation within PcFiml is encapsulated in a simple formula called the estimator generating equation (EGE: see Hendry, 1976, and Hendry *et al.*, 1988). Here we note that OLS and IVE are special cases of the EGE when an individual equation is being studied (even if that equation is implicitly part of a system).

The standard errors of $\hat{\boldsymbol{\theta}}$ are usually calculated from the inverse of the information matrix or the negative inverse of the Hessian, although such a formula assumes a correctly-specified error (that is, a homoscedastic innovation). In PcGive, heteroscedastic-consistent standard errors can be computed for OLS.

The distributional assumptions for $\hat{\boldsymbol{\theta}}$ implicit in inferences within PcGive (other than unit-root tests) are that, conditional on having a congruent representation:

$$\sqrt{T}\mathbf{R}\left(\hat{\boldsymbol{\theta}}-\boldsymbol{\theta}_p\right) \xrightarrow{D} \mathsf{N}_n\left(\mathbf{0},\mathbf{I}\right),$$

where T is the sample size, the probability limit of $\hat{\boldsymbol{\theta}}$ is $\boldsymbol{\theta}_p$ (the invariant parameter of interest), and $\mathbf{V} = \text{plim}\,\mathbf{H}^{-1}$ such that $\mathbf{V}^{-1} = \mathbf{R}'\mathbf{R}$. This assumes that variables are transformed to I(0) and that all the components of congruency are valid. Naturally, these assumptions should be rigorously evaluated in order to sustain such a conditioning claim since 'the three golden rules of econometrics are test, test and test' (see Hendry, 1980). If a function of $\boldsymbol{\theta}$ is of interest, say $\mathbf{g}(\boldsymbol{\theta}) = \boldsymbol{\phi}\,(r \times 1)$ the standard errors of $\hat{\boldsymbol{\phi}} = \mathbf{g}(\hat{\boldsymbol{\theta}})$ are derived from the Taylor-series approximation:

$$\hat{\boldsymbol{\phi}}-\boldsymbol{\phi} = \mathbf{J}\left(\hat{\boldsymbol{\theta}}-\boldsymbol{\theta}\right) \tag{14.10}$$

where

$$\mathbf{J} = \frac{\partial \mathbf{g}\left(\boldsymbol{\theta}\right)'}{\partial \boldsymbol{\theta}}$$

is the Jacobian matrix of the transformation, and hence:

$$\sqrt{T}\left(\hat{\boldsymbol{\phi}}-\boldsymbol{\phi}\right) \xrightarrow{D} \mathsf{N}_r\left(\mathbf{0},\mathbf{JVJ}'\right) \tag{14.11}$$

$\mathbf{J}$ can usually be derived analytically for cases of interest, but otherwise is calculated by numerical differentiation.

The preceding analysis of estimation (and implicitly also of testing) sidesteps an important issue which textbook notation also tends to camouflage, namely that estimation methods and associated tests are applied to the whole sample directly rather than recursively (adding observations one at a time). As stressed above, PcGive incorporates a variety of recursive estimators including RLS and RIV; PcFiml contains the generalization of the former to a system of equations with common regressors (denoted RMLS), and even recursive FIML. Such recursive estimators can yield evaluation information in a powerful way, yet for least squares are not computationally burdensome relative to direct methods (see Hendry and Neale, 1987).

14.9 Conclusion

PcGive explicitly embodies a methodical approach to econometric modelling which seeks to reflect the practical realities confronting the investigation of economic time-series data. This chapter has sketched the principles on which it is based. The next chapter, 15, confronts how PcGive might be used to handle a number of important practical problems.

Part IV completes the econometric discussion by explaining in detail the statistics reported by PcGive. Chapter 16 notes descriptive statistics, and Chapters 17 and 18 discuss statistics associated with single-equation modelling. These chapters could be read in a different order if desired, or left for later reference. The remaining parts provide detailed manuals for PcGive, describing all of the menus that will be encountered during use, and various appendices.

Chapter 15

Nine Important Practical Econometric Problems

Looking back over the sketch of the methodological approach underlying PcGive in Chapters 11–14, it seems worth spelling out how to tackle some of the detailed problems that confront practitioners in many time-series applications, and how the approach differs from that exposited in many econometrics textbooks. The nine issues selected below comprise: §15.1 multicollinearity, §15.2 residual autocorrelation, §15.3 dynamic specification, §15.4 non-nested hypotheses, §15.5 simultaneous equations bias, §15.6 identifying restrictions, §15.7 predictive failure, §15.8 non-stationarity, and §15.9 data mining.

This is not an exhaustive list, but does cover some of the areas of current contention as well as emphasizing the different approach built into PcGive.

15.1 Multicollinearity

The name multicollinearity was coined by Frisch (1934) (in his book on *Confluence Analysis*) to denote the existence of several exact linear relationships connecting a set of theoretical variables: collinearity was the name for when there was only one dependency. As such, the concept was initially unconnected with the present notion of very high correlations between observed variables (see Hendry and Morgan, 1989, for a history of how the present connotations evolved). Perfect collinearity is when an exact linear dependence exists between a set of variables (see §11.10); collinearity, however, is often used to refer to a state of near linear dependence. For linear models, however, collinearity is a property of the way the model is parameterized, not of the model itself. Consider the equation:

$$\mathsf{E}\left[y_t \mid \mathbf{z}_t\right] = \boldsymbol{\beta}'\mathbf{z}_t \tag{15.1}$$

for k elements in $\boldsymbol{\beta}$, expressed in model form as:

$$y_t = \boldsymbol{\beta}'\mathbf{z}_t + \epsilon_t \text{ where } \epsilon_t \sim \mathsf{IN}\left(0, \sigma_\epsilon^2\right). \tag{15.2}$$

Since the model is linear, it is invariant under non-singular linear transformations in that all of its essential properties are unaffected. Let γ denote an arbitrary vector of constants, and $\mathbf{A}$ an arbitrary non-singular $k \times k$ matrix; both γ and $\mathbf{A}$ are chosen by the investigator. Then (15.2) can be transformed linearly to:

$$y_t - \gamma' \mathbf{z}_t = \left((\boldsymbol{\beta} - \gamma)' \mathbf{A}^{-1} \right) \mathbf{A}\mathbf{z}_t + \epsilon_t, \tag{15.3}$$

or:

$$y_t^* = \boldsymbol{\beta}^{*\prime} \mathbf{z}_t^* + \epsilon_t, \tag{15.4}$$

so that

$$\boldsymbol{\beta} = \mathbf{A}' \boldsymbol{\beta}^* + \gamma. \tag{15.5}$$

Transformations like (15.3) are regularly used in practice, as when moving from levels to either differences or differentials between variables. Since $\mathbf{A}$ is non-singular, either $\boldsymbol{\beta}^*$ can be estimated and $\boldsymbol{\beta}$ derived or vice versa: the $\widehat{\boldsymbol{\beta}}$ from least squares estimates of (15.2) is always identical to that derived from $\widehat{\boldsymbol{\beta}}^*$, subject to possible numerical inaccuracies if the problem is extremely ill-conditioned in one parameterization. Direct standard errors of $\widehat{\boldsymbol{\beta}}$ (from (15.2)) or indirect from (15.5) will also be identical.

However, the supposed collinearity in the problem is not at all invariant. For example, let:

$$\mathbf{Q} = T^{-1} \sum_{t=1}^{T} \mathbf{z}_t \mathbf{z}_t',$$

(the sample second moment of the regressors), and select as the $\mathbf{A}$ matrix the inverse of the matrix of eigenvectors of $\mathbf{Q}$ denoted $\mathbf{H}^{-1}$ so $\mathbf{Q} = \mathbf{H}\boldsymbol{\Lambda}\mathbf{H}'$ where $\boldsymbol{\Lambda}$ is diagonal, then:[1]

$$\mathbf{Q}^* = T^{-1} \sum_{t=1}^{T} \mathbf{z}_t^* \mathbf{z}_t^{*\prime} = \mathbf{A}\mathbf{Q}\mathbf{A}' = \mathbf{H}^{-1}\mathbf{H}\boldsymbol{\Lambda}\mathbf{H}'\mathbf{H}^{-1\prime} = \boldsymbol{\Lambda}, \tag{15.6}$$

which is, of course, diagonal (see the related analysis in Leamer, 1983). The eigenvalues in $\boldsymbol{\Lambda}$ are not invariants of the model either, since other choices of $\mathbf{A}$ are admissible (compare Kuh, Belsley and Welsh, 1980).

Thus, the important issue in a model is not the degree of correlation between the variables, which is only loosely associated with the information content of the data, but the precision with which the parameters of interest (for example, $\boldsymbol{\beta}$ or $\boldsymbol{\beta}^*$) can be determined.

Interpretable parameters often correspond to relatively orthogonal variables (see, for example, Davidson, Hendry, Srba and Yeo, 1978), and linear combinations of the original variables which lack variability can be deleted for parsimony. Consequently,

[1]This corresponds to Principal Components analysis but is not recommended as a practical procedure: it is merely one of a class of possible illustrations of the fact that collinearity is not a property of a model, but of a parameterization of that model.

PcGive advises transforming from β to β^* using information gained from previous studies and from theoretical analyses, rather than data-based transformations like Principal Components where the parameters will change if the sample is altered. Then β^*s which are near zero (both in terms of statistical significance and economic importance) can be eliminated. The sequence of reductions and associated transformations is monitored by PcGive so that the validity of any given simplifications can be checked. The final parsimonious, interpretable model will generally not manifest much collinearity (in the sense of high intercorrelations of the z^*s) and can be tested against all the information sets described in §14.5.

15.2 Residual autocorrelation

It should be obvious by this stage how PcGive treats this issue! As discussed in §12.3 (especially §12.3.7), the analysis should commence from a sufficiently general lag specification such that the residuals should be close to white noise. If residual autocorrelation is discovered at any stage, it is taken as a symptom of poor model design, and the whole specification process should be reviewed. It is never arbitrarily assumed to be error autocorrelation, which was shown to correspond to common factors in the dynamics. However, if COMFAC tests suggest that valid common factors can be extracted, then a more parsimonious model with autoregressive errors can be designed and estimated (see Hendry and Mizon, 1978). Both the Wald tests based on Sargan (1980b) and the likelihood-ratio tests of RALS estimates against the general dynamic model should be used prior to imposing common factors owing to the dependence of Wald tests on the formulation and potential multiple optima in the RALS likelihood function.

15.3 Dynamic specification

This is the obverse of §15.2, given the intimate links between dynamic and stochastic specification. PcGive assumes that general lag polynomials will be used for every variable and allows easy creation of any number of lags per variable. The theoretical analysis of the main single-equation dynamic models used in econometrics in §12.3 revealed the many weaknesses of arbitrarily assuming that one particular type happens to apply to the specific measure of the variables used in the problem under study. Consequently, a large section of PcGive is devoted to analysing the empirical results arising from general dynamic models, in terms of long-run responses, roots of lag polynomials, etc. Simple procedures are offered for testing for unit roots.

15.4 Non-nested hypotheses

Many economic phenomena have competing theoretical explanations, especially in macro-economics. The traditional empirical approach in econometrics has been to formulate a model within the given theory framework and test its restrictions against data, corroborating or rejecting as the evidence is favourable or unfavourable. Unfortunately, the same data can corroborate conflicting models (as in Ahumada, 1985, for example). Moreover, if models are redesigned in the light of adverse test results (as happens in practice) then rejection of theory-models rarely occurs. The outcome is a proliferation of non-nested empirical models all claiming to be acceptable, despite being mutually inconsistent.

PcGive confronts this problem from two perspectives, both of which are implications of the theory of reduction discussed in Chapter 14 (for greater detail, see Hendry and Richard, 1983). First, all models are derived from the process that actually generated the data and hence are nested within that process. The model-based analogue is general-to-specific which would eliminate many of the contending hypotheses if the initial general statistical model was formulated so as to embed the contending explanations as special cases: this was discussed in §15.3. Secondly, the traditional 'corroborate or reject' strategy is augmented by the requirement that an acceptable model should be able to account for the results obtained by rival explanations of the same phenomena: this is the theory of encompassing discussed in Chapter 14.5.6. Whether or not other hypotheses are non-nested with respect to the model under study ceases to matter in principle, although there are always practical problems in finite samples. The models must share a common probability framework, as well as seek to explain the same phenomena: the former may not occur, but will do so for any investigators who either claim their models are complete or who accept the need for models to be congruent.

Encompassing is closely related to the well-established class of procedures called mis-specification analysis, where a data generation process (DGP) is assumed known and the consequences of various specification mistakes are studied (such as omitted variables). Since the DGP is indeed correct in such analyses, any specification errors postulated will occur precisely as the analysis predicts. In encompassing, the DGP is not known, but a model (say M_1) is implicitly claiming to represent it adequately. Other models (for example, M_2) are, therefore, mis-specified by hypothesis. The encompassing question is whether or not M_1 mimics the DGP and correctly predicts the results of the mis-specified M_2: that provides a basis for testing if M_1 adequately represents the DGP.

Several encompassing statistics are preprogrammed in PcGive to test such hypotheses, both to evaluate any given model stringently and to help reduce the proliferation of competing explanations. For an exposition, see Hendry and Richard (1989).

15.5 Simultaneous equations bias

The simultaneous equations paradigm is so dominant in both econometrics textbooks and Walrasian equilibrium economics that the prevalence of models with contemporaneous conditioning variables in the earlier analyses needs some comment. First, the theory of weak exogeneity described in §14.5 delineates those cases where contemporaneous conditioning is valid from those where it is not. If weak exogeneity is not sustainable, but the parameters of interest are identifiable (see §15.6 following), then the joint density must be analysed to ensure efficient inference. If y_t depends on x_t and x_t on y_t then conditioning will not yield the parameters of interest. However, in other situations, contemporaneous conditioning can be valid. One sufficient condition is that agents form contingent plans, acting when the necessary information materializes: since the actual joint density $\mathsf{D}_{y,x}(y_t, x_t|\boldsymbol{\theta})$ thereby factorizes into $\mathsf{D}_y(y_t|x_t, \phi_1)$ and $\mathsf{D}_x(x_t|\phi_2)$, and the former captures the parameters of interest, then weak exogeneity holds if the respective parameter spaces also satisfy the requirements for a cut, so that ϕ_1 and ϕ_2 are variation free.

Consider a situation in which both y_t and x_t are interest rates to be modelled, yet y_t is regressed on x_t. At first sight, simultaneity bias seems likely. However, $y_t - x_t$ (a spread) and x_t (a level) equally (and perhaps even more sensibly) could be analysed as functions of past information alone, without any possibility of simultaneity bias. Thus, unless the first regression actually delivers a coefficient larger than unity, it seems odd to categorize it as being biased from y_t and x_t being simultaneous (even though in this example, y_t and x_t are jointly determined).

A more potent analysis ensues if some of the data density parameters vary over the sample, perhaps because of regime shifts. When any coefficients are biased, their bias is dependent on the particular data correlations, and hence will alter as those data correlations change (see, for example, Hendry and Neale, 1988). Thus, no constant conditional model can be obtained, and that is reasonably realistic of many macro-economic time series. Consequently, if a conditional model is constant, yet the marginal model for the conditioning variables is known to vary, this is a strong counter-argument to any claim of simultaneity bias (see Favero and Hendry, 1992). The recursive procedures in PcGive provide a powerful tool for such analyses. Hendry (1988) extends this analysis to models with expectational variables.

15.6 Identifying restrictions

Sims (1980) characterized as 'incredible' many of the over-identifying restrictions imposed in large macro-econometric models, proposing as an alternative a vector autoregression (VAR)-based methodology. The concepts and methods described above offer several insights into Sims' assertions.

One interpretation of Sims' critique is that the restrictions embodied in macro models are often both arbitrarily imposed and untested. This could happen in practice from following a simple-to-general modelling strategy in which the restrictions arose merely because they were not considered. We concur with that criticism under this interpretation in cases where it arises. Nevertheless, we propose an alternative solution, which focuses on two issues:

(1) which model isolates the actual invariants of the economic process (super exogeneity)?
(2) which if any model form (structural system or VAR) encompasses or accounts for the others' results?

Since VARs are derived, rather than autonomous, representations (relative to decision-making structures of economic agents), their constancy necessitates the constancy of every related parameter in the economic system, so they are unlikely to achieve (1). Conversely, their profligate parameterizations virtually ensure an excellent data fit so that they are challenging rivals for any structural model to encompass, noting that variance dominance is necessary but not sufficient for encompassing here (see Hendry and Mizon, 1993).

As before, DGPs where parameters change in some of the marginal processes allow a more penetrating analysis of conditional models which claim to embody constant parameters of interest. Invalid restrictions on models in changing DGPs will generally lead to non-constant relationships, so that constant sub-systems against a background of a changing mechanism offer strong support to any claim about valid specification. Whether or not constant parameters need occur in models is considered in §15.7 below. Constant sub-systems cannot be confounded with any of the changing equations (except by chance cancelling), and are therefore identified relative to them. This last point derives from the analysis in Working's consolidation of identification conditions (Working, 1927). Finally, so-called identifying restrictions are no different in principle from any other form of restriction such as exclusion, linearity, homogeneity etc. Since maximum likelihood methods are equivariant to 1-1 transformations of the parameters (that is, when $\boldsymbol{\theta}$ is mapped to $\boldsymbol{\psi} = \mathbf{f}(\boldsymbol{\theta})$, then $\hat{\boldsymbol{\theta}}$ is mapped to $\hat{\boldsymbol{\psi}} = \mathbf{f}(\hat{\boldsymbol{\theta}})$), estimating a structural model is equivalent to estimating the reduced form subject to certain within- and across-equation restrictions. It is well known that any just-identified model entails an unrestricted reduced form. Thus, unless Sims (1980) either denies the existence of any valid restrictions on reduced forms, which seems inconsistent with his ostensible views on VAR modelling in Doan, Litterman and Sims (1984), or denies that restrictions can ever correspond to a structural parameterization, which would exclude proportionalities between reduced form parameters *inter alia*, then his critique lacks force as an issue of principle, and becomes a practical concern as to whether specific structural models are indeed successful data reductions.

That introduces the topic of testing in simultaneous systems, and there are three related implications from Chapter 14. First, the conventional test of over-identifying restrictions is interpretable as a test of whether the structural model parsimoniously encompasses the unrestricted reduced form, or system as it was denoted above. Secondly, the system must itself be a valid baseline for testing against, which was the thrust of the general-to-specific notion as applied to modelling joint densities (see Hendry, Neale and Srba, 1988). Thirdly, identifying restrictions on structural parameters are meaningless if the claimed parameters are not constant. Consequently, a preferable modelling strategy seems to be: first construct a congruent statistical system (which may well be a VAR), then simplify it via interpretable restrictions (which may be structural), and finally test that the resulting econometric model both is congruent and parsimoniously encompasses the statistical system. This is precisely the strategy adopted in both PcGive for single equations and PcFiml for systems.

15.7 Predictive failure

The prevalence of significant mispredictions and parameter changes in econometric models has been one of the greatest problems confronting applied econometricians (see, for example, Judd and Scadding, 1982, for a history of predictive failure in US money-demand modelling). However, views differ widely as to the explanation for the problem and Baba, Hendry and Starr (1992) propose one constant-parameter model over the period to 1989. To PcGive users, the sheer existence of the phenomenon of predictive failure is important: model discrimination is easier in worlds of parameter change than in constant processes. Next, it behoves modellers to check the historical constancy of any claimed relationship; all too often, public post-sample predictive failures merely highlight previously untested within-sample non-constancies (see Hendry, 1979, 1988): hence the easy-to-use recursive procedures and associated tests in PcGive. Third, the claim that certain predictive failures are owing to confounding expectations and behavioural dynamics (one aspect of the critique in Lucas, 1976) is testable (that is, potentially confirmable or refutable) by employing both encompassing and super exogeneity tests (see Hendry, 1988). Indeed, this point has been exploited in both preceding sections. Finally, it has proved possible in practice to develop models which have good track records over a decade or more (see, for example, Davidson *et al.*, 1978, and Hendry and Ericsson, 1991). Even so, since nothing can guarantee the invariance of human behaviour, regular monitoring for innovation and change is wise. Models are a form of codified accumulated knowledge which progressively increase our understanding of economic behaviour, and consequently have to be adaptive to changing environments.

Some authors have argued for changing-parameter models as a better approximation than constant-parameter models to a reality characterized by predictive failure. It is important to realize that these two types of model only reflect different assumptions about which parameters are constant, as the former do not avoid constancy assumptions. For example, consider the model:

$$y_t = \mathbf{x}_t'\beta_t + \epsilon_t \text{ where } \epsilon_t \sim \underline{\mathsf{IN}}\left(\underline{0}, \underline{\sigma}^2\right)$$

and:

$$\beta_t = \underline{\mathbf{K}}\beta_{t-1} + \nu_t \text{ with } \nu_t \sim \underline{\mathsf{IN}}\left(\underline{\mathbf{0}}, \underline{\mathbf{\Omega}}\right)$$

where $\underline{\beta}_0$ is given. Although the $\{\beta_t\}$ evolve, the new constancies are shown underlined and include assumptions about constant error variances, constant (zero) serial correlation, constant distributional shape etc. Which set of constancies to adopt depends on the specification of the $\mathbf{x}_t$ as determinants of y_t, the functional form linking y_t to $\mathbf{x}_t$ and the constancies in the DGP. There are no principles favouring any particular type of constancy claim. What is important is that evidence should be presented on the actual constancy (or otherwise) of whatever meta-parameters are taken to be the basic constancies of the process being modelled.

At a practical level, the idea of designing models to have nearly orthogonal parameterizations offers some robustness to unmodelled changes since such changes get reflected in increased error variance rather than changing regression parameters.

15.8 Non-stationarity

Three particular forms of non-stationarity have appeared in this book:

(1) I(1), or integrated behaviour, removable by suitable differencing or cointegration transformations;
(2) parameter changes or regime shifts, removable for a subset of parameters of interest by establishing the invariants; and
(3) inherent non-stationarity owing to innovative human behaviour or natural processes, which as yet we do not know how to remove or model.

Concerning (1), it must be stressed that differencing can only remove unit roots and cannot *per se* remove either of (2) or (3) (although it will also mitigate regime shifts in deterministic factors). As noted in Chapter 12, however, analysing only differences also removes all long-run or cointegrating information, and hence is not a sensible generic strategy. Conversely, long-run economic theoretic information should be tested as satisfying cointegration (see Engle and Granger, 1987, Granger, 1986, Johansen, 1988, Phillips, 1991, and Banerjee, Dolado, Galbraith and Hendry, 1993 *inter alia*).

Concerning (2), the establishing of constant and invariant parameters to characterize economic behaviour has been the main thrust of much of the earlier analysis. Many implications of constancy claims are testable and should be tested. Even though every marginal relationship may be affected by structural breaks, linear combinations (perhaps corresponding to conditional relations) need not be, just as linear combinations removed unit roots when cointegration was found: this is called co-breaking in Hendry (1995c).

Finally, (3) raises a number of interesting issues, most as yet unexplored. Can one establish whether or not a process is inherently non-stationary (in the sense of having non-constant unconditional first and second moments)? It is easy to invent complicated mechanisms dependent on mixtures of unlikely but time-independent events, which would seem to be non-stationary despite having constant unconditional moments. How well can learning and innovation themselves be modelled by constant parameter processes? Theoretical analyses of R&D, technical change, financial innovation etc. have progressed, so a constant meta-parameterization in a high dimensional non-linear mechanism cannot be excluded *a priori*. This is especially important now that a theory for analysing integrated processes is available to deal with, for example the accumulation of knowledge and technique. Do the various forms of non-stationarity interact? Here we are on slightly firmer ground – yes they do. A simple I(0) process with a large sustained shift will be quite well described as I(1) since differencing reduces the shift to a one-off blip (see Perron, 1989, and Hendry and Neale, 1991). For example, the artificial data used above have no unit roots, but seem I(1) on conventional scalar unit-root tests. Note, again, that a recursive testing procedure for a unit root may help clarify the relevant state of nature. Alternatively, tests for technical progress changing must allow for the distributional theory to be based on integrated and not on stationary processes. It would seem that lots of interesting findings await discovery in this area.

15.9 Data mining

Data mining has been characterized in many ways, with a common theme being the reuse of the same data to both estimate and revise a model. If that is the intended meaning of data mining, then in economics, either you must be omniscient or you will data mine: unless a model emerges perfect on the first try, it must be revised in the light of data evidence. Leamer (1978) offers an excellent treatment, commenting that his:

> 'book is about "data mining". It describes how specification searches can be legitimately used to bring to the surface the nuggets of truth that may be buried in a data set. The essential ingredients are judgment and purpose...'.

Although the standpoint of PcGive is not Bayesian, much of the analysis, logic, and common sense are similar.

The tools relevant to this issue from Chapter 14 are:

(a) a dichotomy between the contexts of discovery (where you will reuse data in the process of model construction) and of evaluation (where one-off testing on genuinely new information allows valid model destruction);
(b) a theory of reduction to explain how empirical models are derived from the data generating mechanism and hence do not in general have autonomous errors;

(c) a typology of information sets which delineates the necessary conditions for a model to be congruent;
(d) the concept of model design to achieve congruency in the context of discovery, allowing conditioning of later inferences on the congruent model specification as the best representative of the DGP;
(e) a general-to-specific simplification approach to model design, mimicking reduction, moving from a congruent statistical model to a parsimonious and interpretable econometric model thereof, which is theory consistent and encompasses both the general model and other competing models;
(f) the notion that the validity of the chosen model is a property that is intrinsic to the model and not to the process of its discovery; later evaluation will sort the gold from the pyrites.

As a consequence, data mining has to be viewed as an unstructured activity leading some investigators to run 'literally hundreds of regressions' on data sets with fewer than one hundred observations. In such an approach, masses of ore are mined and sifted to pick out the bits of gold which appeal to the particular investigator. As remarked in Hendry (1980), 'econometric fool's gold' is often the result. Gilbert (1986) neatly characterizes the view PcGive takes of such mining: divide all of the output into two piles, one consistent with (and encompassed by) the selected model and one inconsistent with it. 'Weak data mining' is when the second pile has any members and 'strong data mining' is when the anomalous findings are not reported as *caveats* to the claimed model. A related weak form is deliberate non-testing for fear of unfavourable results, so the research assistant does the first pre-filter (or loses the initial sifting sets of runs) – for an interesting analysis of the general problem in science, see Kohn (1987).

Conversely, once a congruent model has been developed by a structured search and rigorously tested, it is sensible to condition further inferences on that congruent model since by definition no better model is currently available. As an aside, all of the numerical values of coefficients, standard errors etc. are the same irrespective of the number of steps in the simplification (or search) process: the only issue is whether the precision recorded should in some sense be discounted because of the search process. If in fact the variances are too small owing to simplifying, over-rejection of such models outside of sample would occur: to date, the evidence is rather the opposite since many of the results seem surprisingly robust over long time periods (see Hendry, 1989).

Part IV

The Statistical Output of PcGive

Chapter 16

Descriptive Statistics in PcGive

The Descriptive Statistics entry on the Data menu gives the first menu which involves the formal calculation of statistics in the PcGive module. Different dialog boxes will appear, depending on which of the data description option is selected. Model-related statistics are considered in Chapters 17 and 18. This chapter provides the formulae underlying the computations. A more informal introduction is given in the tutorial Chapter 4. PcGive will use the largest available sample by default, here denoted by $t = 1, \ldots, T$. It is always possible to graph or compute the statistics over a shorter sample period by clicking the Zoom box, in which case the desired sample will be requested on each occasion.

16.1 Descriptive data analysis

16.1.1 Test for normality

Let μ, σ_x^2 denote the mean and variance of $\{x_t\}$, and write $\mu_i = \mathsf{E}\left[x_t - \mu\right]^i$, so that $\sigma_x^2 = \mu_2$. The skewness and kurtosis are defined as:

$$\sqrt{\beta_1} = \frac{\mu_3}{\mu_2^{3/2}} \text{ and } \beta_2 = \frac{\mu_4}{\mu_2^2}. \tag{16.1}$$

Sample counterparts are defined by

$$\bar{x} = \frac{1}{T}\sum_{t=1}^{T} x_t, \ m_i = \frac{1}{T}\sum_{t=1}^{T}\left(x_t - \bar{x}\right)^i, \ \sqrt{b_1} = \frac{m_3}{m_2^{3/2}} \text{ and } b_2 = \frac{m_4}{m_2^2}. \tag{16.2}$$

A normal variate will have $\sqrt{\beta_1} = 0$ and $\beta_2 = 3$. Bowman and Shenton (1975) consider that the test:

$$\mathsf{e}_1 = \frac{T\left(\sqrt{b_1}\right)^2}{6} + \frac{T\left(b_2 - 3\right)^2}{24} \underset{a}{\sim} \chi^2\left(2\right) \tag{16.3}$$

is unsuitable unless used in very large samples. The statistics $\sqrt{b_1}$ and b_2 are not independently distributed, and the sample kurtosis especially approaches normality very slowly. The test reported by PcGive is fully described in Doornik and Hansen (1994). It derives from Shenton and Bowman (1977), who give b_2 (conditional on $b_2 > 1 + b_1$) a gamma distribution, and D'Agostino (1970), who approximates the distribution of $\sqrt{b_1}$ by the Johnson S_u system. Let z_1 and z_2 denote the transformed skewness and kurtosis, where the transformation creates statistics which are much closer to standard normal. The test statistic is:

$$\mathsf{e}_2 = z_1^2 + z_2^2 \underset{app}{\sim} \chi^2(2). \tag{16.4}$$

Table 16.1 compares (16.4) with its asymptotic form (16.3). It gives the rejection frequencies under the null of normality, using $\chi^2(2)$ critical values. The experiments are based on 10 000 replications and common random numbers.

Table 16.1 Empirical size of normality tests.

	nominal probabilities of e_2				nominal probabilities of (16.3)			
T	20%	10%	5%	1%	20%	10%	5%	1%
50	0.1734	0.0869	0.0450	0.0113	0.0939	0.0547	0.0346	0.0175
100	0.1771	0.0922	0.0484	0.0111	0.1258	0.0637	0.0391	0.0183
150	0.1845	0.0937	0.0495	0.0131	0.1456	0.0703	0.0449	0.0188
250	0.1889	0.0948	0.0498	0.0133	0.1583	0.0788	0.0460	0.0180

PcGive reports the following statistics under this option:

mean	$\bar{x}$
standard deviation	$\sigma_x = \sqrt{m_2}$
skewness	$\sqrt{b_1}$
excess kurtosis	$b_2 - 3$
minimum	
maximum	
normality $\chi^2(2)$	e_2 $\left[\mathsf{P}\left(\chi^2(2) \geq \mathsf{e}_2\right)\right]$
(asymptotic form of normality test)	e_1

16.1.2 Correlations

This reports sample means and standard deviations of the selected variables:

$$\bar{x} = \frac{1}{T}\sum_{t=1}^{T} x_t, \quad s = \sqrt{\frac{1}{T-1}\sum_{t=1}^{T}(x_t - \bar{x})^2}.$$

The correlation coefficient r_{xy} between x and y is:

$$\mathsf{r}_{xy} = \frac{\sum_{t=1}^{T}(x_t - \bar{x})(y_t - \bar{y})}{\sqrt{\sum_{t=1}^{T}(x_t - \bar{x})^2 \sum_{t=1}^{T}(y_t - \bar{y})^2}}. \tag{16.5}$$

The correlation matrix of the selected variables is reported as a lower triangular matrix with the diagonal equal to one. Each cell records the simple correlation between the two relevant variables.

16.1.3 Unit-root tests

A crucial property of any economic variable influencing the behaviour of statistics in econometric models is the extent to which that variable is stationary. If the autoregressive description offered in (16.10) below has a root on the unit circle, then conventional distributional results are not applicable to coefficient estimates. As the simplest example, consider:

$$x_t = \alpha + \beta x_{t-1} + \epsilon_t \text{ where } \beta = 1 \text{ and } \epsilon_t \sim \mathsf{IN}\left(0, \sigma_\epsilon^2\right),$$

which generates a random walk (with drift if $\alpha \neq 0$). Here, the autoregressive coefficient is unity and stationarity is violated. A process with no unit or explosive roots is said to be I(0); a process is I (d) if it needs to be differenced d times to become I(0) and is not I(0) if only differenced $d-1$ times. Many economic time series behave like I(1), though some appear to be I(0) and others I(2).

The Durbin–Watson statistic for the level of a variable offers one simple characterization of this integrated property:

$$DW(x) = \frac{\sum_{t=2}^{T} (x_t - x_{t-1})^2}{\sum_{t=1}^{T} (x_t - \bar{x})^2}. \tag{16.6}$$

If x_t is a random walk, *DW* will be very small. If x_t is white noise, *DW* will be around 2. Very low *DW* values thus indicate that a transformed model may be desirable, perhaps including a mixture of differenced and disequilibrium variables.

An augmented Dickey–Fuller (ADF) test for I(1) against I(0) (see Dickey and Fuller, 1981) is provided by the t-statistic on $\widehat{\beta}$ in:

$$\Delta x_t = \alpha + \mu t + \beta x_{t-1} + \sum_{i=1}^{n} \gamma_i \Delta x_{t-i} + u_t. \tag{16.7}$$

The constant or trend can optionally be excluded from (16.7); the specification of the lag length n assumes that u_t is white noise. The null hypothesis is H_0: $\beta = 0$; rejection of this hypothesis implies that x_t is I(0). A failure to reject implies that Δx_t is stationary, so x_t is I(1). This is a second useful description of the degree of integratedness of x_t. The Dickey–Fuller (DF) test has no lagged first differences on the right-hand side ($n = 0$). On this topic, see the *Oxford Bulletin of Economics and Statistics* (Hendry, 1986a, Banerjee and Hendry, 1992a), and Banerjee, Dolado, Galbraith and Hendry (1993). To test whether x_t is I(1), commence with the next higher difference:

$$\Delta^2 x_t = \alpha + \mu t + \beta \Delta x_{t-1} + \lambda x_{t-1} + \sum_{i=1}^{n} \gamma_i \Delta x_{t-i} + u_t. \tag{16.8}$$

Output of the ADF(n) test of (16.7) consists of:

coefficients	$\hat{\alpha}$ and $\hat{\mu}$ (if included), $\hat{\beta}$, $\hat{\gamma}_1, \ldots, \hat{\gamma}_n$,
standard errors	$\mathsf{SE}(\hat{\alpha})$, $\mathsf{SE}(\hat{\mu})$, $\mathsf{SE}(\hat{\beta})$, $\mathsf{SE}(\hat{\gamma}_i)$,
t-values	t_α, t_μ, t_β, t_{γ_i},
$\hat{\sigma}$	as (16.14),
DW	(16.6) applied to $\hat{u}_t$,
DW(x)	(16.6) applied to x_t,
ADF(x)	t_β,
Critical values	
RSS	as (16.13).

Most of the formulae for the computed statistics are more conveniently presented in the next section on simple dynamic regressions, but the t-statistic is defined (e.g., for $\hat{\alpha}$) as $\mathsf{t}_\alpha = \hat{\alpha}/\mathsf{SE}(\hat{\alpha})$, using the formula in (16.12). Critical values are derived from the reponse surfaces in MacKinnon (1991), and depend on whether a constant, or constant and trend, are included (seasonals are ignored). Under the null ($\beta = 0$), $\alpha \neq 0$ entails a trend in $\{x_t\}$ and $\mu \neq 0$ implies a quadratic trend. However, under the stationary alternative, $\alpha = 0$ would impose a zero trend. Thus the test ceases to be similar if the polynomial in time $(1, t, t^2$ etc.) in the model is not at least as large as that in the data generating process (see, for example, Kiviet and Phillips, 1992). This problem suggests allowing for a trend in the model unless the data is anticipated to have a zero mean in differences. The so-called Engle-Granger two-step method amounts to applying the ADF test to residuals from a prior static regression (the first step). The response surfaces need to be adjusted for the number of variables involved in the first step: see MacKinnon (1991).

The default of PcGive is to report a summary test output for the sequence of ADF(n)...ADF(0) tests. The summary table consists of:

t-adf	the t-value on the lagged level: t_β,
beta Y_1	the coefficient on the lagged level: β,
$\hat{\sigma}$	as (16.14),
lag	j,
t-DY_lag	t-value of the longest lag: t_{γ_j},
t-prob	significance of the longest lag: $1 - \mathsf{P}\left(\lvert\tau\rvert \leq \lvert\mathsf{t}_{\gamma_j}\rvert\right)$,
F-prob	significance level of the F-test on the lags dropped up to that point.

for $j = n, \ldots, 0$. Critical values are listed, and significance of the ADF test is marked by asterisks: * indicates significance at 5%, ** at 1%.

16.2 Autoregressive distributed lag (ADL)

An autoregressive distributed-lag model has the form:

$$y_t = \alpha + \sum_{r=p}^{s} \beta_r x_{t-r} + \sum_{i=m}^{n} \gamma_i y_{t-i} + \epsilon_t \text{ where } \epsilon_t \sim \mathsf{ID}\left(0, \sigma_\epsilon^2\right). \tag{16.9}$$

When no xs are present, an autoregressive model arises, yielding the regression of y_t on a constant and its own lagged values, estimated by ordinary least squares (OLS). The number of lagged values in the autoregression can be specified by the user from m to n; if $m = 1$, an AR(n) model is:

$$y_t = \alpha + \sum_{i=1}^{n} \gamma_i y_{t-i} + u_t. \tag{16.10}$$

Omitting the lagged dependent variables from the ADL specification gives rise to a finite bivariate distributed lag:

$$y_t = \alpha + \sum_{r=p}^{s} \beta_r x_{t-r} + \epsilon_t. \tag{16.11}$$

In addition to the coefficient estimates, PcGive reports their:

16.2.1 Standard errors

Denoted $\mathsf{SE}(\hat{\alpha})$, $\mathsf{SE}(\hat{\gamma}_i)$ etc., these are calculated as (for example):

$$\mathsf{SE}\left(\hat{\gamma}_i\right) = \hat{\sigma}\sqrt{d_{ii}} \tag{16.12}$$

where d_{ii} is the corresponding diagonal element of the inverse sample second-moment matrix of all the variables, and $\hat{\sigma}$ is shown in (16.14).

16.2.2 Residual sum of squares (RSS)

For the example of the simple autoregression, this statistic corresponds to:

$$RSS = \sum_{t=1}^{T} \hat{u}_t^2 \text{ where } \hat{u}_t = y_t - \hat{y}_t \text{ and } \hat{y}_t = \hat{\alpha} + \sum_{i=m}^{n} \hat{\gamma}_i y_{t-i}. \tag{16.13}$$

16.2.3 Standard error of the regression ($\hat{\sigma}$)

This is calculated as:

$$\hat{\sigma} = \sqrt{\frac{1}{T-k} \sum_{t=1}^{T} \hat{u}_t^2}, \tag{16.14}$$

where T is the number of observations and k is the number of regressors, which for the autoregression equals the number of lagged values plus one for the constant term (that is, $n-m+2$). Thus, $\hat{\sigma}$ is the standard deviation of the differences of the actual variable (y_t) from the OLS estimated value $(\hat{y}_t)$, or equivalently the square root of the residual variance.

16.2.4 R^2: the squared coefficient of multiple correlation

The variation in the dependent variable, or the total sum of squares (TSS), can be broken up into two parts: the explained sum of squares (ESS) and the residual sum of squares (RSS). In symbols, $TSS = ESS + RSS$, or:

$$\sum_{t=1}^{T}(y_t-\bar{y})^2 = \sum_{t=1}^{T}(\hat{y}_t-\bar{y})^2 + \sum_{t=1}^{T}\hat{u}_t^2,$$

and hence:

$$\mathsf{R}^2 = \frac{ESS}{TSS} = \frac{\sum_{t=1}^{T}(\hat{y}_t-\bar{y})^2}{\sum_{t=1}^{T}(y_t-\bar{y})^2} = 1 - \frac{\sum_{t=1}^{T}\hat{u}_t^2}{\sum_{t=1}^{T}(y_t-\bar{y})^2},$$

assuming a constant is included. Thus, R^2 is the proportion of the variance of the dependent variable which is explained by the variables in the regression. By adding more variables to a regression, R^2 will never decrease, and it may increase even if nonsense variables are added. Hence, R^2 may be misleading. Also, R^2 is dependent on the choice of transformation of the dependent variable (for example, y versus Δy) – as is the F-statistic below. $\hat{\sigma}$, however, provides a better comparative statistic because it is adjusted by the degrees of freedom. Generally, $\hat{\sigma}$ can be standardized as a percentage of the mean of the original level of the dependent variable (except if the initial mean is zero) for comparisons across specifications. Since many economic magnitudes are inherently positive, that standardization is often feasible. If y is in logs, $100\hat{\sigma}$ is the percentage standard error.

16.2.5 F-statistic

This statistic tests whether the regression explains a significant proportion of the variation in the dependent variable. The formula is:

$$\eta_\beta = \frac{\mathsf{R}^2/(k-1)}{(1-\mathsf{R}^2)/(T-k)} \sim \mathsf{F}(k-1, T-k) \tag{16.15}$$

on H_0: $\beta_p = \beta_{p+1} = \cdots = \beta_s = \gamma_m = \cdots = \gamma_n = 0$ (so all coefficients except α are 0), where k is the number of estimated coefficients ($k = 1 + s - p + 1 + n - m + 1$).

16.2.6 Granger non-causality test

For the ADL model, an F-statistic for testing Granger Causality (G-C) is also given, for which the null of no G-C is H_0: $\beta_p = \beta_{p+1} = \cdots = \beta_s = 0$, together with its probability under H_0.

Chapter 17

Model Estimation Statistics

Individual equation estimation is allowed by:

OLS	ordinary least squares
RLS	recursive OLS
IVE	instrumental variables estimation
RIV	recursive IV
RALS	r^{th} order autoregressive least squares
NLS	non-linear least squares
RNLS	recursive NLS
ML	maximum likelihood estimation

Once a model has been specified, a sample period selected, and an estimation method chosen, the equation can be estimated. For ease of notation, the sample period is denoted $t = 1, \ldots, T+H$, after allowing for any lagged variables created where H is the forecast horizon. The data used for estimation are $\mathbf{X} = (\mathbf{x}_1 \ldots \mathbf{x}_T)$. The H retained observations $\mathbf{X}_H = (\mathbf{x}_{T+1} \ldots \mathbf{x}_{T+H})$ are used for evaluating parameter constancy. Recursive estimation methods are initialized by a direct estimation over $t = 1, \ldots, M-1$, followed by recursive estimation over $t = M, \ldots, T$.

This chapter discusses the statistics reported by PcGive following model estimation. The next chapter presents the wide range of evaluation tools available following successful estimation. Sections marked with * denote information that can be shown or omitted on request.

17.1 OLS/RLS estimation

The algebra of OLS estimation is well established from previous chapters, see, for example, §13.7 and §12.5. RLS formulae were given in §13.7.9. The model is:

$$y_t = \beta' \mathbf{x}_t + u_t, \quad \text{with } u_t \sim \mathsf{IN}\left(0, \sigma^2\right) \quad t = 1, \ldots, T,$$

or more compactly:

$$\mathbf{y} = \mathbf{X}\beta + \mathbf{u}, \quad \text{with } \mathbf{u} \sim \mathsf{N}_T\left(\mathbf{0}, \sigma^2 \mathbf{I}\right). \tag{17.1}$$

The vectors β and $\mathbf{x}_t$ are $k \times 1$. The OLS estimates of β are:

$$\hat{\beta} = (\mathbf{X}'\mathbf{X})^{-1}\,\mathbf{X}'\mathbf{y}, \tag{17.2}$$

with residuals

$$\hat{u}_t = y_t - \hat{y}_t = y_t - \mathbf{x}_t'\hat{\beta}, \quad t = 1, \ldots, T, \tag{17.3}$$

and estimated residual variance

$$\hat{\sigma}_u^2 = \frac{1}{T-k}\sum_{t=1}^{T}\hat{u}_t^2. \tag{17.4}$$

Forecast statistics are provided for the H retained observations (only if $H \neq 0$). For OLS/RLS, these are comprehensive 1-step ahead forecasts and tests, described below.

Two formats for estimation output are available: columnar format, where each row lists information pertaining to each variable (its coefficient, standard error, t-value, etc.), and the equation format, which is of the form coefficient $\times$ variable with standard errors in parentheses underneath.

17.1.1 *Correlations

This reports the sample means and sample standard deviations of the selected variables:

$$\bar{x} = \frac{1}{T}\sum_{t=1}^{T} x_t, \quad s = \sqrt{\frac{1}{T-1}\sum_{t=1}^{T}(x_t - \bar{x})^2}.$$

The correlation matrix of the selected variables is reported as a lower-triangular matrix with the diagonal equal to one. Each cell records the simple correlation between the two relevant variables. The calculation of the correlation coefficient r_{xy} between x and y is:

$$\mathsf{r}_{xy} = \frac{\sum_{t=1}^{T}(x_t - \bar{x})(y_t - \bar{y})}{\sqrt{\sum_{t=1}^{T}(x_t - \bar{x})^2 \sum_{t=1}^{T}(y_t - \bar{y})^2}}. \tag{17.5}$$

17.1.2 The estimated regression equation

The first column of these results records the names of the variables and the second, the estimated regression coefficients $\hat{\beta} = (\mathbf{X}'\mathbf{X})^{-1}\,\mathbf{X}'\mathbf{y}$. PcGive does actually not use this expression to estimate $\hat{\beta}$. Instead it uses the QR decomposition with partial pivoting, which analytically gives the same result, but in practice is a bit more reliable (i.e. numerically more stable). The QR decomposition of $\mathbf{X}$ is $\mathbf{X} = \mathbf{QR}$, where $\mathbf{Q}$ is $T \times T$ and orthogonal (that is, $\mathbf{Q}'\mathbf{Q} = \mathbf{I}$), and $\mathbf{R}$ is $T \times k$ and upper triangular. Then $\mathbf{X}'\mathbf{X} = \mathbf{R}'\mathbf{R}$.

The following five columns give further information about each of the magnitudes described below in §17.1.3 to §17.1.7.

17.1.3 Standard errors of the regression coefficients

These are obtained from the variance-covariance matrix:

$$\mathsf{SE}\left[\hat{\beta}_i\right] = \sqrt{\mathsf{V}\left[\widehat{\beta}_i\right]} = \hat{\sigma}_u \sqrt{d_{ii}} \tag{17.6}$$

where d_{ii} is the ith diagonal element of $(\mathbf{X}'\mathbf{X})^{-1}$ and $\hat{\sigma}_u$ is the standard error of the regression, defined in §17.1.9 below.

17.1.4 *Heteroscedastic-consistent standard errors (HCSEs)

These provide consistent estimates of the regression coefficients' standard errors even if the residuals are heteroscedastic in an unknown way, see (12.19). Large differences between the corresponding values in §17.1.3 and §17.1.4 are indicative of the presence of heteroscedasticity, in which case §17.1.4 provides the more useful measure of the standard errors (see White, 1980). PcGive contains two methods of computing the HCSEs: as described in White (1980), or the Jack-knife estimator from MacKinnon and White (1985) (for which the code was initially provided by James MacKinnon). You can select one of these methods in the profile, or omit computation of the HCSEs altogether (which is the default).

17.1.5 t-values and t-probability

These statistics are conventionally calculated to determine whether individual coefficients are significantly different from zero:

$$\mathrm{t{-}value} = \frac{\hat{\beta}_i}{\mathsf{SE}\left[\hat{\beta}_i\right]} \tag{17.7}$$

where the null hypothesis H_0 is $\beta_i = 0$. The null hypothesis is rejected if the probability of getting a t-value at least as large is less than 5% (or any other chosen significance level). This probability is given as:

$$\mathrm{t{-}prob} = 1 - \mathrm{Prob}\left(|\tau| \leq |\mathrm{t{-}value}|\right) \tag{17.8}$$

in which τ has a Student t-distribution with $T - k$ degrees of freedom. The t-probabilities do not appear when all other options are switched on.

When H_0 is true (and the model is otherwise correctly specified in a stationary process), a Student t-distribution is used since the sample size is often small, and we only have an estimate of the parameter's standard error: however, as the sample size increases, τ tends to a standard normal distribution under H_0. Large t-values reject H_0; but, in many situations, H_0 may be of little interest to test. Also, selecting variables in a model according to their t-values implies that the usual (Neyman–Pearson) justification for testing is not valid (see, for example, Judge, Griffiths, Hill, Lütkepohl and Lee, 1985).

17.1.6 Squared partial correlations

The jth entry in this column records the correlation of the jth explanatory variable with the dependent variable, given the other $k-1$ variables, see §13.7.7. Adding further explanatory variables to the model may either increase or lower the squared partial correlation, and the former may occur even if the added variables are correlated with the already included variables. If the squared partial correlations fall on adding a variable, then that is suggestive of collinearity for the given equation parameterization: that is, the new variable is a substitute for, rather than a complement to, those already included.

17.1.7 *Parameter instability statistics

For each parameter $(\beta_1, \ldots, \beta_k, \sigma^2)$, a parameter instability statistic is computed, based on the approach in Hansen (1992). This final column has the statistics for the βs. Large values reveal non-constancy (marked by * or **), and indicate a fragile model. Note that this measures within-sample parameter constancy, and is computed automatically if numerically feasible (it may fail owing to dummy variables), so no observations need be reserved. The indicated significance is only valid in the absence of non-stationary regressors.

Beneath the columnar presentation an array of summary statistics is also provided as follows:

17.1.8 R^2: squared multiple correlation coefficient

$$\mathsf{R}^2 = \frac{ESS}{TSS} = \frac{\sum_{t=1}^{T}(\hat{y}_t - \bar{y})^2}{\sum_{t=1}^{T}(y_t - \bar{y})^2} = 1 - \frac{\sum_{t=1}^{T}\hat{u}_t^2}{\sum_{t=1}^{T}(y_t - \bar{y})^2}, \tag{17.9}$$

assuming a constant is included. See the discussion in §16.2.4 and §13.7.6. If no intercept is included in $\mathbf{x}_t$, this will be noted in the output, with $\mathsf{R}^2 = 1 - \Sigma\hat{u}_t^2/\Sigma y_t^2$.

17.1.9 Equation standard error $(\hat{\sigma})$

As in §16.2.3, the equation standard error is the square root of the residual variance, which is defined as:

$$\hat{\sigma}_u^2 = \frac{1}{T-k}\sum_{t=1}^{T}\hat{u}_t^2, \tag{17.10}$$

where the residuals are defined as:

$$\hat{u}_t = y_t - \hat{y}_t = y_t - \mathbf{x}_t'\hat{\boldsymbol{\beta}}, \quad t = 1, \ldots, T. \tag{17.11}$$

17.1.10 F-statistic

The formula was already given in (16.15) and (13.94):

$$\eta_\beta = \frac{\mathsf{R}^2 / (k-1)}{(1-\mathsf{R}^2)/(T-k)} \sim \mathsf{F}(k-1, T-k) \tag{17.12}$$

Here, the null hypothesis is that the population R^2 is zero, or that all the regression coefficients are zero (excluding the intercept). The value for the F-statistic is followed by its probability value between square brackets.

17.1.11 Durbin–Watson test (DW)

This is a test for autocorrelated residuals and is calculated as:

$$DW = \frac{\sum_{t=2}^{T} (\hat{u}_t - \hat{u}_{t-1})^2}{\sum_{t=1}^{T} \hat{u}_t^2}. \tag{17.13}$$

DW is most powerful as a test of $\{u_t\}$ being white noise against:

$$u_t = \rho u_{t-1} + \epsilon_t \text{ where } \epsilon_t \sim \mathsf{IID}\left(0, \sigma_\epsilon^2\right).$$

If $0 < DW < 2$, then the null hypothesis is H_0: $\rho = 0$, that is, zero autocorrelation (so $DW = 2$) and the alternative is H_1: $\rho > 0$, that is, positive first-order autocorrelation.

If $2 < DW < 4$, then H_0: $\rho = 0$ and H_1: $\rho < 0$, in which case $DW^* = 4 - DW$ should be computed.

The significance values of DW are widely recorded in econometrics' textbooks. However, DW is a valid statistic only if all the $\mathbf{x}_t$ variables are non-stochastic, or at least strongly exogenous. If the model includes a lagged dependent variable, then DW is biased towards 2, that is, towards not detecting autocorrelation, and Durbin's h-test (see Durbin, 1970) or the equivalent LM-test for autocorrelation in §18.4.3 should be used instead. Also see §16.1.3 and §12.5 .

17.1.12 Residual sum of squares (RSS)

$$RSS = \sum_{t=1}^{T} \hat{u}_t^2. \tag{17.14}$$

17.1.13 *Parameter instability statistics

The remaining parameter instability statistics are reported: first for σ^2, followed by the joint statistic for all the parameters in the model (also see §17.1.7).

17.1.14 *Information criteria

The three statistics reported are the Schwarz criterion (SC), the Hannan–Quinn (HQ) criterion and the Final Prediction Error (FPE). From these, other model selection criteria may be calculated. Here:

$$\begin{aligned} \mathsf{SC} &= \log \tilde{\sigma}^2 + k \, (\log T) / T, \\ \mathsf{HQ} &= \log \tilde{\sigma}^2 + 2k \, (\log (\log T)) / T, \\ \mathsf{FPE} &= (T + k) \, \tilde{\sigma}^2 / (T - k) \, . \end{aligned} \tag{17.15}$$

using the maximum likelihood estimate of σ^2:

$$\tilde{\sigma}^2 = \frac{T-k}{T} \hat{\sigma}^2 = \frac{1}{T} \sum_{t=1}^{T} \hat{u}_t^2 .$$

For a discussion of the use of these and related scalar measures to choose between alternative models in a class, see Judge *et al.* (1985), §12.9.2 and §18.8 below.

17.1.15 *Seasonals means of differences

This shows the seasonal means of the first difference of the dependent variable ($\overline{\Delta y}$ for annual data, four quarterly means for quarterly data, twelve monthly means for monthly data etc.).

17.1.16 *R^2 relative to difference and seasonals

This is a measure of the goodness of fit relative to $\sum(\Delta y_t - \bar{s})^2$ instead of $\sum(y_t - \bar{y})^2$ in the denominator of R^2 (keeping $\sum \hat{u}_t^2$ in the numerator), where $\bar{s}$ denotes the relevant seasonal mean of §17.1.15. Despite its label, such a measure can be negative: if it is, the fitted model does less well than a regression of Δy_t on seasonal dummies.

17.1.17 *Variance-covariance matrix

The matrix of the estimated parameters' variances is reported as lower triangular. Along the diagonal, we have the variance of each estimated coefficient, and off the diagonal, the covariances. The $k \times k$ variance matrix of $\hat{\boldsymbol{\beta}}$ is estimated by:

$$\widehat{\mathsf{V}\left[\hat{\boldsymbol{\beta}}\right]} = \hat{\sigma}^2 \left(\mathbf{X}'\mathbf{X}\right)^{-1}, \tag{17.16}$$

where $\hat{\sigma}^2$ is the full-sample equation error variance. The variance-covariance matrix is only shown when requested, in which case it is reported before the equation output.

The remaining statistics only appear if observations were withheld for forecasting purposes:

17.1.18 Analysis of 1-step forecasts

Following estimation over $t = 1, \dots, T$, 1-step forecasts are given by:[1]

$$\hat{y}_t = \mathbf{x}_t'\hat{\boldsymbol{\beta}}, \quad t = T+1, \dots, T+H, \tag{17.17}$$

which requires the observations $\mathbf{X}_H' = (\mathbf{x}_{T+1}, \dots, \mathbf{x}_{T+H})$. The 1-step forecast error is the mistake made each period:

$$e_t = y_t - \mathbf{x}_t'\hat{\boldsymbol{\beta}}, \quad t = T+1, \dots, T+H, \tag{17.18}$$

which can be written as:

$$e_t = \mathbf{x}_t'\boldsymbol{\beta} + u_t - \mathbf{x}_t'\hat{\boldsymbol{\beta}} = \mathbf{x}_t'\left(\boldsymbol{\beta} - \hat{\boldsymbol{\beta}}\right) + u_t. \tag{17.19}$$

Assuming that $\mathsf{E}[\hat{\boldsymbol{\beta}}] = \boldsymbol{\beta}$, then $\mathsf{E}[e_t] = 0$ and:

$$\mathsf{V}[e_t] = \mathsf{E}\left[e_t^2\right] = \mathsf{E}\left[\left(\mathbf{x}_t'\left(\boldsymbol{\beta} - \hat{\boldsymbol{\beta}}\right)\right)^2 + u_t^2\right] = \sigma_u^2\mathbf{x}_t'\left(\mathbf{X}'\mathbf{X}\right)^{-1}\mathbf{x}_t + \sigma_u^2. \tag{17.20}$$

This corresponds to the results given for the innovations in recursive estimation, see §13.7.9. The whole vector of forecast errors is $\mathbf{e} = (e_{T+1}, \dots, e_{T+H})'$. $\mathsf{V}[\mathbf{e}]$ is derived in a similar way:

$$\mathsf{V}[\mathbf{e}] = \sigma^2\mathbf{I}_H + \mathbf{X}_H\mathsf{V}\left[\hat{\boldsymbol{\beta}}\right]\mathbf{X}_H' = \sigma_u^2\left(\mathbf{I}_H + \mathbf{X}_H\left(\mathbf{X}'\mathbf{X}\right)^{-1}\mathbf{X}_H'\right). \tag{17.21}$$

Estimated variances are obtained after replacing σ_u^2 by $\hat{\sigma}_u^2$.

The columns respectively report the date for which the forecast is made, the realized outcome (y_t), the forecast ($\hat{y}_t$), the forecast error ($e_t = y_t - \hat{y}_t$), the standard error of the 1-step forecast ($\mathsf{SE}(e_t) = \sqrt{\mathsf{V}[e_t]}$), and a t-value (that is, the standardized forecast error $e_t/\mathsf{SE}(e_t)$).

17.1.19 Forecast test

A χ^2 statistic follows the 1-step analysis, comparing within and post-sample residual variances. Neither this statistic nor η_3 below measure absolute forecast accuracy. The statistic is calculated as follows:

$$\xi_1 = \sum_{t=T+1}^{T+H} \frac{e_t^2}{\hat{\sigma}_u^2} \underset{app}{\sim} \chi^2(H) \text{ on } \mathsf{H}_0. \tag{17.22}$$

The null hypothesis is 'no structural change in any parameter between the sample and the forecast periods' (denoted 1 and 2 respectively), H_0: $\boldsymbol{\beta}_1 = \boldsymbol{\beta}_2; \sigma_1^2 = \sigma_2^2$. A rejection of

[1] Dynamic forecasts are needed when the xs are also predicted for the forecast period. Dynamic forecasts are implemented in PcFiml.

the null hypothesis of constancy by ξ_2 below implies a rejection of the model used over the sample period – so that is a model specification test – whereas the use of ξ_1 is more as a measure of numerical parameter constancy, and it should not be used as a model-selection device (see Kiviet, 1986). However, persistently large values for this statistic imply that the equation under study will not provide very accurate *ex ante* predictions, even one step ahead. An approximate F-equivalent is given by:

$$\eta_1 = \frac{1}{H}\xi_1 \underset{app}{\sim} \mathsf{F}\left(H, T-k\right) \text{ on } \mathsf{H}_0. \tag{17.23}$$

17.1.20 Chow test

This is the main test of parameter constancy and has the form:

$$\eta_3 = \frac{\left(RSS_{T+H} - RSS_T\right)/H}{RSS_T/(T-k)} \underset{app}{\sim} \mathsf{F}\left(H, T-k\right) \text{ on } \mathsf{H}_0 \tag{17.24}$$

where H_0 is as for ξ_1. For fixed regressors, the Chow (1960) test is exactly distributed as an F, but is only approximately (or asymptotically) so in dynamic models.

Alternatively expressed, the Chow test is:

$$\eta_3 = H^{-1}\xi_3 = H^{-1}\mathbf{e}'\left(\widehat{\mathsf{V}[\mathbf{e}]}\right)^{-1}\mathbf{e}. \tag{17.25}$$

We can now see the relation between ξ_3 and ξ_1: the latter uses $\widehat{\mathsf{V}[\mathbf{e}]} = \hat{\sigma}_u^2\mathbf{I}$, obtained by dropping the (asymptotically negligible) term $\mathsf{V}[\hat{\beta}]$ in (17.21). In small samples, the dropped term is often not negligible, so ξ_1 should not be taken as a test. The numerical value of ξ_1 always exceeds that of ξ_3: the difference indicates the relative increase in prediction uncertainty arising from estimating, rather than knowing, the parameters.

PcGive computes the Chow test efficiently, by noting that:

$$\hat{\sigma}_u^2\mathbf{e}'\left(\widehat{\mathsf{V}[\mathbf{e}]}\right)^{-1}\mathbf{e} = \mathbf{e}'\left(\mathbf{I}_H - \mathbf{X}_H\left(\mathbf{X}'\mathbf{X} + \mathbf{X}_H'\mathbf{X}_H\right)^{-1}\mathbf{X}_H'\right)\mathbf{e}. \tag{17.26}$$

17.1.21 t-test for zero forecast innovation mean (RLS)

The recursive formulae from §13.7.9 are applicable over the sample $T+1, \ldots, T+H$, and under the null of correct specification and H_0 of ξ_1 above, then the standardized innovations $\{\nu_t/(\omega_t)^{1/2}\}$ in (13.111) are distributed as $\mathsf{IN}(0, \sigma_u^2)$. Thus:

$$\sqrt{H}\frac{\frac{1}{H}\sum_{t=T+1}^{T+H}\nu_t/(\omega_t)^{1/2}}{\hat{\sigma}_u} \sim \mathsf{t}\left(H-1\right) \text{ on } \mathsf{H}_0. \tag{17.27}$$

This tests for a different facet of forecast inaccuracy in which the forecast errors have a small but systematic bias. This test is the same as an endpoint CUSUM test of recursive residuals, but using only the forecasts sample (see Harvey and Collier, 1977).

17.2 IV/RIV estimation

Instrumental variables estimation was considered in §12.7. Here we write the model as:

$$y_t = \beta_0' \mathbf{y}_t^* + \beta_1' \mathbf{w}_t + \epsilon_t, \tag{17.28}$$

in which we have $n-1$ endogenous variables $\mathbf{y}_t^*$ and q_1 non-modelled variables $\mathbf{w}_t$ on the right-hand side (the latter may include lagged endogenous variables). We assume that we have q_2 additional instruments, labelled $\mathbf{w}_t^*$. Write $\mathbf{y}_t = (y_t : \mathbf{y}_t^{*\prime})'$ for the $n \times 1$ vector of endogenous variables. Let $\mathbf{z}_t$ denote the set of all instrumental variables (non-endogenous included regressors, plus additional instruments): $\mathbf{z}_t = (\mathbf{w}_t' : \mathbf{w}_t^{*\prime})'$, which is a vector of length $q = q_1 + q_2$.

17.2.1 Reduced form estimates

First the reduced form (RF) estimates are printed. If $\mathbf{Z}' = (\mathbf{z}_1 \dots \mathbf{z}_T)$, and $\mathbf{y}_t$ denotes all the n endogenous variables including y_t at t with $\mathbf{Y}' = (\mathbf{y}_1, \dots, \mathbf{y}_T)$, then the RF estimates are:

$$\hat{\mathbf{\Pi}}' = (\mathbf{Z}'\mathbf{Z})^{-1} \mathbf{Z}'\mathbf{Y}, \tag{17.29}$$

which is $q \times n$. The elements of $\hat{\mathbf{\Pi}}'$ relevant to each endogenous variable are written:

$$\pi_i = (\mathbf{Z}'\mathbf{Z})^{-1} \mathbf{Z}'\mathbf{Y}_i,\ i = 1, \dots, n, \tag{17.30}$$

with $\mathbf{Y}_i' = (y_{i1}, \dots, y_{iT})$ the vector of observations on the ith endogenous variable. Standard errors etc. all follow as for OLS above (using $\mathbf{Z}$, $\mathbf{Y}_i$ for $\mathbf{X}, \mathbf{y}$ in the relevant equations there).

17.2.2 GIV estimates

Generalized instrumental variables estimates for the $k = n - 1 + q_1$ coefficients of interest $\beta = (\beta_0' : \beta_1')'$ are:

$$\tilde{\beta} = \left(\mathbf{X}'\mathbf{Z}\,(\mathbf{Z}'\mathbf{Z})^{-1}\,\mathbf{Z}'\mathbf{X}\right)^{-1} \mathbf{X}'\mathbf{Z}\,(\mathbf{Z}'\mathbf{Z})^{-1}\mathbf{Z}'\mathbf{y}, \tag{17.31}$$

using $\mathbf{x}_t = (\mathbf{y}_t^{*\prime} : \mathbf{w}_t')'$, $\mathbf{X}' = (\mathbf{x}_1 \dots \mathbf{x}_T)$, $\mathbf{y} = (y_1 \dots y_T)'$, which is the left-hand side of (17.28), and $\mathbf{Z}$ is as in (17.29). This allows for the case of more instruments than explanatory variables ($q > k$), and requires rank$(\mathbf{X}'\mathbf{Z}) = k$ and rank$(\mathbf{Z}'\mathbf{Z}) = q$. If $q = k$ the equation simplifies to that of (12.22):

$$\tilde{\beta} = (\mathbf{Z}'\mathbf{X})^{-1} \mathbf{Z}'\mathbf{y}. \tag{17.32}$$

As for OLS, PcGive does not use expression (17.31) directly, but instead uses the QR decomposition for numerically more stable computation. The error variance is given by

$$\tilde{\sigma}_\epsilon = \frac{\tilde{\epsilon}'\tilde{\epsilon}}{T-k}, \quad \text{where } \tilde{\epsilon} = \mathbf{y} - \mathbf{X}\tilde{\beta}. \tag{17.33}$$

The variance of $\tilde{\beta}$ is estimated by:

$$\widehat{\mathsf{V}\left[\tilde{\beta}\right]} = \tilde{\sigma}_\epsilon \left(\mathbf{X}'\mathbf{Z}\left(\mathbf{Z}'\mathbf{Z}\right)^{-1}\mathbf{Z}'\mathbf{X}\right)^{-1}. \tag{17.34}$$

Again the output is closely related to that reported for least squares except that the columns for HCSE, partial r^2 and instability statistics are omitted. However, RSS, $\tilde{\sigma}$ and DW are recorded, as is the reduced form $\hat{\sigma}$ (from regressing y_t on $\mathbf{z}_t$, already reported with the RF equation for y_t). Additional statistics reported are :

17.2.3 Specification χ^2

This tests for the validity of the choice of the instrumental variables as discussed by Sargan (1964). It is asymptotically distributed as $\chi^2(q_2 - n + 1)$ when the $q_2 - n + 1$ overidentifying instruments are independent of the equation error. It is also interpretable as a test of whether the restricted reduced form of the structural model (y_t on $\mathbf{x}_t$ plus $\mathbf{x}_t$ on $\mathbf{z}_t$) parsimoniously encompasses the unrestricted reduced form (y_t on $\mathbf{z}_t$ directly):

$$\frac{\hat{\pi}'\left(\mathbf{Z}'\mathbf{Z}\right)\hat{\pi} - \tilde{\beta}'\left(\mathbf{X}'\mathbf{Z}\left(\mathbf{Z}'\mathbf{Z}\right)^{-1}\mathbf{Z}'\mathbf{X}\right)\tilde{\beta}}{\tilde{\epsilon}'\tilde{\epsilon}/T} \underset{app}{\sim} \chi^2(q_2 - n + 1), \tag{17.35}$$

with $\hat{\pi} = \left(\mathbf{Z}'\mathbf{Z}\right)^{-1}\mathbf{Z}'\mathbf{y}$ being the reduced form estimates.

17.2.4 Testing $\beta = 0$

Reported is the χ^2 test of $\beta = \mathbf{0}$ (other than the intercept) which has a crude correspondence to the earlier F-test. On H_0: $\beta = \mathbf{0}$, the reported statistic behaves asymptotically as a $\chi^2\,(k-1)$. First define

$$\xi_\beta = \tilde{\beta}'\left(\mathbf{X}'\mathbf{Z}\left(\mathbf{Z}'\mathbf{Z}\right)^{-1}\mathbf{Z}'\mathbf{X}\right)\tilde{\beta}. \tag{17.36}$$

Then $\xi_\beta/\tilde{\sigma}_\epsilon \underset{app}{\sim} \chi^2(k)$ would test whether all k coefficients are zero (*cf.* equation (13.58)). To keep the intercept separate, we compute:

$$\frac{\xi_\beta - T\bar{y}^2}{\tilde{\sigma}_\epsilon} \underset{app}{\sim} \chi^2(k-1). \tag{17.37}$$

This amounts to using the formula for $\tilde{\beta}$ (eq. (17.31)) in ξ_β with $\mathbf{y} - \bar{y}\iota$ instead of $\mathbf{y}$.

17.2.5 Forecast test

A forecast test is provided if H observations are retained for forecasting. For IV/RIV there are endogenous regressor variables: the only interesting issue is that of parameter constancy and correspondingly the output is merely ξ_1 of (17.22) using $\tilde{\sigma}_\epsilon$ and:

$$e_t = y_t - \mathbf{x}_t'\tilde{\beta}, \quad t = T+1, \ldots, T+H. \tag{17.38}$$

Dynamic forecasts (which require forecasts of the successive $\mathbf{x}_{T+1},\ldots,\mathbf{x}_{T+H}$) could be obtained from PcFiml where the system as a whole is analysed.

17.3 RALS estimation

As discussed in the typology in §12.3, if a dynamic model has common factors in its lag polynomials, then it can be re-expressed as having lower-order systematic dynamics combined with an autoregressive error process (called COMFAC: see model type §12.3.7, and §12.5.6). If the autoregressive error is of rth order, the estimator is called r^{th}-order Autoregressive Least Squares or RALS, and it takes the form:

$$\beta_0 (L)\, y_t = \sum_{i=1}^{m} \beta_i (L)\, z_{it} + u_t \text{ with } \alpha (L)\, u_t = \epsilon_t, \tag{17.39}$$

when:

$$\alpha (L) = 1 - \sum_{i=s}^{r} \alpha_i L^i. \tag{17.40}$$

This can be written as:

$$y_t = \mathbf{x}_t'\boldsymbol{\beta} + u_t, \quad u_t = \sum_{i=s}^{r} \alpha_i u_{t-i} + \epsilon_t, \quad t = 1,\ldots,T, \tag{17.41}$$

with $\epsilon_t \sim \mathsf{IN}\left(0, \sigma_\epsilon^2\right)$.

Minimizing:

$$f\left(\boldsymbol{\beta}, \boldsymbol{\alpha}\right) = \sum_{t=1}^{T} \epsilon_t^2 \tag{17.42}$$

as a function (denoted Phi in the output) of the $(\boldsymbol{\beta}, \boldsymbol{\alpha})$ parameters yields a non-linear least squares problem necessitating iterative solution. However, conditional on values of either set of parameters, $f(\cdot)$ is linear in the other set, so analytical first and second derivatives are easy to obtain. There is an estimator-generating equation for this whole class (see Hendry, 1976, Section 7), but as it has almost no efficient non-iterative solutions, little is gained by its exploitation. Letting $\boldsymbol{\theta}$ denote all of the unrestricted parameters in $\beta_0(\cdot)$, $\{\beta_i(\cdot)\}$ and $\alpha(\cdot)$, then the algorithm programmed in PcGive for minimizing $f(\cdot)$ as a function of $\boldsymbol{\theta}$ is a variant of the Gauss–Newton class. Let:

$$\mathbf{q}(\boldsymbol{\theta}) = \frac{\partial \mathbf{f}}{\partial \boldsymbol{\theta}} \text{ and } \mathbf{Q} = \mathsf{E}\left[\mathbf{q}\mathbf{q}'\right], \tag{17.43}$$

so that negligible cross-products are eliminated, then at the ith iteration:

$$\boldsymbol{\theta}_{i+1} = \boldsymbol{\theta}_i - s_i \mathbf{Q}_i^{-1} \mathbf{q}_i, \quad i = 0,\ldots,I, \tag{17.44}$$

where s_i is a scalar chosen by a line search procedure to minimize $f(\boldsymbol{\theta}_{i+1}|\boldsymbol{\theta}_i)$. The convergence criterion depends on $\mathbf{q}_i'\mathbf{Q}_i^{-1}\mathbf{q}_i$ and on changes in $\boldsymbol{\theta}_i$ between iterations. The bi-linearity of $f(\cdot)$ is exploited in computing $\mathbf{Q}$.

17.3.1 Initial values for RALS

Before estimating by RALS, OLS estimates of $\{\beta_i\}$ are calculated, as are LM-test values of $\{\alpha_i\}$, where the prespecified autocorrelation order is 'data frequency+1' (for example, 5 for quarterly data). These estimates are then used to initialize $\boldsymbol{\theta}$. However, the $\{\alpha_i\}$ can be reset by users. Specifically, for single-order processes, $u_t = \alpha_r u_{t-r} + \epsilon_t$, then α_r can be selected by a prior grid search. The user can specify the maximum number of iterations, the convergence tolerance, both the starting and ending orders of the polynomial $\alpha(L)$ in the form:

$$u_t = \sum_{i=s}^{r} \alpha_i u_{t-i} + \epsilon_t,$$

and whether to minimize $f(\cdot)$ sequentially over $s,\ s+1,\ldots,r$ or merely the highest order, r.

17.3.2 Final estimates

On convergence, the variances of the θs are calculated (from $\mathbf{Q}^{-1}$), as are the roots of $\alpha(L) = 0$. The usual statistics for $\hat{\sigma}$, RSS (denoted ϕ for function value, as this can be used in likelihood-ratio tests between alternative nested versions of a model), t-values etc. are reported, as is $\Sigma(y_t - \bar{y})^2$ in case a pseudo-R^2 statistic is desired.

17.3.3 Significance tests

Likelihood ratio tests of $\alpha_i = 0, i = s, s+1, \ldots, r$, are shown if sequential optimization was selected and $r - s \geq 2$. These are set out in tabular form as $\chi^2(m)$ (to be additive) so the first (top left) element tests $\alpha_s = 0$ by $\chi^2(1)$, the next row tests $\alpha_s = \alpha_{s+1} = 0$ by $\chi^2(2)$, followed by $\alpha_{s+1} = 0$ by $\chi^2(1)$ etc. Going down rows increases the order m; going along rows reduces the number of terms tested. Thus if $s = 1$, and $r = 3$ the hypotheses being tested are:

$$\left.\begin{array}{l|l|l}
\alpha_1 = 0 & & \\
\alpha_1, \alpha_2 = 0 & \alpha_2 = 0 & \\
\alpha_1, \alpha_2, \alpha_3 = 0 & \alpha_2, \alpha_3 = 0 & \alpha_3 = 0
\end{array}\right| \sim \left|\begin{array}{l|l|l}
\chi^2(1) & & \\
\chi^2(2) & \chi^2(1) & \\
\chi^2(3) & \chi^2(2) & \chi^2(1)
\end{array}\right.$$

COMFAC restrictions are not tested at this stage but can be for the general model using OLS-based Wald tests, or by likelihood-ratio tests comparing residual sums of squares from $f(\cdot)$ with those from the general unrestricted model.

17.3.4 Analysis of 1-step forecasts

Rewrite the RALS model as:

$$y_t = \mathbf{x}_t'\boldsymbol{\beta} + \sum_{i=s}^{r} \alpha_i u_{t-i} + \epsilon_t \tag{17.45}$$

with:

$$\hat{y}_t = \mathbf{x}_t'\hat{\boldsymbol{\beta}} + \sum_{i=s}^{r} \hat{\alpha}_i \hat{u}_{t-i} \tag{17.46}$$

where $\hat{\boldsymbol{\beta}}$ and $\{\hat{\alpha}_i\}$ are obtained over $1, \ldots, T$. The forecast error is:

$$e_t = y_t - \hat{y}_t = \epsilon_t + \mathbf{x}_t'\left(\boldsymbol{\beta} - \hat{\boldsymbol{\beta}}\right) + \sum_{i=s}^{r} \left(\alpha_i u_{t-i} - \hat{\alpha}_i \hat{u}_{t-i}\right) \tag{17.47}$$

or:

$$e_t = \epsilon_t + \mathbf{x}_t'\left(\boldsymbol{\beta} - \hat{\boldsymbol{\beta}}\right) + \sum_{i=s}^{r} \left[\left(\alpha_i - \hat{\alpha}_i\right) \hat{u}_{t-i} + \alpha_i \left(u_{t-i} - \hat{u}_{t-i}\right)\right]. \tag{17.48}$$

Now:

$$u_{t-i} - \hat{u}_{t-i} = \left(y_{t-i} - \mathbf{x}_{t-i}'\boldsymbol{\beta}\right) - \left(y_{t-i} - \mathbf{x}_{t-i}'\hat{\boldsymbol{\beta}}\right) = -\mathbf{x}_{t-i}'\left(\boldsymbol{\beta} - \hat{\boldsymbol{\beta}}\right). \tag{17.49}$$

Consequently:

$$e_t = \epsilon_t + \left(\mathbf{x}_t' - \sum_{i=s}^{r} \alpha_i \mathbf{x}_{t-i}'\right)\left(\boldsymbol{\beta} - \hat{\boldsymbol{\beta}}\right) + \sum_{i=s}^{r} \left(\alpha_i - \hat{\alpha}_i\right) \hat{u}_{t-i}. \tag{17.50}$$

Thus:

$$e_t = \epsilon_t + \mathbf{x}_t^{+\prime}\left(\boldsymbol{\beta} - \hat{\boldsymbol{\beta}}\right) + \hat{\mathbf{u}}_r'\left(\boldsymbol{\alpha} - \hat{\boldsymbol{\alpha}}\right) = \epsilon_t + \mathbf{w}_t'\left(\boldsymbol{\theta} - \hat{\boldsymbol{\theta}}\right), \tag{17.51}$$

where we define $\mathbf{x}_t^{+\prime} = \mathbf{x}_t - \Sigma_s^r \alpha_i \mathbf{x}_{t-i}$, $\hat{\mathbf{u}}_r' = (\hat{u}_{t-s} \ldots \hat{u}_{t-r})$, $\mathbf{w}_t' = \left(\mathbf{x}_t^{+\prime} : \hat{\mathbf{u}}_r'\right)$, and $\boldsymbol{\theta}' = (\boldsymbol{\beta}' : \boldsymbol{\alpha}')$ when $\boldsymbol{\alpha}' = (\alpha_s \ldots \alpha_r)$. $\mathsf{E}\left[e_t\right] \simeq 0$ for a correctly-specified model. Finally, therefore (neglecting the second-order dependence of the variance of $\mathbf{w}_t'(\boldsymbol{\theta} - \hat{\boldsymbol{\theta}})$ on $\hat{\boldsymbol{\theta}}$ acting through $\mathbf{w}_t$):

$$\mathsf{V}\left[e_t\right] = \sigma^2 + \mathbf{w}_t'\mathsf{V}\left[\hat{\boldsymbol{\theta}}\right]\mathbf{w}_t. \tag{17.52}$$

$\mathsf{V}[\hat{\boldsymbol{\theta}}]$ is the RALS variance-covariance matrix, and from the forecast-error covariance matrix, the 1-step analysis is calculated, as are parameter-constancy tests.

The output is as for OLS: the columns respectively report the date for which the forecast is made, the realized outcome (y_t), the forecast ($\hat{y}_t$), the forecast error ($e_t = y_t - \hat{y}_t$), the standard error of the 1-step forecast ($\mathsf{SE}\left(e_t\right) = \sqrt{\widehat{\mathsf{V}\left[e_t\right]}}$), and a t-value (that is, the standardized forecast error $e_t/\mathsf{SE}\left(e_t\right)$).

17.3.5 Forecast tests

The RALS analogues of the forecast test ξ_1 of (17.22), and of the Chow test η_3 in (17.25), are reported. The formulae follow directly from (17.47) and (17.52).

17.4 NLS/RNLS estimation

The non-linear regression model is written as

$$y_t = f\left(\mathbf{x}_t, \boldsymbol{\theta}\right) + u_t, \quad t = 1, \ldots, T, \text{ with } u_t \sim \mathsf{IN}\left(0, \sigma_u^2\right). \tag{17.53}$$

We take $\boldsymbol{\theta}$ to be a $k \times 1$ vector. For example:

$$y_t = \theta_0 + \theta_1 x_t^{\theta_2} + \theta_3 z_t^{1-\theta_2} + u_t.$$

Note that for fixed θ_2 this last model becomes linear; for example, for $\theta_2 = \frac{1}{2}$:

$$y_t = \theta_0 + \theta_1 x_t^* + \theta_3 z_t^* + u_t, \quad x_t^* = \sqrt{x_t},\ z_t^* = \sqrt{z_t},$$

which is linear in the transformed variables x_t^*, z_t^*. As for OLS, estimation proceeds by minimizing the sum of squared residuals:

$$\hat{\boldsymbol{\theta}} = \underset{\boldsymbol{\theta}}{\operatorname{argmin}} \sum_{t=1}^{T} u_t^2 = \underset{\boldsymbol{\theta}}{\operatorname{argmin}} \sum_{t=1}^{T} \left(y_t - f\left(\mathbf{x}_t, \boldsymbol{\theta}\right)\right)^2. \tag{17.54}$$

In linear models, this problem has an explicit solution; for non-linear models the minimum has to be found using iterative optimization methods.

Instead of minimizing the sum of squares, PcGive maximizes the sum of squares divided by $-T$:

$$\hat{\boldsymbol{\theta}} = \underset{\boldsymbol{\theta}}{\operatorname{argmax}}\, g\left(\boldsymbol{\theta} \mid y_t, \mathbf{x}_t\right) = \underset{\boldsymbol{\theta}}{\operatorname{argmax}} \left\{ -\frac{1}{T} \sum_{t=1}^{T} u_t^2 \right\}. \tag{17.55}$$

As for RALS, an iterative procedure is used to locate the maximum:

$$\boldsymbol{\theta}_{i+1} = \boldsymbol{\theta}_i + s_i \mathbf{Q}\left(\boldsymbol{\theta}_i\right)^{-1} \mathbf{q}\left(\boldsymbol{\theta}_i\right), \tag{17.56}$$

with $\mathbf{q}\left(\cdot\right)$ the derivatives of $g(\cdot)$ with respect to θ_j (this is determined numerically), and $\mathbf{Q}\left(\cdot\right)^{-1}$ a symmetric, positive definite matrix (determined by the BFGS method after some initial Gauss-Newton steps). Practical details of the algorithm are provided in §20.3.3; PcFiml gives a more thorough discussion of the subject of numerical optimization. Before using NLS you are advised to study the examples given in tutorial Chapter 9, to learn about the potential problems.

Recursive estimation is achieved by the brute-force method: first estimate for the full sample, then shrink the sample by one observation at a time. At each step the $\hat{\theta}$ and $\mathbf{Q}(\hat{\theta})^{-1}$ of the previous step are used as starting values, resulting in a considerably faster algorithm.

Output is as for OLS, except for the instability tests and HCSEs which are not computed. The variance of the estimated coefficients is determined numerically, other statistics follow directly, for example:

$$\hat{\sigma}_u^2 = \frac{1}{T-k}\sum_{t=1}^{T}\hat{u}_t^2, \quad \text{with } \hat{u}_t = y_t - f\left(\mathbf{x}_t, \hat{\theta}\right). \tag{17.57}$$

Forecasts are computed and graphed, but the only statistic reported is the ξ_1 test of (17.22), using 1-step forecast errors:

$$e_t = y_t - f\left(\mathbf{x}_t, \hat{\theta}\right), \quad t = T+1, \ldots, T+H. \tag{17.58}$$

17.5 ML estimation

Maximum likelihood estimation was established in Chapter 13. We saw in (13.28) that for an independent sample of T observations and k parameters $\boldsymbol{\theta}$:

$$\hat{\theta} = \underset{\boldsymbol{\theta}}{\operatorname{argmax}}\, \ell\left(\boldsymbol{\theta} \mid \mathbf{X}\right) = \underset{\boldsymbol{\theta}}{\operatorname{argmax}} \sum_{t=1}^{T} \ell\left(\boldsymbol{\theta} \mid \mathbf{x}_t\right). \tag{17.59}$$

This type of model can be estimated with PcGive, which solves the problem:

$$\max_{\boldsymbol{\theta}} \sum_{t=1}^{T} \ell\left(\boldsymbol{\theta} \mid \mathbf{x}_t\right). \tag{17.60}$$

Models falling in this class are, for example, binary logit and probit, ARCH, GARCH, Tobit, Poisson regression. Extensive examples are given in tutorial Chapter 9. As an example, consider the linear regression model. PcGive gives three ways of solving this:

(1) direct estimation (OLS);
(2) numerical minimization of the residual sum of squares (NLS);
(3) numerical maximization of the likelihood function (ML).

Clearly, the first method is to be preferred when available.

Estimation of (17.60) uses the same technique as NLS. The output is more concise, consisting of coefficients, standard errors (based on the numerical second derivative), t-values, t-probabilities, and 'loglik' which is $\sum_{t=1}^{T}\ell(\hat{\theta}|\mathbf{x}_t)$. Forecasts are computed and graphed, but no statistics are reported.

Chapter 18

Model Evaluation Statistics

18.1 Graphic analysis

Graphic analysis focuses on graphical inspection of individual equations. Let y_t, $\hat{y}_t$ denote respectively the actual (that is, observed) values and the fitted values of the selected equation, with residuals $\hat{u}_t = y_t - \hat{y}_t$, $t = 1, \ldots, T$. When H observations are retained for forecasting, then $\hat{y}_{T+1}, \ldots, \hat{y}_{T+H}$ are the 1-step forecasts. NLS/RNLS/ML use the variables labelled 'actual' and 'fitted' for y_t, $\hat{y}_t$.

Eight different types of graph are available:

(1) *Actual and Fitted Values*
$(y_t, \hat{y}_t)$ over t. This is a graph showing the fitted ($\hat{y}_t$) and actual values (y_t) of the dependent variable over time, including the forecast period;

(2) *Cross-plot of Actual and Fitted Values*
$\hat{y}_t$ against y_t, also including the forecast period;

(3) *Scaled Residuals*
$(\hat{u}_t/\hat{\sigma})$ over t, where $\hat{\sigma}^2 = (T-k)^{-1}RSS$ is the full-sample equation error variance. As indicated, this graph shows the scaled residuals given by $\hat{u}_t/\hat{\sigma}$ over time;

(4) *Forecasts and Outcomes*
The 1-step forecasts can be plotted in a graph over time: y_t and $\hat{y}_t$ are shown with error bars of $\pm 2\mathsf{SE}(e_t)$ centered on $\hat{y}_t$ (that is, an approximate 95% confidence interval for the 1-step forecast); e_t are the forecast errors.

(5) *Residual Correlogram*
This plots the correlogram using $\hat{u}_t$ as the x_t variable in (18.13).

(6) *Residual Spectrum*
This plots the estimated spectral density (see the GiveWin book) using $\hat{u}_t$ as the x_t variable.

(7) *Residual Density Optionally with Histogram and Normal*
By default the histogram of the standardized residuals $\hat{u}_t/\sqrt{(T^{-1}RSS)}$, $t = 1, \ldots, T$, and the estimated density $\widehat{f_{\mathsf{u}}(\cdot)}$ are graphed using the settings described in the GiveWin book.

(8) *Residual QQ Plot*
The estimated QQ plot of the residuals is shown with a standard normal for comparison.

The residuals can be saved to the database for further inspection.

18.2 Recursive graphics

Recursive methods estimate the model at each t for $t = M-1, \ldots, T$. RNLS does this directly. RLS and RIV initialize the process by estimation over $1, \ldots, M-1$, which is followed by recursive updating over $M, \ldots, T$. The output generated by the recursive procedures is most easily studied graphically, possibly using the facility to view multiple graphs together on screen. The dialog has a facility to write the output to the editor, instead of graphing it. The recursive estimation aims to throw light on the relative future information aspect (that is, parameter constancy).

Let $\hat{\beta}_t$ denote the k parameters estimated from a sample of size t, and $y_j - \mathbf{x}_j'\hat{\beta}_t$ the residuals at time j evaluated at the parameter estimates based on the sample $1, \ldots, t$ (for RNLS the residuals are $y_j - f(\mathbf{x}_j, \hat{\beta}_t)$).

We now consider the generated output:

(1) *Coefficients* ± 2 *Standard Errors*
The graph shows $\hat{\beta}_{it} \pm 2\mathsf{SE}(\hat{\beta}_{it})$ for each selected coefficient $i \quad (i = 1, \ldots, k)$ over $t = M, \ldots, T$.

(2) t-*values*
$\hat{\beta}_{it}/\mathsf{SE}(\hat{\beta}_{it})$ for each selected coefficient $i \;\; (i = 1, \ldots, k)$ over $t = M, \ldots, T$.

(3) *Residual Sum of Squares*
The residual sum of squares at each t is $RSS_t = \sum_{j=1}^{t}(y_j - \mathbf{x}_j'\hat{\beta}_t)^2$ for $t = M, \ldots, T$.

(4) *Standardized Innovations*
The standardized innovations (or standardized recursive residuals) for RLS are: $\nu_t = (y_t - \mathbf{x}_t'\hat{\beta}_{t-1})/(\omega_t)^{1/2}$ where $\omega_t = 1 + \mathbf{x}_t'\left(\mathbf{X}_{t-1}'\mathbf{X}_{t-1}\right)^{-1}\mathbf{x}_t$ for $t = M, \ldots, T$.
As pointed out in §13.7.9, $\sigma^2\omega_t$ is the 1-step forecast error variance of (17.20), and $\hat{\beta}_{M-1}$ are the coefficient estimates from the initializing OLS estimation.

(5) *1-Step Residuals* $\pm 2\hat{\sigma}$
The 1-step residuals $y_t - \mathbf{x}_t'\hat{\beta}_t$ are shown bordered by $0 \pm 2\hat{\sigma}_t$ over $M, \ldots, T$. Points outside the 2 standard-error region are either outliers or are associated with coefficient changes.

(6) *1-Step* F-*Tests (1-Step Chow-Tests)*
1-step forecast tests are $\mathsf{F}(1, t-k-1)$ under the null of constant parameters, for

$t = M, \ldots, T$. A typical statistic is calculated as:

$$\frac{(RSS_t - RSS_{t-1})(t-k-1)}{RSS_{t-1}} = \frac{\nu_t^2/\omega_t}{\hat{\sigma}_{t-1}^2}. \tag{18.1}$$

Normality of y_t is needed for this statistic to be distributed as an F.

(7) *Break-point* F-Tests ($N\downarrow$-Step Chow-Tests)
Break-point F-tests are $\mathsf{F}(T-t+1, t-k-1)$ for $t = M, \ldots, T$. These are, therefore, sequences of Chow tests and are called $N\downarrow$ because the number of forecasts goes from $N = T - M + 1$ to 1. When the forecast period exceeds the estimation period, this test is not necessarily optimal relative to the covariance test based on fitting the model separately to the split samples. A typical statistic is calculated as:

$$\frac{(RSS_T - RSS_{t-1})(t-k-1)}{RSS_{t-1}(T-t+1)}. = \frac{\frac{1}{T-t+1}\sum_{m=t}^{T}\nu_m^2/\omega_m}{\hat{\sigma}_{t-1}^2}. \tag{18.2}$$

This test is closely related to the CUSUMSQ statistic in Brown, Durbin and Evans (1975).

(8) *Forecast* F-Tests ($N\uparrow$-Step Chow- Tests)
Forecast F-tests are $\mathsf{F}(t-M+1, M-k-1)$ for $t = M, \ldots, T$, and are called $N\uparrow$ as the forecast horizon increases from M to T. This tests the model over 1 to $M-1$ against an alternative which allows any form of change over M to T. A typical statistic is calculated as:

$$\frac{(RSS_t - RSS_{M-1})(M-k-1)}{RSS_{M-1}(t-M+1)}. \tag{18.3}$$

The statistics in (18.1)–(18.3) are variants of Chow (1960) tests: they are scaled by 1-off critical values from the F-distribution at any selected probability level as an adjustment for changing degrees of freedom, so that the significant critical values become a straight line at unity. Note that the first and last values of (18.1) respectively equal the first value of (18.3) and the last value of (18.2).

Test statistics from (18.1)–(18.3) are not calculated for RIV; (1), (2) and (4) are not calculated for RNLS.

18.3 Dynamic analysis

The general class of models estimable in PcGive was discussed in Chapter 12 in the form:

$$b_0(L)\, y_t = \sum_{i=1}^{q} b_i(L)\, z_{it} + \epsilon_t \tag{18.4}$$

where $b_0(L)$ and the $b_i(L)$ are polynomials in the lag operator L. Now $q+1$ is the number of distinct variables (one of which is y_t), whereas k remains the number of estimated coefficients. For simplicity we take all polynomials to be of length m:

$$b_i(L) = \sum_{j=0}^{m} b_{ij} L^j, \quad i = 0, \ldots, q.$$

With $b_{00} = 1$ and using $a(L) = -\sum_{j=1}^{m} b_{0j} L^{j-1}$ we can write (18.4) as:

$$y_t = a(L)\, y_{t-1} + \sum_{i=1}^{q} b_i(L)\, z_{it} + \epsilon_t. \tag{18.5}$$

Finally, we use $\mathbf{a} = (b_{01}, \ldots, b_{0m})'$ and $\mathbf{b}_i = (b_{i0}, \ldots, b_{im})$, $i = 1, \ldots, q$.

In its unrestricted mode of operation, PcGive can be visualized as analysing the polynomials involved, and it computes such functions as their roots and sums. This option is available if a general model was initially formulated, and provided OLS/RLS or IV/RIV was selected.

18.3.1 Static long-run solution

When working with dynamic models, concepts such as equilibrium solutions, steady-state growth paths, mean lags of response etc. are generally of interest. In the simple model:

$$y_t = \beta_0 z_t + \beta_1 z_{t-1} + \alpha_1 y_{t-1} + u_t, \tag{18.6}$$

where all the variables are stationary, a static equilibrium is defined by:

$$\mathsf{E}[z_t] = z^* \text{ for all } t$$

in which case, $\mathsf{E}[y_t] = y^*$ will also be constant if $|\alpha_1| < 1$, and y_t will converge to:

$$y^* = Kz^* \text{ where } K = \frac{(\beta_0 + \beta_1)}{(1 - \alpha_1)} \tag{18.7}$$

(cf. §12.3.8). For non-stationary but cointegrated data, reinterpret expression (18.7) as $\mathsf{E}[y_t - Kz_t] = 0$.

PcGive computes estimates of K and associated standard errors. These are called static long-run parameters. If $b_0(1) \neq 0$, the general long-run solution of (18.4) is given by:

$$y^* = \sum_{i=1}^{q} \frac{b_i(1)}{b_0(1)} z_i^* = \sum_{i=1}^{q} K_i z_i^*. \tag{18.8}$$

The expression $y_t - \Sigma K_i z_{it}$ is called the equilibrium-correction mechanism (ECM) and can be stored in the data set. If common-factor restrictions of the form $b_j(L) =$

$\alpha(L)\gamma_j(L)$, $j = 0, \ldots, q$ are imposed, then $\alpha(1)$ will cancel, hence enforced autoregressive error representations have no impact on derived long-run solutions.

The standard errors of $\hat{\mathbf{K}} = \left(\hat{K}_1 \ldots \hat{K}_q\right)'$ are calculated from:

$$\widehat{\mathsf{V}\left[\hat{\mathbf{K}}\right]} = \hat{\mathbf{J}}\widehat{\mathsf{V}\left[\hat{\beta}\right]}\hat{\mathbf{J}}' \text{ when } \mathbf{J} = \frac{\partial \mathbf{K}}{\partial \beta'}. \tag{18.9}$$

PcGive calculates $\mathbf{J}$ using numerical differentiation. PcFiml, on the other hand, computes the multivariate analogue analytically (which extends the algorithm proposed by Bårdsen, 1989).

PcGive outputs the solved static long-run equation, with standard errors of the coefficients. This is followed by a Wald test of the null that all of the long-run coefficients are zero (except the constant term). The lower diagonal of the $\widehat{\mathsf{V}[\hat{\mathbf{K}}]}$ matrix is optionally printed.

18.3.2 Analysis of lag structure

The $\hat{b}_i(L)$, $i = 0, \ldots, q$ of (18.4) and their standard errors are reported in tabular form with the $\hat{b}_i(1)$ (their row sums) and associated standard errors.

18.3.2.1 Tests on the significance of each variable

The first column contains F-tests of each of the $q + 1$ hypotheses:

$$\mathsf{H}_{v0} : \mathbf{a} = \mathbf{0};\ \mathsf{H}_{vi} : \mathbf{b}_i = \mathbf{0} \text{ for } i = 1, \ldots, q.$$

These test the significance of each basic variable in turn. The final column gives the PcGive unit-root tests:

$$\mathsf{H}_{ui} : b_i(1) = 0 \text{ for } i = 0, \ldots, q.$$

If H_{ui}: $b_i(1) = 0$ cannot be rejected, there is no significant long-run level effect from z_{it}; if H_{vi}: $\mathbf{b}_i = \mathbf{0}$ cannot be rejected, there is no significant effect from z_{it} at any (included) lag. Significance is marked by * for 5% and ** for 1%. Critical values for the PcGive unit-root test (H_{u0}: $b_0(1) = 0$) are derived from a response surface fitted to the results in Banerjee, Dolado and Mestre (1992). For the unit root test, only significance of the dependent variable is reported (not the remaining variables!),

Conflicts between the tests' outcomes are possible in small samples.

Note that $b_i(1) = 0$ and $\mathbf{b}_i = \mathbf{0}$ are not equivalent; testing $K_i = 0$ is different again. Using (18.6) we can show the relevant hypotheses:

significance of each variable	$\mathsf{H}_{v0} : \alpha_1 = 0;\ \mathsf{H}_{v1} : \beta_0 = \beta_1 = 0,$
PcGive unit root test	$\mathsf{H}_{u0} : \alpha_1 - 1 = 0,$
Additional unit root tests	$\mathsf{H}_{u1} : \beta_0 + \beta_1 = 0,$
t-values from static long run	$\mathsf{H}_l : (\beta_0 + \beta_1)/(1 - \alpha_1) = 0.$

18.3.2.2 Tests on the significance of each lag

F-tests of each lag length are shown, beginning at the longest (m) and continuing down to 1. The test of the longest lag is conditional on keeping lags $(1, \ldots, m-1)$, that of $(m-1)$ is conditional on $(1, \ldots, m-2, m)$ etc.

18.3.3 Tests on the significance of all lags

Finally, F-tests of all lags up to m are shown, beginning at the longest $(1, \ldots, m)$ and continuing further from $(2, \ldots, m)$ down to $(m, \ldots, m)$. These tests are conditional on keeping no lags, keeping lag 1, down to keeping $(1, \ldots, m-1)$. Thus, they show the marginal significance of all longer lags.

18.3.4 COMFAC tests

First, the roots of lag polynomials are calculated, followed by COMFAC tests for the legitimacy of common-factor restrictions of the form:[1]

$$\alpha(L)\, b_0^*(L)\, y_t = \alpha(L) \sum_{i=1}^{k} b_i^*(L)\, x_{it} + u_t \tag{18.10}$$

where $\alpha(L)$ is of order r and * denotes polynomials of the original order minus r. The degrees of freedom for the Wald tests for COMFAC are equal to the number of restrictions imposed by $\alpha(L)$ and the Wald statistics are asymptotically χ^2 with these degrees of freedom if the COMFAC restrictions are valid. It is preferable to use the incremental values obtained by subtracting successive values of the Wald tests. These are χ^2 also, with degrees of freedom given by the number of additional criteria. Failure to reject common-factor restrictions does not entail that such restrictions must be imposed. For a discussion of the theory of COMFAC, see Hendry and Mizon (1978) and §12.3.7, §12.5.6; for some finite-sample Monte Carlo evidence see Mizon and Hendry (1980). COMFAC is not available for RALS.

When the minimum order of lag length in the $b_i(L)$ is unity or larger (m say), the Wald test sequence for $1, 2, \ldots, m$ common factors is calculated. Variables that are redundant when lagged (Constant, Seasonals, Trend) are excluded in conducting the Wald test sequence since they always sustain a common-factor interpretation.

18.3.5 Lag weights

Consider the simple model:

$$(1 - \alpha_1 L)\, y_t = (\beta_0 + \beta_1 L)\, z_t + u_t. \tag{18.11}$$

[1] Using Sargan's Wald algorithm (see Hendry, Pagan and Sargan, 1984 and Sargan, 1980b). Note that this non-linear Wald test is susceptible to formulation, so depends on the order of the variables.

With $|\alpha_1| < 1$ this can be written as:

$$y_t = w(L)\, z_t + v_t,$$

when:

$$w(L) = (\beta_0 + \beta_1 L) / (1 - \alpha_1 L) = (\beta_0 + \beta_1 L)\left(1 + \alpha_1 L + \alpha_1^2 L^2 + \cdots\right).$$

Starting from an equilibrium z^* at $t = 0$, a one-off increment of δ to z^* has an impact on y^* at $t = 0, 1, 2, \ldots$ of $w_0\delta$, $w_1\delta$, $w_2\delta$, $w_3\delta, \ldots$ with the ws defined by equating coefficients of powers of L as:

$$w_0 = \beta_0, \quad w_1 = \beta_1 + \beta_0\alpha_1, \quad w_2 = \alpha_1 w_1, \quad w_3 = \alpha_1 w_2, \ldots$$

PcGive can graph the normalized lag weights $w_0/w(1)$, $w_1/w(1)$,..., $w_s/w(1)$ and the cumulative normalized lag weights $w_0/w(1)$, $(w_0 + w_1)/w(1)$,..., $(w_0 + \cdots + w_s)/w(1)$.

Lag weights are available for models estimated by OLS/RLS or IV/RIV.

18.4 Diagnostic tests

18.4.1 Introduction

Irrespective of the estimator selected, a wide range of diagnostic tests is offered, intimately related to the model evaluation criteria discussed in Chapter 14, also see §12.5 and §12.8. Tests are available for residual autocorrelation, conditional heteroscedasticity, normality, unconditional heteroscedasticity/functional form mis-specification and omitted variables. Recursive residuals can be used if these are available. Tests for common factors and linear restrictions are discussed in §18.3.4 and §18.5 below, encompassing tests in §18.9. Thus, relating this section to the earlier information taxonomy in §14.5, the diagnostic tests of this section concern the past (checking that the errors are a homoscedastic, normal, innovation process relative to the information available), whereas the forecast statistics discussed in Chapter 17 concern the future and encompassing tests concern information specific to rival models.

Many test statistics in PcGive have either a χ^2 distribution or an F distribution. F-tests are usually reported as:

```
F(num,denom)   =  Value  [Probability]  /*/**
```

for example:

```
F(1, 155)      =  5.0088 [0.0266] *
```

where the test statistic has an F-distribution with one degree of freedom in the numerator, and 155 in the denominator. The observed value is 5.0088, and the probability of getting a value of 5.0088 or larger under this distribution is 0.0266. This is less than 5% but more than 1%, hence the star. Significant outcomes at a 1% level are shown by two stars.

χ^2 tests are also reported with probabilities, as for example:

```
Normality Chi²(2)=  2.1867 [0.3351]
```

The 5% χ^2 critical values with two degrees of freedom is 5.99, so here normality is not rejected (alternatively, Prob($\chi^2 \geq 2.1867$) = 0.3351, which is more than 5%).

The probability values for the F-test are calculated using an algorithm based on Majunder and Bhattacharjee (1973a) and Cran, Martin and Thomas (1977).[2] Those for the χ^2 are based on Shea (1988). The significance points of the F-distribution derive from Majunder and Bhattacharjee (1973b).

Some tests take the form of a likelihood ratio (LR) test. If ℓ is the unrestricted, and ℓ_0 the restricted log-likelihood, then $-2(\ell_0 - \ell)$ has a $\chi^2(s)$ distribution, with s the number of restrictions imposed (so model ℓ_0 is nested in ℓ).

Many diagnostic tests are calculated through an auxiliary regression. In the case of single-equation tests, they take the form of $T\mathsf{R}^2$ for the auxiliary regression so that they are asymptotically distributed as $\chi^2\left(s\right)$ under their nulls, and hence have the usual additive property for independent $\chi^2 s$. In addition, following Harvey (1990) and Kiviet (1986), F-approximations of the form

$$\frac{\mathsf{R}^2}{1-\mathsf{R}^2} \cdot \frac{T-k-s}{s} \sim \mathsf{F}\left(s, T-k-s\right) \tag{18.12}$$

are calculated because they may be better behaved in small samples.

18.4.2 Residual correlogram and residual autoregression

The correlogram of a variable x_t is the series $\{\mathsf{r}_j\}$ where r_j is the correlation coefficient between x_t and x_{t-j} for $j = 1, \ldots, s$:

$$\mathsf{r}_j = \frac{\sum_{t=j+1}^{T}\left(x_t - \bar{x}_0\right)\left(x_{t-j} - \bar{x}_j\right)}{\sqrt{\sum_{t=j+1}^{T}\left(x_t - \bar{x}_0\right)^2 \sum_{t=j+1}^{T}\left(x_{t-j} - \bar{x}_j\right)^2}}. \tag{18.13}$$

Here $\bar{x}_0 = \frac{1}{T-j}\sum_{t=j+1}^{T} x_t$ is the sample mean of x_t, $t = j+1, \ldots, T$, and $\bar{x}_j = \frac{1}{T-j}\sum_{t=j+1}^{T} x_{t-j}$ is the sample mean of x_{t-j}, so that r_j corresponds to a correlation coefficient proper. Note the difference with the definition in many time-series text books, where the denominator is defined as $\sum_1^T (x_t - \bar{x})^2$. This difference tends to be small, and vanishes asymptotically. Also see the GiveWin book.

---

[2] As recommended in Cran *et al.* (1977), the approach in Pike and Hill (1966) is used for the logarithm of the gamma function.

The residual correlogram is defined as above, but using the residuals from the econometric regression, rather than the data. Thus, this reports the series $\{\mathsf{r}_j\}$ of correlations between the residuals $\hat{u}_t$ and $\hat{u}_{t-j}$.

It is possible to calculate a statistic based on 'T $*$ (sum of s squared autocorrelations)', with s the length of the correlogram, called the Portmanteau statistic:

$$\mathsf{LB}\,(s) = T^2 \sum_{j=1}^{s} \frac{\mathsf{r}_j^2}{T-j}. \tag{18.14}$$

This is corresponds to Box and Pierce (1970), but with a degrees of freedom correction as suggested by Ljung and Box (1978). It is designed as a goodness-of-fit test in stationary, autoregressive moving-average models. Under the assumptions of the test, $\mathsf{LB}(s)$ is asymptotically distributed as $\chi^2(s-n)$ after fitting an AR(n) model. A value such that $\mathsf{LB}(s) \geq 2s$ is taken as indicative of mis-specification for large s. However, small values of such a statistic should be treated with caution since residual autocorrelations are biased towards zero (like *DW*) when lagged dependent variables are included in econometric equations. An appropriate test for residual autocorrelation is provided by the LM test in §18.4.3 below.

The Residual Autoregression is identical to §16.2 but again using the residuals $\hat{u}_t$ of the econometric regression as the y_t variable in (16.10); it provides further descriptive information about residual autocorrelation. The approximate F-test reported has the same advantages and disadvantages as the $\mathsf{LB}\,(s)$ statistic just above, and should be treated as descriptive information about the residuals.

18.4.3 LM test for autocorrelated residuals (not for RALS, ML)

This is the Lagrange-multiplier test for r^{th} order residual autocorrelation, distributed as $\chi^2\,(r)$ in large samples, under the null hypothesis that there is no autocorrelation (that is, that the errors are white noise). In standard usage, $r \simeq \frac{1}{2}s$ for s in §18.4.2 above, so this provides a type of Portmanteau test (see Godfrey, 1978). However, any orders from 1 up to 12 can be selected to test against:

$$u_t = \sum_{i=p}^{r} \alpha_i u_{t-i} + \epsilon_t \text{ where } 0 \leq p \leq r.$$

As noted above, the F-form suggested by Harvey (1981, see Harvey, 1990) is the recommended diagnostic test. Following the outcome of the F-test (and its p-value), the error autocorrelation coefficients are recorded. For an autoregressive error of order r to be estimated by RALS, these LM coefficients provide good initial values, from which the iterative optimization can be commenced. The LM test is calculated by regressing the residuals on all the regressors of the original model and the lagged residuals for lags p to

r (missing residuals are set to zero). The LM test $\chi^2(r-p+1)$ is $T\mathsf{R}^2$ from this regression (or the F-equivalent), and the error autocorrelation coefficients are the coefficients of the lagged residuals. For an excellent exposition, see Pagan (1984).

18.4.4 LM test for autocorrelated squared residuals

This is the ARCH (AutoRegressive Conditional Heteroscedasticity) test: see Engle, 1982) which in the present form tests the hypothesis $\boldsymbol{\gamma} = \mathbf{0}$ in the model:

$$\mathsf{E}\left[u_t^2 \mid u_{t-1}, \ldots, u_{t-r}\right] = c_0 + \sum_{i=1}^{r} \gamma_i u_{t-i}^2$$

where $\boldsymbol{\gamma} = (\gamma_1, \ldots, \gamma_r)'$. Again, we have $T\mathsf{R}^2$ as the χ^2 test from the regression of $\hat{u}_t^2$ on a constant and $\hat{u}_{t-1}^2$ to $\hat{u}_{t-r}^2$ (called the ARCH test) which is asymptotically distributed as $\chi^2(r)$ on H_0: $\boldsymbol{\gamma} = \mathbf{0}$. The F-form is also reported. Both first-order and higher-order lag forms are easily calculated (see Engle, 1982, and Engle, Hendry and Trumbull, 1985).

18.4.5 Test for normality

This is the test statistic described in §16.1.1, which amounts to testing whether the skewness and kurtosis of the residuals corresponds to that of a normal distribution.

18.4.6 Test for heteroscedasticity using squares (not for ML)

This test is based on White (1980), and involves an auxiliary regression of $\{\hat{u}_t^2\}$ on the original regressors (x_{it}) and all their squares (x_{it}^2). The null is unconditional homoscedasticity, and the alternative is that the variance of the $\{u_t\}$ process depends on $\mathbf{x}_t$ and on the x_{it}^2. The output comprises $T\mathsf{R}^2$, the F-test equivalent, the coefficients of the auxiliary regression, and their individual t-statistics, to help highlight problem variables. Variables that are redundant when squared are automatically removed.

18.4.7 Heteroscedasticity using squares and cross-products (not for ML)

This test is that of White (1980), and only calculated if there is a large number of observations relative to the number of variables in the regression. It is based on an auxiliary regression of the squared residuals $\left(\hat{u}_t^2\right)$ on all squares and cross-products of the original regressors (that is, on $r = \frac{1}{2}k(k+1)$ variables). That is, if $T >> k(k+1)$, the test is calculated; redundant variables are automatically removed. The usual χ^2 and F-values are reported; coefficients of the auxiliary regression are also shown with their t-statistics to help with model respecification. This is a general test for heteroscedastic errors: H_0 is that the errors are homoscedastic or, if heteroscedasticity is present, it is unrelated to the *x*s.

In previous versions of PcGive this test used to be called a test for functional form mis-specification. That terminology is criticised by Godfrey and Orme (1994), who show that the test does not have power against omitted variables.

18.4.8 RESET (OLS/RLS only)

The RESET test (Regression Specification Test) due to Ramsey (1969) tests the null of correct specification of the original model against the alternative that powers of $\hat{y}_t$ such as $(\hat{y}_t^2,\ \hat{y}_t^3 \ldots)$ have been omitted. This tests to see if the original functional form is incorrect, by adding powers of linear combinations of xs since by construction, $\hat{y}_t = \mathbf{x}_t'\hat{\boldsymbol{\beta}}_t$. As in §18.7, partitioned inversion is used for accurate calculation of the F-statistic.

18.4.9 Diagnostic tests for NLS/RNLS

The LM tests for autocorrelation, heteroscedasticity and functional form require an auxiliary regression involving the original regressors x_{it}. RNLS and NLS use $\partial f(\mathbf{x}_t, \boldsymbol{\theta})/\partial \theta_i$ (evaluated at $\hat{\boldsymbol{\theta}}$) instead. The auxiliary regression for the autocorrelation test is:

$$\hat{u}_t = \sum_{i=1}^{k} \beta_i \left(\frac{\partial f(\mathbf{x}_t, \boldsymbol{\theta})}{\partial \theta_i} \right)_{\rfloor \hat{\boldsymbol{\theta}}} + \sum_{i=p}^{r} \alpha_i \hat{u}_{t-i} + \epsilon_t. \tag{18.15}$$

These three tests are not computed for models estimated using ML.

18.5 Linear restrictions test

Writing the model in matrix form as $\mathbf{y} = \mathbf{X}\boldsymbol{\beta} + \mathbf{u}$, the null hypothesis of p linear restrictions can be expressed as H_0: $\mathbf{R}\boldsymbol{\beta} = \mathbf{r}$, with $\mathbf{R}$ a $(p \times k)$ matrix and $\mathbf{r}$ a $p \times 1$ vector. This test is well explained in most econometrics textbooks, and uses the unrestricted estimates (that is, it is a Wald test).

The subset form of the linear restrictions tests is: H_0: $\beta_i = \cdots = \beta_j = 0$: any choice of coefficients can be made, so a wide range of specification hypothesis can be tested.

18.6 General restrictions

Writing $\hat{\boldsymbol{\theta}} = \hat{\boldsymbol{\beta}}$, with corresponding variance-covariance matrix $\mathsf{V}\left[\hat{\boldsymbol{\theta}}\right]$, we can test for (non-) linear restrictions of the form (see §19.1 for the syntax):

$$\mathbf{f}(\boldsymbol{\theta}) = \mathbf{0}.$$

The null hypothesis $\mathsf{H}_0 : \mathbf{f}(\boldsymbol{\theta}) = \mathbf{0}$ will be tested against $\mathsf{H}_1 : \mathbf{f}(\boldsymbol{\theta}) \neq \mathbf{0}$ through a Wald test:

$$\mathsf{w} = \mathbf{f}\left(\hat{\theta}\right)'\left(\hat{\mathbf{J}}\mathsf{V}\left[\widetilde{\hat{\theta}}\right]\hat{\mathbf{J}}'\right)^{-1}\mathbf{f}\left(\hat{\theta}\right)$$

where $\mathbf{J}$ is the Jacobian matrix of the transformation: $\mathbf{J} = \partial\mathbf{f}(\boldsymbol{\theta})/\partial\boldsymbol{\theta}'$. PcGive computes $\hat{\mathbf{J}}$ by numerical differentiation. The statistic w has a $\chi^2(s)$ distribution, where s is the number of restrictions (that is, equations in $\mathbf{f}(\cdot)$). The null hypothesis is rejected if we observe a significant test statistic.

Output consists of:

(1) *Wald test for general restrictions*, this is the statistic w with its p-value;

(2) **Restricted variance*, the matrix $\hat{\mathbf{J}}\mathsf{V}\left[\widetilde{\hat{\theta}}\right]\hat{\mathbf{J}}'$. This requires Covariance matrix to be set in the Profile.

18.7 LM tests for omitted variables (OLS/RLS/IV/RIV)

Lag polynomials of any variable in the database can be tested for omission. Variables that would change the sample or are already in the model are automatically deleted. The model itself remains unchanged. If the model is written in matrix form as $\mathbf{y} = \mathbf{X}\boldsymbol{\beta} + \mathbf{Z}\boldsymbol{\gamma} + \mathbf{u}$, then H_0: $\boldsymbol{\gamma} = \mathbf{0}$ is being tested. The test exploits the fact that on H_0:

$$\sqrt{T}\hat{\gamma} \xrightarrow{D} \mathsf{N}_p\left(\mathbf{0}, \sigma^2\left(\mathbf{Z}'\mathbf{M}_X\mathbf{Z}/T\right)^{-1}\right) \text{ with } \mathbf{M}_X = \mathbf{I}_T - \mathbf{X}\left(\mathbf{X}'\mathbf{X}\right)^{-1}\mathbf{X}', \quad (18.16)$$

then:

$$\frac{\hat{\gamma}'\left(\mathbf{Z}'\mathbf{M}_X\mathbf{Z}\right)\hat{\gamma}}{\hat{\sigma}^2} . \frac{T-k-p}{p} \sim \mathsf{F}\left(p, T-k-p\right) \quad (18.17)$$

for p added variables.

Since $\left(\mathbf{X}'\mathbf{X}\right)^{-1}$ is precalculated, the F-statistic is easily computed by partitioned inversion. Computations for IV/RIV are more involved.

18.8 Progress: the sequential reduction sequence

Finally, because of the methodological arguments advanced in Chapter 14, PcGive has specific procedures programmed to operate when a general-to-specific mode is adopted.[3] In PcGive, when a model is specified and estimated by least squares or instrumental variables, then the general dynamic analysis is offered: see §18.3.

[3]Note that PcGive does not *force* you to use a general-to-specific strategy. However, we hope to have given compelling arguments in favour of adopting such a modelling strategy.

However, while the tests offered are a comprehensive set of Wald statistics on variables, lags and long-run outcomes, a reduction sequence can involve many linear transformations (differencing, creating differentials etc.) as well as eliminations. Consequently, as the reduction proceeds, PcGive monitors its progress, which can be reviewed at the progress menu. The main statistics reported comprise:

(1) The number of parameters, the residual sum of squares, the equation standard error, and the Schwarz criterion for each model in the sequence.
(2) F-tests of each elimination conditional on the previous stage.

18.9 Encompassing and 'non-nested' hypotheses tests

Once appropriate data representations have been selected, it is of interest to see whether the chosen model can explain (that is, account for) results reported by other investigators. Often attention has focused on the ability of chosen models to explain each other's residual variances (variance encompassing), and PcGive provides the facility for doing so using test statistics based on Cox (1961) as suggested by Pesaran (1974). Full details of those computed by PcGive for OLS and IV are provided in Ericsson (1983). Note that a badly-fitting model should be rejected against well-fitting models on such tests, and that care is required in interpreting any outcome in which a well-fitting model (which satisfies all of the other criteria discussed in Chapter 14) is rejected against a badly-fitting, or silly, model (see Mizon, 1984, Mizon and Richard, 1986, and Hendry and Richard, 1989). The Sargan test is for the restricted reduced form parsimoniously encompassing the unrestricted reduced form, which is implicitly defined by projecting y_t on all of the non-modelled variables. The F-test is for each model parsimoniously encompassing their union. This is the only one of these tests which is invariant to the choice of common regressors in the two models.[4] Thus, the F-test yields the same numerical outcome for the first model parsimoniously encompassing either the union of the two models under consideration, or the orthogonal complement to the first model relative to the union. In PcGive, tests of both models encompassing the other are reported.

[4]For example, if either the first or both models have the lagged dependent variable y_{t-1}, the same F-value is produced. However, a different value will result if only the second model has y_{t-1}.

Part V

Manuals

Chapter 19

PcGive Languages

PcGive is mostly menu-driven for ease of use. To add flexibility, certain functions can be accessed through entering commands. The syntax of these commands, which can be seen as little computer languages, is described in this chapter.

Algebra is described in the GiveWin manuals. Algebra commands are executed in GiveWin, via the Calculator, the Algebra editor, or as part of a batch run.

19.1 General restrictions

Restrictions have to be entered when testing for parameter restrictions and for imposing parameter constraints for estimation. The syntax is similar to that of algebra, albeit more simple.

Restrictions code may consist of the following components:

(1) *Comment*
(2) *Constants*
(3) *Arithmetic operators*

These are all identical to algebra. In addition there are:

(4) *Parameter references*
Parameters are referenced by an ampersand followed by the parameter number. Counting starts at 0, so, for example, &2 is the third parameter of the model. What this parameter is depends on your model. Make sure that when you enter restrictions through the batch language, you use the right order for the coefficients. In case of IV estimation PcGive will reorder your model so that the endogenous variables come first.

Consider, for example, the following unconstrained model:

$$\text{CONS}_t = \beta_0\text{CONS\_1}_t + \beta_1\text{INC}_t + \beta_2\text{INC\_1}_t + \beta_3\text{INFLAT}_t + \beta_4 + u_t.$$

Then &0 indicates the coefficient on CONS_1, etc.

Restrictions for *testing* are entered in the format: $f(\theta) = 0$;. The following restrictions test the significance of the long-run parameters in this unconstrained model:

```
(&1 + &2) / (1 - &0) = 0;
&3 / (1 - &0) = 0;
```

19.2 Non-linear models

19.2.1 Non-linear least squares

A non-linear model is formulated in Algebra code. The following extensions are used:

(1) *parameter references*
Parameters are referenced by an ampersand followed by the parameter number. The numbering does not have to be consecutive, so your model can use for example `&1`, `&3` and `&4`.
Consider, for example, the following specification of the fitted part:

```
fitted = &0*lag(CONS,1) + &1*INC + &3*INFLAT + &4;
```

(2) *starting values*
Starting values are entered in the format: *&parameter=value*;. For example:

```
&0 = 0;   &1 = 1;   &3 = -1;   &4 = 1;
```

The following two variables must be defined for NLS to work:

(1) `actual`
Defines the actual values (the y variable).
(2) `fitted`
Defines the fitted values (the $\hat{y}$ variable).

Together, these formulate the whole non-linear model, as in the following example:

```
actual = CONS;
fitted = &0 + &1*lag(CONS,1) + &2*INC - &1*&2*lag(INC,1);
```

You are advised to work through the examples in Chapters 6 and 9 before trying to estimate models by NLS or RNLS. Also see §17.4.

19.2.2 Maximum likelihood

Maximum likelihood models are defined using the three variables:

(1) `actual`
(2) `fitted`
(3) `loglik`

Both `actual` and `fitted` only define the variables being used in the graphic analysis and the residual based tests. The `loglik` variable defines the function to be maximized. Parameters and starting values are as for NLS. See Chapter 9 and §17.5.

19.3 PcGive batch language

PcGive allows models to be formulated, estimated and evaluated through batch commands. Such commands are entered in GiveWin. Certain commands are intercepted by GiveWin, such as those for loading and saving data, as well as blocks of algebra code. The remaining commands are then passed on to the active module, which is PcGive in this case.

This section gives an alphabetical list of the PcGive batch language statements. There are two types of batch commands: function calls (with or without arguments) terminated by a semicolon, and commands, which are followed by statements between curly brackets.

Table 19.1 Batch language syntax summary.

algebra { ...}
appenddata("*filename*", "*group*");
appresults("*filename*");
arorder(*ar1*, *ar2*);
break;
comfac;
database(*year1*, *period1*, *year2*, *period2*, *frequency*);
dynamics;
encompassing;
estsystem("*method*", *year1*, *period1*, *year2*, *period2*, *forc*, *init*, 0);
exit;
loaddata("*filename*");
module("*name*");
nonlinear { ...}
profile("*option*", *argument*);
progress;
savedata("*filename*");
saveresults("*filename*");
store("*name*");
system { ...}
testlinrestr { ...}
testrestr { ...}
testsummary;
usedata("*databasename*");

Anything between /* and */ is considered comment. Note that this comment cannot be nested. Everything following // up to the end of the line is also comment.

GiveWin allows you to save the current model as a batch file, and to rerun saved batch files. If a model has been created interactively, it can be saved as a batch file for further editing or easy recall in a later session. This is also the most convenient way to create a batch file.

If an error occurs during processing, the batch run will be aborted and control returned to GiveWin. A warning or out of memory message will have to be accepted by the user (press `Enter`), upon which the batch run will resume.

In the following list, function arguments are indicated by *words*, whereas the areas where statement blocks are expected are indicated by .... Examples follow the list of descriptions. For terms in double quotes, the desired term must be substituted and provided together with the quotes. A command summary is given in Table 19.1. For completeness, the Table 19.1 also contains the commands which are handled by GiveWin. Consult the GiveWin book for more information on those commands.

arorder(*ar1*, *ar2*);
: Specifies the starting and ending order for RALS estimation. Note that the estimation sample must allow for the specified choice.

comfac;
: Tests for common factors.

dynamics;
: Does part of the the dynamic analysis: the static long-run solution and the lag structure analysis.

encompassing;
: Tests the two most recent models for encompassing.

estsystem("*method*", *year1*, *period1*, *year2*, *period2*, *forc*, *init*, 0);
: Estimate a system.
The *method* argument is one of: OLS, IVE, RLS , RIVE, RALS, NLS, RNLS, ML.
year1(period1) – year2(period2) is the estimation sample. Setting year1 to zero will result in the earliest possible year1(period1), setting year2 to zero will result in the latest possible year2(period2).
forc is the number of observations to withhold from the estimation sample for forecasting.
init is the number of observations to use for initialization of recursive estimation (*method* must be RLS or RIVE); if *init* = 0 the default number of inits will be used.
The final argument is 0 for compatibility with PcFiml.

nonlinear { ... }
: Formulates a non-linear model. The code between { } must conform to the syntax of §19.2.

profile("*option*", *argument*);

option	*argument*
HCSE	0 to switch off, 2,1 to switch on, 1 for Jackknife,
descriptive	0 to switch off, 1 to switch on,
correlation	0 to switch off, 1 to switch on,
covariance	0 to switch off, 1 to switch on,
eqnmodel	0 to switch off, 1 to switch on,
r2seasonals	0 to switch off, 1 to switch on,
instability	0 to switch off, 1 to switch on,
infcrit	0 to switch off, 1 to switch on.

progress;

Reports the modelling progress.

store("*name*");

Use this command to store residuals, etc. into the database, the default name is used. The *name* must be one of: residuals, fitted, res1step, stdinn, rss, eqse, innov, loglik.

system { Y=...; Z=...; U=...; A=...; }

Specify the system, consisting of the following components:

- Y endogenous variables;
- A additional instruments (optional);
- Z non-modelled variables;
- U unrestricted variables (optional, treated as Z).

The variables listed are separated by commas, their base names (that is, name excluding lag length) must be in the database. If the variable names are not a valid token, the name must be enclosed in double quotes.

The following special variables are recognized: Constant, Trend, Seasonal and CSeason.

Note that when IVE/RIVE are used PcGive reorders the model as follows: the endogenous variables first and the additional instruments last. This reordering is relevant when specifying restrictions.

testlinrestr { ...}

Test for linear restrictions. The content is the matrix dimensions followed by the $(R : r)$ matrix.

testrestr { ...}

Used to test for general restrictions: specify the restrictions between { }, conforming to §19.1.

testsummary;

Do the test summary.

We finish with an annotated example using most commands. To run this file, we assume that GiveWin is loaded with DATA.IN7, and that PcGive has been started.

```
system
{
    Y = CONS, INC;            // endogenous variables
    Z = CONS_1, INC_1,        // non-modelled variables
        Constant;
    A = OUTPUT, OUTPUT_1;  // additional instruments, optional
}
estsystem("IVE", 0, 0, 0, 0, 8, 0, 0);
                      // Estimate by IV over maximum sample:
                      // 1953(2)-1992(3), use 8 forecasts
testsummary;          // Do the test summary.
dynamics;             // Do dynamic analysis.
store("residuals");   // store the residuals
testrestr             // Test for general restrictions.
{
    &1 - &2 = 0;      // coeff of CONS_1 - coeff of INC_1.
}
testlinrestr          // Test for linear restrictions.
{                     // same restriction
    1 5
    0 1 -1 0 0
}
```

Two points are worth stressing. First, that an error will lead to abortion of the batch run. If we had written line 6 as:

```
A = OUTPU, OUTPUT_1;
```

this would result in the following three error messages:

OUTPU not found in database data.in7

PcGive Batch error: system: failed to get data and sample

Batch error: error on line 1

Note that the line number reported in the error message is that of the start of the command.

Chapter 20

PcGive Menus

This chapter describes each menu option in the PcGive menu structure. From the menu bar at the top of the screen, pull-down menus give access to all the actions in PcGive. Examples of most options were given in the tutorial chapters of Part II. Often, after selecting a menu option, a dialog will take over to request the information needed to perform the requested task. Only a few dialogs are discussed in this chapter, but remember that all dialogs are featured in the tutorial chapters. Moreover, on-line help is available in each dialog by pressing `F1` or the help button.

20.1 The File menu (Alt+f)

The main function of the File command is to provide access to the Exit command.

20.2 The Data menu (Alt+d)

20.2.1 Descriptive statistics

The data description statistics are all defined in Chapter 16. The following options are available:

(1) Normality tests
A χ^2 test is reported (with two degrees of freedom), and the output includes all moments up to the fourth. The null hypothesis is normality, which will be rejected at the 5% level, if a test statistic of more than 5.99 is observed.

(2) Correlations
The correlation matrix of selected variables is reported as a lower triangular matrix, with the diagonal equal to one. Each cell records the simple correlations between the two relevant variables. The mean and standard deviation of the variables are also given.

(3) Unit-root tests

You can choose whether to include a constant or constant+trend, and the lag length s. The Dickey–Fuller test arises with $s = 0$. The null hypothesis is that of a unit root. This is rejected if the coefficient on the lagged level is negative and significantly different from zero. Note that its t-statistic does not have the conventional t-distribution.

PcGive can produce a table of ADF tests, dropping one lag at a time. Reported are:

t-adf	ADF t-statistic;
beta Y_1	the coefficient on the lagged level,
$\hat{\sigma}$	equation standard error;
lag	highest lag used (value of s);
t-DY_lag	t-value on longest lag;
t-prob	significance level of t-DY_lag, which is t-distributed.
F-prob	significance level of the F-test on the lags dropped up to this point.

The critical values reported by PcGive are based on a response surface developed by MacKinnon (1991). The presence of seasonals does not change the reported critical values.

20.2.2 Autoregressive-distributed lag

We shall give three examples of bivariate autoregressive-distributed lag (ADL) models:

(1) a finite distributed lag:

$$\text{CONS}_t = \beta_0 + \beta_1\text{INC}_t + \beta_2\text{INC}_{t-1};$$

(2) an autoregression:

$$\text{CONS}_t = \beta_0 + \text{CONS}_{t-1}\beta_1 + \beta_2\text{CONS}_{t-2};$$

(3) an autoregressive-distributed lag:

$$\text{CONS}_t = \beta_0 + \beta_1\text{INC}_t + \beta_2\text{CONS}_{t-1} + \beta_3\text{INC}_{t-1}.$$

A bivariate ADL model is specified by:

(1) which two variables are involved;
(2) the orders of the lag polynomials;
(3) the sample period.

Note:

(1) A constant is always included in ADL models.
(2) The sample size will be set to the maximum available as a default. If you have activated the Zoom sample check box on the dialog, you will be asked to select a sample period.

20.3 The Model menu (Alt+m)

Single equation modelling is described in detail in Chapter 17.

20.3.1 Formulate (Alt+y)

The Formulate command is used for dynamic model formulation: formulate (or reformulate) a model for estimation by selecting variables and lag lengths in the Formulate a model dialog. When you press OK, you will be taken automatically to the Estimation dialog. For instrumental variables estimation, mark variables in the model as endogenous or instruments. The remaining variables will be assumed exogenous. A model in PcGive is formulated by:

(1) Which variables are involved;
(2) The orders of the lag polynomials;
(3) The status of variables (only when it is not legitimate to treat all regressors as valid conditioning variables, and you wish to use Instrumental Variables).

Recall

Up to 100 estimated models are remembered during a session. The Recall command lets you recall any of these through the Recall dialog box. This requires that the variables involved are still at the same position in the database.

20.3.2 Estimate (Alt+l)

The following information is needed to estimate an equation:

(1) The model formulation.
(2) The initial and final observation of the sample.
(3) The number of forecasts to be withheld for testing parameter constancy.
PcGive allows you to retain observations to compute forecast statistics. For OLS/RLS/RALS these are comprehensive 1-step-ahead forecasts. For IV/RIV, since there are endogenous regressor variables, the only interesting issue is that of parameter constancy, and the only output is the forecast χ^2 test. RLS/RNLS also just reports the forecast χ^2 test.
(4) The method of estimation:

    (a) Ordinary Least Squares (OLS)
    Ordinary Least Squares is the standard textbook method. OLS is valid if the data model is congruent. The requirements for congruency are:

        (i) Homoscedastic innovation errors;
        (ii) Weakly exogenous regressors;
        (iii) Constant parameters;

(iv) Theory consistency;
(v) Data admissibility;
(vi) Encompassing rival models.

PcGive provides tests of most of the aspects of model congruency

(b) Instrumental Variables (IV)

A structural representation is parsimonious with parameters but has regressors which are correlated with the error term. IV requires that the reduced form is a congruent data model. The instrumental variables are the reduced form regressors. Instrumental variables estimation includes two stage least squares (2SLS) as a special case. PcGive needs to know the status of the variables in the model:

(i) At least one endogenous variable on the right-hand side;
(ii) At least as many instruments as endogenous rhs variables.

(c) Autoregressive Least Squares (RALS)

RALS requires that the restricted dynamic model is data congruent, where the restrictions correspond to COMFAC constraints selected (since an autoregressive error is a more parsimonious representation). Various orders of autoregression can be selected

(i) Different initial delays (s);
(ii) Different highest orders (r);
(iii) All orders sequentially fitted;
(iv) Only the general r^{th} order case estimated;
(v) A grid is estimable for single orders.

Multiple optima to the likelihood function commonly occur in the COMFAC class, thus (v) is recommended. Direct use of (iv) may not find the global optimum.

(5) Whether to use recursive estimation, and if so, the number of observations to be used to initialize the recursive estimation (RLS and RIV only). This results in one of:

(a) Recursive Least Squares (RLS)

Recursive Least Squares is OLS where coefficients are estimated sequentially and is a powerful tool for investigating parameter constancy. The sample starts from a minimal number of observations and statistics are recalculated adding observations one at a time. The recursive output is analysed graphically. The algorithm was initially written by Adrian Neale.

(b) Recursive Instrumental Variables (RIV)

Recursive Instrumental Variables operates like RLS but using IV methods.

PcGive will elicit information on all these aspects. Models may be revised interactively after formulation and after estimation.

The Profile command can be used to influence the computation of statistics, as well as automatic evaluation. By default, the items labelled optional do not appear.

Once a model has been specified, a sample period selected, and an estimation method chosen, the output appears:

(1) Descriptive statistics (optional, OLS/RLS only)

(a) Means and standard deviations
These are calculated for all the variables involved over the relevant sample for direct methods and over initial observations for recursive methods, if correlation output is selected in the profile.

(b) Correlation matrix
This is reported (if selected in the profile) as a lower triangular array with unity on the diagonal and each off-diagonal element being the simple correlation between the two associated variables.

(c) Variance-covariance matrix
This matrix of the estimated parameters' variances is reported as lower triangular, if selected in the profile. Along the diagonal, we have the variance of each estimated coefficient and off the diagonal, the covariances.

(2) OLS/RLS estimation

(a) Estimated regression equation
The first column of these results records the names of the variables and the second, the estimated regression coefficients values. The following five columns give further information about each of the magnitudes described below in 2 to 6.

(b) Standard errors of the regression coefficients
These are the square roots of the diagonal of the variance-covariance matrix.

(c) Heteroscedastic-consistent standard errors (optional)
The HCSEs provide consistent estimates of the regression coefficients' standard errors even if the residuals are heteroscedastic in an unknown way. Large differences between the corresponding values in (a) and (c) are indicative of the presence of heteroscedasticity, in which case (c) provides the more useful measure of the standard errors (see White, 1980). These are also optional. The formulae in PcGive are from White (1980) and the Jackknife estimator in MacKinnon and White (1985) (for which the code was initially provided by James MacKinnon).

(d) t-statistics and t-probabilities
These statistics are conventionally calculated to determine whether individual coefficients are significantly different from zero (called the null hypothesis, H_0). When H_0 is true (and the model is otherwise correctly specified), a Student t-distribution is used since the sample size is often small, and we only have an estimate of the parameter's standard error. However,

as the sample size increases, t tends to a standard normal distribution under H_0. Large values of t reject H_0.

(e) Squared partial correlations
The jth entry in this column records the correlation of the jth explanatory variable with the dependent variable, given the other $k-1$ variables. Adding further explanatory variables to the model may either increase or lower the squared partial correlation, and the former may occur even if the added variables are correlated with the already included variables. If the squared partial correlations fall on adding a variable, then that suggests a collinear parameterization: that is, the new variable is a substitute for, rather than a complement to, those already included.

(f) Parameter instability statistics (optional)
This is based on the result in Hansen (1992). Large values reveal non-constancy (marked by * or **) and indicate a fragile model. This measures within-sample parameter constancy, and is computed automatically if numerically feasible (may fail owing to dummy variables), so no observations need be reserved.
Beneath the columnar presentation an array of summary statistics is also provided as follows:

(g) Squared multiple correlation Coefficient R^2
If no intercept is included as a regressor, this will be noted on the screen.

(h) Residual standard deviation σ
This is the standard deviation of the difference between the actual and fitted values in the regression. Since many economic magnitudes are inherently positive, σ often can be standardized as a percentage of the mean of the original level of the dependent variable y for comparisons across specifications.

(i) F-statistic
The null hypothesis is that the population β vector is zero or that all the regression coefficients except the intercept are zero. The probability value for the F-test is shown in square parentheses, calculated using an algorithm based on Majunder and Bhattacharjee (1973a) and Cran, Martin and Thomas (1977).

(j) Durbin–Watson test (DW)
This is a test for autocorrelated residuals. DW is most powerful as a test of white noise against a first-order autoregressive error. The significance values of DW are widely recorded in most econometrics' textbooks. However, DW is a valid statistic only if all the regressor variables are strongly exogenous. If the model includes a lagged dependent variable, then DW is biased towards 2, that is, towards not detecting autocorrelation, and Durbin's h-test (see Durbin, 1970) or the equivalent LM test for autocorrelation should be used instead.

(k) Residual sum of squares RSS

(l) Remaining parameter instability statistics (optional)
The test on the variance, and the joint test.

(m) Information criteria (optional)
The three statistics reported are the Schwarz Criterion (SC), the Hannan–Quinn (HQ) Criterion and the Final Prediction Error (FPE). From these, other model selection criteria may be calculated. These, and related scalar measures, are often used to choose between alternative models in a class. The Progress output reports σ, RSS and SC, where smaller values of all three are preferable, *ceteris paribus*. These three measures differ in the 'penalty' they impose for more parameters.

(n) R^2 relative to difference and seasonals (optional)
This is a measure of the goodness of fit of the present regression relative to the first difference of y adjusted for seasonal means (that is, the overall mean for annual data, but the monthly mean for monthly data etc.). Despite its label, such a measure can be negative: if it is, the fitted model does less well than a regression of the first difference of y on seasonal dummies.

(3) IV/RIV estimation

(a) Reduced form estimates
After the output up to the end of (1) above, the reduced form estimates are reported. Let z denote the set of instrumental variables (non-endogenous included regressors plus additional instruments), then the regression of every endogenous variable on z is written to the Results window.

(b) GIVE estimates
The output is similar to that reported for least squares except that the columns after HCSE are omitted. However, RSS and DW and a χ^2 statistic are recorded. The last of these has a crude correspondence to the earlier F-test. On $\mathsf{H}_0 : \beta = 0$, the reported statistic would asymptotically behave as a $\chi^2(k-1)$, assuming a constant term is included. Additional statistics reported are the reduced form σ (from regressing y on z) and:

(c) Specification χ^2
This tests for the validity of the choice of the instrumental variables as discussed by Sargan (1964). It is asymptotically distributed as $\chi^2(m)$ when the m over-identifying instruments are independent of the equation error. It is also interpretable as a test of whether the restricted reduced form of the structural model parsimoniously encompasses the unrestricted reduced form.

(4) RALS output
The output is similar to that reported for least squares except that the columns after HCSE are omitted. The estimates of the autoregressive error coefficients are reported with standard errors. If all orders were estimated, a table of tests of each

restriction on order is reported. The roots of the error autoregressive lag polynomial are also calculated.

20.3.3 Non-linear model

PcGive can estimate three types of non-linear model:

(1) Non-linear least squares (NLS);
(2) Recursive non-linear least squares (RNLS).
(3) Maximum likelihood (ML).

These models are formulated in algebra code. NLS requires the definition of a variable called `actual`, and one called `fitted`. It uses these to maximize minus the residual sum of squares divided by T:

$$-\frac{1}{T}\sum_{t=1}^{T}\left(actual_t - fitted_t\right)^2 .$$

An example for NLS is:

```
actual = CONS;
fitted = &0 + &1 * INC + &2 * lag(INC,1);
&0   = 400;
&1   = 0.8;
&2   = 0.2;
```

This is just a linear model, and much more efficiently done using the normal options.

Models can be estimated by maximum likelihood if they can be written as a sum over the observations (note that the previous concentrated log-likehood cannot be written that way!). An additional algebra line is required, to define a variable called `loglik`. PcGive maximizes:

$$\sum_{t=1}^{T} loglik_t.$$

Consider, for example, a binary logit model:

```
actual = vaso;
xbeta = &0 + &1 * Lrate + &2 * Lvolume;
fitted = 1 / (1 + exp(-xbeta));
loglik = actual * log(fitted) + (1-actual) * log(1-fitted);
&0   = 0.74;
&1   = 1.3;
&2   = 2.3;
```

Here `actual` and `fitted` are not really that, but these variables define what is being graphed in the graphic analysis.

Note that algebra is a vector language without temporary variables, restricting the class of models that can be estimated. Non-linear models are *not* stored for recall and progress reports.

After correct model specification, the method is automatically set to Non-linear model (using ML if `loglik` is defined, NLS/RNLS otherwise); in addition, the following information needs to be specified:

(1) Estimation sample.
(2) The number of forecasts; enter the number of observations you wish to withhold for forecasting.
(3) Whether to use recursive estimation, and if so, the number of observations you wish to use for initializing RNLS.

NLS, RNLS and ML estimation require *numerical optimization* to maximize the likelihood $\log \mathsf{L}(\phi(\theta)) = \ell(\phi(\theta))$ as a non-linear function of θ. PcGive maximization algorithms are based on a Newton scheme:

$$\theta_{i+1} = \theta_i + s_i \mathbf{Q}_i^{-1} \mathbf{q}_i \tag{20.1}$$

with

- θ_i parameter value at iteration i;
- s_i step length, normally unity;
- $\mathbf{Q}_i$ symmetric positive-definite matrix (at iteration i);
- $\mathbf{q}_i$ first derivative of the log-likelihood (at iteration i) (the score vector);
- $\delta_i = \theta_i - \theta_{i-1}$ is the change in the parameters;

PcGive uses the quasi-Newton method developed by Broyden, Fletcher, Goldfarb, Shanno (BFGS) to update $\mathbf{K} = \mathbf{Q}^{-1}$ directly. It uses numerical derivatives to compute $\partial\ell(\phi(\theta))/\partial\theta_i$. However, for NLS, PcGive will try Gauss-Newton before starting BFGS. In this hybrid method, Gauss-Newton is used while the relative progress in the function value is 20%, then the program switches to BFGS.

Starting values must be supplied. The starting value for $\mathbf{K}$ consistes of 0s off-diagonal. The diagonal is the minimum of one and the inverse of the corresponding diagonal element in the matrix consisting of the sums of the outer-products of the gradient at the parameter starting values (numerically evaluated).

RNLS works as follows: starting values for θ and $\mathbf{K}$ for the first estimation ($T-1$ observations) are the full sample values (T observations); then the sample size is reduced by one observation; the previous values at convergence are used to start with.

Owing to numerical problems it is possible (especially close to the maximum) that the calculated δ_i does not yield a higher likelihood. Then an $s_i \in [0,1]$ yielding a higher function value is determined by a line search. Theoretically, since the direction is upward, such an s_i should exist; however, numerically it might be impossible to find one. When using BFGS with numerical derivatives, it often pays to scale the data so that the initial gradients are of the same order of magnitude.

The *convergence* decision is based on two tests. The first uses likelihood elasticities ($\partial\ell/\partial\log\boldsymbol{\theta}$):

$$\begin{aligned} |q_{i,j}\theta_{i,j}| \leq \epsilon \quad & \text{for all } j \text{ when } \theta_{i,j} \neq 0, \\ |q_{i,j}| \leq \epsilon \quad & \text{for all } j \text{ with } \theta_{i,j} = 0. \end{aligned} \tag{20.2}$$

The second is based on the one-step-ahead relative change in the parameter values:

$$\begin{aligned} |\delta_{i+1,j}| \leq 10\epsilon\,|\theta_{i,j}| \quad & \text{for all } j \text{ with } \theta_{i,j} \neq 0, \\ |\delta_{i+1,j}| \leq 10\epsilon \quad & \text{for all } j \text{ when } \theta_{i,j} = 0. \end{aligned} \tag{20.3}$$

The status of the iterative process is given by the following messages:

(1) No convergence!
(2) Aborted: no convergence!
(3) Function evaluation failed: no convergence!
(4) Maximum number of iterations reached: no convergence!
(5) Failed to improve in line search: no convergence!
The step length s_i has become too small. The convergence test (20.2) was not passed, using tolerance $\epsilon = \epsilon_2$.
(6) Failed to improve in line search: weak convergence
The step length s_i has become too small. The convergence test (20.2) was passed, using tolerance $\epsilon = \epsilon_2$.
(7) Strong convergence
Both convergence tests (20.2) and (20.3) were passed, using tolerance $\epsilon = \epsilon_1$.

The chosen default values for the tolerances are:

$$\epsilon_1 = 10^{-4},\ \epsilon_2 = 5 \times 10^{-3}. \tag{20.4}$$

You can:

(1) set the initial values of the parameters to zero or the previous values;
(2) set the maximum number of iterations;
(3) write iteration output;
(4) change the convergence tolerances ϵ_1 and ϵ_2. Care must be exercised with this: the defaults are 'fine-tuned'; some selections merely show the vital role of sensible choices!
(5) plot a grid of the log-likelihood. The 'fineness', number of points and centre can be user-selected. Up to 16 grids can be plotted simultaneously. A grid may reveal potential multiple optima.

NOTE 1: NLS, RNLS, ML estimation can only continue after convergence.
NOTE 2: Restarting the optimization process leads to a Hessian reset.
NOTE 3: RNLS can be interrupted at each T, just press any key and confirm to abort. In that case the recursive results up to that point are used.

20.3.4 Profile

The Profile command sets automatic estimation evaluation, and some estimation options:

(1) Output generation

  (a) Correlation matrix
  Includes means and standard deviations (OLS/RLS only).

  (b) Covariance matrix
  Prints out the covariance matrix of the estimated coefficients prior to the estimate model, and the covariance matrix of the long-run coefficients following dynamic analysis, as well as the restricted covariance matrix following general restrictions.

  (c) Heteroscedastic-consistent standard errors
  When this option is selected (OLS only), the HCSEs are computed using the White (1980) formulae. Optionally, you can choose compution by Jackknife (again OLS only), see MacKinnon and White (1985).

  (d) Instability tests;

  (e) Information criteria;

  (f) R^2 about seasonals;

  (g) Equation format
  This is of the form coefficient × variable with standard errors in parentheses underneath.

(2) Automatic evaluation
If any of the boxes are checked, PcGive will automatically call up these dialogs upon successful estimation:

  (a) Graphic analysis;

  (b) Dynamic analysis;

  (c) Test summary.

20.3.5 Progress

The Progress command reports on the progress made in the general to simple modelling strategy. A more recent model (Model 2) is nested in an older (Model 1) if:

(1) Model 2 is derived from a parameter restriction on Model 1;
This entails:

(2) Model 2 is estimated over the same period, using the same method (where OLS=RLS, and IV=RIV);

(3) Model 2 has fewer coefficients than Model 1;

(4) Model 2 has a higher RSS than Model 1;
But not necessarily:

(5) both models have the same dependent variable, and the set of explanatory variables of Model 2 is a subset of that of Model 1.

For example, $\Delta\text{CONS}_t = \beta_0+\beta_1\Delta\text{INC}_t$ is nested in $\text{CONS}_t = \alpha_0+\alpha_1\text{CONS}_{t-1}+\alpha_2\text{INC}_t + \alpha_3\text{INC}_{t-1}$, through two restrictions: $\alpha_1 = 1$ and $\alpha_3 = -\alpha_2$.

PcGive will offer you a default nesting sequence based on (2)-(5), but since it cannot decide on (1) itself, you will have the opportunity to change this nesting sequence. However, model sequences which do not satisfy (2)-(4) will always be deleted. The progress report consists of:

(1) Residual Sums of Squares, equation standard error (σ) and Schwarz criterion for each model, displayed in a bar chart.
(2) F-tests of each reduction.

The Progress dialog box is used to change the default model nesting sequence.

20.3.6 Encompassing

Encompassing evaluates against rival models to see if they embody specific information excluded from the model under test. Encompassing is not available for models estimated by RALS. Four tests are calculated:

(1) The Cox non-nested hypotheses test (Cox, 1961)
This tests whether the adjusted likelihoods of two rival models are compatible. It is equivalent to checking variance encompassing.
(2) The Ericsson instrumental variables test (Ericsson, 1983)
This is an IV equivalent to the Cox test.
(3) The Sargan restricted/unrestricted reduced form test (Sargan, 1964)
This checks if the restricted reduced form of a structural model encompasses the unrestricted reduced form including exogenous regressors from rival models.
(4) The joint model F-test
This checks if each model parsimoniously encompasses the linear nesting model.

The F-test is invariant to variables in common between the rival models. The Cox and the Ericsson tests are not invariant: their values change with the choice of overlapping variables. Consult, for example, Ericsson (1983) or Hendry and Richard (1989) for details.

PcGive checks for valid choices of variables and sample:

(1) Endogenous variables are matched.
(2) Instruments in Model 1 are treated as exogenous in Model 2 even if you denote them as endogenous.
(3) The models must be non-nested.
(4) The sample is automatically adjusted to incorporate both models.

The output is summarized in an encompassing table:

(1) The type of test statistic;
(2) The value of each outcome;
(3) The degrees of freedom of each test;
(4) The null that Model 1 is valid is on the left;
(5) The null that Model 2 is valid is on the right.

If the left-side tests are insignificant, Model 1 encompasses Model 2. If the left-side tests are significant, Model 1 fails to encompass Model 2. Similarly for the right-side tests with Models 1 and 2 interchanged. Model 1 encompasses Model 2 $\Rightarrow$ Model 1 also parsimoniously encompasses the linear nesting model. If not, Model 2 contains specific data information not captured by Model 1. The algorithm incorporated in PcGive was initially written by Neil Ericsson.

20.4 The Test menu (Alt+t)

The mathematics of all statistics are described in Chapter 18.

20.4.1 Graphic analysis

The Graphic analysis command gives various options to graph actual and fitted values, forecasts and residuals. Use the Zoom button to graph for periods other than the default.

(1) Actual values (time-plots)
(2) Cross-plots
(3) Residual correlogram
This plots the series r_j where r_j is the correlation coefficient between x_t and x_{t-j}. The length s of the correlogram is chosen by the user, leading to a figure which shows $(\mathsf{r}_1, \mathsf{r}_2, \ldots, \mathsf{r}_s)$ plotted against $(1, 2, \ldots, s)$.
(4) Residual spectrum
A stationary series can be decomposed in cyclical components with different frequencies and amplitudes. The spectral density gives a graphical representation of this. It is symmetric around 0, and only graphed for $[0, \pi]$ (the horizontal axis in the PcGive graphs is scaled by π, and given as $[0, 1]$).
(5) Non-parametric density estimation and histograms
Histograms are a way of looking at the sample distributions of statistics. Then on the basis of the original data, density functions may be interpolated to give a clearer picture of the implied distributional shape and similarly, QQ plots may be constructed (and compared on-screen to a Normal density).

20.4.2 Recursive graphics (Alt+r)

The Recursive graphics command graphs the recursive output as generated by a recursive estimation. Multiple graphs allow for condensation of the information. For T observations and M observations for initialization, that output is:

(1) Beta coefficient $\pm 2 \times$ Standard Errors;
(2) The 't-statistic' for any coefficient;
(3) Residual Sums of Squares;
(4) Standardized innovations;
(5) 1-step residuals with $0 \pm 2\sigma$; This will reveal any model deficiencies.
(6) 1-step Chow tests scaled by their critical values at the 5% level (or a user defined probability level, with 0% leading to unscaled Chows) at each t, so the 5% value is a straight line independent of t and the changing degrees of freedom, but does not allow for the number of tests conducted.
(7) N decreasing Chow tests (again scaled by their critical values), so that the value shown at t tests for constancy from t to T.
(8) N increasing Chow tests (again scaled by their critical values), so that the value shown at t tests for constancy from M to t.

RIV does not calculate (5)-(7) (the Chow tests), owing to endogenous regressors. RNLS does not calculate (1), (2) or (4).

20.4.3 Dynamic analysis

The dynamic analysis is only available when the model has been estimated by OLS, RLS, IV or RIV. The following are reported:

20.4.3.1 Static long-run solution

A Wald test is reported which tests the joint significance of all the variables (excluding the constant) in the long-run solution. You can optionally save the error correction mechanism (ECM).

20.4.3.2 Lag structure analysis

(1) Significance of basic variables
(2) Significance of each lag when the relevant lag is present.
(3) Unit-root statistics

20.4.3.3 Test for common factors

The common-factor test (COMFAC test) evaluates error-autocorrelation claims by checking if the model's lag polynomials have factors in common. If so, the model's lags can be simplified with an autoregressive error; if not, the model cannot be re-expressed with an autoregressive error. χ^2 tests of each possible common factor and of sequences are shown. The COMFAC test option is only feasible for unrestricted dynamic models (which have a closed lag system), which are not estimated by RALS. The algorithm was originally developed and written by Denis Sargan and Juri Sylvestrowicz.

20.4.3.4 Lag weights

The Lag weights option allows you to graph or write the normalized and/or cumulative lag weights. The option is only available when the model has been estimated by OLS, RLS, IV or RIV.

20.4.4 Test

Many diagnostic tests are done through an auxiliary regression. In this case two forms of the test are reported:

(1) $T\mathsf{R}^2$, which has a $\chi^2(r)$ distribution for r restrictions;
(2) $(T-k-r)\,\mathsf{R}^2/r\left(1-\mathsf{R}^2\right)$, which has an $\mathsf{F}(r, T-k-r)$ distribution.

The F-form may be better behaved in small samples.

The Test command offers a range of diagnostic tests:

(1) Residual correlogram
Gives a correlogram of the residuals with Portmanteau statistic, and fits an autoregression to describe the autocorrelation structure of the residuals.
(2) Error autocorrelation (not for RALS, ML)
Yields a Lagrange-Multiplier (LM) test for serial correlation. This test is done through the auxiliary regression of the residuals on the original variables and lagged residuals (missing lagged residuals at the start of the sample are replaced by zero, so no observations are lost). χ^2 and F-statistics and the coefficients on the lagged residuals are shown. The null hypothesis is no autocorrelation, which would be rejected if the test statistic is too high. This LM test is valid for models with lagged dependent variables, whereas neither the DW nor the residual correlogram provide a valid test in that case.
(3) Autoregressive conditional heteroscedasticity (ARCH)
Checks whether the residuals have an ARCH structure. This test is done by regressing the squared residuals on a constant and lagged squared residuals (now some observations are lost at the beginning of the sample). An F-statistic and the estimated coefficients on the lagged squared residuals are reported. The null hypothesis is no ARCH, which would be rejected if the test statistic is too high.
(4) Normality test
Runs a normality test on the residuals.

(5) Heteroscedasticity (using squares) (not for ML)
Tests if the disturbances have constant variances against the alternative that the squared disturbance depends on the original and squared regressors. The null hypothesis is no heteroscedasticity, which would be rejected if the test statistic is too high. This test is done by regressing the squared residuals on a constant, the original regressors, and the original regressors squared. An F-test and the auxiliary regression coefficients are reported.
(6) Heteroscedasticity (using squares and cross-products) (not for ML)
This is the test of White (1980), and checks if homoscedasticity is reasonable against the squared disturbance depending on squares and cross-products of the regressors. The null hypothesis is no heteroscedasticity, which would be rejected if the test statistic is too high. This test is done by regressing the squared residuals on a constant, the original regressors, the original regressors squared and all the cross-products. An F-test and the auxiliary regression coefficients are reported.
(7) RESET (OLS/RLS only)
The auxiliary regression amounts to adding powers (2, 3 or 4) of the fitted values to the original regression; however, partitioned inversion is used to calculate the F-test. The null hypothesis is no functional form mis-specification, which would be rejected if the test statistic is too high.

Notes:

(1) Residual correlogram, autoregression and Durbin–Watson test are not valid for models with lagged dependent variables or only weakly (as opposed to strongly) exogenous variables, whereas the LM test for autocorrelation is.
(2) If the model has been estimated recursively (RLS, RIV), you can ask for the above tests to be based on the 1-step residuals, instead of the normal residuals.
(3) The values for lag lengths and RESET order are set for the first model, and thereafter only reset when loading a new data set. If you specify the value 0, PcGive will substitute the default.

20.4.5 Test summary (Alt+u)

The Test summary command does tests automatically, using the current settings in the Test dialog. The following diagnostic testing is done:

(1) Error autocorrelation (not for RALS, ML)
(2) ARCH
(3) Normality
(4) Heteroscedasticity (not for ML)
(5) Functional form (not for ML)
(6) RESET (OLS/RLS only)

Only the F-forms of the statistics are reported. More extensive output is generated with the Test command.

20.4.6 Linear restrictions (subset)

The Linear restrictions (Subset) command allows you to select explanatory variables and test whether they are jointly significant. A more general form of the test for linear restrictions is:

20.4.7 Linear restrictions ($R\beta = r$)

Restrictions are given in the form of a matrix **R**, and a vector **r**. These are entered as one matrix $(\mathbf{R} : \mathbf{r})$ in the Matrix Editor.

For example, the two restrictions $\alpha_1 = 1$ and $\alpha_3 = -\alpha_2$ in

$$\text{CONS}_t = \alpha_0 + \alpha_1 \text{CONS}_{t-1} + \alpha_2 \text{INC}_t + \alpha_3 \text{INC}_{t-1}$$

can be expressed as:

$$\mathbf{R} = \begin{pmatrix} 0 & 1 & 0 & 0 \\ 0 & 0 & 1 & 1 \end{pmatrix}; \quad \mathbf{r} = \begin{pmatrix} 1 \\ 0 \end{pmatrix}.$$

The null-hypothesis $\mathsf{H}_0 : \mathbf{R}\boldsymbol{\beta} = \mathbf{r}$ is rejected if we observe a significant test statistic. The matrix entered into PcGive is:

$$(\mathbf{R} : \mathbf{r}) = \begin{pmatrix} 0 & 1 & 0 & 0 & 1 \\ 0 & 0 & 1 & 1 & 0 \end{pmatrix}.$$

The most general form of testing restrictions is:

20.4.8 General restrictions

Here (non-)linear restrictions on the coefficients can be tested using a Wald test. Such restrictions are expressed as $\mathbf{f}(\boldsymbol{\beta}) = \mathbf{0}$; The Wald test has a $\chi^2(r)$ distribution where r is the number of restrictions (i.e. equations in $\mathbf{f}()$). The null hypothesis is rejected if we observe a significant test statistic.

For example the two restrictions implied by the long-run solution of:

$$\text{CONS}_t = \beta_0 \text{CONS\_1}_t + \beta_1 \text{INC}_t + \beta_2 \text{INC\_1}_t + \beta_3 \text{INFLAT}_t + \beta_4 + u_t$$

are expressed as

$$(\beta_1 + \beta_2)/(1 - \beta_0) = 0;$$
$$\beta_3/(1 - \beta_0) = 0;$$

Which has to be specified in PcGive as (coefficient numbering starts at 0!):

```
(&1 + &2) / (1 - &0) = 0;
&3  / (1 - &0) = 0;
```

20.4.9 Omitted variables

This tests if some variables should be added to the model; these variables can be any variables in the database matching the present sample. This test is not available for models estimated by RALS.

20.4.10 Store in database

The Store in database command allows you to save in the database:

(1) Residuals
(2) Fitted values
Following a recursive estimation, you can also save:
(3) 1-step residuals
(4) Standardised innovations (not for RNLS)
(5) Residual sums of squares
(6) Equation standard errors
(7) Innovations (not for RNLS)
Following ML estimation:
(8) Log-likelihood.

You will be prompted for a variable name.

20.5 The Help menu (Alt+h)

20.5.1 Help topics

20.5.2 Help topics

The Help topics command describes all the available topics in the Help system.

20.5.3 Contents

The Help Index lists the subjects covered in the Help database. You can go directly to a subject from the index by selecting the subject's name.

20.5.4 About

The About command displays a message that tells you what the application is.

Part VI

Appendices

Appendix A1

PcGive Artificial Data Set (data.in7/data.bn7)

The following four-equation log-linear artificial data generation process was created using DAGER (see Hendry and Srba, 1980):

$$\begin{aligned}
\Delta c_t &= -0.9 + 0.4\,\Delta y_t + 0.15\,(y-c)_{t-1} - 0.9\,\Delta p_t + \epsilon_{1t} && \text{(A1.1)}\\
\Delta y_t &= -75.0 + 0.3\,\Delta c_t + 0.25\,(q-y)_{t-1} + 0.25\,\Delta q_t + \epsilon_{2t} && \text{(A1.2)}\\
\Delta p_t &= 0.3 + 0.7\,\Delta p_{t-1} + 0.08\,(q-1200)_{t-1} + \epsilon_{3t} && \text{(A1.3)}\\
\Delta q_t &= 121.3 - 0.1\,q_{t-1} - 1.30\,\Delta p_{t-1} + \epsilon_{4t} && \text{(A1.4)}
\end{aligned}$$

The $\{\epsilon_{it}\}$ were generated as $\mathsf{IN}\left(0, \sigma_{ii}^2\right)$ where $(\sigma_{11}, \sigma_{22}, \sigma_{33}, \sigma_{44}) = (1, 3, 0.25, 4)$ with zero covariances. The variables are interpreted such that $x_t = 100 \log X_t \; (\forall x)$. The conditional latent roots of the dynamics for the 'domestic' economy (c_t, y_t) are $0.8 \pm 0.044i$, so the modulus is 0.80 and the period 115 'quarters', whereas for the world economy $(\Delta p_t, q_t)$ the roots are $0.8 \pm 0.31i$, with modulus 0.86 and period 17.2 'quarters'. Data were generated for a sample supposed to represent 1953(1) to 1992(3), with an 'oil crisis' in 1973(3). Thus, there were 159 observations on $(c_t, y_t, \Delta p_t, q_t)$ with an autonomous shock to the world economy intercepts (equations (A1.3) and (A1.4)) at observation 83. This shock left the system dynamics unaltered and only directly affected Δp_t and q_t. The long-run equilibrium of the system was shifted from:

	$c = y - 6\Delta p - 6$	$[C = \exp(-6\Delta p - 0.06)\, Y]$
	$y = q - 300$	$[Y = 0.05\, Q]$
with:	$\Delta p = 1$	$[\dot{p} = 1\%$ per quarter$]$
	$q = 1200$	$[Q = 162,755]$
to:	$\Delta p = 2$	$[\dot{p} = 2\%$ per quarter$]$
	$q = 1180$	$[Q = 133,252]$

Thus, 'equilibrium' inflation ($\dot{p}$) doubled and world output fell by about 18%. Correct modelling of the system necessitates different intercepts pre/post-1973(3) in equations (A1.3) and (A1.4). The structural break was included so that issues of predictive failure would be meaningful (see Hendry, 1979).

To ease recognition of the variables, they were respectively named CONS, INC, INFLAT and OUTPUT. PcFiml closely replicates these coefficients of the DGP and the long-run solutions. Note that estimating (A1.2) by OLS yields a spectacular example of simultaneity bias and (A1.3) without the oil dummy shows massive predictive failure. Also, (A1.1) by RLS indicates evidence of parameter non-constancy owing to the change in the simultaneity bias at the oil crisis: most mis-specifications also lead to predictive failure.

Appendix A2

Numerical Changes From Previous Versions

A2.1 From version 7 to 8

The numerical results generated by PcGive version 8 are unchanged from version 7, apart from a marginal increase in accuracy of several diagnostic tests. Also, a new version of the normality test is used now, which uses a small sample correction.

A2.2 From version 8 to 9

The major change is the adoption of the QR decomposition with partial pivoting to compute OLS and IV estimates. There are also some minor improvements in accuracy, the following tests are the most sensitive to such changes: encompassing, heteroscedasticity and RESET. The heteroscedasticity tests could also differ in the number of variables removed owing to singularity.

References

Ahumada, H. (1985). An encompassing test of two models of the balance of trade for Argentina, *Oxford Bulletin of Economics and Statistics*, **47**, 51–70.

Amemiya, T. (1981). Qualitative response models: A survey, *Journal of Economic Literature*, **19**, 1483–1536.

Amemiya, T. (1985). *Advanced Econometrics*. Oxford: Basil Blackwell.

Anderson, T. W. (1971). *The Statistical Analysis of Time Series*. New York: John Wiley & Sons.

Baba, Y., Hendry, D. F. and Starr, R. M. (1992). The demand for M1 in the U.S.A., 1960–1988, *Review of Economic Studies*, **59**, 25–61.

Banerjee, A., Dolado, J. J., Galbraith, J. W. and Hendry, D. F. (1993). *Co-integration, Error Correction and the Econometric Analysis of Non-Stationary Data*. Oxford: Oxford University Press.

Banerjee, A., Dolado, J. J., Hendry, D. F. and Smith, G. W. (1986). Exploring equilibrium relationships in econometrics through static models: Some Monte Carlo evidence, *Oxford Bulletin of Economics and Statistics*, **48**, 253–277.

Banerjee, A., Dolado, J. J. and Mestre, R. (1992). On some simple tests for cointegration: The cost of simplicity, Mimeo, Institute of Economics and Statistics, University of Oxford.

Banerjee, A. and Hendry, D. F. (1992a). Testing integration and cointegration, *Oxford Bulletin of Economics and Statistics*, **54**. Special issue.

Banerjee, A. and Hendry, D. F. (1992b). Testing integration and cointegration: An overview, *Oxford Bulletin of Economics and Statistics*, **54**, 225–255.

Bårdsen, G. (1989). The estimation of long run coefficients from error correction models, *Oxford Bulletin of Economics and Statistics*, **50**.

Bentzel, R. and Hansen, B. (1955). On recursiveness and interdependency in economic models, *Review of Economic Studies*, **22**, 153–168.

Bollerslev, T., Chou, R. S. and Kroner, K. F. (1992). ARCH modelling in finance – A review of the theory and empirical evidence, *Journal of Econometrics*, **52**, 5–59.

Bowman, K. O. and Shenton, L. R. (1975). Omnibus test contours for departures from normality based on $\sqrt{b_1}$ and b_2, *Biometrika*, **62**, 243–250.

Box, G. E. P. and Jenkins, G. M. (1976). *Time Series Analysis, Forecasting and Control*. San Francisco: Holden-Day.

Box, G. E. P. and Pierce, D. A. (1970). Distribution of residual autocorrelations in autoregressive-integrated moving average time series models, *Journal of the American Statistical Association*, **65**, 1509–1526.

Breusch, T. S. and Pagan, A. R. (1980). The Lagrange multiplier test and its applications to model specification in econometrics, *Review of Economic Studies*, **47**, 239–253.

Brown, R. L., Durbin, J. and Evans, J. M. (1975). Techniques for testing the constancy of regression relationships over time (with discussion), *Journal of the Royal Statistical Society B*, **37**, 149–192.

Chambers, E. A. and Cox, D. R. (1967). Discrimination between alternative binary response models, *Biometrika*, **54**, 573–578.

Chow, G. C. (1960). Tests of equality between sets of coefficients in two linear regressions, *Econometrica*, **28**, 591–605.

Cochrane, D. and Orcutt, G. H. (1949). Application of least squares regression to relationships containing auto-correlated error terms, *Journal of the American Statistical Association*, **44**, 32–61.

Cox, D. R. (1961). Tests of separate families of hypotheses, In *Proceedings of the Fourth Berkeley Symposium on Mathematical Statistics and Probability*, Vol. 1, pp. 105–123 Berkeley: University of California Press.

Cramer, J. S. (1991). *The LOGIT Model: An Introduction for Economists.* London: Edward Arnold.

Cran, G. W., Martin, K. J. and Thomas, G. E. (1977). A remark on algorithms. AS 63: The incomplete beta integral. AS 64: Inverse of the incomplete beta function ratio, *Applied Statistics*, **26**, 111–112.

D'Agostino, R. B. (1970). Transformation to normality of the null distribution of g_1, *Biometrika*, **57**, 679–681.

Davidson, J. E. H., Hendry, D. F., Srba, F. and Yeo, S. (1978). Econometric modelling of the aggregate time-series relationship between consumers' expenditure and income in the United Kingdom, *Economic Journal*, **88**, 661–692. Reprinted in Hendry D. F. (1993), *Econometrics: Alchemy or Science?* Oxford: Blackwell Publishers.

Dickey, D. A. and Fuller, W. A. (1981). Likelihood ratio statistics for autoregressive time series with a unit root, *Econometrica*, **49**, 1057–1072.

Doan, T., Litterman, R. and Sims, C. A. (1984). Forecasting and conditional projection using realistic prior distributions, *Econometric Reviews*, **3**, 1–100.

Doornik, J. A. and Hansen, H. (1994). A practical test for univariate and multivariate normality, Discussion paper, Nuffield College.

Doornik, J. A. and Hendry, D. F. (1992). *PcGive 7: An Interactive Econometric Modelling System.* Oxford: Institute of Economics and Statistics, University of Oxford.

Doornik, J. A. and Hendry, D. F. (1994a). *PcFiml 8: An Interactive Program for Modelling Econometric Systems.* London: International Thomson Publishing.

Doornik, J. A. and Hendry, D. F. (1994b). *PcGive 8: An Interactive Econometric Modelling System.* London: International Thomson Publishing, and Belmont, CA: Duxbury Press.

Durbin, J. (1970). Testing for serial correlation in least squares regression when some of the regressors are lagged dependent variables, *Econometrica*, **38**, 410–421.

Durbin, J. and Watson, G. S. (1951). Testing for serial correlation in least squares regression II, *Biometrika*, **38**, 159–178.

Eicker, F. (1967). Limit theorems for regressions with unequal and dependent errors, In *Proceedings of the Fifth Berkeley Symposium on Mathematical Statistics and Probability*, Vol. 1, pp. 59–82 Berkeley: University of California.

Eisner, R. and Strotz, R. H. (1963). *Determinants of Business Investment.* Englewood Cliffs, NJ: Prentice-Hall.

Emerson, R. A. and Hendry, D. F. (1994). An evaluation of forecasting using leading indicators, Mimeo, Nuffield College, Oxford.

Engle, R. F. (1982). Autoregressive conditional heteroscedasticity, with estimates of the variance of United Kingdom inflations, *Econometrica*, **50**, 987–1007.

Engle, R. F. (1984). Wald, likelihood ratio, and Lagrange multiplier tests in econometrics, in Griliches and Intriligator (1984), Ch. 13.

Engle, R. F. and Granger, C. W. J. (1987). Cointegration and error correction: Representation, estimation and testing, *Econometrica*, **55**, 251–276.

Engle, R. F., Hendry, D. F. and Richard, J.-F. (1983). Exogeneity, *Econometrica*, **51**, 277–304. Reprinted in Hendry D. F. (1993), *Econometrics: Alchemy or Science?* Oxford: Blackwell Publishers.

Engle, R. F., Hendry, D. F. and Trumbull, D. (1985). Small sample properties of ARCH estimators and tests, *Canadian Journal of Economics*, **43**, 66–93.

Ericsson, N. R. (1983). Asymptotic properties of instrumental variables statistics for testing non-nested hypotheses, *Review of Economic Studies*, **50**, 287–303.

Ericsson, N. R. (1992). Cointegration, exogeneity and policy analysis: An overview, *Journal of Policy Modeling*, **14**, 251–280.

Escribano, A. (1985). Non-linear error correction: The case of money demand in the UK (1878–1970), Mimeo, University of California at San Diego.

Favero, C. and Hendry, D. F. (1992). Testing the Lucas critique: A review, *Econometric Reviews*, **11**, 265–306.

Finney, D. J. (1947). The estimation from individual records of the relationship between dose and quantal response, *Biometrika*, **34**, 320–334.

Fletcher, R. (1987). *Practical Methods of Optimization* 2nd edition. New York: John Wiley & Sons.

Friedman, M. and Schwartz, A. J. (1982). *Monetary Trends in the United States and the United Kingdom: Their Relation to Income, Prices, and Interest Rates, 1867–1975*. Chicago: University of Chicago Press.

Frisch, R. (1934). *Statistical Confluence Analysis by means of Complete Regression Systems.* Oslo: University Institute of Economics.

Frisch, R. (1938). Statistical versus theoretical relations in economic macrodynamics, Mimeograph dated 17 July 1938, League of Nations Memorandum. Reproduced by University of Oslo in 1948 with Tinbergen's comments. Contained in Memorandum 'Autonomy of Economic Relations', 6 November 1948, Oslo, Universitets Økonomiske Institutt.

Gilbert, C. L. (1986). Professor Hendry's methodology, *Oxford Bulletin of Economics and Statistics*, **48**, 283–307. Reprinted in Granger C. W. J. (ed.) (1990), *Modelling Economic Series.* Oxford: Clarendon Press.

Godfrey, L. G. (1978). Testing for higher order serial correlation in regression equations when the regressors include lagged dependent variables, *Econometrica*, **46**, 1303–1313.

Godfrey, L. G. (1988). *Misspecification Tests in Econometrics*. Cambridge: Cambridge University Press.

Godfrey, L. G. and Orme, C. D. (1994). The sensitivity of some general checks to omitted variables in the linear model, *International Economic Review*, **35**, 489–506.

Granger, C. W. J. (1969). Investigating causal relations by econometric models and cross-spectral methods, *Econometrica*, **37**, 424–438.

Granger, C. W. J. (1986). Developments in the study of cointegrated economic variables, *Oxford Bulletin of Economics and Statistics*, **48**, 213–228.

Granger, C. W. J. and Newbold, P. (1974). Spurious regressions in econometrics, *Journal of Econometrics*, **2**, 111–120.

Granger, C. W. J. and Newbold, P. (1977). The time series approach to econometric model building, In Sims, C. A. (ed.), *New Methods in Business Cycle Research*, Ch. 1. Minneapolis: Federal Reserve Bank of Minneapolis.

Gregory, A. W. and Veale, M. R. (1985). Formulating Wald tests of non-linear restrictions, *Econometrica*, **53**, 1465–1468.

Griliches, Z. and Intriligator, M. D. (eds.)(1984). *Handbook of Econometrics*, Vol. 2–3. Amsterdam: North-Holland.

Hansen, B. E. (1992). Testing for parameter instability in linear models, *Journal of Policy Modeling*, **14**, 517–533.

Harvey, A. C. (1981). *The Econometric Analysis of Time Series*. Deddington: Philip Allan.

Harvey, A. C. (1990). *The Econometric Analysis of Time Series* 2nd edition. Hemel Hempstead: Philip Allan.

Harvey, A. C. (1993). *Time Series Models* 2nd edition. Hemel Hempstead: Harvester Wheatsheaf.

Harvey, A. C. and Collier, P. (1977). Testing for functional misspecification in regression analysis, *Journal of Econometrics*, **6**, 103–119.

Hendry, D. F. (1976). The structure of simultaneous equations estimators, *Journal of Econometrics*, **4**, 51–88. Reprinted in Hendry D. F. (1993), *Econometrics: Alchemy or Science?* Oxford: Blackwell Publishers.

Hendry, D. F. (1979). Predictive failure and econometric modelling in macro-economics: The transactions demand for money, In Ormerod, P. (ed.), *Economic Modelling*, pp. 217–242. London: Heinemann. Reprinted in Hendry D. F. (1993), *Econometrics: Alchemy or Science?* Oxford: Blackwell Publishers.

Hendry, D. F. (1980). Econometrics: Alchemy or science?, *Economica*, **47**, 387–406. Reprinted in Hendry D. F. (1993), *Econometrics: Alchemy or Science?* Oxford: Blackwell Publishers.

Hendry, D. F. (1986a). Econometric modelling with cointegrated variables, *Oxford Bulletin of Economics and Statistics*, *48*(3). Special issue.

Hendry, D. F. (1986b). Econometric modelling with cointegrated variables: An overview, *Oxford Bulletin of Economics and Statistics*, **48**, 201–212.

Hendry, D. F. (1986c). Using PC-GIVE in econometrics teaching, *Oxford Bulletin of Economics and Statistics*, **48**, 87–98.

Hendry, D. F. (1987). Econometric methodology: A personal perspective, In Bewley, T. F. (ed.), *Advances in Econometrics*, Ch. 10. Cambridge: Cambridge University Press.

Hendry, D. F. (1988). The encompassing implications of feedback versus feedforward mechanisms in econometrics, *Oxford Economic Papers*, **40**, 132–149.

Hendry, D. F. (1989). Comment on intertemporal consumer behaviour under structural changes in income, *Econometric Reviews*, **8**, 111–121.

Hendry, D. F. (1993). *Econometrics: Alchemy or Science?* Oxford: Blackwell Publishers.

Hendry, D. F. (1995a). *Dynamic Econometrics.* Oxford: Oxford University Press.

Hendry, D. F. (1995b). On the interactions of unit roots and exogeneity, *Econometric Reviews.* Forthcoming.

Hendry, D. F. (1995c). A theory of co-breaking, Mimeo, Nuffield College, University of Oxford.

Hendry, D. F. and Anderson, G. J. (1977). Testing dynamic specification in small simultaneous systems: An application to a model of building society behaviour in the United Kingdom, In Intriligator, M. D. (ed.), *Frontiers in Quantitative Economics*, Vol. 3, pp. 361–383. Amsterdam: North Holland Publishing Company. Reprinted in Hendry D. F. (1993), *Econometrics: Alchemy or Science?* Oxford: Blackwell Publishers.

Hendry, D. F. and Doornik, J. A. (1994). Modelling linear dynamic econometric systems, *Scottish Journal of Political Economy*, **41**, 1–33.

Hendry, D. F. and Ericsson, N. R. (1991). Modeling the demand for narrow money in the United Kingdom and the United States, *European Economic Review*, **35**, 833–886.

Hendry, D. F. and Mizon, G. E. (1978). Serial correlation as a convenient simplification, not a nuisance: A comment on a study of the demand for money by the Bank of England, *Economic Journal*, **88**, 549–563. Reprinted in Hendry D. F. (1993), *Econometrics: Alchemy or Science?* Oxford: Blackwell Publishers.

Hendry, D. F. and Mizon, G. E. (1993). Evaluating dynamic econometric models by encompassing the VAR, In Phillips, P. C. B. (ed.), *Models, Methods and Applications of Econometrics*, pp. 272–300. Oxford: Basil Blackwell.

Hendry, D. F. and Morgan, M. S. (1989). A re-analysis of confluence analysis, *Oxford Economic Papers*, **41**, 35–52.

Hendry, D. F. and Morgan, M. S. (1995). *The Foundations of Econometric Analysis.* Cambridge.

Hendry, D. F. and Neale, A. J. (1987). Monte Carlo experimentation using PC-NAIVE, In Fomby, T. and Rhodes, G. F. (eds.), *Advances in Econometrics*, Vol. 6, pp. 91–125. Greenwich, Connecticut: Jai Press Inc.

Hendry, D. F. and Neale, A. J. (1988). Interpreting long-run equilibrium solutions in conventional macro models: A comment, *Economic Journal*, **98**, 808–817.

Hendry, D. F. and Neale, A. J. (1991). A Monte Carlo study of the effects of structural breaks on tests for unit roots, In Hackl, P. and Westlund, A. H. (eds.), *Economic Structural Change, Analysis and Forecasting*, pp. 95–119. Berlin: Springer-Verlag.

Hendry, D. F., Neale, A. J. and Ericsson, N. R. (1991). *PC-NAIVE, An Interactive Program for Monte Carlo Experimentation in Econometrics. Version 6.0.* Oxford: Institute of Economics and Statistics, University of Oxford.

Hendry, D. F., Neale, A. J. and Srba, F. (1988). Econometric analysis of small linear systems using PC-FIML, *Journal of Econometrics*, **38**, 203–226.

Hendry, D. F., Pagan, A. R. and Sargan, J. D. (1984). Dynamic specification, in Griliches and Intriligator (1984), Ch. 18. Reprinted in Hendry D. F. (1993), *Econometrics: Alchemy or Science?* Oxford: Blackwell Publishers.

Hendry, D. F. and Richard, J.-F. (1982). On the formulation of empirical models in dynamic econometrics, *Journal of Econometrics*, **20**, 3–33. Reprinted in Granger C. W. J. (ed.) (1990), *Modelling Economic Series.* Oxford: Clarendon Press and in Hendry D. F. (1993), *Econometrics: Alchemy or Science?* Oxford: Blackwell Publishers.

Hendry, D. F. and Richard, J.-F. (1983). The econometric analysis of economic time series (with discussion), *International Statistical Review*, **51**, 111–163. Reprinted in Hendry D. F. (1993), *Econometrics: Alchemy or Science?* Oxford: Blackwell Publishers.

Hendry, D. F. and Richard, J.-F. (1989). Recent developments in the theory of encompassing, In Cornet, B. and Tulkens, H. (eds.), *Contributions to Operations Research and Econometrics. The XXth Anniversary of CORE*, pp. 393–440. Cambridge, MA: MIT Press.

Hendry, D. F. and Srba, F. (1980). AUTOREG: A computer program library for dynamic econometric models with autoregressive errors, *Journal of Econometrics*, **12**, 85–102. Reprinted in Hendry (1993), *Econometrics: Alchemy or Science?* Oxford: Blackwell Publishers.

Hendry, D. F. and von Ungern-Sternberg, T. (1981). Liquidity and inflation effects on consumers' expenditure, In Deaton, A. S. (ed.), *Essays in the Theory and Measurement of Consumers' Behaviour*, pp. 237–261. Cambridge: Cambridge University Press. Reprinted in Hendry D. F. (1993), *Econometrics: Alchemy or Science?* Oxford: Blackwell Publishers.

Hendry, D. F. and Wallis, K. F. (eds.)(1984). *Econometrics and Quantitative Economics*. Oxford: Basil Blackwell.

Hooker, P. H. (1901). Correlation of the marriage rate with trade, *Journal of the Royal Statistical Society*, **64**, 485–492.

Johansen, S. (1988). Statistical analysis of cointegration vectors, *Journal of Economic Dynamics and Control*, **12**, 231–254.

Johansen, S. (1995). *Likelihood based Inference on Cointegration in the Vector Autoregressive Model*: Oxford University Press. Forthcoming.

Johansen, S. and Juselius, K. (1990). Maximum likelihood estimation and inference on cointegration – With application to the demand for money, *Oxford Bulletin of Economics and Statistics*, **52**, 169–210.

Judd, J. and Scadding, J. (1982). The search for a stable money demand function: A survey of the post-1973 literature, *Journal of Economic Literature*, **20**, 993–1023.

Judge, G. G., Griffiths, W. E., Hill, R. C., Lütkepohl, H. and Lee, T.-C. (1985). *The Theory and Practice of Econometrics* 2nd edition. New York: John Wiley.

Kiviet, J. F. (1986). On the rigor of some mis-specification tests for modelling dynamic relationships, *Review of Economic Studies*, **53**, 241–261.

Kiviet, J. F. (1987). *Testing Linear Econometric Models*. Amsterdam: University of Amsterdam.

Kiviet, J. F. and Phillips, G. D. A. (1992). Exact similar tests for unit roots and cointegration, *Oxford Bulletin of Economics and Statistics*, **54**, 349–367.

Kohn, A. (1987). *False Prophets*. Oxford: Basil Blackwell.

Koopmans, T. C. (ed.)(1950). *Statistical Inference in Dynamic Economic Models*. No. 10 in Cowles Commission Monograph. New York: John Wiley & Sons.

Kuh, E., Belsley, D. A. and Welsh, R. E. (1980). *Regression Diagnostics. Identifying Influential Data and Sources of Collinearity*. Wiley Series in Probability and Mathematical Statistics. New York: John Wiley.

Leamer, E. E. (1978). *Specification Searches. Ad-Hoc Inference with Non-Experimental Data*. New York: John Wiley.

Leamer, E. E. (1983). Let's take the con out of econometrics, *American Economic Review*, **73**, 31–43. Reprinted in Granger C. W. J. (ed.) (1990), *Modelling Economic Series*. Oxford: Clarendon Press.

Ljung, G. M. and Box, G. E. P. (1978). On a measure of lack of fit in time series models, *Biometrika*, **65**, 297–303.

Lucas, R. E. (1976). Econometric policy evaluation: A critique, In Brunner, K. and Meltzer, A. (eds.), *The Phillips Curve and Labor Markets*, Vol. 1 of *Carnegie-Rochester Conferences on Public Policy*, pp. 19–46. Amsterdam: North-Holland Publishing Company.

MacKinnon, J. G. (1991). Critical values for cointegration tests, In Engle, R. F. and Granger, C. W. J. (eds.), *Long-Run Economic Relationships*, pp. 267–276. Oxford: Oxford University Press.

MacKinnon, J. G. and White, H. (1985). Some heteroskedasticity-consistent covariance matrix estimators with improved finite sample properties, *Journal of Econometrics*, **29**, 305–325.

Majunder, K. L. and Bhattacharjee, G. P. (1973a). Algorithm AS 63. The incomplete beta integral, *Applied Statistics*, **22**, 409–411.

Majunder, K. L. and Bhattacharjee, G. P. (1973b). Algorithm AS 64. Inverse of the incomplete beta function ratio, *Applied Statistics*, **22**, 411–414.

Marschak, J. (1953). Economic measurements for policy and prediction, In Hood, W. C. and Koopmans, T. C. (eds.), *Studies in Econometric Method*, No. 14 in Cowles Commission Monograph. New York: John Wiley & Sons.

McFadden, D. L. (1984). Econometric analysis of qualitative response models, in Griliches and Intriligator (1984), Ch. 24.

Mizon, G. E. (1977). Model selection procedures, In Artis, M. J. and Nobay, A. R. (eds.), *Studies in Modern Economic Analysis*, Ch. 4. Oxford: Basil Blackwell.

Mizon, G. E. (1984). The encompassing approach in econometrics, in Hendry and Wallis (1984), pp. 135–172.

Mizon, G. E. (1993). A simple message to autocorrelation correctors: Don't, Discussion paper, European University Institute, Florence.

Mizon, G. E. and Hendry, D. F. (1980). An empirical application and Monte Carlo analysis of tests of dynamic specification, *Review of Economic Studies*, **49**, 21–45. Reprinted in Hendry D. F. (1993), *Econometrics: Alchemy or Science?* Oxford: Blackwell Publishers.

Mizon, G. E. and Richard, J.-F. (1986). The encompassing principle and its application to non-nested hypothesis tests, *Econometrica*, **54**, 657–678.

Nelson, C. R. (1972). The prediction performance of the FRB-MIT-PENN model of the U.S. economy, *American Economic Review*, **62**, 902–917.

Nickell, S. J. (1985). Error correction, partial adjustment and all that: An expository note, *Oxford Bulletin of Economics and Statistics*, **47**, 119–130.

Pagan, A. R. (1984). Model evaluation by variable addition, in Hendry and Wallis (1984), pp. 103–135.

Perron, P. (1989). The great crash, the oil price shock and the unit root hypothesis, *Econometrica*, **57**, 1361–1401.

Pesaran, M. H. (1974). On the general problem of model selection, *Review of Economic Studies*, **41**, 153–171.

Phillips, P. C. B. (1986). Understanding spurious regressions in econometrics, *Journal of Econometrics*, **33**, 311–340.

Phillips, P. C. B. (1987). Time series regression with a unit root, *Econometrica*, **55**, 277–301.

Phillips, P. C. B. (1991). Optimal inference in cointegrated systems, *Econometrica*, **59**, 283–306.

Pike, M. C. and Hill, I. D. (1966). Logarithm of the gamma function, *Communications of the ACM*, **9**, 684.

Ramsey, J. B. (1969). Tests for specification errors in classical linear least squares regression analysis, *Journal of the Royal Statistical Society B*, **31**, 350–371.

Richard, J.-F. (1980). Models with several regimes and changes in exogeneity, *Review of Economic Studies*, **47**, 1–20.

Sargan, J. D. (1958). The estimation of economic relationships using instrumental variables, *Econometrica*, **26**, 393–415.

Sargan, J. D. (1959). The estimation of relationships with autocorrelated residuals by the use of instrumental variables, *Journal of the Royal Statistical Society B*, **21**, 91–105. Reprinted as pp. 87–104 in Sargan J. D. (1988), *Contributions to Econometrics*, Vol. 1, Cambridge: Cambridge University Press.

Sargan, J. D. (1964). Wages and prices in the United Kingdom: A study in econometric methodology (with discussion), In Hart, P. E., Mills, G. and Whitaker, J. K. (eds.), *Econometric Analysis for National Economic Planning*, Vol. 16 of *Colston Papers*, pp. 25–63. London: Butterworth Co. Reprinted as pp. 275–314 in Hendry D. F. and Wallis K. F. (eds.) (1984). *Econometrics and Quantitative Economics*. Oxford: Basil Blackwell, and as pp. 124–169 in Sargan J. D. (1988), *Contributions to Econometrics*, Vol. 1, Cambridge: Cambridge University Press.

Sargan, J. D. (1980a). The consumer price equation in the post-war British economy. An exercise in equation specification testing, *Review of Economic Studies*, **47**, 113–135.

Sargan, J. D. (1980b). Some tests of dynamic specification for a single equation, *Econometrica*, **48**, 879–897. Reprinted as pp. 191–212 in Sargan J. D. (1988), *Contributions to Econometrics*, Vol. 1, Cambridge: Cambridge University Press.

Shea, B. L. (1988). Algorithm AS 239: Chi-squared and incomplete gamma integral, *Applied Statistics*, **37**, 466–473.

Shenton, L. R. and Bowman, K. O. (1977). A bivariate model for the distribution of $\sqrt{b_1}$ and b_2, *Journal of the American Statistical Association*, **72**, 206–211.

Sims, C. A. (1980). Macroeconomics and reality, *Econometrica*, **48**, 1–48. Reprinted in Granger C. W. J. (ed.) (1990), *Modelling Economic Series*. Oxford: Clarendon Press.

Spanos, A. (1986). *Statistical Foundations of Econometric Modelling*. Cambridge: Cambridge University Press.

White, H. (1980). A heteroskedastic-consistent covariance matrix estimator and a direct test for heteroskedasticity, *Econometrica*, **48**, 817–838.

White, H. (1984). *Asymptotic Theory for Econometricians*. London: Academic Press.

White, H. (1990). A consistent model selection, In Granger, C. W. J. (ed.), *Modelling Economic Series*, pp. 369–383. Oxford: Clarendon Press.

Working, E. J. (1927). What do statistical demand curves show?, *Quarterly Journal of Economics*, **41**, 212–235.

Yule, G. U. (1926). Why do we sometimes get nonsense-correlations between time-series? A study in sampling and the nature of time series (with discussion), *Journal of the Royal Statistical Society*, **89**, 1–64.

Author Index

Subject Index